PAUL VERLAINE

PAUL VERLAINE

HIS LIFE—HIS WORK

BY
EDMOND LEPELLETIER

TRANSLATED BY E. M. LANG

AMS PRESS
NEW YORK

Reprinted from a copy in the collections of the Harvard College Library
From the edition of 1909, New York
First AMS EDITION published 1970
Manufactured in the United States of America

International Standard Book Number: 0-404-03968-5

Library of Congress Card Catalog Number: 79-128938

AMS PRESS, INC.
NEW YORK, N.Y. 10003

PAUL VERLAINE

HIS LIFE—HIS WORK

BY

EDMOND LEPELLETIER

TRANSLATED BY E. M. LANG

ILLUSTRATED

LONDON

T. WERNER LAURIE

CLIFFORD'S INN, FLEET STREET

INTRODUCTORY NOTE

PAUL VERLAINE, in one of the most critical hours of his troubled existence, a prey to melancholy, only too well justified, isolated, forgotten, or remembered by comrades and contemporaries only to be contemned, calumniated, and disowned, wrote from his cell in the prison at Mons on the margin of a letter addressed to his mother this despairing appeal to the one whom he knew to be always his friend:

". . . Let Lepelletier defend my reputation. He is able to clear what will soon be my memory. I rely upon him to make me known as I was in reality, when I am no longer here. . . ."

EDMOND LEPELLETIER.

BOUGIVAL.

TRANSLATOR'S NOTE.

It has been found necessary, for purposes of space, to abridge a few passages in this volume.

CONTENTS

EDMOND LEPELLETIER.
Député de Paris.

ILLUSTRATIONS

à Edmond Lepelletier

Mon plus vieil ami survivant
D'un groupe déjà de fantômes
Qui dansent comme des atômes
Dans un rais de lune devant

Nos yeux assombris et rêvant
Sous les ramures polychrômes
Que l'automne assouplit en dômes
Funèbres où gémit le vent,

Bah! la vie est si courte, en somme,
On se réveil après quel somme!
Qu'il ne faut plus songer aux morts

Que pour les plaindre et pour les
De regrets exempts de remords
Car n'allons nous pas les rejoindre

H. Cochin, juillet 90

Paul Verlaine

PAUL VERLAINE

CHAPTER I

THE LEGEND OF PAUL VERLAINE

It was at the Lycée Bonaparte, formerly known as Bourbon, later as Fontanes, which is now under the republican patronage of the Marquis de Condorcet, that my friendship with Paul Verlaine began; it lasted without a single break for thirty-six years, from 1860 until the fatal 9th of January 1896. I was concerned in the most decisive events of his troublous career; and although we were separated for various periods by the exigencies of life I never lost touch nor ceased to correspond with him. His real confidences were for my ear alone. It is true the poor fellow loved open confession, to pour out his heart in prose and verse. A table in a café would serve him as confessional, and there to any chance acquaintance he would reveal what appeared to be the inmost secrets of his soul in long, long talks far into the night—particularly during his later years. But, as a matter of fact, these statements of his about himself were mostly exaggerations. He would accuse, judge, and condemn himself with naïve humility

A

and unnecessary frankness. Seldom did he make excuses, and never did he cast the responsibility for his misdeeds on other shoulders save in the case of the woman, whom in one breath he would curse and regret, that Delilah who had delivered him over, helpless, unarmed, unready, to vice and temptation. In such moments of excitement, when the sting of his secret sorrow grew unbearable, he would lash himself into a passion of self-condemnation that was only half genuine. These confessions, begun in the flaring gaslight of the Café Rouge or François Premier, continued into the grey light of dawn, and not ended till a final halt was made at some wine-shop just taking down its shutters, were doubtless partly for effect whether his listeners were sceptics or so-called disciples.

Verlaine was gifted with the romantic temperament. Victor Hugo, Calderon, Pétrus Borel, and Barbey d'Aurevilly were the literary influences of his most impressionable years. Gongora he admired to the extent of desiring to translate him, but the elements of Spanish grammar proved a stumbling - block ; contact with this exuberant genius, however, fostered in him a tendency to exaggeration and reckless bravado. His religious emotions, which were little more than a pose, for Verlaine's faith was more theoretical than practical, were the result of the deep draughts he had drunk from the intoxicating founts of romanticism ; and the avowals he made in those wanderings of his among the drinking-shops of the Quartier Latin, punctuated by the tap of his stick on resounding pavements, across piles of saucers on stained marble-topped tables, or in the precious pages of delightful but fictitious autobiography, must be accepted not without reservation, and largely discounted. The confession is often objective and the fault imaginary. Fancy played a large part in these outpourings of his. There was something of the playhouse in this pose of Verlaine's, not that he wished to create a sensation, his taste was too good for that, but he enjoyed the dramatic effect of himself as a past master of vice, a St Augustine of the wine-shop, who did not lack a St Monica, for he frequently invoked the name of his good and pious mother.

Thus a legend grew up around him ; all the more persistent and enduring from the fact that Verlaine himself was largely its author, and dug the grave of his own reputation. His disciples widely disseminated the gospel of depravity it amused him to preach ; some even transformed into realities his literary parables, and the public have taken too literally the creed of the master, paraphrased by the apostles of fantasy, and denounced by emphatic hypocritical pharisees. It ought to be revised, and its commentators kept within bounds. Verlaine's signature at the foot of his numerous printed confessions is no proof of the correctness of the facts. Before everything else, he was a poet ; therefore he exaggerated, amplified, enlarged. Sentiments and sensations alike he peered at through a microscope. Under the eyes of a too credulous public he advanced into the lists of publicity, sounding his trumpet and presenting himself as a knight of depravity. He beat a drum around the imaginary debaucheries with which he publicly reproached himself, while regretting in his inmost heart that he was utterly innocent of them. He boasted of impurities that existed solely in his own imagination. In fact he was a great romancer.

It is far from my desire to present Verlaine as a saint, an exemplary citizen, and model husband. He was not, as will presently appear, even a good patriot; the banalities of ordinary epitaphs are not for him. At the same time he was not the graceless vagabond, the licentious reprobate that the middle-class public, who have literary pretensions, imagine to themselves, with interest or disgust, as best suits their varying temperaments.

I contradicted the legend when I stood by the grave which swallowed up my friend; but in the little cemetery of the Batignolles I was too much overcome for a set speech. I had followed the bier, which bore away with it a part of my own being, with heart oppressed and mind charged with sad memories, without having taken the precaution of furnishing myself with a little bouquet of the flowers of rhetoric, conventionally arranged in accordance with the taste of the day, such as is usually placed on the tombs to which oratorical access is afforded. In the sorrowful and sincere little speech I improvised, I endeavoured to refute all idle tales, and present Verlaine as he really was, the son of a provincial family, his father an officer in the army, his mother a landed proprietress educated as beseemed his condition, provided with diplomas, the possessor of a competency from his cradle, having led a conventional existence for twenty years, and, in fact, having adopted the Bohemian habits of his later days solely because his income had vanished, and literature provided

him with but an intermittent and insufficient livelihood.   He held in horror and contempt the poets
of old who, miserable, suffering, and destitute,
knocked at the doors of friends, and clamoured
for admittance to hospitals.   He escaped the
lamentable reputation of the Malfilâtres and the
Gilberts.   Certainly he was a poet, and unlucky,
but never a beggar.   If, in the last stage of his
life, he was helped, it was quite voluntarily by some
friends, and if Paris furnished him with a refuge,
was she not bound to help him or any other of
her children attacked by illness and misfortune?
He never sought a permanent dependence on the
hospital, and experienced profound relief in his
last hours in that they were not spent on a
pauper's bed.

When his resources were exhausted, and his
patrimony consumed—partly by his own extra-
vagance, and partly by the fault of others—he
intended to earn his own living.   He imagined
that his poems, books, and articles would yield
the equivalent of the capital that had been so
easily dissipated, believing, perhaps, in his artistic
unworldliness, that they represented a competency
which would endure till he died or grew rich.
He was rapidly disillusioned.   The capital upon
which he had imprudently subsisted, instead of
contenting himself with its dividends, was not to
be replaced by the daily use of his pen.   That
instrument was a marvel, but the work it produced
unremunerative to the astonishment and dis-
comfiture of the poet; fame not money resulted
from the furrow he had laboriously traced.   It
was then that he resolved to tear himself away

from the famine-struck hazardous path of literature and the futile quest for a price for his copy;
to quit the paltry battlefield whereon fights are
waged for 100 sous. The painful bargaining he
had already endured with the publisher Vanier;
the entreaties, delays, and humiliations attendant
on literary commerce filled him with apprehension.
He begged me, most wisely, to endeavour to
obtain his re-installation in Government employ.
Was not this an indication of his desire for decency
and order? It was only when official hostility shut
this door of escape in the face of the anxious poet,
that Verlaine, feeling himself caught in the toils
of fate and misery, ceased to aspire after that life
of conventional regularity in which the table is laid
every day, and money comes in as if by clockwork
at the end of the month. Disheartened, he allowed
himself to drift into disorder and drunkenness,
aimlessness, and unproductiveness. To this extent
and no more was the legend founded on fact, and
comparison made between one "poor Lelian" and
Villon, poet and rascal.

Verlaine the modern Villon! It is one of those
coined phrases which, having apparently been cast
in the mint of observation and truth, is passed from
hand to hand, and accepted without being subjected
to the test which would have proved its falseness.
Yet from a literary point of view the comparison is
not unkindly, but even flattering.

François Villon, that poet most human and
original, who first sounded the note of melancholy
among the frivolities, satires, and insipid allegories
of the meaningless songsters and arid and argu-
mentative poets of the fifteenth century, heads the

magnificent dynasty of our monarchs of wit. He was the Pharamond, the ancestor, the father of our poetical *noblesse*. To be ranked with him is to be placed at the summit of the aristocracy of letters. But with the gratifying literary comparison is an unpleasant hint of resemblance in life and habits; Villon was the king of vagabonds, and from this point of view, rather than that of his poetical talent, has Verlaine been confounded with him.

Such confusion cannot withstand analysis, although personal virtues have nothing in common with poetical talents. The misdeeds of a man of genius ought not to prejudice us; even his crimes should not be taken into account when his work only is in question. A literary critic is not a criminal jury. What matters an error of conduct on the part of the artist to the egotistical public who delight in his masterpiece? They suffer no inconvenience, have incurred no injury, be he ever so debauched, violent, covetous or dishonest. The artist must be judged by his work alone, quite apart from his responsibilities as a man. If he sets an example of all the domestic virtues, do the public obtain any advantage? Should he not, in the interests of humanity, set himself apart from common morality, if by so doing his brain is stimulated, rather than leave behind him the best of reputations and the worst literature. He may have committed all the sins in the decalogue, and yet have made both his own and the generations which follow him heirs of a marvellous and immortal kingdom. And it is well. Around him the shadow may lie deep, but he has illuminated the world. For mankind

as a whole this is clear gain. Our sympathy
and gratitude should not be confined to the light-
house keeper in Maeterlinck's tale, who, too
virtuous to permit his neighbours to suffer, divided
among them the oil from his lamps, thus neglecting the illumination of the ocean in order to light
a few cabins. Virtue may or may not be allied
with genius. If Verlaine had been worthy of the
Monthyon prize, or if he had merited the halter
Villon so narrowly escaped, it would not have
altered one verse of *Sagesse* nor modified one
stanza of the *Fêtes galantes*.

But one is not necessarily a rascal in order to
be classed with the great artists, and there is no
reason why offences from which Verlaine was quite
free should be attributed to him. That is what
happens when he is lightly compared to Villon;
for the author of the *Grand* and the *Petit
Testament* left behind him a most unenviable
reputation besides his superb literary renown. It
is well known to all he consorted with shameless
highwaymen; that he swindled trusting innkeepers;
that even to theft by violence he was no stranger.
In our day he would have been counted a hooligan
and an *apache*. Caught redhanded in a highway
robbery, he was tried and condemned to be hanged
with his comrades; and to this we owe the fine
epitaph: "In the rain have we been washed and
made clean . . ."

Verlaine, too, had his moods of melancholy
and remorse, in which he mournfully asked himself
"what he had done with his youth"; but he had
no highway robbery on his conscience; he had
never committed the smallest act of dishonesty;

by birth, breeding, instinct, and inclination he was absolutely upright. Family tradition, early influences, the scrupulously detailed accounts kept by his mother, the untarnished record of his father, all combined to protect him against the temptations of cupidity, the degrading effects of want. No doubt he sought to materialise the pure gold of his verses, and practised the art of dedication to moneyed friends, but this was only following the example of the greatest writers of the time of Louis XIV., who unblushingly dedicated their work to the most influential nobles. But his life might be examined through a microscope, and although it will be found to contain plenty of faults, follies and weaknesses, and also many sufferings, with fate at the bottom of them all, nothing shameful, not one really vile nor unworthy action, would be discovered. The true friends of the poet may therefore rightly claim for him the epithet of honest man, commonplace enough perhaps, but yet, in the eyes of many, of sterling value; and with it may be coupled, even as Léon Cladel united the two on the tomb of Albert Glatigny, that of great artist, of which he was equally worthy.

Verlaine never came within an ace of the halter like the poet bandit with whose memory he has been associated. Villon escaped the gallows simply through the favour of Louis XI., who chanced to be passing through Meung; Verlaine incurred the anger of the law through an accident that could hardly be regarded as criminal. If he were constrained to stand in the prisoner's dock, it was in a foreign land, and at a most unpropitious moment.

The independent air and French nationality of the aimless traveller who followed no regular calling—at the police station in Brussels he stated that he was "lyrical poet to his country"—and above all information from Paris representing him as a dangerous republican who had served under the Commune, prejudiced the Brabançon jury against him, and he received a heavy sentence—several years' imprisonment. It all arose out of a slight quarrel with a comrade, Arthur Rimbaud — the result of too liberal libations of gin. A revolver, imprudently carried, foolishly produced and pointed threateningly by way of emphasising an argument, unfortunately exploded, the ball grazing Rimbaud's hand. This insignificant injury would perhaps in France have entailed a week's imprisonment, or more probably a police summons for carrying arms prohibited by law, and a sentence of two or three days' "hard labour"; the maximum for small injuries which do not incapacitate for work.

It is true that alcohol—that worst of devils according to Edgar Allan Poe, a most competent judge,—had a malign influence over Verlaine, and caused pernicious suggestions to enter his head. Temperamentally inclined to excess and morbidity, as he confesses in his preface to the *Poèmes Saturniens*, under the influence of alcoholic intoxication Verlaine became a caricature of himself. Hence the aforesaid avowals of vice. He had always a weakness for drink, but during his travels, after his separation from his wife, he developed an almost chronic drunkenness. Who will ever know what mental hell he strove to escape by seeking at the bottom of a glass for a satanically artificial paradise ?

It was in England especially, the land of whisky, which overwhelms, and gin which stupefies, that he acquired the habit of steady drinking, of hurried glasses "on draught" at the bar, of fits of exaltation followed by prolonged torpors. Far from all he loved, his home broken up, exiled from his native land, with the sole prospect of a wandering life and its necessarily frequent stoppages at inns, accompanied by Rimbaud who was a precocious and steady drinker, what wonder that he sought forgetfulness in heady liquids and their mental stimulation. Alcohol had, as it were, the effect of doubling his personality so that for the time being he lived another life. The existence circumstances had ordained for him was so melancholy, so uncomfortable, that surely he may be excused for endeavouring to construct another habitation for his mind, foolish though it was. More than once in his sober moments he thought of suicide. The after-effect of intoxication is depression, when the brain is often obsessed by the desire for annihilation; to rid himself of his temptation he would raise the cheering cup again to his tremulous lips, and like Anthea and the earth, contact with the liquid re-invested him with an ephemeral but brilliant vigour. In the union of cup and lips he found life; depression vanished, and, warming his numbed will before the fire of alcohol he recovered force to support destiny for yet another day. As Baudelaire says, "alcohol made the universe less hideous to him, and time hung less heavy on his hands." Let us not reproach him overmuch for these moments of forgetfulness. Perhaps to him they were the most endurable of his sad life, the only ones, save those of work, in which he savoured anything of happiness. At one time when immured in the oppressive solitude of a Belgian prison he sought and found both peace and excitement in devotion, prayer, and religious exaltation. To this we owe *Sagesse* ; but once at liberty again he returned to alcohol.

During the last phase of his life, in his years of Bohemianism and want, was he not, in spite of himself, poor wanderer, almost irresistibly urged towards cafés and wine-shops ? Homeless, penniless, and companionless save for fallen creatures like himself, he found in them the parody of a home, company, comparative comfort, and a shelter from rain, snow, and especially solitude. They afforded a means of escape from a miserable garret, and had almost the semblance of a familiar sitting-room. A photograph, one of a series of famous literary men in their well-furnished homes, exhibits the poet of the *Romances sans Paroles* lounging on a bench in a café evolving verses, his elbow supported on the marble-topped table, a glass of absinthe within reach, and underneath is written "Paul Verlaine at home."

It is surely the fault of a society which like ours pretends to be literary, artistic, intellectual, and refined when so gifted a poet has not at his command a modest lodging and bread sufficient for each day, while many a scandalous sinecure is lavished upon writers, destitute of talent or worth, but masters of intrigue, obsequious, and distinguished.

One last word regarding the accusation of unnatural vice which has been hurled against Verlaine. He would foolishly joke on this dangerous subject, smiling equivocally and cynically when allusions were made to any of those notorious friendships of his which were considered compromising, apparently with the desire to brave public opinion. He gave vent to paradoxical theories on the subject, and indulgent, even favourable, appreciations, in audacious conversations at table, which were borne out and corroborated in more than one of his poems. Did he confine himself to a theory which seemed to him amusing, and one to be rather proud of, or did he succumb to a desire to put it into practice? I emphatically assert the former. He made no confession of such lapse to me; on the contrary, on a certain serious occasion, entirely laying aside his usual pleasantries on the subject, he indignantly protested against it, and his innocence was proved in a letter he wrote to me at the time when his wife was suing for a separation. I am compelled to believe that any such licentiousness on his part was purely cerebral. He surrounded it with mystery. He wished to impress his contemporaries by endowing himself with imaginary vices, and clothing himself in a garment of depravity which only existed in his imagination.

I have already enumerated his earliest literary influences, Pétrus Borel, Barbey d'Aurevilly, and Baudelaire. Their pompously expounded eccentricities, serious farces, outrageous criticisms of accepted truths, and pedantic method of sneering at current morality, had greatly biassed his judgment. The fantastic and extravagant Prudhomme owed a number of his strange ideas to the nocturnal conversation of Verlaine and Villiers de l'Isle-Adam. These men of exuberant imagination,

among other unexpected tolerations, had none of
the usual indignation and disgust for the debauchery
practised and vaunted among the ancients. The
tranquillity with which many of the literary men
of the time expressed themselves on the subject
would seem to argue practical experience. The
complaisance written and spoken of Verlaine and
some of his friends gave rise to various suppositions
and presumptions which formed the basis of a
reputation quite undeserved, and of which no proof
in support was ever brought against Verlaine. The
legend, however, grew up and spread, owing its
inception and circulation largely to the extraordinary
fatuity and bravado of him who was and is its
victim.

One fact I may mention, viz. : that Verlaine's
whole heart was filled with an immense love for
one woman alone, and that love was betrayed.
His originality is apparent not only in his work
but in his life. In default of the absent, whose
memory, tantalising and enthralling, was always
with him, and whose face adored, yet hated,
haunted his sorrowful dreams, he sought relief
for his aching heart elsewhere, particularly during
the latter years of his life. His loves were lowly ;
but what choice had he ? Their very degradation
proved his need, his yearning for feminine companionship. A hundred poems, to say nothing of
his purely erotic works, bear witness to the strength
of his feelings, and exhibit him as an ardent lover
of woman. His tendency to sentimental love was
slight, it was the material woman alone which
appealed to, and interested him. His last adventures were truly despicable ; and the poor loiterers

on the pavement whom he accosted could neither understand nor console him.

Although he was never an ecstatic lover, after the manner of romantic swains, and demanded nothing from the women he met, after the loss of the adored one, except to share in his revelries, he had several sentimental friendships of a particularly refined and subtle nature; another proof of what I have already asserted—the perfect innocence of his masculine affections.

Among the cherished comrades who at various periods of his life inspired him with very warm sentiments, I remember first of all one of his cousins, named Dujardin of Lécluse, near Arleux in the north, where he spent his holidays. It was a very ardent, youthful friendship, and he wrote to me about it in his letters of September and October 1862 with enthusiasm. It was of a different character altogether from the intellectual affection which already existed between him and me. He expressed himself regarding this young cousin like a lover vaunting his mistress, and in those days the schoolboy Verlaine was absolutely innocent. A contemporary of ours at the Lycée Bonaparte, a delicate and melancholy young man, named Lucien Viotti, to whom Verlaine alludes with regret in his *Mémoires*, was another of these friends of his.

Viotti took part with me in the commencement of the war of 1870. He was enrolled in my regiment, but during the affair at Chevilly on 30th September he disappeared, and was either killed or wounded and captured. We heard that he died in hospital at Mayence, but the exact end of our brave and gentle comrade was never known; Verlaine was deeply afflicted by his loss, and always spoke of him with emotion and regret.

Arthur Rimbaud was Verlaine's last obsession; he was a sinister character, an extraordinary young man, whose strange verses, barbaric in colour and of bizarre force, have recently been exhumed. He had all the appearance of a youth escaped from a reformatory; slender, pale, awkward, endowed with a robust appetite and an unquenchable thirst, cold, contemptuous, cynical, he rapidly dominated the weak Verlaine. As they say in melodramas, he was the poet's evil genius.

Arthur Rimbaud was the chief instrument in Verlaine's misfortunes. It was he who lured the poet to cafés, and kept him there, while the table at home was spread for him in vain; and when he accompanied Verlaine to the Rue Nicolet, his want of breeding and arrogance made him a most unwelcome guest. Finally, having been the cause of numerous quarrels between husband and wife, he induced the poet to quit the conjugal hearth and wander with him in England and Belgium.

During these roamings, beyond the range of home ties and friends, Verlaine became more than ever under the influence of the bizarre abnormal being, the unhealthy genius whose sensational originality and extraordinary speculations greatly impressed him, and altered his poetic temperament. The shock of arrest, imprisonment, and isolation, and the sudden impulse towards religion which followed in their train, undoubtedly played a large part in the transformation of the talent and poetical productions of Verlaine; but the effect of the capricious and original intellectuality of his fatal

mentor was very strong, and gave another direction
to his ideas, opinions, dreams of art, and methods
of interpreting the world within him.

Unhappily the malignity of the compelling and
baneful dominion Rimbaud exercised over him
extended to the domain of reality.   This pernicious
adviser effected a radical alteration in the life and
habits of the impressionable and weak Verlaine, who
allowed himself to be guided towards perdition by
the superior will and precocious energy of Rimbaud,
poet, dreamer, idler, one day to develop into explorer,
merchant, man of business, pursuing an adventurous
caravan life, in which arguments regarding rhymes
and alliterations were replaced by the special pleadings
of commerce, discussions with printers on the choice
of lettering and typographical ornament, by bargains
concluded at the point of the revolver, and literary
fortunes by those obtained from wielding the hatchet
in forests of precious woods.   Rimbaud, poetical
guide, destined to become a slave-driver, was the
cause of Verlaine's arrest at Brussels ; and after thus
completing his ruin he abandoned the unfortunate
poet, and abruptly disappeared.   He burnt his
poems, obtained an appointment as manager to a
factory in Abyssinia, made money, and eventually
returned to France to die of a gangrenous wound in
a hospital at Marseilles.   A statue has been raised
to him in Charleville, his native town.

In the course of his varied career, Verlaine
formed other sincere and extravagant attachments
for certain young poets, artists, and scholars, whom
he designated as his disciples, and memories of
whom he has preserved in one or other of his
books.

B

The Pharisees, fools, and slanderers of this world may put an evil construction on the invincible attraction his chosen friends always had for Verlaine. The legend of which he is the victim almost seems to be confirmed by his emotional relations with them. Yet these friendships of his are not without precedent. Ancient history is full of tales of ideal affection between pure-minded heroes and reverend sages, untouched by a single breath of calumny. Nisus and Euryalus, whose friendship provided Virgil with a theme for an epic, Achilles mourning and avenging Patroclus, and the heroic Theban legion, which allowed itself to be massacred at Cheronesus, are all examples of that platonic affection between members of the same sex, for which Verlaine has been reproached, not only in whispers but on the housetop, Verlaine, who loved one woman and that one his wife, with his whole heart, and never ceased to suffer because she had abandoned him.

Paul Verlaine has become famous. Literature mourned his loss, and his obsequies had the character-istics of an apotheosis. He is regarded as the founder of a school, and one of the revivalists of modern poetry. His renown is considerable abroad ; in France he has not yet received the official and popular recognition due to his genius.

PAUL VERLAINE'S MOTHER

CHAPTER II

(1844-1862)

PAUL MARIE VERLAINE was born at Metz on the
30th March 1844, in a house, middle - class in
appearance, of several stories, No. 2 in the Rue
Haute-Pierre, now known as Hochsteinstrasse, near
the Esplanade ; it is still standing.

Here is an extract from the birth certificate
of the poet which I copied at the Hôtel-de-Ville
of Metz :—

". . . Nicolas Auguste Verlaine, aged forty-six,
born at Bertrix (Belgium) Captain Adjutant-Major
in the second regiment of Engineers, Chevalier
of the Legion-d'Honneur and of Saint-Ferdinand
d'Espagne, residing at Metz, Rue Haute-Pierre,
who presented to us a male child, which, on the
30th March last at nine o'clock in the evening was
born in his house to him and his wife, Elisa Julie
Josèphe Stéphanie Dehée, aged thirty-two years,
born at Fampoux (Pas-de-Calais), of no profession,
and to which he states he has given the names
of Paul Marie. . . ."

Verlaine was therefore a Messin, in accordance

19

with the custom of calling the town in which an
individual is born his native place.   The regiments
of Engineers were quartered at Arras, Montpellier,
and Metz, each in turn furnishing the garrison,
and military routine had assigned Metz to Captain
Verlaine at the time of his child's birth.   Victor
Hugo, by an analogous chance, was a Bisontin.
As his father was again quartered at Metz, Verlaine
knew the town well, and never spoke of it, after the
annexation, without sincere emotion.   There his
child life began and his intellect awakened; in the
old episcopal city he received his first impressions,
which he has related in some delightful pages.
His sketch of the Esplanade, where the officers
and the ladies of Metz society were wont to meet
and the children to play, is full of life and colour.

"The Esplanade, a very fine promenade, is a
terrace above the Moselle, which flows, a wide and
limpid stream, at the foot of hills, covered with
vineyards, most pleasing to behold.   Against this
background, rising above the town, the cathedral
uprears its lace-like architecture, and towards night-
fall the tranquil cawing of the rooks is heard, as
they return like a cloud to roost upon the innumerable towers and turrets clearly outlined against the
purple sky.   In the centre of the promenade is a
bandstand of elegant design where military concerts
used to take place on Thursdays and Sundays,
and were attended by all the unoccupied of
Metz.   Toilettes, greetings, conversations, flirtations, waving of fans and brandishing of lorgnons,
in those days square monocles or eyeglasses of
mother-of-pearl and tortoise-shell, which an effort
has since been made to revive among other fashions
of the past.   All these things were intensely

interesting to my boyish and rather mischievous observation. I said little, but sometimes a terrible remark would escape me regarding the worn-out gloves of Madame So - and - So, or the shrunken nankeen trousers of Monsieur Such-and-Such, whilst my youthful love of melody was intoxicated by the dance music of Pilodo, clarionet solos, or a selection of airs from the latest comic opera of Auber or Grisar. . . ." (*Confessions*, Part I.)

On this Esplanade the poet experienced one of those childish loves, the remembrance of which endures and perfumes the whole of a lifetime. Among the many children who played around the bandstand under their parents' watchful eyes, was the little daughter of a magistrate with whom Verlaine quickly made friends. She was called Mathilde, a name the poet was to meet with again in after days.

" She might have been eight," he said, "while I was just entering my seventh year. She was not pretty with the prettiness usually associated with that age. Auburn-hued hair falling in ringlets round an animated face with eyes of golden brown, the full lips of kindness and of health, and complexion lightly touched with sun stains made up, it seemed to me, a physiognomy all alight with fire and sparkle, and in her eager gait there was an abounding youthfulness — all this caught hold of me, ensnared my heart and, shall I say, my senses? Immediately we were friends. What had we to say to one another? I do not know, yet we always talked on the frequent occasions when we did not play. When one of us was late in arriving, for I pleased her I must confess, fully as much as she pleased me, the waiting was charged with anxious expectancy, and then what joy, what haste to meet, what numerous and resounding kisses on both cheeks! Sometimes there were reproaches for delay, miniature scenes, shadows of jealousy, when another boy or girl joining in our play found too warm a welcome on one side or the other. Our very demonstrative friendship was commented upon with much interest, and greatly amused, among others, the officers who formed a large part of the audience at these concerts. 'Paul and Virginia' said the commandants and captains, who did not go further back than modern classics, while the lieutenants and sub-lieutenants, more scholarly and with truer instinct, laughingly insinuated 'Daphnis and Chloe!' My father's colonel, who was later to become Marshal Niel, was greatly diverted by these youthful enthusiasms, and our parents, recognising their utter innocence and naïveté, willingly permitted our charming relations. . . ." (*Confessions*, Part I.)

Softened by this unsullied incident of happy childhood, and reviving the idyll after thirty-five years, he added, addressing the little girl, now a woman, a mother doubtless, even grandmother, of whose fate he was ignorant, lost as she was to him in the whirlpool of life, perhaps dead, and surviving only in the heart of the poet :

"Madame, if ever your eyes chance upon these lines you will smile kindly, will you not? Just as they smiled who were witnesses of our pure childish love, as I do myself at these memories, still fresh and filled with the perfume of innocence and early impulse, flowering of a sudden in the mind, which marvels at their exquisite charm, of the poet, who wishes, alas! he had only such sweet sincerities to relate." (*Confessions*, Part I.)

Lives, like rivers, are only limpid near their source. Recollections such as these, chaste and delicate, are but rarely to be met with in the biography, too often soiled and sullen, of the Daphnis of 1850. Only once again does Chloe appear at his side during the few fleeting hours of *La Bonne Chanson.*

Verlaine twice resided at Metz with his parents, and these memories, which he evoked after long years of absence, have to do with his second stay in the town. Not long after the birth of his son Captain Verlaine's regiment went to Montpellier. Of that great southern town Verlaine retained only a confused recollection, blurred pictures of religious processions with penitents in white, black, and grey, threading their way through the streets, their heads enveloped in the sinister cowls, like those of phantoms, which recall the times of the Inquisition.

On another occasion he was taken to Nîmes, his father having been sent there to maintain order during the revolution of 1848. They remained in the town a very short time, and the only remembrance retained by Verlaine was that of being present at the ceremony of the proclamation of the Republic, in the great square, dressed in his best clothes : embroidered collar, knickerbockers half - way down his legs, and cap with a long tassel falling to one side.

It was after this that the Verlaine family returned to Metz with the regiment, and the period began when the childish mind of the poet first received definite impressions—when his imagination awoke and his brain acquired the qualities of comprehension and comparison.

" I did not live there many years, it is true,"
he said, " but it was certainly at this time that
my mind and senses opened to the life which, on
the whole, I have found deeply interesting. Since
those days the noble and ill-fated town has fallen,
has it not, gloriously and tragically—abominably
tragically, after what immortal combats, by treason,
unparalleled in history, at the hands of its hereditary
foe. Therefore, in order to remain French, at the
age of twenty-eight, after having fulfilled all my
civic and social duties in France and as a
Frenchman, and taking part, uncompelled save
by patriotism, when the war broke out, in the
national defence to the utmost of my powers, I
was obliged, in 1872, when in London, whither
I had been hurried in consequence of the social
war, after the civil war and the foreign war, to
make a choice in favour of the nationality . . . of
my birth." (*Confessions*, Part I.)

Thus the poet chose France, under the conditions imposed by the Treaty of Frankfort. Except
for certain periods of relaxation and reaction,
Verlaine was always imbued with patriotic, even
militant sentiments. He might be called a chauvin
without hint of ridicule; his chauvinism was genuine
and active, at once instructive and calculated,
hereditary and acquired, in contrast with the
opinions, indifferent, sceptical, cosmopolitan, and
even anarchist, expressed, particularly during the
last years of his life, by his acquaintances, associates
on decadent reviews, colleagues on symbolist newspapers, and those whom he called his disciples.
He protested against these negations of patriotism,
to him blasphemies, evincing the very real emotion
he always felt when there was question, however

slight, of Alsace-Lorraine, already half forgotten, or regarded as a negligable quantity. His vigorous ode to Metz testifies to his national sentiments; it is a virile poem, a rousing salutation to the battalions of posterity rising up to avenge the defeat of the armies of the past. The persistent note of revenge that animates it places Verlaine in the front rank of patriot poets.

These martial and warlike ideas of his were doubtless the result both of heredity and environment, as the son of an officer brought up under the flag. He loved and admired his father, and retained a proud recollection of the handsome paternal uniform, recalling its details with pleasure in after life, and alluding with fond pride, as he completed his portrait of the Captain, to " his superb carriage and great height, such as we do not see nowadays," and his visage stern yet gentle, whereon the habit of command had imprinted a look of authority which inspired respect.

When his father died one 31st December, although Verlaine was then an ardent Republican and full of respect for Marat, Babeuf, and the more extreme Revolutionists, he put aside his grief in order to call upon the officers in command, they having refused to allow the usual military honours to take place at the funeral, under the pretext that the date was the 1st January. Verlaine insisted, however, and Captain Verlaine received all the marks of respect due to his rank and decorations, exacted by the son who for himself was totally indifferent to dignities, distinctions, and honours of every kind.

Verlaine's father, when I knew him, was a

fine old man, upright and spare, his face thin and
bronzed, the skin like parchment, with a short
white moustache, and a stern but not ill-tempered
expression. He never dilated upon his military
experiences. He adored his son, although strict
with him, particularly in public. When the boy
was at boarding - school, however, in the Rue
Chaptal, he used to go every day and enquire
after his health and progress, and always took
with him some dainty set aside for the purpose
from dinner the previous night, to supplement the
somewhat meagre school fare. Paul experienced
deep grief when he lost the excellent man. I
was present, and consoled him as well as I could,
having suffered a similar bereavement three years
before. One small detail serves to show the
intensity of Verlaine's affliction : he was a great
smoker, but, during the two days before the
funeral, he never even thought of lighting a pipe
or cigarette. Impressionable and stirred to the
depths of his being, it was weeks before he shook
off the effects of his grief.

Bertrix, where the Captain was born, is situated
between Bouillon and Paliseul, quite near the frontier,
and Paul often spent his vacations at the latter place,
having kept up with his paternal relations, Mme.
Grandjean, the widow of a colonel, and Mme.
Evrard, also a widow at Jehonville and Paliseul.
Verlaine's father was the son of a notary, who held
a position in the chief town of the Department.
At sixteen he joined Napoleon's army and took
part in the last campaigns of the Empire, 1814
and 1815. He remained French, after his birth-
place had become, under the treaty of 1815, Luxem-

bourgeois. He gradually rose in the Engineers until he was Captain Adjutant - Major, when he resigned on account of the unjust treatment he considered he had received. His Colonel, afterwards Marshal Niel, who liked and esteemed him, wrote a complimentary letter urging him to withdraw his resignation ; but the Captain, who was exceedingly obstinate, persisted, and retiring into civil life quitted Metz for Paris.

The Verlaines were an ancient Ardennaise family. One biographer claims for them a seigneurial origin, but I am rather inclined to the opinion of M. Saint - Pol - Roux, who stated in *La Plume* for February 1896 that Verlaine's great-grandfather after having served in the army settled at Arville, where he was dispensed from paying titles by the Abbé of Saint-Hubert, in consideration of his attending High Mass at the Abbey in uniform. This modest and rustic origin seems to me more in accordance with known facts than the theory of nobility. All Verlaine's relations were farmers and small landed proprietors, and neither Paul nor his mother ever alluded to a title having existed in the family, nor to documents substantiating such a claim.

The poet, moreover, kept silence in his writings regarding his birth and ancestors, which proves his lack of information on the subject, as he was very careful to keep in touch with his connections, and had the sentiment of kinship and soil largely developed.

Verlaine's mother had numerous relatives at Fampoux, Lécluse, Arleux - du - Nord, and Arras. Belonging to a family of landowners, farmers, and sugar manufacturers, she brought her husband, besides the usual dowry, a certain fortune, and in all the Verlaines had about 400,000, francs. This competency was threatened by the unfortunate speculations of Verlaine's father. The Captain was acquainted with M. Michel Chevalier, ex-Saint-Simonien, economist and senator, and as this personage was one of the Board of Directors of the Crédit Mobilier, founded by the Péreiras, Captain Verlaine thought he ought to invest his fortune in the concern, the shares in which went up to a fabulous extent on the Bourse for a brief space, 500 franc shares being quoted at 2,000 francs. Captain Verlaine unfortunately deferred consulting my father who, occupying a high position in a great banking-house, at the head of which was one of the Directors of the Banque de France, was able to give most excellent advice. He counselled the Captain to sell out at once, as the shares had already suffered considerable depreciation, and would soon fall even lower, but the old soldier hesitated; he could not comprehend that the shares for which he had paid between 1,300 and 1,400 francs, and which had gone up in price for a time on the Bourse to 1,900 and 2,000 francs, must now be sold at 800 francs. He hoped they would go up again, and it was only with the greatest difficulty that my father could prevail upon him to sell out while there was yet time. The Crédit Mobilier in fact was declining every day, and it was impossible to tell when it would cease to fall. Thanks to this sale, which took place almost at the last moment, a portion of the Verlaines' fortune was preserved, but their capital, of course, was sensibly diminished.

I believe Captain Verlaine obtained about 700 francs per share. He made two or three other unfortunate speculations. Having a pleasant recollection of Spain where he had been on a campaign he determined to invest in the railways of Séville-Xérès, and this, too, underwent a rapid and large depreciation.

These losses hastened the death of the Captain, and he succumbed to an attack of apoplexy on 31st December 1865. I have already spoken of Paul's acute sorrow; his father, though sometimes severe, after the manner of an old soldier, had loved him tenderly and !given him a hundred repeated proofs of his affection. His loss was the poet's first grief.

His mother was a woman of middle height, thin, upright, energetic, dignified in aspect, cold and calm in manner. She always dressed in black, even in her husband's lifetime; having many relations she was often obliged to go into mourning, and for the sake of economy continued to wear her sable garments after the conventional period had elapsed. She was pious, thrifty, and highly respectable in every sense of the word. In Paris she did not discard her provincial habits as an officer's wife. She affected a ceremonious air even on the most ordinary occasions, and in the suburb of the Batignolles was considered very well bred. She spoke seldom and with precision, and had little customs of her own; for instance, at the middle-class dinners to which she was invited, she always wore a hat trimmed with great bows of grey watered-silk. She knew nothing of literature and admired everything her son wrote, without in the least understanding it; I am not certain that she read his works. She adored Paul, spoilt him, and forgave him everything. Afterwards she had often to repent her too great indulgence, enduring in silence the bad habits he acquired; she dared not scold him even when he came home drunk, which happened rather often. She would help him to bed, bring him *eau sucrée* and *tisane* and then, retiring to her own room, burst into tears. But the next day she was always ready with excuses for the dear drunkard, throwing the blame on his comrades—of whom I was one—for the excesses to which Verlaine spontaneously abandoned himself without even the example of his friends, for we were far from drinking as deeply as he did. Some of our little circle were, on the contrary, excessively sober, L. - Xavier de Ricard drank nothing but water, and Coppée and Dierx only went to the cafés to meet their friends and talk.

Madame Verlaine did not leave her son until his marriage. They lived together at 26 Rue Lécluse, after the death of the Captain. Afterwards she accompanied him when he went to stay with his relations in the north, and on several occasions took part in his adventurous wanderings. She was near him at the time of the trouble in Brussels; she lived with him at Boulogne-sur-Seine, on his return from Belgium; and during the last years of her life she lodged in the Rue de la Roquette, then the Rue Moreau, near the Cour Saint-François, where Verlaine had rooms behind a wine-merchant's shop.

Her death on the 21st January 1886 broke the last link between the poor exile and his own

people. The month of January was particularly
fatal for the family; Captain Verlaine was buried
on the 1st, his wife on the 23rd, and Verlaine
himself on the 10th.

The loss of his best friend left Paul very
desolate, totally abandoned to his own devices,
without ties, a prey to all the allurements of
drink, the irregularities of a Bohemian life, evil
associations, degrading pleasures, misery and
sickness.

Verlaine's youth, except for visits to his relatives
at Fampoux, Lécluse, and Paliseul, was spent partly
at the house in the Batignolles, and partly at a
school in the 19th *arrondissement* (then the 2nd)
quartier Saint-Georges. When Captain Verlaine
resigned he came to Paris, and at first, while
awaiting his household effects, stayed at a hotel
in the Rue des Petites-Ecuries. Paul was seven
years old, and his first impression of Paris, which
he has described with an exactitude probably
derived from further acquaintance, was unfavourable. He found "the network of very high
houses, with their mouldy walls of a doubtful
grey, and yellow stucco façades, covered with dust
and greenish stains" very miserable. It is true
that the district in which the family were staying
is one of the least attractive in Paris. The Rue
des Petites-Ecuries is crowded, noisy, narrow, and
gloomy, full of warehouses, trucks, packers nailing
up wooden cases on the footpath and sheds, in
which impatient horses keep striking their hoofs
on the resounding pavements.

When the furniture, forwarded by slow train,
arrived from Metz, they quitted the hotel, and

Captain Verlaine, attracted by the hope of finding
some brothers-in-arms in the Batignolles, a district
largely frequented in those days by retired army
men, went to live at No. 10 Rue Saint-Louis,
not No. 2, as the *Confessions* erroneously states.
The Rue Saint-Louis is now called the Rue
Nollet. The Verlaines occupied an apartment on
the second floor of a house with a decent, middle-
class exterior, unchanged in the present day.

Paul was sent as a day boy to a little school,
still in existence, in the Rue Hélène, where he
learned to read, to write, and the four rules of
arithmetic. Carle des Perrières, afterwards a well-
known journalist, was a school-fellow of his in
these early days. About this time the boy was
attacked by one of those fevers, so serious in
childhood and dreaded by mothers, and Mme.
Verlaine tended him with the whole-souled devotion
of which she afterwards gave many proofs. During
his convalescence Paul felt the growth in his heart
of an entirely new sentiment—that of filial love.
Hitherto he had loved his mother, as all children
do, with a sort of animal instinct, from habit, but
now he realised his affection, he understood how
much his mother loved him, and with what tenderness he ought to repay that love; to the natural
and almost, if not altogether, unconscious attachment of the child for its mother, succeeded a filial
love both human and genuine.

"This sentiment, powerful and sweet, and,
above everything, good," wrote Verlaine, "showed
itself first of all by a surprising and heartfelt
submission, accompanied by a delicious desire to
weep. No *tisane* was too bitter, no medicine too

disagreeable to draw from me, when offered by my mother, aught else than a smile, almost I might say of beatitude, and when the cure was complete, ardent embraces, warm and tender kisses, moistened with burning tears on her cheeks and her hands; how refreshing to my poor childish heart, so pure then and always when I think of my mother; to my poor man's heart, unhappy through my own fault and the fault of having her always with me, especially now that she is dead. . . . But no, she lives, my mother, in my heart, and I swear to her here that her son lives with her, cries upon her breast, suffers for her, and has never for an instant, even in his worst errors, or rather weaknesses, felt himself without her protection, her reproaches, and her encouragements." (*Confessions*, Part I.)

These are excellent words. Perhaps Verlaine, writing forty years afterwards, may have exaggerated the gratitude and love he felt at eight years of age for his kind mother. Like sorrow, filial love is a fruit that needs a good strong branch to sustain it.

In this veneration, very lawful and laudable for his adorable mother, of which Verlaine afterwards gave many proofs, particularly in his writings, there was a touch of literary recollection. We know what admiration, perhaps excessive, he expressed for Mme. Desbordes - Valmore, and perhaps a certain filial canticle of the sweet Marceline's sometimes sounded in his ears. The perfume of filial love, with which he was wholly impregnated, particularly at the time when he wrote his *Confessions*, was intermittent, and at times evaporated, but only to reappear shortly;

it was a persistent aroma. It even happened that
Verlaine was once accused by an over-zealous
magistrate of having desired to make his mother
die—of sorrow perhaps! Not otherwise, assuredly.
No matter how quarrelsome he might be, in
consequence of inflaming libations, anger, and
still less hatred, never found a place in his heart.
Verlaine had the warmest sentiments of affection
for his family. His grief at the death of his
father was sincere and deep; and afterwards he
experienced great sorrow when he heard of the
loss of his cousin Elisa. This young woman,
older than himself, had always loved and spoiled
him, had had a hand in his bringing up, and
furnished the necessary funds for printing the
Poèmes Saturniens. She married, rather late,
a sugar manufacturer in the north, near Douai,
and died in childbed. Verlaine has described his
mournful sensations during his miserable journey,
in the rain and icy wind of winter, through the
sad Douaisian country, and his arrival, covered
with mud and soaked with rain, at the house of
mourning, from whence he followed through the

"incessant downpour, his cousin, his dear, ever
regretted, good, well-beloved Elisa, borne by
eight old women, in long, black mantles with
immense hoods like nuns, and unaffected sorrow
on their faces, for she had been very kind to
the poor! . . ."

Although he had caught glimpses of rather than
known his son Georges, an infant at the time of
the separation, Verlaine felt a real affection for
the child. It was not only a conventional and

correct sentiment, a paternal pose, but a genuine instinctive tenderness, unreasoning and impulsive.

After the little school in the Rue Hélène, where the scholars were mere babes, Paul was sent to a large and important establishment in the Rue Chaptal, the Institution Landry, which has only recently been broken up. The pupils were prepared by classes at the Lycée Bonaparte, and the College Chaptal, for the *baccalauréat* and special schools. The head of the establishment, M. Landry, was ill, it was therefore conducted by his brother, M. Fortuné, a great mathematician, irreverently nicknamed by the boys the "Père Pointu." He was an excellent man, very strong in "x y z," cosinus and logarithms, but rather ignorant of other things. One prize distribution day (I was for some time a day boy at this school), I asked him if I might recite a poem by Victor Hugo (*Le Régiment du Baron Madruci*). He scratched his head and asked: "Whose is the poem?" "Victor Hugo's." "Ah! Victor Hugo? The one who writes in the newspapers? . . ."

The school, however, prided itself on having turned out some remarkable men, notably Sainte-Beuve, and the engineer C. de Lapparent. Paul Verlaine was an ordinary pupil to begin with. He found it difficult at first to become accustomed to boarding-school life, and even went so far as to escape on the day of his arrival, taking advantage of the door by which the day boys went out. He ran off home, his hair disordered by his haste, and throwing himself into his parents' arms began to cry. They lectured him till he promised to allow himself to be taken back to school; and the next day he was re-installed at the Institution Landry, where he was to remain for several years and make his first communion.

He belonged to a circle which reverenced the Catholic traditions. If Captain Verlaine, like many officers, was rather indifferent to the things of religion, although maintaining a respectful attitude towards the Church, and her time - honoured authority, Mme. Verlaine, on the contrary, was pious, and carefully observed all solemn days. Although as yet the ideas and mystical emotions he was afterwards to experience in the prison of Mons were quite unknown to him, Verlaine made what is customarily called a good first communion, and after this initiation he entered the Lycée Bonaparte, class No. 7.

The pupils of the Institution Landry were taken twice a day to the Lycée. In a long, noisy and rather disorderly file the boys trooped down the Rue Blanche, the Rue Saint-Lazare, and the Rue Caumartin, under the guidance of a bearded, badly-shod usher, who was impatient for the cigarette and *absinthe-anis* in the Place Sainte-Croix, which whiled away the time until ten o'clock, when the return journey was made.

It was at the Lycée Bonaparte that, as I have said, I first made friends with Verlaine, when we were in the second class (1860). He was two years older than me. I was only fourteen while he was a big boy turned sixteen—somewhat young for his years. Our relations were hindered by the school routine. I was a day boy and free from all supervision out of hours, could return home-wards just as I liked, idling along the boulevards, looking in the shops, buying chestnuts in the winter and iced drinks in the summer, according to the fancy of the moment and the state of my purse; whilst poor Paul, still a prisoner, returned with the other boarders to the Rue Chaptal.

The Lycée Bonaparte was composed of free day boys, supervised day boys, and pupils from institutions on the right bank of the river, who all attended the various classes. We had little opportunity to make friends with the last-mentioned, but the bond of literature drew Verlaine and me together.

The professor of the second class was M. Perrens, a distinguished university man, author of a history of Savonarola and a conscientious work on modern Italy, a defence of Etienne Marcel, the great head of the merchants of the fourteenth century. Verlaine said of him: "M. Perrens detested me and detests me still." He exaggerated the facts of the case. Our professors were majestic personages, indifferent to the conduct and application of the greater number of their pupils. They took their classes in cap and gown, some of them having palms in violet embroidered on the latter, a distinction in those days peculiar to the University. They rarely deigned to supervise their classes, occupying themselves almost exclusively with ten of the older and more studiously inclined boys who figured regularly in the lists of honours. Their exercises were read, their compositions carefully examined, and they were questioned. The others, the insignificants as they were called, might read novels, papers, and magazines during the class, or, like Verlaine and me, write verses and

draw figures on the margins of exercise books,
without fear of interruption or reprimand.

One master alone formed an exception to these
eminent pedants with their disdainful apathy; the
good, gentle, and slightly grotesque English
master, M. Spiers. With an originality for which
he was held in derision in the Lycée, even by
his colleagues, M. Spiers directed and followed
all his pupils, questioning them and correcting
their exercises. I owe a debt to the excellent
man for his conscientious supervision; it helped
me to take more trouble over my exercises, to
pay more attention to the lessons, and afterwards
to continue the study of English. It is impossible
to learn a living language at a Lycée, but the
first idea of a foreign idiom can be acquired,
together with the inclination to master it more
completely.

Verlaine, like myself, felt the influence of the
good M. Spiers. He acquired the elements of
the English language sufficiently to be able, afterwards in England, when led thither by events,
to make himself understood, and even to achieve
a certain acquaintance with English. When, as
a man, he set himself to study it with enthusiasm
during his stay in London, he regretted more than
once that he had not taken greater advantage of
the lessons of the excellent M. Spiers, to whom
justice for the first time is doubtless now rendered.
The good man has been dead a long time, and
this eulogy is simply an act of homage to truth.

If each of our professors had taken as much
pains with his pupils as the English master did,
we might have been average scholars and escaped

the trouble we afterwards had to obtain our diplomas, and to learn, unaided, Latin, Greek, and many other things quite as unnecessary for success in life as for happiness.

Good M. Spiers, in spite of his zeal and the care with which he poured instruction into the little brain pans inclined towards him in the rows of the English class, was often obliged to close his ears to certain shufflings of feet, rustlings, and buzzings, transforming the place into a hive in which the bees were drones. When the noise became too perceptible, he distributed irregular verbs to be copied out right and left. Sometimes he would stop in the middle of the lesson and cry out with comical solemnity that he regarded all conversation among the pupils as a "tacit" demand to be sent out of the room.

The professor of history was M. Camille Rousset, the author of various historical works on Louvois, the volunteers of the Republic, and the conquest of Algeria, who was afterwards made an academician in consequence. Our literature master was M. Deltour, who has left a name in the scholastic world. Young, dark, bearded, with a thin ascetic face, he recalled a Sorbonnian of the sixteenth century. He had, moreover, adopted for the authorship of his works the name of a celebrated scholar of the Renaissance, "Tournebœuf" or "Turnèbe." Racine was his favourite author and he quoted him on every occasion, appropriate or otherwise. Naturally we preferred the long-haired romantics to the tragic bewigged one, and scandalised our Racinian professor by approving Auguste Vacquerie's blasphemy that "in the forest of art Shakespeare was a tree and Racine a stake." We did not always persist, however, in this unjust comparison, and the penetrating analyst of *Bajazet*, the subtle psychologist of *Andromaque*, and the bold physiologist of *Phèdre*, received from us due meed of admiration.

Verlaine soon returned to his allegiance for Racine, impelled thereto by the delicate intoxication he experienced from inhaling the aroma of the poesies of Madame Desbordes-Valmore, that sweet violet in the field of poetry, for whom he had always an admiration which amounted to a cult.

Our class numbered more than fifty pupils. I have discovered a list of the places obtained for a composition in which I was sixth and Verlaine fourteenth. Several names figure in it which have since become known : Richelot, famous surgeon and physician ; Humbert, also a surgeon ; Paul Stapfer, well-known University man ; Marius Sépet, religious publicist and biographer of Joan of Arc ; Abel d'Avrecourt, poet and critic ; Albert Millaud, one of the chief editors of the *Figaro*, parliamentary reporter and dramatic author, whose joyous *répertoire* made, with the aid of Judic, the fortune of the Variétiés ; Ducloux, accomplished notary ; Destailleurs, orientalist ; Marzoli, republican publicist ; Vernhes, pastor ; Hayem, *dilettante* and humorist ; Heugel, music publisher ; Lespérut, distinguished diplomatist ; and lastly, that excellent Antony Jeunesse, who, under the nickname of the *propriétaire*, had the happiest of reputations in the Quartier Latin, where he was for a number of years the leading spirit, while at the same time one of the most active of republican agitators. It will thus be seen that in the rhetoric class alone, in the Lycée Bonaparte in 1862, there were many budding notorieties. Two of our comrades committed suicide—one from want. This unfortunate, named James de Rothschild, lost money—thirty-five millions at cards. He was the son of Nathaniel de Rothschild, a fair, timid, amiable young man, who studied law and figured in the list of solicitors. Being unable to pay, and his family considering thirty-five millions was too large a sum for them to think of furnishing, the poor heir of so many millionaires blew out his brains—the victim of a name. A Rothschild cannot play for ordinary stakes.

I stated elsewhere that our poet was an assiduous student, sometimes one of the best, and was confronted with Verlaine's own contradiction, he having confessed himself an idler, to whom punishments were not wanting. This was true, generally speaking, yet especially in rhetoric he studied well. Latin greatly interested him; he made rapid progress, and at the prize distribution received rewards for Latin translation and French composition.

I can positively assert that he seriously went in for rhetoric, and was really interested in that branch of knowledge, instruction in which was given more in the form of a lecture than of a class. He paid great attention to any information which went beyond the range of the day's lesson, M. Deltour being wont to dwell upon subjects outside the particular one he was explaining. For instance, one day he read us a piece of verse by a poet who, far from being classical, was a revolutionary and a romanticist : Hégésippe Moreau, a poet of the people. The piece was entitled " Recollections of a Hospital," and was a ballad with a melancholy refrain, after Villon, in which the poet, comparing his own case with that of his predecessor when he was expiring in the hospital, bemoans his wretchedness and desolation, curses the age in which he lives and weeps. Verlaine did not appreciate this lachrymose verse, and later on declared that he took little interest in suffering in a hospital. The remembrance of M. Deltour must have counted for something in his persistent reprobation afterwards.

Without being very strong in themes Paul was a good enough rhetorician, and the list of honours bears witness to the fact that the University did recognise now and then in both of us youthful knowledge and aptitude which, it must be confessed, were somewhat irregular and intermittent. We put into practice Fourier's theory with regard to attractive work, and did our tasks in rhetoric well because rhetoric pleased us.

My powers, however, like Verlaine's, were restricted, and in Latin declamation, Latin translation, and more especially French composition alone did we rank with the promising pupils. In the sciences, and principally geometry and trigonometry, we were absolute failures, whence it happened that in our finals we got ill-omened red marks for the science oral examination.

I became fast friends with Verlaine in consequence of a school task, a French composition which he rendered in verse, attracting thereby the sarcasm of M. Deltour and all my sympathy. I waited for the author of the poem when the class was over and congratulated him. We at once exchanged our last attempts at poetry, freshly blown, and by the evening seemed like old friends.

After this we kept up our relations by the interchange of books, copies of poems, and confidences. We showed one another our effusions, and discussed their merits.

To complete these details of Verlaine's student life I may say that the Bachelor of Letters degree was rather difficult to obtain in those days, and that Verlaine took it by storm on leaving the Lycée, *i.e.*, on the strength of his University training alone ; while I thought it prudent to cram up in two months special classes with the excellent professor, M. Herbault, the examiner at Chaptal and Fontanes, who died nine years ago, and whom I had the pleasure of knowing up to the end.

A certificate delivered to the Hôtel-de-Ville when Verlaine's application for employment was being considered, stated that—

"I, the undersigned, head of the institution, certify that the young Paul Verlaine studied in this institution from October 1853 to July 1862 ; that he attended with the success indicated by several prizes the courses of instruction at the Lycée Bonaparte, from the sixth to philosophy exclusively ; that his conduct was that of a good pupil, and that he has completed excellent studies, receiving the degree of Bachelor of Letters at the end of his rhetoric. I have only an excellent report to make of this pupil, who is one of the many distinguished students the establishment can number.

"*Signed:* Landry, 32, Rue Chaptal."

It may be seen from this sort of certificate of

study which without being compulsory, was advantageous for the classification of candidates for the
Government offices that Verlaine was by no means
the idler and ignoramus he made out. It was
always his pleasure to make the worst of himself.
His biographers, M. Ch. Donos among others, has
been wrong in attaching too much credence to his
Confessions, in which he often poses as one of the
most deplorable of failures. His good work as
a student gave him a real appreciation for the
classics. He often expressed his liking for Latin!
Everything he wrote was certainly influenced by
his excellent and arduous University studies, unsuspected as they were by several of his disciples,
and by a singular perversity concealed by himself.

PAUL VERLAINE.
Aged Two Years.

CHAPTER III

(1862-1864)

HAVING finished his studies, and obtained his degree, Paul Verlaine went into the country to spend his vacations with his mother's relatives at Artois. He also went to see his Aunt Grandjean, in the Ardennes.

Verlaine was intensely patriotic, both in the wide and the narrow sense, as citizen and as native. Just as his love for his mother in no way diminished his affection for his father, and the reverent esteem in which he held his memory, so his attachment to Arras, Fampoux, Arleux, and Roeux, his mother's country, did not prevent his finding pleasure in the country round Bouillon and Sedan, near the banks of the Semoy, where his father was born. He divided his love for his native land between the plains of the north and the wooded slopes of the Ardennes.

He has several times affectionately described the scenery of Bouillon with its aisles of greenery of every shade, affording glimpses of the blue sky beyond; fir trees, beeches, and ash trees, and above them the feudal castle with its heavy posterns and thick walls, once furnished with oubliettes which are

45

now mere purposeless cavities. He has, although not much of a gastronomist, lauded the trout of the Semoy, calling them divine. Later on will be found letters in which he vaunts the charm of the plains of Artois and the marshes of Fampoux.

He had a strong feeling for the land which had given him birth ; and, in spite of his irregular habits, errors of conduct, singularities of character, vices real and imaginary ; in spite, moreover, of those friends and circumstances of his which would seem most likely to destroy such sentiments, he always retained his respect for the flag, his love for his fatherland, his hope, as his Ode to Metz proves, for the renaissance, military territorial, and moral, of France. He became an outcast, a vagabond, a pariah, but never a cosmopolitan, a renegade, nor a bad patriot. As long as patriotism is honoured as a noble sentiment and a virtue, Paul Verlaine must be regarded from this point of view as an honourable and virtuous citizen.

Verlaine often stayed in Artois, where his mother was born ; its melancholy had a charm for him—particularly in early life. He loved to wander through the fields, breathing the morning air and brushing through the dew. At one time he even went in for shooting, and after such expeditions with what satisfaction he would sit down to table in the inn ! He loved all the life of the north : the warm smoky interiors, which Van Ostade has painted ; the beer, a horrible bitter Flemish drink which has no point of resemblance with the creamy beer of Bavaria ; the great draughts of sourish black coffee in which chicory predominated ; the tobacco which he obtained at a very cheap price—thanks to the smugglers. How he would smoke and break the brown and red clay pipes with their protruding tufts of tobacco, lighting them again and again at the brazier with its glowing cinders, for the nicotian weed is always rather damp in that part of the country.

In the village ale-house he would spend long hours dressed like a rustic seated at a table, his legs stretched out in the attitude of one of Adrian Brauwer's figures, smoking and sipping with evident satisfaction the bitter draughts of coffee, mingled with brandy, which are called " Bistouille." He had no affinity with the south; he used to declare that he did not like the sun, and that the full noontide dizzied and overwhelmed him; I do not think he ever passed the southern boundary of Paris except for a cure at Aix-les-Bains and his short stay at Montpellier as a child. He never visited Spain, although he had a great admiration for Castilian literature, and placed Calderon de la Barca almost above Shakespeare. He once determined to learn Spanish by himself, and wrote to me on the 10th September 1864 to ask me to lend him my Spanish dictionary. But I do not believe he made any serious progress in the language of Cervantes, and certainly afterwards he forgot all he had ever learned. He intended to translate Calderon's drama *For Secret Outrage, Secret Vengeance*, but this project was never realised. His access of Hispaniolatry was confined to admiration, proved and reiterated for the author of *The Physician of His Honour*, and to the loan of my Spanish dictionary, to which I added *Sobrino*, a grammar of the Castilian language.

Longer than his love for Spain Verlaine retained his rural tastes. During the last years of his life he could only gratify them to the extent of choosing in preference to any other hospital that of Tenon, which is situated on the heights of Belleville, near the fortifications. Although I did my utmost to persuade him to come for a rest to my house on the outskirts of Paris, and he promised a hundred times to accept my cordial hospitality, he could never make up his mind to board the train for Bougival. Everything was ready for his reception; a room fresh and gay looking out upon the Seine, with the green poplars of the Isle of Croissy opposite, a table for work with French and English dictionaries, and a collection of ancient and modern poets; moreover, a jar of tobacco, a choice of pipes, clay, wood, and meerschaum, a divan for siestas, a boat in which to idle along the banks, and cool green arbours wherein to enjoy a drink and listen to the song of the birds. But all this was powerless to move him; he remained rooted in the Quartier Latin. Once I really thought I had succeeded in enticing him; he even accompanied me to the Gare Saint-Lazare, but at the last moment left me under the pretext of posting a letter, and I did not come across him again until half an hour later when, tired of waiting, I went for my train. He was seated at a table in a café near the station before a large glass containing a jade-coloured fluid, evidently the successor of several others. Intoxication had already set in, and he obstinately refused to accompany me, alleging an important appointment with a publisher for that evening, but faithfully promising to come the next day. I went off shaking my head. . . . He never came.

Although he seldom wrote sylvan verse he always yearned after the life of the fields, and that he appreciated rustic pleasures when he was quite young the following letters written in 1862 testify. A portrait taken at this period represents him clad in a blouse, and having all the appearance of a countryman.

"LÉCLUSE, 16*th September* 1862.

"MY DEAR LEPELLETIER,—As I do not know your address (I was then spending my vacation at Riceys) I write on the chance to the Rue Laffitte in the hope that as soon as my letter is received you will answer it, if only with a few words. Without further preamble I may tell you that I have been accepted (as a *Bachelier-ès-Lettres*), fortune favouring me on 16th August, the day of my oral. I had white for my translation and red for my discourse. For the oral I had all red except one, generously conceded me by the history examiner ; one is not a pupil of Rousset's for nothing. The next day I packed up, and the day after I was in the country. I have therefore one month in which to breathe pure air and clear my head and lungs, all dizzy yet with Greek and mathematics, in the atmosphere of the fields ; here without more thought than Colin Tampon has for Demosthenes and his logic, or the sum of the angles of a triangle, free as air, my dear fellow, and joyful as a liberated prisoner, I am giving myself up to the pleasures of the country, to wit—walking, fishing, and shooting. Walking and fishing were set aside when hunting began, which in this fortunate northern district is on 6th September, and truly I am not so bad at it. I came home yesterday with an enormous rabbit I had shot ; but there is a knack in it as Gavroche would say.

"What I shall do after the holidays I have not made up my mind. My parents are in favour of the law, and I think on the whole they are right, so I may keep my terms. However, as I said, nothing is decided at present.

"And you, my dear Lepelletier, what are you doing? Are you still in the country? If so, and you fish, shoot, or ride, give me in your next full details of your exploits in these several directions. Or have you gone back to Paris? Oh, in that case send me a whole budget at once. I am a Tantalus thirsting for news; do not withhold the fruit and water from my parched mouth; write to me at the earliest possible moment, tell me all about the new publications, acquaint me with every-thing that is going on in town, let me know all there is to be known—the more the better.

"Tell me also a little about yourself. Are you working up for your degree? When do you go up? What do you intend to do when you have passed? Have you finished reading *Les Misérables*? What is your opinion of that splendid epic? For my part, I have arrived at the end of the second volume of the *Idylle Rue Plumet*, so that I cannot pass a final judgment on it. Up to the present my impression is favourable; it is great, fine, and, above all, it is good. Christian charity illuminates the gloomy drama. Even its faults, and they are enormous, have an air of greatness which attracts. This hoary book, compared with *Notre Dame de Paris*, Victor Hugo's undoubted masterpiece, gives me the impression of an old man, but a fine old man, with white hair and beard, of commanding figure and sonorous voice like the Job of the *Burgraves*, beside a young man with aristocratic features, proud and courtly manners, waxed moustache, his rapier drawn ready for the fray. The young man pleases the most, he is more brilliant, more attractive, handsomer, but the old man, lined and furrowed though he be, is more majestic, and his gravity has something holy in it, which the liveliness of the young man lacks.

> "'A flame glows in the eyes of the young,
> But in the eyes of the old there is light.'

At this point, my dear Lepelletier, I must leave you. You will write to me very soon, will you not? My respects to your parents, and for yourself a hearty shake of the hand.—Thy friend,

"VERLAINE.

"My address is: M. Paul Verlaine, chez M. Dujardin, à Lécluse (Nord), par Arleux."

Here is the second letter of those holidays, mingling regret for town and literature with pleasure in life in the country. In this second letter a landscape is described in the classic manner by the escaped rhetorician.

"LÉCLUSE, *4th October* 1862.

"MY DEAR LEPELLETIER,—At last I can take up my pen for a little talk with you; I may tell you that latterly my time has been entirely occupied with the *Ducasses*. These are the village *fêtes* which succeed one another with a rapidity, which, by my faith, is highly injurious to the legs and stomach—the former especially. So if I have been rather dilatory in writing to you it has not been my fault, and I hope you will not be angry with me. With these words of excuse, let us to our subject. You are right, there are a hundred things to say, and one forgets ninety-nine. Thus, for example, in my quality as a more or less descriptive poet do I not owe you a picture of the 'place which holds me,' as Boileau romantically puts it? Here it is ; with it I will commence my letter, and after such splendour of colouring it will seem to you a veritable *desinere in piscem.*

"Lécluse is a large town of nearly two thousand inhabitants, furnished with a mayor and two assistants. The town is not in itself of an exclusively transcendental picturesqueness. The one street of which it is composed is implacably straight and clean as a new pin, with two gutters if you please, and two footpaths—the Rue de Rivoli in miniature! The roofs are red tiled. As to the surrounding country, it has nothing remarkable except some marshes shaded by trees of all sorts, poplars, elms, willows, set about with reeds and water - lilies, white and yellow, and bordered all round with chickweed, cress, and forget-me-not.

"Sometimes I go, book in hand, and seat myself before the melancholy Flemish landscape, remaining there for hours, dreamily following in their uncertain flight the blue king-fisher, the green dragon-fly, or the pearl-hued wood-pigeon. The fields, properly speaking, are fertile but monotonous. Picture to yourselves entire plains of beetroot, intersected occasionally by roads, scantily shaded by aspen trees, standing something like thirty feet apart.

"However, I must be just; manufacture, which reigns despotically in this Department, has not yet chased away all poetry, and I have two woods, not large it is true, but charming; up hill and down dale, with many a shady path and glade echoing with the song of blackbirds and doves. They might be the scene, these woods that I love, of those delightful fairy plays of the great William's wherein Oberon and Titania dance, Rosalind bewitchingly torments her Orlando, trees produce sonnets, and madrigals spring up like mushrooms. I am compelled to confess that Nature is not so poetical as that here, and there are more nuts than sonnets, and black-

berries than madrigals; but that does not prevent
these woods from delighting me, nor me from losing
my way very often for the pleasure of losing it,
just like one of George Sand's heroes.

"Now, shall I tell you of my *Ducasses*? Of
Homeric feasts and impossible balls? It would
need the irony of Heinrich Heine, or the pencil
of Hogarth, to give you an idea of the fantastic
quadrilles in which whirl round, moved as by strings,
big creatures clasping plump beauties clad in light
robes (my love of truth prevents me from adding,
O Scribe!) 'of an extreme whiteness.' All this to
the noise of a chaotic orchestra: mad clarionet,
hoarse piston, intemperate violin and triangle, yes,
triangle, held by a child who strikes it noisily,
neither more nor less than the little Bohemian his
kettle in *Notre Dame de Paris*. That, my dear
friend, is the orchestra which has made me dance
for six consecutive days. But spare your pity, there
were not only red-cheeked, untidy peasants, but
several charming girls—Parisians—and among them
the daughter of the head of one of the institutions
whose pupils attend Bonaparte, Mdlle. Hiolle,
with whom I had the honour of dancing several
quadrilles.

"As to my return, I have not made up my mind.
I think, however, the time is not far distant; indeed,
it is very possible that in a fortnight I shall see
this overgrown Paris of ours again, and shake your
hand in person. Meanwhile, write to me as soon
as you can. Have you seen *Dolores*, Bouilhet's
new drama? The papers speak in praise of it.
There is in the second act a serenade which
Roqueplan of the *Constitutionnel* quotes at length
in his paper, and which is charming. My father,
although his pains have not left him since we came,
is a little better, and we all hope for a speedy
recovery.

"Adieu, dear friend, excuse this rigmarole, and answer it soon.—Your friend,

"Paul Verlaine.

"Chez M. Dujardin, à Lécluse, par Arleux (Nord)."

Our schoolboy friendship was strengthened and placed on a regular footing by the establishment of relations between our two families. My mother, daughter of an army man, promoted to the Légion d'Honneur, made great friends with Mme. Verlaine, and my father, whose brother was an officer in the Zouaves in Africa, was soon on good terms with the Captain, who, much preoccupied with his unfortunate investments, demanded endless appreciations of the shares on the Bourse. After formal calls we exchanged invitations and afterwards every week, and almost regularly every Wednesday evening, the day on which my mother held her modest weekly receptions, the Verlaines came to take a cup of tea, preceded by a little music. I was one of the instrumentalists. I avoided the musical section as much as possible, being a very unenthusiastic pianist, and awaited with impatience the commencement of the customary game of whist or loo, the predecessor of poker, which constituted one of the amusements of these middle-class parties. On another day the Lepelletiers went up the Rue Saint-Louis to the Batignolles; and there was another edition, with the exception of the piano, of our evenings. From time to time we dined with one another.

We took advantage generally, Paul and I, in the course of these visits and homely receptions of the

noise of conversation or interest in the entertainment, to retire to our own rooms in order to talk
freely on literary subjects, and show one another
our attempts at verse, while smoking many pipes—
for already we had discarded the youthful aspirations
of the cigarette.   We always went to one another's
houses laden with books.   Verlaine's little library
was, if not better furnished, at least in a different
manner from mine, more classical and historical.   It
included a certain number of new books, which were
a sort of initiation for me.   On the other hand, the
volumes which Verlaine found in my shelves certainly
had an influence on his culture.   I lent him Victor
Hugo, of which I possessed a complete set, *i.e.*, up to
Les Misérables in the edition Hachette; Jean Jacques
Rousseau, then my favourite author ; and the book
which was at that time the catechism of unbelievers,
Force et Matière, by Dr Büchner.   We had some
odd volumes of Balzac, Cadot edition, which we
completed as far as we could on the quays.   He
made me acquainted with *Les Fleurs du Mal*,
edition Poulet-Malassis, which I was eager to buy
in order to have for my own so precious a treasure ;
the *Ensorcelée* by Barbey d'Aurevilly ; two volumes
of a poet then altogether unknown ; the *Poèmes
Antiques*, and the *Poèmes Barbares*, by Leconte
de Lisle ; the *Emaux et Camées*, by Théophile
Gautier, in a little edition in-18 with a rose-
coloured cover, very rare nowadays ; the *Cariatides*,
by Théodore de Banville ; the *Vignes Folles*, by
Albert Glatigny ; and last of all a work which I
considered very wearisome, but which Verlaine
seemed to prize highly, the *Histoire de Port Royal*,
by Sainte-Beuve.

This hotch-potch of books, which formed our
earliest reading, is interesting in the analysis of
the formation of an intellect. We read with
avidity anything that fell into our hands. The
library of Sainte-Geneviève and a reading-room
facing the Sorbonne supplied us with the material
for the foundation on which a literary future was
to be built. We read pell-mell, telling each other
of books, and passing them on : the Greek classics
badly translated at the Lycée and regarded as im-
positions ; the historians Michelet, Henri Martin,
Vaulabelle, Louis Blanc; the philosophers Descartes,
Nicole ; one or two works by Proudhon, whose
Justice dans la Révolution et dans l'Eglise had been
suppressed ; Emile Saisset ; Jules Simon ; many
books of criticism ; Villemain and his pictures of the
literature of the sixteenth century ; Philarète Chasles
and his *Moyen-Age* ; Sainte-Beuve and his *Lundis* ;
Taine and his *Histoire de la Littérature Anglaise* ;
the ancient chroniclers : Palma Cayet, Montluc,
and D'Aubigné whom we admired especially as the
passionate poet of the *Tragiques*, forerunners of
the *Châtiments* ; the Vedic poems which M. Fauche
had just translated ; the *Ramayana* or some parts
of the *Maha-Bharata* ; foreign drama : Shakespeare,
Calderon, Lope de Véga, Goethe ; all sorts of
publications with regard to the French Revolution
and some English novels : *Dombey and Son*, and
David Copperfield, by Dickens, and *Vanity Fair*,
by Thackeray. We possessed nearly all the classics
Latin and French ; and some second - rate but
picturesque and imaginative authors, such as Petrus
Borel and Aloysius Bertrand, the delicate fantasist,
whose *Gaspard de la Nuit* in the original edition,

procured at Angers, enchanted Verlaine. The poet's private literary education, in reaction against the University teaching was almost exclusively romantic. It was the fashion at this period to swear by Victor Hugo; exile adding majesty to the authority of genius. There was more Hugolatry in 1860 than at any other time since 1830. The *Contemplations* seemed to us the very Bible of poetry. In spite of party spirit the *Châtiments* was less admired; its poetical inspiration degenerating too often into gross invective. The plays of Victor Hugo were considered the last word of scenic art. We despised Ponsard, Scribe, Emile Augier, Octave Feuillet, and all the "common-sense" school, and backed the passionate effusions of Auguste Vacquerie against everything that was not disorderly, violent, truculent and enthusiastic. It was the epoch of the sonnet *A Don Quichotte*. Barbey d'Aurevilly who was afterwards to laugh at the *Parnasse*, and to caricature us individually, delighted us, and, in spite of the retrograde opinions he vaunted, his articles in the *Pays* were devoured every week. But his diatribes against Victor Hugo, keeping pace with the publication of the volumes of *Les Misérables*, aroused indignation. We forgave them, however, because of his many brilliant acute criticisms, which branded feeble writers and thieves of fame with a red-hot iron.

Verlaine was a Republican, with a certain leaning towards those in authority and mystics. He greatly admired Joseph de Maistre. The *Rouge et Noir* of Stendhal's made a strong impression upon him. He unearthed, I do not know where, a *Life of St Theresa*, which he read with a rapture I was far from sharing. Yet he was not a believer in those days; if he frequently visited the churches, it was as an artist, and for the objects of art they contained. Saint - Séverin, Saint-German-des-Prés, and Saint-Sulpice with its two superb frescoes by Eugène Delacroix, received his especial homage. He also liked to listen at this period to two famous preachers, Père Monsabré and Père Minjard.

Verlaine's literary *début*, when he first came before the public in the form of print, took place in 1866 (in the journal *L'Art*, and verses published in *Le Hanneton*), but his first attempts date back at least to the year 1860. They were only crude, unpolished efforts, the disjointed, stammering phrases of a child in the world of literature. Of these rough drafts, torn up, burnt and lost, no trace now remains. Verlaine preserved nothing, not even a memory of these poetic babblings. The first piece of verse that he afterwards considered worth printing was entitled *Nocturne Parisien*. It is a picturesque and detailed description of the Seine, dedicated to me, and included in *Poèmes Saturniens*. I carefully preserved the original, or at least a fair copy of the rough draft which Verlaine had thrown away, so that when the idea of including it in his first volume of poems occurred to him, he had to apply to me. He had passed it to me in class, hidden in some book while the professor of Latin rhetoric, the good M. Durand, initiated us, in a gentle unconvincing voice, in the beauties of the *Electra* of Sophocles.

Jules de Goncourt, referring to this first attempt,

wrote to Verlaine when thanking him for the *Poemès Saturniens* :

"You have this real gift, originality of idea and exquisite arrangement of words. Your poem on the Seine is a fine thing, sinister and menacing as a morgue at Notre Dame. You feel for, and suffer with Paris, and the age in which you live. . . ."

Verlaine, alluding to these destroyed efforts which he called detestable, speaks of a sketch of a drama on Charles VI., the first act of which takes place at a masked ball when the king is on the verge of madness. The legendary forest where the monarch is assailed by a savage, half-crazed charcoal burner whose appearance provokes the royal dementia, and episodes in the Hundred Years' War were to constitute the principal scenes in the piece. He also mentioned his idea for a play in which Charles V., Etienne Marcel, and King John were to be the principal characters. Finally, he dreamed of a *Louis XV.* in six acts, in which Damiens would appear avenging, with his pocket-knife, the sister carried off and shut up in the Parc-aux-Cerfs.

None of these projects were realised. His dramatic work was confined to the comedy *Les Uns et les Autres* which, except for his unlucky benefit at the Vaudeville, and private performances among friends, was not played in a regular manner. I have the commencement of a play entitled the *Forgerons*, our collaboration in which was interrupted by the war, the Commune, Verlaine's marriage, and the events following after it ; and the *scenario* of a

fairy play. He also began a *Louis XVII.*, of
which a fragment has been published, the only
part, I believe, he completed. The first act of
the *Forgerons* was written, and a little more of
the dialogue, while the rest had not got beyond
the stage of analysis and *scenario*. Perhaps some
day I shall complete this interesting and original
play which, as a psychological picture of the
working-man, was a forerunner of *L'Assommoir*.

No unpublished dramatic MSS. by Verlaine
are therefore in existence. On the other hand,
there must be in the portfolios of old friends
fragments of unpublished verse—perhaps complete
short poems. The poet in his youth, and even
later, for he sent me from the prisons of Mons
and Brussels, enclosed in his letters, a large number
of fragments of *Sagesse*, had a habit of slipping
verses and drawings into his correspondence with
his friends. In later life he was careful not to
lose literature which might be transmuted into
gold, although sometimes, unfortunately, containing
alloy; but in those days he scattered at random in
his letters pieces of verse, often of a high standard,
which he could have included in his printed volumes
without a blush. He was later to regret this waste
of good material. After having declared in his
Confessions that he had not cared to publish anything bearing too evident traces of youthfulness,
he altered his opinion.

"Since changing my mind, I hardly know why,
I have searched among the not inconsiderable
remainder of my old papers, once innumerable and
in what disorder! with the intention of giving some
idea of my style of writing in those days, but found

absolutely no trace of any early attempts. Yet there must have been at least as much interesting material as was contained in the *Poèmes Saturniens* when they appeared in the first collection of *Poètes Contemporains*, Alphonse Lemerre, in the last month of 1867." (*Confessions*, Part I.)

This should read in the last months of 1866 or the first months of 1867, for the original edition of the *Poèmes Saturniens* bears this statement on the last sheet : "*Imprimé par D. Jouaust le vingt Octobre mil huit cent soixante-six pour A. Lemerre, libraire à Paris.*" The volume which appeared on the same day as *Le Reliquaire* by François Coppée, and after *Ciel, Rue et Foyer*, by L.-X. de Ricard, was the third issued by Lemerre, after his *début* as publisher, and his shop was indicated as the editing and publishing office of the paper *L'Art*, December to January 1866.

Verlaine added to the above statement :

"All that has survived this not very regretable shipwreck is two sonnets, one of which was published two years ago, at the time of a series of lectures in a Liège paper—if I am not in error! What devil unearthed the ancient raven? It was entitled *L'Enterrement*, and the first line ran :

"'Je ne sais rien de gai comme un enterrement!'

The other was published recently in the literary column of an evening paper by some one signing himself 'Pégomas,' whom I thank for his good intention." (*Confessions*, Part I.)

Always careless, and scarcely following the newspapers, Verlaine had not read the *Echo de*

Paris, in which, in a sympathetic article about himself, I had reproduced the sonnet *L'Enterrement*, found amongst my papers, very carefully preserved, classified, and arranged in packets since 1871 ; but, previous to that date, scattered, lost, or destroyed by my agitated mother on the eve or subsequent to political investigations or researches of which I was the object, under the Empire and after the Commune. A large number of letters and unpublished poems and fragments of Verlaine's, going back over the years before the war, that I possessed had thus disappeared.

The sonnet *L'Enterrement*, which was reproduced in *La Plume* of 1st July 1896, was reprinted in the völume of *Œuvres Posthumes*. Librairie Léon Vanier, A. Messein, successeur, 1903. This sonnet, dated 5th July 1864, is in the ironic and morbid style to which Verlaine frequently resorted afterwards. The piece is a rather precise composition, the details of the funeral ceremony paving the way for the final breakdown of the covetous heirs, who find it impossible to dissimulate their joy, in spite of the solemn demeanour proper for the occasion.

As to the other sonnet, *A Don Quichotte*, I published it in my literary column in the journal *Paris*, which I signed with the pseudonym Pégomas, and Verlaine afterwards reproduced it with comments. With regard to the un-Spanish "Hurrah!" in the first triplet, he said:

"Now better informed, and understanding that the local colour makes me appear as ridiculous as when I first wrote the sonnet, I have replaced the British exclamation by the proper 'Ollé!'" (*Confessions*, Part I.)

In regard to the *Vers de Jeunesse*, which figure in the edition of the *Œuvres Posthumes*, I will say, for the sake of accuracy, and without attaching any other importance to it, that the sonnet *A Don Juan* is by me. It appeared, under the pseudomyn " Fulvio," in the journal *L'Art* (1866), and was the first thing of mine published. The poet mentions, among these efforts of his early youth, another piece of verse and a poem :

"An imitation, oh, so unconscionably audacious, and oh, so bad of the *Petites Vieilles* by Baudelaire and a *Crepitus*, in the pessimistic manner, in which after a description of the interior of a ditch, out of malodorous mud — naturally — supernaturally appears the God who delivers a very bitter speech utterly disdaining humanity, his mother included! Here, again, I can only recall the first two lines of the long, perhaps too long, harangue of the strange divinity. But these lines, they are good are they not ?

" ' Je suis l'Adamastor des cabinets d'aisance,
  Le Jupiter des lieux bas . . . ' " (*Confessions*, Part I.)

Verlaine had a great taste for parody. He wrote, in a spasm of gaiety, the day after an excursion we had made to l'Villette, *L'Ami de la Nature*, a song in realistic slang, a forerunner of the Montmartrois species, and I remember we composed, in collaboration with François Coppée, two laments to the air of Fualdès, one at the time of Berézowsski's attempt, in the Bois de Boulogne, on the Emperor of Russia, and the other in connection with a notorious crime, the Frigard poisoning case, at Fontainebleau. Verlaine, moreover, published various triolets and satiric quatrains, such as the epigram on the photograph representing Alexandre Dumas, in shirt sleeves, holding Miss Ada Menkin, the lovely horsewoman of the *Pirates de la Savane*, on his knees, in a very suggestive attitude.

Verlaine spasmodically loved broad farce, and some time before the war, after having carefully wrought the delicate *Fêtes galantes*, and rendered enthusiastic by an idiotic vaudeville played at the Gaîté-Rochechouart called *La Famille Beau-trouillard*, he determined, with his friend Viotti, to undertake a similar farce to be called *Veau-cochard et Fils Ier*.

He wrote to me (no date; I imagine from the allusion to the *Fêtes galantes* that this letter was written at the end of the year 1869):

"*Friday 5th.*

"MY DEAR COLLABORATOR.—Does it not appear to you time to announce those *Forgerons* (the play of which I have already made mention)? Therefore could you not write to the address of the clock-man (Victor Cochinat, dramatic critic to the *Nain Jaune*, an allusion to the sign of the clock-shop of the Porte-Saint-Denis, Victor Cochinat being a black man) who finds the Parnassians such '*vilains bonshommes*' (an epithet from which resulted the monthly meeting of poets and artists, known as the dinner of the *Vilains Bonshommes* [wicked good-men]), a note something like the following: 'Our colleague, M. Edmond Lepelletier (I was then editor of the *Nain Jaune*) is now putting the finishing touches to a great prose drama in five acts and 40,000 *tableaux* entitled the *Forgerons*, which he has written in collaboration with the celebrated Paul Verlaine. The latter, a delicate poet, the much praised author of that great work, the *Poèmes Saturniens*, and that charming fantasy, the *Fêtes galantes*, is also the author, in collaboration with M. Lucien Viotti, of an opera-bouffe, which we believe will be a startling success, and the title of which is, up to the present, *Veaucochard et Fils Ier*. The manner of the telling I leave to you, MM. Offre - un - bock (Jacques Offenbach), Hervé, Léo Delibère, Lecoq, and *tutti quanti* . . . I count on you.

"I did not come on Wednesday, and shall not go out again for ninety-nine days, because *Veaucochard* must be finished, produced, and played here in a month or two. I am going to break this rule to-day by going to dine in the Quartier Ninacum (at Mme. Nina de Callias's house in the Rue Chaptal) with Sivrot (Ch. de Sivry) and Cross Carolus (Charles Cros, author of the *Coffret de santal*, and one of the inventors of the telephone). Moreover on Wednesday I intend to honour your rooms with the presence of your grudging

"P. VERLAINE.

"*P.S.* — Come and see me at the 'Ville', why not?"

This *Veaucochard et Fils Ier* was it ever completed? I am not even certain that it was seriously commenced. Lucien Viotti was a charming young man, but indolent in the extreme. With his leisurely manner and his melancholy sweetness I cannot easily imagine him making Veaucochard and his son talk in burlesque couplets. I have not an idea what this operetta, qualified as comic, could be like. Verlaine was at the time very much taken with the musical comedies of Offenbach and

E

Hervé. *Le Serpent à Plumes* enchanted him, and he greatly admired the *Ile de Tulipatan*. He was often with Charles de Sivry, his future brother-in-law, an accomplished musician, playing all sorts of parts, parodying all the masters, and a very clever counter-pointest composing mad galops and brisk refrains in polka time. It was undoubtedly this gay composer who aroused in him his taste for operettas.

Later on Verlaine gave Emmanuel Chabrier, the composer of *Espana*, the *scenario* of an operetta, which was re-written and re-staged and played under the title of *L'Etoile*, and under the name of another author. Paul was to have written specially for this piece the song of the *Pal*, the first couplets of which Chabrier sang to us; they began thus :

> " Le Pal
> Est de tous les supplices
> Le principal
> Il commence en délices
> Le Pal,
> Mais il finit fort mal. . . ."

Verlaine, besides deigning, in an interval between two delicate or powerful poems, to offer sacrifices to the frivolous, sometimes vulgar muse of the operetta and the café-concert, occasionally took part in burlesque charades which we improvised. Once he even sang a small rôle in a musical burlesque entitled the *Rhinocéros*, of which I was the author, and which was afterwards played more than a hundred times at the Théâtre des Délassements Comiques, its bright gay music being by Charles de Sivry. This was the only occasion on which Verlaine ever sang in public, or even among friends, for Nature had not endowed him with any of the gifts of a tenor; his voice being false, discordant, and impossible. My reason for relating this artistic episode is because the performance, and in particular its several rehearsals, had a decisive influence on Verlaine's destiny; it was the occasion of his being introduced to Charles de Sivry, whose sister he was soon to espouse.

I had met the strange little musician, Charles de Sivry, a long time before at the house of some friends, M. and Mme. León Bertaux, sculptors. Mme. León Bertaux, afterwards President of the Union of Women Painters and Sculptors, and the creator of a remarkable *Baigneuse*, for which she received a medal from the *Salon* of 1872, used to hold receptions in her studio in the Rue Gabrielle at Montmartre. These *soirées*, half suburban, half artistic, were amusing on account of their impromptu programmes, the medley of performers, and their most unusual eclecticism. The notabilities of the Butte found themselves cheek by jowl with the Bohemians of the Quartier Pigalle. There were performances of music and charades, and once for a more formal occasion, with written invitations, a platform for the performers, artists engaged and poets recruited, when François Coppée recited his fine piece the *Aïeules*, which he had just composed, I was asked to compose a libretto for which Sivry would write the music.

I concocted the *Rhinocéros* (afterwards enlarged and adapted for the stage), which only contained three characters. One of my friends, an amateur comedian with a pleasant voice, accustomed to perform Berthelier's *répertoire* at our little *soirées*, was

to fill the rôle of tenor ; but he was a traveller for a
great silk house in the Rue des Jeûneurs, and was
most inopportunely compelled to set out on a journey
some days before the performance was to be given.
Who was to replace him ? I took Verlaine to a
rehearsal in the Bertaux studio, and quite at a loss
how to fill up the vacancy I said to him : " You help
us, old man, you read the part, and the rehearsals can
go on just the same while I look about for a tenor."
My suggestion was agreed to, and Verlaine read
the part, by my faith, in a manner so comic and
with such burlesque intonations, passing from the
deep bass of a cathedral chorister to the falsetto
of a ventriloquist, that he bewildered and astonished
us. His performance was a blend of frigid burlesque,
and airy tragedy. What an unforgettable tenor
and singular comedian he made. Mac-Nab afterwards reminded me of him on this occasion. He
was a cross between a clown and an undertaker.
All those who were present at the rehearsal were
enormously amused (perhaps the actual performance was not quite so funny), burst out laughing,
and complimented the unexpected actor. " You
resemble Grassot," said a painter named Pécrus.
The compliment was a broad one, Grassot being
at the time the leading comedian at the Palais-
Royal and the king of buffoons with his famous
gnouf ! gnouf ! which Verlaine unconsciously reproduced, by reason of a little hoarse cough which
punctuated his words.

It must be confessed that in those days Verlaine's
physiognomy was one of the most extraordinary it
is possible to conceive. When he was first introduced to my parents, his close-cropped head, beard-

less chin, deep-set eyes, thick straight eyebrows, Mongolian cheek-bones and flat nose, so took my mother aback that she uttered an ejaculation of terror. "*Mon Dieu!*" she said to me after he had gone, "your friend made me think of an orang-outang escaped from the Jardin des Plantes."

At the time of the performance of the *Rhinocéros* a beard had begun to clothe Verlaine's chin, his eyes had acquired the expression of a faun's, his smile— and he laughed often and heartily—extended his mouth from ear to ear, which made it irresistibly comic; and lastly he affected the Banvillesque method of speech, clipping his words with his teeth, and emphasising them with his forefinger pointed forward and then solemnly uplifted. Clad in a tan-coloured macfarlane, dirty from long usage, with a tall, black hat on his head and a cane in his pocket, he produced a regular sensation. This *début* remarked, if not remarkable, led to nothing. Verlaine never even saw the *Rhinocéros* on the stage.

Among the audience, crowded together on the chairs which furnished the Bertaux studio, were the entire family Mauté, invited as belonging to the Montmartrois notabilities; the young Mathilde Mauté, half-sister of Charles de Sivry, being one of them. This was the first time she saw her future husband. He doubtless paid scarcely any attention to the little girl, then classed among the insignificant, and lost in the crowd, whom nobody troubled about. Perhaps, on the other hand, the strangeness of the poet, performing absurdities in the rôle of grotesque lover, made an impression on her, and later, when they met in the Rue Nicolet

and were introduced, as if they had never seen one
another before, the recollection of the *soirée* at the
Bertaux studio won doubtless for the saturnine
poet, doubled by a clown, a look of curiosity and
an amiable reception.   Clowns, comedians, and
stage buffoons, even the ugliest, perhaps especially
when they are very ugly, have always an inex-
plicable attraction, and their conquests are innumerable.   It was probably the comic character in the
Rhinocéros, rather than the poet of the *Fêtes
galantes*, who won for Verlaine the smile and soft
pressure of the hand, with a compliment at the
initial interview.   Perhaps, but for the *Rhinocéros*,
the tenor on journey, and the chance rôle confided
to him, Verlaine would never have been led into
crossing the threshold of the house in the Rue
Nicolet, a paradise soon to be transformed into
hell.   But, like books, operettas have their endings,
and our comic opera was, for one of its characters,
to be turned into a drama.

Verlaine, being full of the desire to write plays,
assiduously attended alternately at Montmartre and
the Batignolles the performances of the troupe
Chotel.   At that time, in the two local theatres
which were under the same management, the bill
was changed every week.   The troupes exchanged
theatres, taking with them the play they had
been performing all the week, and so both the
Batignollais and the Montmartrois had a first night
every Saturday.   They played the dramas and
comedies which had been successful at the Paris
theatres, and when there was a scarcity of novelties
they performed plays from the *répertoires* of the
Ambigu and the *Porte-Saint-Martin*, for the pieces

in vogue would not have sufficed, by reason of the
weekly change of bill, to supply these two local
theatres. Good artistes, with Chotel, the manager,
at their head, were to be met with in this
suburban company. On these remote boards,
Parade, Daubray, Nertann, Priston, and many
others whose names I forget, then beginners and
unknown, afterwards favourites at the Vaudeville,
the Gymnase, and the Palais - Royal, were
applauded.

Verlaine attended the performances in the
musicians' orchestra, into which he was introduced
by a friend, an amateur violinist, a very original
young man, even a trifle fantastic, called Ernest
Boutier, who disappeared without ever having
published anything, although he was for a time
one of the budding group of Parnassians, and had
doubtless, like the rest of us, in his portfolio,
lucubrations in prose and verse. Boutier played
a part in the literary life of our youth; he it was
who introduced us to the bookseller Alphonse
Lemerre, and guided the Parnassian band to the
Passage Choiseul, from whence issued the poetic
flight of 1869.

The suburban drama, the café - concerts of
Rochechouart, and chamber operettas, did not by
any means occupy Verlaine's whole attention.
His vast brain was open to all branches of art.
We made frequent visits to the Louvre and the
Musée du Luxembourg, and he did not miss any
of the picture exhibitions then held in the Palais
de l' Industrie.

"Come here on Sunday between two and a
quarter past," he wrote to me in May 1864, "and

we will go, if you are agreeable, to the *Salon*, although it is very bad this year." I have given the date, to be precise, for Verlaine's negative appreciation might be equally applied to other years. This was the habitual attitude. It is a fact that he went to the *Salon* from habit and for the sake of having been there.

He loved good music and was one of the first who assiduously attended the *concerts populaires* established by Pasdeloup, which have so greatly contributed to the expansion and elevation of musical taste in France. At these concerts in the Cirque du Boulevard des Filles-du-Calvaire, where for the first time the masterpieces of classical music, symphonies by Beethoven, Haydn, and Mozart, restricted up to that time to the aristocratic subscribers of the Société du Conservatoire, were performed before the public for a very small fee—it was cheap seats which made the success and fortune of Pasdeloup—and the attendance was large, as the following letter shows :

" *Saturday*, 24*th* (*October* 1864 ?).

" *MI BUENO*,—This is what has been decided by the most reverend Ernest (the violinist Boutier), and your humble servant, with regard to the concert to-morrow. I will be with you about half-past twelve. We will go and fetch Ernest in the Passage Verdeau, and from there we will go to the Cirque Napoleon, where we ought to arrive about half-past one, which is not too early ; it is better to wait half an hour and get good seats than have to stand for three consecutive hours, or to find the box - office shut, which might easily happen to-morrow, as it is the opening day,

PAUL VERLAINE—TERRITORIAL (1879).

PAUL VERLAINE AT 22.
(When Clerk at the Hôtel-de-Ville).

unless we are there beforehand. So be ready at half-past twelve; I shall knock at your door rather before than afterwards. Till to-morrow, and kindest regards. PAUL."

With the Bertaux *soirée*, when Paul Verlaine was first introduced to the Mauté family (1867), a new era in the poet's life commenced. But we must go back to Verlaine as clerk, a period of his life which lasted seven years, from 1864 to 1871.

CHAPTER IV

(1864-1871)

VERLAINE was for seven years a Government official. Having obtained his diploma as *Bachelier ès-Lettres*, and satisfied the conscription—the day before the ballot his parents had insured themselves against the unlucky number, and he drew an excellent one—it became necessary to think of finding regular and lucrative employment for the big lad of twenty. His parents, not without reason, considered poetry an unremunerative employment, and cast about for some other opening. A young man cannot remain idle. He was allowed several weeks' holiday, which he spent very happily at Lécluse and Fampoux with the Dujardins and Dehées, wandering through the fields, drinking the bitter beer he found so delicious, flirting with the girls in the inns he encountered on his walks, reviving himself with gin pick-me-ups, shooting, smoking, inhaling through every pore the vigorous country life he loved and, between times, reading for the satisfaction of his intellect the *Ramayana* of which he said: "By Indra! it is fine; how it puts the Bible, the Gospel, and all the effusions of the Fathers of the Church in the shade."

On his return to Paris while awaiting something better, he began to study law. He showed no special professional aptitude ; it seemed doubtful whether he would ever make a lawyer or a man of business ; vague official functions were thought of. The diploma of licentiate might be useful to him in a Government office, and he therefore began to go to the school of law, but stopped half way and devoted himself to the study of the drinking-shops on the left bank of the Seine, and the examination of the ale-houses in the Quartier Latin, where twenty years later he was to submerge will, talent, strength, and health.

Captain Verlaine knew nothing of these divergences beyond the range of his attentive vigilance. He spoke to every one of his desire to "start Paul." On the recommendation of one of his old comrades-in-arms, M. Darcet, a retired officer, who was one of the Directors of an Insurance Company, Paul presented himself and was accepted at the offices of the "Aigle" and the "Soleil" Insurance Companies, now amalgamated, and having their headquarters in the Rue du Helder. The combination was managed by a M. Thomas, who styled himself " De Colmar " until he became " M. le duc de Boïano."

In order to obtain an appointment Verlaine had been subjected to a course of professional training in writing, book-keeping, and accounts, by a special tutor named Savouret in the Rue Faubourg-St-Honoré, and in the course of several months he learned how to "write." The *Bacheliers ès-Lettres* who are turned out by the Lycées have no aptitude for gaining their bread by the use of their pens in an office. It was impossible to admit the young rhetorician into any Government office whatsoever, his tortured handwriting at best being only good enough for copy for the printers, who are wonderful at deciphering hieroglyphics.

After having undergone this necessary preparation, and been instructed in the profound art of writing a business letter, Verlaine was at length installed in front of the rows of green pasteboard boxes in the offices of the " Aigle " and the " Soleil." This business appointment had a more considerable influence than might be supposed upon the poet's existence. He was perforce sober, and in our leisure time we used to ramble together along the quays, turning over the cases of dusty books, and hunting for pictures in the museums and churches, and penetrating, without any educational aim, into the heart of the cafés. We had to find places where little or no expense was entailed, for our parents left us, from motives both of prudence and economy, with a very slender purse.

At the end of his first month in business Verlaine received his first instalment of salary. It was a day of days. It had been arranged that he should hand half of it over to his parents, retaining the remainder for his personal expenses : dress, pleasure, books, and amusements. Returning homewards on this thrice happy evening of Sainte-Touche, we stopped once or twice at various cafés, and finding this a pleasant relaxation, repetition soon converted it into a habit. I used to meet him coming out of his office about five o'clock, and we would turn our steps towards the Café d'Orient, a vast establishment in the Rue de Clichy. There during the prolonged process of having a drink we talked on every subject that interested us—literature, art, and politics—and Verlaine, falling into the habit of renewing his glass of green liquid, contracted the desire for drink which at a later date service on the ramparts during the siege was to develop into what seemed at certain periods of his life a regular disease. This craving for drink, which bordered on dipsomania, undermined his moral and cerebral stamina, and eventually led to his social and even intellectual downfall.

He had entered the service of the Insurance Company while awaiting an appointment in the Government Offices for which he had made a formal application, supported by M. Tassin, a friend of my father's, head of the Custom House. After having passed an examination in writing and book-keeping, exhibited his diploma, and furnished the requisite papers, he was admitted in March 1864 and appointed clerk in the municipal offices of the 9th *arrondissement*, Rue Drouot, in connection with the marriage bureau. After a certain time in this department he passed into the central offices, and was appointed clerk in the Bureau of Budgets and Accounts.

Verlaine certainly was not a very zealous clerk at the Hôtel-de-Ville; his assiduity was intermittent. On arrival at a quarter past ten he signed the book, cast an apprehensive glance at the pile of documents before him, pushed them gently aside, and, hidden from view by the heaps of green pasteboard boxes which stood on his bureau, unfolded the morning's paper, drew silhouettes, or lazily rhymed a quatrain. At noon he escaped, bareheaded, from the office, leaving his hat on the peg as an assurance of his presence in case of a visit from the assistant chief. He was supervised only by the head clerk named Guy, an honest, careful, and hard-working man, who, being chiefly desirous of obtaining supplementary work, was naturally pleased with a colleague unlikely to hinder him. Verlaine's duties consisted in issuing orders for the payment of the salaries of ministers officiating in Paris and curés in the suburbs.

Once out of office Verlaine made his way with a light footstep to the Café du Gaz, Rue de Rivoli, where a numerous and poetical company assembled every day. The Hôtel-de-Ville, under Baron Haussmann, was exceedingly hospitable to literary men. It is common knowledge that Rochefort passed through the offices, working about as hard as Verlaine. Georges Lafenestre, Ormand Renaud, Léon Valade, Albert Mérat, all poets destined to achieve a certain degree of literary fame in the course of a prolonged official career, were among the municipal employees who regularly frequented the Café du Gaz. Later on, when I was at the Palais I lunched there sometimes. Many were the conversations that took place in this café among poets, youthful literary aspirants, and masters in the art, who came by invitation. Rising above the voices of contractors who, after lunching at the Belle-Gabrielle, were wont to discuss tenders and contracts over their coffee, could be heard noisy and heated discussions, on the full rhyme the "e" mute, blank verse, and all the other details of verse-making, which for us were of enthralling interest. We read letters of literary advice; we listened to travellers, such as Emile Blémont, then a young barrister lately returned from Italy, who spoke with enthusiasm of that country favoured by art; we recapitulated what had been said at the Saturdays of Leconte de Lisle, down there by the side of the Gros-Caillou; we spoke of those strange early poems by a young professor of English, named Stéphane Mallarmé, whose obscure and studied style Verlaine admired, and we excitedly read the reviews and newspapers in which questions of poetry and literature were dealt with. This was undoubtedly a pleasanter way of spending the hour after midday than in filling up order forms in company with good M. Guy.

Verlaine's career at the Hôtel-de-Ville could hardly be called brilliant. He had not even obtained promotion when the war broke out. He could not make up his mind to go in for the necessary examination, very easy, but indispensable, for advancement. He by no means regarded Government service as the ideal employment for himself, yet he made no attempt to look for another appointment, nor to engage in literature from the point of view of making money. He never thought of leaving the "Ville." He believed himself tied to his stool for life like so many others, and awaited with a clerkly fatalism the triennial increase in his salary, composing verses meanwhile, and not making the slightest effort to climb higher. At no period of his life did Verlaine evince ambition; he never expressed a desire to attain any distinction whatever. Towards the end of his life, inflamed by alcohol, he certainly conceived the idea of applying for admittance into the Académie, instigated by some joke on the part of his companions, which for the

moment he appeared to treat seriously; but only
for the moment, the impulse ceased with the conversation which gave it birth. He had not to
regret any aspiration unfulfilled, any favour postponed or denied, because even at the time when
no objection on the score of his irregularities could
be raised against him, he asked for nothing.

After the publication of the *Poèmes Saturniens*
and the *Fêtes galantes*, he might have claimed the
academic honours recently instituted by M. Duruy;
he even refused to be put up for membership in
the Société des Gens de Lettres when Charles Joliet
offered to nominate him. He was indifferent to
money. He had the prospect of a reasonable competency in the future, and that, doubtless, caused
him to neglect occasions for advancement; yet
by passing an easy examination he might have
increased his limited salary to 1,800 francs. He
made no more effort to gain money by his pen than
to improve his official position. Now and again
he would place some article in a literary paper, but
it would be only an ephemeral publication which
did not pay for contributions like *Le Hanneton*.
His productions, whether verse or essays in criticism,
did not come within the realm of regular marketable
journalistic work. At no period of his life, not even
when I opened up to him the columns of the *Echo
de Paris*, was he capable of doing anything in the
way of journalism. It requires a special knack to
be able to turn out copy likely to be appreciated
by thousands of readers. Moreover, journalism,
even of an exclusively literary character, such as
that into which some of Verlaine's companions,
Mendès, Coppée, and Armand Silvestre — then

riding an independent Pegasus, were afterwards
drawn, requires special qualifications, precision of
mind, fit choice of subjects, power of expression,
etc., etc., which Verlaine, irregular in everything
and a vagrant even in intellect, could never force
himself to acquire. He was always the exact
opposite of a professional man of letters, and had
neither the taste nor the *technique* of a writer
who lives by his writings. Amateur *virtuoso*, intermittent observer, fantastic dreamer, he produced
literature as a briar wild roses, and never troubled
to obtain from it any sort of profit. He wanted
his productions to be read, but gave no thought
to the number of his readers. He published collections of verse, because manuscript poems cannot
be distributed among one's comrades, critics, and
masters. He printed all his first volumes at his
own expense, and received very little money from
the booksellers, Lemerre, Palmè, and Savine.

Except with Fasquelle and Vanier in his later
years his copyrights represented nothing. The
press, so ready to hint evil of symbolists and
decadents, having created round the name, work,
and life of Verlaine that atmosphere of infamous
notoriety which condenses into paying advertisement, it was possible for him to make money out
of his later and inferior verse; and then only did
the unfortunate poet set about turning into gold the
dry leaves of his manuscripts. He achieved his
purpose laboriously, for he had neither custom nor
tact to guide him in his relations with publishers.
They did not hasten to open their purses, for they
had doubts as to the punctual delivery and sale of
any work they might acquire. If Verlaine succeeded

F

in extracting a few hundred sous pieces from Vanier, who having published the greater number of his works, did not desire a competitor to appear with the unpublished, more saleable ones, it was after much bargaining and many entreaties, vituperations, and threats not very creditable to either party. These bargains, generally concluded in the street or in front of a marble-topped table, resembled a second-hand sale or distribution of charity rather than a literary man's formal contract with his publisher.

His existence as Government clerk was tranquil and untroubled by official incident, yet in the meanwhile three events occurred, which had a decisive effect on the private life of the poet: he married (August 1870), the war broke out, and was followed by the siege and the Commune.

Freed from military service by his ballot number, and having moreover furnished a substitute, belonging by his class (1864) to the reserve list, and as a married man exempt from inclusion in the effective force of the national guard, Verlaine was perfectly at liberty to follow the example of many other municipal clerks and take refuge in some duty which, while it necessitated the wearing of uniform, made no other call upon him. But he was a Republican, a good patriot all aflame with zeal and ardour for the defence of his duty, so he got himself appointed to the 160th battalion of the Rapée-Bercy. At this time he was living at No. 2 Rue du Cardinal-Lemoine, Quartier de la Halle-aux-Vins (5th *arrondissement*, Panthéon).

Honest Paul had the heart of a hero, but the physical capacities of a pantaloon, which was the mocking nickname given to the sedentary National Guards. Great drawers of corks were they in their enthusiasm for their country, and the boldest of strategists in front of any counter or table where drink was to be had; but these soldier citizens were not entrusted with any very important duties. They were neither drilled nor commanded, and their devotion found no practical outlet. A clever and bold general would have subjected them to a severe course of discipline, and transformed them into effective belligerents—but Trochu was not such a one.

Verlaine's battalion was stationed among the southern forts between Issy and Montrouge. We did not meet during the war, although when the 13th Corps de Mézières returned we were not far from one another. My regiment the 69th of the line, defended the redoubt of the Hautes-Bruyères between Montrouge and Villejuif. Armed with a heavy gun, Verlaine gloomily mounted guard with a resignation less and less patriotic. He was quickly discouraged, and very soon tired out; and only too willing to rest from the warlike exercises, he considered superfluous and harassing, in the friendly shelter of some canteen. National defence made the soldier citizens very thirsty, and Verlaine was promptly put at the head of the deep drinkers of the battalion, the majority of which were men of Bercy connected in some way or other with the wine trade. It was not long before he returned home drunk and worried his wife—perhaps he was over affectionate—and one fine evening she quitted the conjugal hearth for the first time, and took refuge with her parents at Montmartre. They had been scarcely six months married, and the ink had not yet dried on the glowing sheets of *La Bonne Chanson.*

In consequence of an attack of bronchitis, stated to have been brought on by sentry duty on a cold night—the which was attested by the major of the battalion — Verlaine was allowed to retire from active service, and invited to resume his official duties, a place having been kept open for him at the Hôtel-de-Ville. So not without a certain feeling of relief he put down the gun of a national defender, never to take it up again.

Although favouring in principle the movement of the 18th of March, and sharing the sentiments of the majority of Parisians, who dreaded the restoration of the monarchy, he took no part in the insurrection. If afterwards he was classed among the Communists, it was only by putting a very broad interpretation upon that dangerous appellation. He did not go to Versailles—that was the whole of his crime. Moreover he was not at any time the object of a judicial ban for taking part in the Commune. These facts have often been misstated.

M. Thiers quitted Paris precipitately on the 18th March 1871 in a carriage, which to the gallop of two excited horses carried him far away from the tumultuous city. The little man left all the public services to shift for themselves. His flight was so prompt that he did not even remember to give orders for the evacuation of the offices of the ministry and prefecture. Gradually the adminis- trative chiefs departed in their turn for Versailles quite spontaneously, and of their own free will. It was not until some days after the stampede that the heads of departments went thither also by special command, to organise provisional services. No regular instructions were given to the inferior employees at the Hôtel-de-Ville; no one ordered them to cease from their daily routine and await at home an invitation to rejoin their chiefs at Versailles. The Government of Versailles afterwards published in the newspapers it controlled, which naturally were little read in Paris, a notice recommending the Government employees to abstain from all their functions, and to await the orders of their official heads. Some obsequious clerks, in order to curry favour and merit, favourable notice and advancement, without awaiting the orders which after all were never sent, packed their bags at the end of a fortnight and fled from rebellious Paris, in imitation of M. Thiers. Arriving at Versailles in a state of affright, they exaggerated the cause of their alarm, enlarged upon the perils from which they had escaped, and put their glossy silk sleeves at the entire disposition of the Government. M. Thiers would have preferred a regiment of artillery, and little notice was taken of these useless quill-drivers. Some wandered about Versailles until the entry of the troops, but the greater number returned unobtrusively to Paris, and, benefiting by the holiday, awaited the course of events, uneasy only as to whether their arrears of salary would be paid up. After the downfall of the Commune they all returned to their desks.

Verlaine alone took a different but perfectly natural course. The distastefulness of leaving Paris for a place overrun with soldiers and officials, and some friendships among the leaders of the movement, notably Raoul, Rigault, Andrieu, and

Léo Meillet, decided him to remain. His wife, besides, did not wish to leave her parents, and he would have been obliged to take his mother with him. The Hôtel-de-Ville had not budged, and he returned to it with the docility of custom, seated himself in his usual chair in the room to which he had been allotted, and went on with the regular routine as if nothing had occurred to disturb it. He was perfectly logical in his attitude. An employee ought to know nothing beyond the seat, writing - desk, and register that has been assigned to him. He is part of a complicated machine, and as long as it stands he must perform his functions regardless of political events. The only authority he has to recognise is that of the being who sits in the chief's armchair and issues orders. The Government had undoubtedly changed since the 18th of March; but was this any reason why the daily routine should be disturbed?

There were precedents, on the 4th of September the Government had been changed as completely as on the 18th March. Not a single employee of the Hôtel-de-Ville, however, had ceased to occupy his stool; nothing had been altered except the notepaper headings and stamps representing the imperial eagle. M. Thiers had been removed from the head of the state like Napoleon III., Charles X., and Louis Philippe, and he would be replaced. It was nothing to do with the employees, and the idea that any harm could come to them from remaining at their posts would not be expected to enter any reasonable brain.

The employee who continued at his post, in spite of the political upheaval, was naturally made

much of by the new masters of the Hôtel-de-Ville.
It was impossible at such a time to regulate the
administration perfectly. The more urgent matters
had to be attended to first. There were municipal
functions which could not be interrupted, for they
had to do with the events of every day—births,
deaths, police, commerce, customs, etc., etc. The
department to which Verlaine was attached was
not one of these; the salary sheets of ministers
and curés could wait, and he was accordingly transferred to the Press bureau; his literary qualifications causing him to be chosen for this employment,
which consisted in making cuttings from newspapers. Verlaine received no promotion in this
department; had he done so he would certainly
have been charged at a later date with usurping
the position.

Verlaine took no part in the political and
military affairs of the Commune. He made verses
to the noise of the cannonade of the Point-du-Jour,
imitating Goethe, who, according to Théophile
Gautier, during the wars of the empire at Weimar,
shut himself up, and, deaf to the thunder of the
cannon, gathered the roses of Hafiz, and composed
the *Divan Oriental.* He had not even the curiosity
to descend into the street as a spectator during the
great and terrible days when Paris was taken, in
order to contemplate the sublime horror of civil
war.

His wife, who had returned to her husband on
the preceding 22nd of May, hurried off to her
parents in the Rue Nicolet, directly the news
spread that the Versaillais had passed the Porte
d'Auteuil, and shooting had begun in the Champs-

Elysées; she left her husband and home to the care of a smart little servant girl, her filial sentiments being more developed than those of wifely anxiety or even jealousy.

Verlaine has described in his *Confessions* our meeting on that fatal Wednesday, 24th May 1871; but as some of his facts are not altogether precise, I will go over it again, for it is a fragment of actual history.

I found myself on that day with my friend Emile Richard, afterwards President of the Municipal Council of Paris, and now dead, in the neighbourhood of the blazing Hôtel-de-Ville. We were almost shut in between two fires; the troops from Versailles having gained the banks of the Seine, and the Federates still occupying the barricades in the Rue des Nonnains d'Hyères, Rue Monge, Boulevard Saint - Germain, and Boulevard Bourdon. It was as dangerous to go back as to go forward, and I suggested to my companion that we should take refuge with Paul Verlaine, as we were near his house, and I thought it improbable that he would be out.

I happened to be right in my supposition; he had passed the previous day in a windowless dressing-room scared by the cannonade, and had endeavoured to persuade the little servant to bear him company, to reassure her, he said, and himself also—doubtless one feels braver with a companion.

We were neither begrimed with powder nor in the uniform of the National Guards, as Verlaine states in the *Confessions*; he probably retained but a hazy recollection of the facts, for the emotion under which he was labouring was strong, and our arrival

increased it. Emile Richard wore a *képi* and
breeches with a purple stripe; for he was then
a medical student, and had been on ambulance
duty during the war. We had been in the act,
Richard and I, of returning to the Rue d'Aboukir,
to make up the last number of our newspaper
the *Tribun du Peuple.* I was dressed in the attire
I had worn throughout the whole of the Commune,
viz. : ordinary civilian clothes, without badge or
scarf, although I was a delegate of the Council
of State.

Poor Paul was so frightened, that after a repast
sent to the devil, omelette, salad, and all, he could
not be induced to go out on the balcony and
contemplate the hideous magnificence of the
spectacle which was the veritable panorama of a
Roman emperor!

He lodged on the fourth floor of No. 2 Rue
Cardinal-Lemoine, and the balcony of the apartment gave on the Quai de la Tournelle, opposite
the Pont Marie; spread out, therefore, before us
was a vast space all in a blaze of sun and fire.

Beyond the Seine rose the heights of Passy,
Montmartre, Belleville, and where the river disappeared, Ivry and Charenton. In the foreground
stood Nôtre Dame, a huge bulk of unrelieved
shadow, with the Hôtel-de-Ville on one side a
glowing, red-hot mass, and the Palais de Justice
on the other enshrouded in a thick pall of smoke,
from which darted at intervals enormous tongues
of blue flame. There was a roar as of furnaces,
splitting, crashing, rending, and the sky grew
overcast with the smoke on to which were thrown
gigantic crimson reflections. Ever and again, like

a flight of crows or bats, uprose a cloud of bits of paper, blackened, charred, shrivelled, which soared aloft, whirled around, and darting into the masses of smoke disappeared from view. They were the remnants of the archives of the Exchequer, the Council of State, and the Prefecture of Police. Although the Hôtel-de-Ville waxed red-hot, with banners of flame floating from its high roof like the flags of some festival, the edifice remained almost intact except for its emptied windows, and was reflected upon the surface of the Seine vibrating with the thunder of continual explosions.

On the left, on the right, on the south, and on the north, the colours of the sunset glowed at full noon; a study in ochre, bitumen, and vermilion. Columns of vapour were continually uprising as far as the eye could reach, like screens between each glowing brazier. Clear and distinct alone rose up the delicate point of the gilded spire of Sainte-Chapelle, emerging as if mysteriously protected from the falling roofs of the blazing prefecture. Suddenly, in the east an enormous volume of flames burst out: green, blue, purple, red, and yellow, they darted forth like gigantic sword-blades, discordantly painted in barbaric hues; the great granary, filled to overflowing against a time of scarcity, had taken fire. I cried to Verlaine to come out, if only for an instant, on to the balcony, but could not prevail upon him to do so; he pretended he must remain with the frightened Louise in the dark dressing-room.

From Père-la-Chaise and the Buttes-Chaumont came the muffled roar of cannons, the last volleys of the conquered, while the fusillade of the conquerors at the Bastille rent the air, and added to the horror of the scene; savage music accompanying a terrible yet superb drama. The powder magazine at the Luxembourg blew up just as we were seating ourselves in the *salle* for *déjeuner*, and the whole quarter trembled, the windows shook, the dishes rattled. "Ah," cried Verlaine, "the Panthéon falls into my plate!" and he took refuge anew in the dressing-room.

Every now and then he plaintively referred to his mother, and less frequently to his wife, calling himself a wretch to be there in safety when he ought to be out searching for them. At last they arrived, his mother coming in first from the Batignolles. She must have traversed the whole of Paris on foot, right through the half-destroyed barricades, picking her way among ruins, ashes, and smoking fire-brands, and the still warm bodies of those who had just been shot, holding up her skirts lest they should be soiled in the pools of blood. Verlaine's mother, an officer's widow, did not approve of the Commune. She could not conceal the feelings of horror inspired in her by this struggle, then only in its initial stages, legitimate or at least justifiable and excusable though it was.

Mme. Verlaine's narration warned Emile Richard and me that it was time to depart, the place was not safe, Verlaine's apartment was only a temporary refuge, no matter how favourable the landlord and other tenants might be; there were no signs that any one intended to denounce the two intruders as yet; but this happy state of affairs might not continue, and when it was apparent that the Commune was definitely worsted, our presence

might become a danger.   The most prudent course
was to decamp; yet retreat was perilous.   The
infantry were winding their way along the quay in
Indian file, close to the houses, evidently making
for the Place du Trône (now the Place de la Nation),
where, as I learned afterwards, they were to meet
some other regiments of the division Susbielle.

If we fell in with these men, weary, irritated as
they were, and ready to shoot or run through the
body any suspicious person who passed within
range of their at last victorious armies, we should
have short shrift.   They would not wait for any
explanations, all they would ask of us was that we
should allow ourselves to be pinned unresistingly
to the wall.   To remain at Verlaine's, on the other
hand, was to expose ourselves to the probability
of being arrested by the police following behind the
soldiers, besides compromising the excellent fellow
who, after all, had given us an asylum wherein to
rest and gain time, which sometimes means life.
The luck I have encountered twice or thrice, on
decisive occasions, now intervened in my favour.

Leaning half over the balcony I was anxiously
watching the soldiers as they defiled past the
house, when I suddenly caught sight of some
faces I knew.   "Richard," I said, "you have
excellent sight, can you tell me the number of this
regiment?"   "The 110th," he answered quickly,
withdrawing his head as a shot whistled past his
ear, aimed intentionally perhaps.   "Quick, quick,"
I cried joyfully; "let us go down without an instant's
delay," and dragging Richard towards the Verlaines
I briefly explained my reason for insisting on an
immediate retreat; the 110th was the regiment to

which I had belonged when I had served as a volunteer, and the men who were passing under the windows were my old companions-in-arms. I had left them two months before at the end of the war, and had nothing to fear from them as I was neither a national guard nor a combatant, and they did not even know that I had performed certain official functions under the Commune. They would in all probability help me to pass through the cordons of troops surrounding the little island in which we were enclosed; in any case they would tell me how to gain some quarter already occupied and settled down. There was nothing in my civilian costume to arouse suspicion; with a badge round my arm I might easily have passed for an *Ami de l'Ordre*.

It was quite otherwise with Emile Richard with his *képi* and purple - striped trousers. He loudly asserted that the dress of a doctor would pass him in safety anywhere, but I replied with an equal conviction that his *képi* would instantly proclaim him a Federate; and even if he were recognised as belonging to the ambulance corps, I was sure that to soldiers exasperated by the resistance they had encountered a Communist doctor would be as fair a mark as an ordinary Federate. Giving in to this reasoning Richard commenced to tear off his stripes, assisted by the scissors of the little maid, while Verlaine's wife borrowed from the landlord a black felt hat, with which my friend covered his thick head of hair. It was rather a tight fit, but Richard kept taking it off to wipe his heated brow. We now took leave of our hosts, and were soon in the midst of the column, the battalion coming to a halt at that moment. Calling by name the first man I recognised I asked him to direct me to Sergeant-Major Broca, the chief of my Company. "There he is, quite close," answered my one-time comrade, adding : "You mean Lieutenant Broca. . . ."

Two minutes later I was shaking the hand of the excellent Broca (now a retired commandant living at Ajaccio, his native town), and congratulating him upon his promotion, while all my old friends crowded round me, officers, corporals, and privates. A wine merchant on the quay had begun to open his shop. I offered refreshments. "We are forbidden to accept drinks from the Parisians," said Sergeant Peretti ; "but that does not apply to you who belong to the Company." Another sergeant, Arrio, who afterwards assisted with me at a patriotic ceremony at the Hague in 1905, offered to go in search of the liquid.

We drank merrily, and, needless to say, to the success of the Versaillaise troops. My comrades, tired and confused by the recent fighting, never thought to ask me what I was doing among the deserted barricades and troops on the march, and, in order to forestall any awkward questions, I told them that I had come to enquire after some relations in the Quarter, about whom I felt uneasy, and was now desirous of regaining my home with the friend who accompanied me, and we were expected at the Batignolles. "You could not get through by yourselves," said one of the officers, "but I will send a man with you to the Pont-Neuf, and once over the bridge, you will find the roads open."

I gladly accepted the offer, thanking him, but not

too warmly, lest he should suspect the importance of a military escort, and off we went, encountering at every step greetings and exclamations of surprise and pleasure from others of my old comrades, standing or sitting on the edge of the footpath. We were stopped at the pumps of the fire-brigade in the Place Dauphine, and had to run the gauntlet of the eyes of suspicious police officers; a critical moment, for we might be recognised and pointed out, which meant instant death. The Pont-Neuf crossed, we separated, and I went on towards the 9th *arrondissement* by way of almost deserted streets, Rues Sainte-Anne, Grammont, Taitbout, d'Aumale, and La Rochefoucauld. I knocked at the door of Charles de Sivry, Verlaine's brother-in-law, No. 65 Rue La Rochefoucauld, to give him news of his sister and Paul, and at the same time to send a message to my mother that I was safe and well, as she had heard nothing of me for three days. This is an exact account of what occurred at the end of the Commune. It differs in a few details only from Paul's sympathetic account in the *Confessions*.

Verlaine did not return to his office when, after six days' fighting in the streets of Paris, the defeat of the last defenders of the Commune, intrenched among the tombs of Père-la-Chaise, was completed. He could have presented himself at the Luxembourg, where the Government offices were now installed, without running any risk. In the general confusion it is probable that hardly any attention would have been paid to him, and in any case, a certificate from a friendly doctor would have furnished him with a reason for having remained in Paris, and as there would have been only his attendance at the Press bureau in the Hôtel-de-Ville to reproach him with, he would have come out of the affair with an admonition, or, at the worst, a bad mark against his name. But he alarmed himself.

He was of a nervous and very impressionable temperament, and believed that to present himself before the head of his department would be to court disaster — Caledonia at the very least. Therefore, he resigned, *i.e.*, he disappeared from the Government offices. At the bottom of his heart, perhaps, he was not very sorry for this opportunity to resume his liberty. He had had enough of office life, he said. He made no attempt to hide, which proves that his political terrors were exaggerated. He and his wife lived in the Rue Nicolet with her parents, and from the date of his resignation his misfortunes began. Scenes at home became frequent, for although he had no office to which to repair, Verlaine went out as usual, and his visits to cafés and wine-shops increased in number and length. After a time he left Paris with his wife to go north. There were hints of denunciation, even arrest, in the air; he grew frightened and decamped as rapidly as possible.

Circumstances separated me from Verlaine during part of that sad year 1871. I did not know where he was, and he could not write to me. He spent the summer partly with M. Julien Dehée at Fampoux, and partly with M. Dujardin at Lécluse. He wrote from thence to our mutual friend, Emile Blémont, who had recently married, and gave him impressions of the rural life in the north he loved so much, similar to those already quoted in letters from the same localities. Among other detailed and picturesque descriptions he dashed off the following sketch of his cousin's sugar manufactory :

"Our window looks out upon a large court, in the centre of which rises up a *Vendôme* column which, less pretentious and more useful than the defunct (here we recognise the Parisian who had lived for two months in the midst of the communal fever), is content with the humble name of chimney. Beyond it are brick roofs, pierced with a thousand pipes, each more bizarre than the other, and then vats, more vats, and yet more vats ; and if you like treacle, it is everywhere to be found.

"These surroundings, industrial to a degree, are happily compensated for by the near vicinity of a charming little wood which abounds in strawberries, nuts, and views. Moreover, my cousin possesses a *very comfortable* garden where pear-trees standing erect, peach-trees against the wall, and vines over arches, make a very impressive background for magnificent roses and enormous lilies. To smoke two pipes here after dinner (at twelve), to have seven or eight drinks at the inn (from four till five), and to see night fall in the woods while reading some tranquillising book, this is my new life, different indeed from that of Paris. We intend to return shortly to Fampoux."

These interesting letters to Emile Blémont appeared in the *Revue du Nord* on 1st February 1896.

Verlaine paid these visits chiefly to get away from Paris, still in a state of upheaval, also for a rest, to gaze upon the monotonous landscapes of the north, and finally to introduce his young wife to his relations at Fampoux, Lécluse, and Arleux.

G

He returned to Paris in September, a few days
before me, and I wrote to inform him of the sudden
death of my mother, which took place at Arcueil
on the 29th September.   He did not come to the
funeral, but sent a rather enigmatical letter of
excuse instead.   I greatly regretted his absence.
On a day of mourning such as this, it is a consolation to be surrounded by one's dearest friends.
Besides, I had only returned the day before from
an enforced stay at Versailles, and had not seen
Paul since our rapid adieux in the Rue du Cardinal-
Lemoine amid the roar of cannons and blazing fires
of Paris.   I knew nothing of his domestic affairs,
but suspected my friend was not happy, which added
to my trouble.   We should have had many things
to say to one another.   This is the letter Paul
wrote me :

" 30th *September* 1871.

" MY DEAR FRIEND,—My mother has told you,
has she not, the reasons which prevent my being
present on the sad occasion ?   Out of your old
friendship you will pardon, I am sure, my enforced
absence, and understand how deeply I sympathise
with your great sorrow.

" Please accept and ask Laura (my sister) to do
likewise, my sincerest condolences on the death of
your excellent mother.   Write to me I entreat, to
let me know either when I may come and see you,
or when you will come and see me.   Looking
forward to meeting you soon.—Your devoted friend,

" PAUL VERLAINE.

" 14 Rue Nicolet, Paris-Montmartre."

What was the real reason of his absence ?   Had
his mother informed me, and was I too greatly

overwhelmed by my grief to take it in? I have never been able to recollect any explanation being given, but imagine some domestic quarrel kept Verlaine away. Later on we will speak of the misunderstandings of the young couple and the unhappy epilogue to *La Bonne Chanson* ; at present we have only to do with Verlaine's official career.

His resolution not to return to the " Ville " was a hasty one. He did not consult his friends nor make any attempt to obtain information or an interview with his chiefs. He was merely influenced by the idle statement of outsiders that he would be arrested if he had the audacity to reappear at the office. This most unfortunate determination of his had a decisive and disastrous effect upon his destiny, and with it commenced the second stage, an unhappy and homeless one, of Verlaine's career. Although not yet the Bohemian and outcast of later years, he was no longer the man in easy circumstances who could occupy himself with Art and literature, and publish poems and fancies while retaining a regular employment and fixed salary. He had quitted the organised ranks of Society, but not to enter the independent company of literary men, which also has its own methods, order, tasks to be accomplished, and discipline to be maintained. He did not abandon his official career, as did many of his friends for the purpose of having more time to devote to literature ; they found more independence doubtless in their new sphere, but at the same time harder work. They endeavoured to import official regularity into the free world of literature, and to turn out a certain amount of copy in order to make up by their

literary earnings for the official salary no longer
to be expected at the end of the month.   Verlaine
published nothing and produced little during his
first months of liberty and complete leisure.   *La
Bonne Chanson* appeared not long after, but the
poems which made up this song of happiness so
long delayed as to be the *De Profundis* of a
defunct domestic bliss, were composed at a much
earlier date.   Paul might publish his lover's dithy-
ramb at this period, but he would have found it
difficult to revive the sentiment which had given
it birth in the preceding year.

More than once afterwards during self-examina-
tion Verlaine regretted that he had not tried to
retain or recover his position.   His official duties
would not have prevented him from rhyming and
publishing his rhymes.   Albert Mérat, Valade, and
Armand Renaud, all clerks at the " Ville," Armand
Silvestre in the Finance Department, Coppée for
a long time attached to the War Office, proved that
there was no incompatibility between the service
of the Muses and that of the State or the Prefecture.
In alluding to this regret of Verlaine's for employment lost, or rather foolishly abandoned, I am
not dealing with a mere supposition, neither am I
biassed by personal affection, I am merely stating
the subsequent opinion of Verlaine himself.   Many
years after these events, Verlaine permanently
settled in France, at the end of his resources,
without aptitude for productive literary labours,
aged, ill, or at least with health undermined, evinced
a desire to recover the tranquillity of mind, security
for the future, and regular salary of an official, and
he asked me to endeavour to obtain his reinstate-

ment in Government employ. He had neither been the object of any judicial enquiry, nor regularly and officially dismissed ; he ought to be considered simply as having resigned, having been absent from office since May 1871. His request was therefore quite feasible. Charles Floquet, with whom I had most friendly relations, was then Prefect of the Seine, and I addressed myself to him on the subject of the poet's reinstatement. Paul's application to the Prefect, which I supported, was as follows :

" To Monsieur le Prefet de la Seine, Paris.

" Monsieur Paul Verlaine asks to be reinstated in the Government employ, having fulfilled the duties of clerk for seven years. His last position was that of assistant editor. Dismissed in 1871 for having remained under the Commune. All the papers are in the hands of the staff."

This peculiar circumstance in the haphazard existence of the poet, and his desire to resume his employment, are not generally known. The facts I state herein, with a view to making clear the real character and life of Verlaine, have often been misrepresented and misconstrued, but they are established by numerous letters. On the 22nd October 1882, for example, he wrote to me :

" Dear Friend,—I would ask you to be so kind as to write on the return of the prefect to Paris, in accordance with your promise, with a view to my speedy reinstatement. . . .—Your old friend,
" P. V."

I put the matter in train at once. Verlaine was very impatient. He wrote to me again on

7th January 1883, probably in consequence of a difficulty raised by the Board:

" My case is as complete as possible. It cannot be expected that I should obtain certificates of good conduct from a number of inn-keepers whose names and addresses I will put down in the many towns I have happened to pass through in the last ten years! I have already had enough trouble to get a certificate from the Corporation at Arras, a town where I spent more than a year chiefly, it is true, with my mother, the mayor objecting that this was not enough. You can imagine therefore how the burgomaster of Machin or the Chief Alderman of Chose, where I spent a month in three or four hotels, would answer me. Tibi.   P. V.

" *P.S.*—I omitted in my note to you regarding M. de B——, to send you my new address: 17 Rue de la Roquette."

This M. de B——, to whom Verlaine alluded, was the President of the Municipal Council of Paris Jehan de Bouteiller, my colleague on the *Mot d'Ordre*. Verlaine wrote to me on the same subject in an undated letter:

" MY DEAR EDMUND,—As I told you the other day all the papers necessary for my application are ready—not one is missing. Nothing remains therefore except to clinch the matter, but time presses; circumstances may favour us if we act at once. Will you therefore see if you can say a word for me to M. de Bouteiller whose influence would doubtless be decisive if he would kindly speak to the head of the staff and the prefect in person. I shall be exceedingly grateful to you. . . ."

Some days afterwards he added: " You are going to put in a good word for me with M. de Bouteiller as soon as possible, are you not? "

These letters surely show how greatly he desired to resume his position under Government, to become once more a regular clerk, and thus escape the unhealthy influence of the wine-shops and saloons in which he afterwards, save for his long sojourns in hospital, dragged out his miserable days. But disease and disaster had their claws in him. The very day on which I was to obtain from my friend, the Prefect of the Seine, the poet's reinstatement in office, Verlaine wrote to me :

" An attack of fever, inflammation and coughing having seized me and reduced me to a mere wreck, I am putting myself in the hands of the medicine men for eight or ten days for a course of prudence, fumigation, pill - swallowing, draught - quaffing, *clysterium donare, ensuita purgare,* etc. After which seriously I hope to be all right again."

But Verlaine's hope was not to be realised. He renewed his application, but Floquet having left the prefecture, the heads of the staff and prefectoral departments put their veto upon it, the ignorant and erring judgment of Belgian justice being as usual brought up against him, together with the undoubted fact of his adhesion to the Commune and bohemian habits.

Verlaine therefore resumed his starved and disreputable existence. Official hostility threw him back, an outcast from ordinary society, into a life of misery and want. Yet he had greatly desired to re-enter the plane of respectability, and had every right to do so. The Prefecture of the Seine was in fault, and assumed a great moral responsibility in thus repulsing its former employee, who had committed no disqualifying offence. He had been condemned, it is true, but in a foreign land, by judges prejudiced against a Frenchman, and for a quarrel prodigiously exaggerated, and punished with excessive severity. He was guilty only, as far as the Government was concerned, of practical resignation, of an absence which the exceptional circumstances of 1871 might have well excused. Floquet's successor should have considered it as an amnesty. There was yet time to preserve his health, and give a new direction to his talent, by securing to the poet his daily bread, and replacing him in a sphere necessitating sufficient regularity of habit and life to prevent the degeneration of his poetic faculty and the consequent lack of adequate production which resulted from the refusal of his application.

Under the ancient monarchy pensions from the Exchequer, or great personages, or official sinecures, kept men of letters from want, and enriched our literary patrimony with many a precious treasure. It is much to be deplored that a great poet like Paul Verlaine, a Republican and patriot who had even suffered for excess of zeal, should not have been allowed to re-enter the service of a democratic Government. Reinstated in his position with its attendant literary and social life, Paul would have retained his health and added to his list of works masterpieces as exquisite as *Sagesse* or the *Romances sans Paroles*. He would have written in the tranquillity ensured in this age of manufacture and commerce by an official sinecure, which scholars and chroniclers of old found in the cloister.

CHAPTER V

LITERARY BEGINNINGS—THE *SALON* OF THE MARQUISE DE RICARD—THE *POÈMES SATURNIENS*—THE *FÊTES GALANTES*

(1864-1869)

IT no longer sufficed us, towards 1864, to read to each other our ingenuous poems in the solitude of the rooms allotted to us by our parents, apart from all other literary contemporaries. Our sphere was too restricted. Doubtless we found a certain satisfaction in the exchange of projects, opinions, ideas, paradoxes, criticisms, and fancies in our long walks, interrupted by halts at various cafés, either at the corners of the boulevards or in the Rue de Clichy, whither we went on purpose. Our favourite haunt was the Café d'Orient, no longer in existence, which used to stand at the top of the street near the Place Clichy. We began to desire a larger audience, and sought for one of those circles of which we had learned from Balzac and Joseph Delorme. We felt there must be something of the kind still in existence where we could encounter other young minds, poetry - struck like our own, eager to discuss literature and the possibility of opening up a new path towards Art. What is the use of poetry if there is no one to hear, admire, and criticise it? Chance provided us with the opportunity we sought.

A school-fellow, P.-L. Miot-Frochot, an amiable,
self-satisfied, and not particularly gifted youth, who
went in for work of an erudite character, mediæval
research, the romances of chivalry, etc., took us
to the house of a new writer, who was already
beginning to make a mark, Louis-Xavier de Ricard,
son of a general of the empire, the Marquis de
Ricard, formerly Governor of Martinique and ex-
aide-de-camp to Prince Jerome. Louis-Xavier de
Ricard was at this time quite young, dark, bearded,
grave, and devoured by a very fever of compilation, annotation, criticism, and lay exegesis; he
accumulated every kind of learning, his desire
embraced the whole cosmos of the intellect by turns,
sometimes simultaneously; poet, novelist, dramatist,
historian, philosopher, critic, journalist, popular
scientist, and politician, he seemed destined for
an encyclopædic career—as a matter of fact it has
been a chequered and unlucky one.

After having played a very active part in the
formation of the *Félibres*, and organised Latin *fêtes*
at Montpellier, where he played Aubanel in the *Pain
du Péché*, in the Languedoc *patois* he became chief
editor of the *Dépêche*, an important newspaper in
the south. His next proceeding was to put himself
up as candidate for the Hérault; but being beaten
by a minister, M. Devès, and at the same time
much cast down by a domestic calamity, he left
the country. It is known that he founded an agricultural institution in Paraguay. But further troubles
overtook him, and leaving Asunçion he returned
to France, wearied, aged, but not beaten. He
resumed his obscure and ill-paid literary labours,
and at present he is working on various socialistic

papers, besides occupying a position as curator in a new museum at Azay-le-Rideau. He was like a literary sun in the morning of our youth, which as it proceeded on its journey was obscured by clouds, and reappeared only at intervals.

In 1863 Louis - Xavier de Ricard, whose prestige as a writer of published works, was great in our eyes, but who, nevertheless, possessed neither the authority nor the desire to found a new literary group, employed a legacy left him by an aunt to start a philosophic and rather heavy review called the *Revue du Progrès*, which had the honour of being subjected to judicial enquiry. The case was in connection with an article, which nowadays would be considered absolutely innocuous, on a worthless book by Saturnin Morin, signed " Miron " and entitled *L'Examen du Christianisme*. Ricard was defended by a very energetic young barrister from the south named Léon Gambetta, whose admirable talents and prodigious good luck were not yet recognised—but the result was eight months imprisonment, which he spent at Sainte-Pélagie ; the manager of the *Revue*, Adolphe Racot, afterwards editor of the *Figaro*, having managed to get his sentence abated.

Ricard having met in court, when his case was on, some young men particularly interested in politics, and no strangers to literature, invited them to his mother's apartment. This was the commencement of a literary and political *salon* at No. 10 Boulevard des Batignolles, and although it might be regarded almost as a suburban one, for Batignolles had only recently become part of Paris, and still preserved some of its suburban features,

it exercised a decisive influence upon the movement
of ideas, and more especially the formation of a new
school of poetry among the literary youths of 1866-
1870. It was here that the *Parnassus* had its cradle.

Madame de Ricard was an amiable but rather
coquettish and flighty woman, who knew little of
literature and was suspicious of politics, but adored
her son, and was delighted that he should receive
his friends, and attract famous and interesting
visitors to the house. She liked to listen, without
joining in, to our eager and sometimes noisy discussions. She was passionately fond of youth, and
the noise suited her; we were all very young and
tolerably noisy, and were therefore welcome. Her
husband, the old general, allowed his apartment
to be invaded, retiring into his own room without
much fuss. In the daytime he wrote his indiscreet
recollections of the great personages of the imperial
family with whom he had come into contact. In the
evenings he tried to sleep, but could not close his
ears like his eyes, and our near vicinity was far
from soothing. Poor general, we certainly disturbed
the last nights of his life. Madame Ricard, who
survived him many years, died in 1905 at the age
of eighty-four.

This improvised *salon*, bohemian in character,
especially in later years, witnessed the first introduction of a rough-headed poet, whose appearance
had the effect of a dawn, viz., the brilliant and
sparkling Catulle Mendès: refinement in ringlets.
He was credited in those days with vices of
which he was probably ignorant, and the talent
of which he already showed signs was not properly
appreciated. Mendès, in his turn, introduced a

young man, pale and thin, with brilliant, deep-set eyes and inscrutable expression, whom he presented to us as a clerk in the War Office, desirous of reciting some verses. The newcomer rapidly won our admiration and friendship. After reciting some unpublished poems he announced the near appearance of his volume of verse *Le Reliquaire*; his name was François Coppée (familiarly Francis).

At his side might be seen a youth of serene aspect and tranquil mien, with a small nose, somewhat sententious speech, circumspect regard, and prudent handshake, Anatole France, who delivered himself of a sonnet, which had something to do with a turbot, placed by a decree of the Senate before Cæsar with *sauce piquante*. Sully-Prudhomme, the oldest of us all, grave and gentle, surrounded by the prestige of a volume of verse, *Stances et Poèmes*, published some months previously by Achille Faure, and recently returned from Italy, also recited in a slow, monotonous sing-song the admirable philosophical sonnets which later on were collected and published under the title *Les Epreuves*. One by one they leant against the mantelpiece to enunciate their verses, retiring afterwards to a corner in silence.

The strangest and most curious of the guests at Mme. Ricard's *salon* was undoubtedly Auguste Villiers de l'Isle-Adam. He was gifted with a genius that bordered on madness, trivial and sublime, cynical and enthusiastic; for his daring flights towards the infinite and the bizarre he mounted alternately Pegasus and a broom handle. He had in him something of the magician, something of the mountebank. He seemed intoxicated with air;

some said he smoked opium. We listened with astonishment, admiration, even fear. We almost dreaded when he narrated some strange tale, emphasised by fantastic gesture, some crisis that would cause him to fall down in a fit of epilepsy or hurl himself bodily upon his auditors. He affected a strange pronunciation, punctuating his phrases, emphasising his verbs, and sounding his adjectives, his many and rounded periods ringing out like a clarion. He borrowed his gestures and attitudes from Rouvière's *Hamlet*, who, it is well known, was mistaken for an actual madman.

José - Maria de Heredia, sonorous, exuberant, amiable, well-dressed, displaying a gold chain on his evening waistcoat, with his handsome brown beard, would declaim sounding verses and reproduce the cries with which Artemis filled Ortygia as she chased the wild leopards. *Les Trophées* with its note of triumph, published twenty-five years later, dates from this period.

The musician, Emmanuel Chabrier, would place himself at the piano and drown with his chords and harmonies the voices of the poets as they discussed questions of metre. He had written original and effective music to Victor Hugo's ballad, *Le Pas d'Armes*, and often sang it to his own accompaniment, oblivious of our presence.

Some celebrated men came to this Batignolles *salon*, but not till later when its frequenters had conquered fame — Edmond de Goncourt among others; he took part in a performance of the first act of *Marion Delorme*, when Coppée played "Didier." Théodore de Banville, Paul de Saint-Victor, Xavier Aubryet, each put in an appearance.

Verlaine and I specialised in charades, which we improvised at the expense of the personages and doings of the Empire. My hairless face lent itself easily to an impersonation of Napoleon I., and by adding moustaches and a small beard, made with burnt cork, I presented a fairly good imitation of Napoleon III., of whom every good policeman seems the counterpart. Verlaine was always a revolutionary, a conspirator, who wanted to violate the majesty of the throne, and change the order of succession, as the attorneys of the Palais de Justice say. These buffooneries, which, however, bore the stamp of a biting and satirical actuality, were not altogether free from danger. The police who were then very much on the alert might listen at doors and cause us, thanks to a devoted magistracy, to reflect on the perils of charades too much up to date on " wet straw." These charades were wont to terminate with mad gallops and *farandoles*, improvised by Charles de Sivry, at breakneck speed.

Our comrade, Ernest Boutier, knew a bookseller in the Passage Choiseul, whose customers mostly purchased books of prayer and first communion, which he displayed at No. 45, the corner-shop, where the passage opens out into the Place Ventadour, in which the Italian theatre then stood. This bookseller was young, intelligent, enterprising, ambitious, and dreamed of something better than being the mere successor of a certain Percepied. He therefore lent an ear to the tentative suggestions of Ernest Boutier, backed up by Verlaine, Ricard, and myself; and finally consented to publish certain volumes of poetry, which it was understood were to be printed at the expense of the authors, and to act as agent for a literary journal we were contemplating.

Preceded by an edition of *Ciel, Rue et Foyer*, by L.-X. de Ricard, in which the publisher's name only appeared on the cover, two volumes of poetry were issued on the same day, viz., *Le Reliquaire* by François Coppée, and the *Poèmes Saturniens* by Paul Verlaine, a triple commencement, and also the first essay of the excellent Alphonse Lemerre, who was before long to conquer fame and fortune by publishing poetry, an undertaking at all times hazardous, and in those days regarded as absolutely mad.

The journal, of which Ricard was editor-in-chief, was called *L'Art*, and had but a short existence. It attracted most notice when *Henriette Maréchal* was produced. Verlaine was loudest among the supporters of this piece of Edmond de Goncourt's, a proof of the eclecticism of the young Parnassian school. Nothing could be more remote from the poetic spirit of the Parnassians than the modernity, brutality, and lack of artistic finish of the Goncourts; yet they one and all echoed Verlaine's plaudits, and were present at the tumultuous performance of the play which, as a matter of fact, was second-rate, and rather banal, and famous merely because its career was suddenly cut short by a violent and unreasonable cabal. Leconte de Lisle, who was seated behind me in the orchestra, said to me in the midst of the uproar : " I am not very certain what we are doing here ; " to which I replied that " Pipe-en-bois (the originator of the cabal) knows no more about it than we do, and we are here to answer him back."

The motive of the squabble was always rather obscure, it was probably more political than literary ; Pipe - en - bois and the students reproached the Goncourts with the fact that it was owing to the favour of the Princesse Mathilde that their play was performed at the Théâtre-Français. Now we were not generally friendly to the princess, and would not have thought of backing up her patronage. As to the brothers Goncourt, they belonged to another literary generation, and their style, altogether opposed to romanticism, harmony, and poetry, was not calculated to arouse us to enthusiastic partisanship. The real truth was, we wanted an opportunity to create a sensation, to make known our existence, to attract the public eye—*Henriette Maréchal* was a mere pretext. The papers were full of the students who hissed, and the poets who applauded. Moreover we saw that the *éclat* attending this invasion of a theatre by an uproarious *coterie*, eager to prove its existence by making a noise like the romanticists in the days of *Hernani*, would react favourably on our recently started journal, which so far had received scarcely any notice, in spite of the talent and audacity of its contributors. *Henriette Maréchal* ran a very short time, its first performance only, like that of *Hernani*, being noteworthy from the point of view of noise be it understood. Twenty-five years later, when it was revived, it became clear how little the piece merited such violent attack and ardent defence.

Verlaine had a very real sympathy for the realist school, remote as it was from him. He had no contempt for the inaccurate and imperfect works of Champfleury, and pointed out to me as having

H

afforded him pleasure the adventures of *Mademoiselle Mariette* and *Les Amoureux de Sainte-Périne*. I need hardly say that he prostrated himself before the majestic genius of Balzac. A novel, now completely forgotten, by Ch. Bataille and Ernest Rasetti, entitled *Antonie Quérard*, was singled out by him, and not without reason, as one of the most vigorous productions of the time.

His conception of poetry, at this period of his life, was descriptive objectivity, an adaptation of the methods of Leconte de Lisle, and even more, of Victor Hugo. The *Poèmes Saturniens* include a large number of pieces which are purely descriptive and objective ; yet here and there is perceptible a personal note, feeling, or sentimental impression.

The *Poèmes Saturniens* on its appearance made no impression, and was passed over by the critics. *Le Reliquaire*, published on the same day, obtained greater notoriety, chiefly owing to the wonderful success of the *Passant*. The sensation made by that little poetical play was like the sound of a drum which attracts the multitude, and all Coppée's friends, the young poets who had already formed themselves into a group, and were beginning to be talked about, benefited. The eyes of the public were turned to them ; they existed. It was thirty years and more since the public had been known to pay any attention to versifiers, or to be interested in a poetic revival.

The original edition of the *Poèmes Saturniens* was a volume in-18 of 163 pages, with the imprint ; Alphonse Lemerre, publisher, Paris, 47 Passage Choiseul, 1866, and his trade mark (then without the rising sun), a labourer digging, and the motto *Fac et Spera*.

Verlaine received flattering eulogies from the friends and famous poets to whom he sent his volume. Leconte de Lisle declared that "these poems were written by a true poet, an artist already very clever, who has early acquired the art of 'expression.'" Théodore de Banville rather affectedly asserted that, although literally a wreck, he had read and re-read the *Poèmes Saturniens* ten times consecutively, so great a hold had it upon him both as man and artist, and, moreover, that Verlaine was a poet of true originality: "We are all wearied to such an extent by every kind of jingle that we cannot be moved by anything except real poetry." The poet of the *Cariatides* quoted with particular appreciation three choice pieces which were somewhat in his own style, for instance *La Chanson des Ingénues*, and he ended up with this opinion, which the future has confirmed and posterity ratified: "I am sure I do not deceive myself when I say that among contemporary poets you will hold one of the most assured and prominent places."

Of course Victor Hugo despatched his paternal blessing from Guernsey, somewhat after this fashion:

"*Confrère*, for you are my *confrère*, and in *confrère* there is *frère* (brother). My setting sun salutes your dawn. You are beginning to climb the Golgotha of the Idea, as I descend. I watch your ascension as I go down, and smile upon it. Art is infinite, you are a ray upon the great unknown. I press your poet hands. *Ex imo.* V. H."

This is not an exact reproduction of what the great man wrote, but this parody, with which we

have often amused ourselves, represents the manner
of compliment which the "Père" from his island
forwarded to all who sent him verses. It was
like a benevolent circular which we each received
from the master we one and all admired, although
his stereotyped compliments certainly afforded us
entertainment. Sometimes the eulogistic auto-
graphed letter which was generally written either
by Mme. Drouet or François Victor Hugo was
accompanied by a precious photograph like the
one which occupies a place of honour in my
study. The writing on this was the work of two
hands; the signature and dedication "To M——"
were written by Victor Hugo himself, and the name
left blank was filled in by Paul Meurice to whom
the exile, for safety's sake, sent the whole parcel
of portraits, the author of *Fanfan-la-Tulipe* duly
apportioning them out. There is no occasion for
excessive mirth over this method of concocting
felicitations beforehand, and distributing portraits
like prospectuses. Victor Hugo was simply overwhelmed with poems, books, novels, magazine
articles, political pamphlets and revolutionary
schemes; he could not read and reply to every
one. As to the photographs, the inconsiderate
police would doubtless have confiscated them if
posted direct, and, under suspicion of disseminating
republican propaganda, these acts of courtesy on
the part of the exile, might often have drawn down
persecution upon the recipients.

However, if Victor Hugo did not read the *Poèmes
Saturniens* on publication, and praised them merely
on trust, in accordance with his usual custom, it was
evident he had become acquainted with them when

Verlaine called on him in Brussels at a later date. Victor Hugo received the young poet in the famous lodging in the Place des Barricades, which was afterwards offered as a shelter to the proscribed Communists — a perilous hospitality indeed, for it led to a disgraceful storming of the great man's windows. The Brabançon populace were, at the time, in a fever of reaction, and furious against every one who had taken part in the Parisian insurrection, or seemed to countenance it. It is necessary to take into account this treatment to which Victor Hugo was subjected, and his compulsory retirement from Belgium on account of the Commune, when we attempt to appreciate the heavy sentence passed upon Paul Verlaine, a reputed Communist, by the Belgian magistrates.

The great poet, forewarned of the coming of the author, was doubtless prepared for him; flatteringly he quoted some of his visitor's verses. This delicate personal tribute made Verlaine very happy, although, as a rule, he cared little for compliments. In the course of this visit, made in 1868, Verlaine was presented to Madame Victor Hugo, the romantic Muse, the immortal Adèle, who had inspired not only her husband's great passion of which his *Lettres à la Fiancée*, recently published, bears ample testimony, but also the famous and mysterious collection of burning verse entitled, *Le Livre d'Amour*, in which Sainte-Beuve celebrated the most beautiful and desirable of his *inconnues*.

Verlaine went away enchanted with the cordial, simple, and familiar reception, almost excessive in its warmth, of the great man. But simplicity is sometimes disconcerting, and it is possible there

may have been some slight feeling of disillusion-
ment, consequent upon a too glorified expectation
in this first contact of a young writer with a master
in the zenith of his glory. Victor Hugo's characteristic simplicity and admirable familiarity, in strong
contrast with the majesty of his genius, did not
astonish Verlaine alone, and it led to a rather
amusing passage of arms between François Coppée
and Victor Noir, a young journalist, the future unfortunate victim of Pierre Bonaparte's pistol shot
in the memorable house at Auteuil. An article
in itself harmless, but interpreted offensively by
Coppée, appeared in connection with a visit similar
to that of Verlaine, paid by the author of the
Passant, to the illustrious outlaw. "You have
returned from Guernsey. How did you find Victor
Hugo?" Victor Noir made an interlocutor say to
Coppée in the newspaper *Le Corsaire*. "Very well
indeed," Coppée was supposed to have replied,
"but his air seemed to me rather provincial."

This remark was absolutely denied, yet there was
truth in it, and Victor Hugo retained his provincial
manner and characteristic good nature throughout
his productive and glorious old age. He did not
try to distinguish himself in dress or manner, nor to
assume the air of a celebrated man. He was one
of those who pass unnoticed in a crowd. Although
for many years he went twice a day in an omnibus
from Batignolles to the Jardin-des-Plantes, none of
the conductors nor passengers on the line, which
was frequented by artists, writers, and political men,
ever suspected that the old gentleman with a fine,
white beard, who sat unassumingly in his place
looking like a good, ordinary citizen, was one of

the greatest writers of the age. This commonplace air in no way detracted from Victor Hugo's
greatness ; on the contrary, it enhanced it if that
were possible. He was formal, perhaps emphatically so, only on the occasions when he took pen
in hand to reply to some admirer. His speeches,
political manifestoes, proclamations, and appeals to
the Ministers of State and nations, the composition
of which is always grandiloquent, gave an impression of simplicity. Pierre Dupont's superb verses
on the fir trees might well be applied to him.

Of the large number of complimentary letters,
some of them mere courteous banalities, but others
evidently sincere, which reached the young poet,
now become quietly famous, the fine letter of
Sainte-Beuve, which is included in his *Correspondence*, should have a place apart. Coming from
the great, almost the only literary critic France
could boast in the nineteenth century, the only one,
perhaps, who will remain, whose documented mono-
graphs and studied and condensed opinions will be
re-read, combined with the fantastic yet ofttimes true
pronouncements of the extravagant and captivating
Barbey d'Aurevilly, such homage ought to count.
The spontaneous appreciation of Sainte-Beuve for
a beginner, an unknown, proves that we were not
deceived, nor under an illusion concerning one of
our own set, when we declared after a first rapid
hearing that the majority of the poems were fine,
and Paul Verlaine was at twenty a true poet who
would develop into a great poet.

This is the letter Sainte-Beuve wrote to
Verlaine in December 1866, *i.e.*, when the volume
appeared :

"Sir and dear Poet,—I wished to read the *Poèmes Saturniens* before thanking you for the volume. The critic and poet in me are at war in regard to it. Talent there is, and to it first of all I render my homage. Your aspiration is elevated, and as you say in your epilogue, in words that may not be forgotten, you are not contented with that fugitive thing, inspiration. In your descriptions of scenes you have produced some altogether brilliant sketches and night effects; and, like all who are worthy of the laurel, you strive after that which is fresh and untouched. All this is good. . . ."

After some remarks anent metre and certain cæsuras he considered irregular or too far-fetched, which he quoted, giving page and line, Sainte-Beuve added, particularising the objects of his praise:

"I rather like *Dahlia*, and am especially pleased when you apply your serious manner to subjects which demand grave treatment—*César Borgia* and *Philippe II*. You need not shrink from being at times more harmonious, more suave, and rather less gloomy and hard in the matter of emotion. We should not take poor, good Baudelaire as our starting-point, and endeavour to outdo him."

This fine letter of criticism, which shows a perfect appreciation of Verlaine's talent and style at that time: "You need not shrink from being . . . less hard in the matter of emotions," ends up with encouragement. Sainte-Beuve advises the young poet to continue unflinchingly in his present manner, endeavouring to render it more facile, but not less strong, and to extend and adapt it to worthy subjects. Verlaine, however, later on, driven by circumstances, ceased to follow his counsel, and definitely determined to abandon the objective and descriptive method employed in *César Borgia* and *Philippe II.*, which the eminent critic had urged him to continue. The letter confers true brevet rank upon the poet and artist, discovered by a competent critic and recognised master. Verlaine was justly flattered by it, and we, his friends, delighted.

The *Poèmes Saturniens* have a twofold inspiration, and are of a composite character : two or three of the pieces, and those not the least beautiful, among them the poems specially quoted and praised by Sainte-Beuve, *César Borgia* and *La Mort de Philippe II.*, are entirely in the descriptive and pompous manner of *La Légende des Siècles* and the *Poèmes Barbares*. Others show signs of the influence of Baudelaire, *Mon Rêve familier*, *e.g.*, evokes a recollection of some piece out of *Les Fleurs du Mal*, in spite of the lucidity and precision which Verlaine introduced into the expression, however studied and subtle, of exquisite sensations, mysterious correspondences, and mental affinities. The lines, charged with ideas and suggestions, with which the poem ends, are of a consistent and original beauty very characteristic of the author, and have no trace of the influence of Baudelaire. There was, moreover, in the *Poèmes Saturniens*— I was at hand when most of the poems which make up the volume were conceived—an intent to dogmatise and create a poetic creed. Verlaine was in fact the first to formulate the theory of the *Impassibles* (the immovable ones), as the poets

of the new school were called to begin with;
afterwards the term " Parnassiens " carried the day,
although less appropriate and more pedantic.

In the introductory poem, as in that which
forms the epilogue, he rebels against the school
of Lamartine (and delights in Madame Desbordes-
Valmore), the unlyrical brilliance of Alfred de
Musset (" *Allons ! dieu mort descends de ton autel
d'argile !* " he cries furiously to the shade of Rolla),
and the political satire of Auguste Barbier,
Barthélemy, Hégésippe Moreau, and even Victor
Hugo. He proclaims the abstention of the poet,
in the midst of struggles for public office, his
indifference to the quarrels which agitate states-
men and citizens. He preaches isolation, and
admires the ivory tower. The world, troubled by
the fervid language of the poets, has exiled them,
and in their turn they shut out the world. The
artist must not mingle his song with the clamours
of the crowd, which he qualifies, regardless of
universal suffrage, as obscene and violent. The
eye of the poet must not look down upon vulgar
things. The priest of the beautiful has the blue
sky for altar and infinity for temple. He must
participate in no earthly passion, nor mingle in
the commonplace doings of other men. He does
not share their griefs, and should abstain from
their joys. Their quarrels, their wars, the pride
of republics, the arrogance of monarchies, military
glory, industrial power, the prodigious extension
of science, commercial expansion, the common
weal, instruction within reach of all thirst for
knowledge, the amelioration of labour, the diminish-
ment of social wretchedness, and individual suffer-

ing—all these things, which go to make up the democratic and civilising work of modern society—should leave him unmoved. Dream must not take part in action.

This theory, then new and even daring, since it contradicted public opinion, and clashed with legitimate admiration for Victor Hugo, the educator, philanthropist, humanitarian, socialist, and theoretical demagogue, was soon taken up, developed, remarked upon, and vulgarised. The press had a good deal to say about it, laughed and approved, attributing the originality of the doctrine and the initiative of its formula to various contemporary personages, Leconte de Lisle, Alfred de Vigny, and Victor de Laprade. But it was Verlaine who first presented, in the strong, lucid verse of the prologue to the *Poèmes Saturniens* the theory of poetical abstraction, the isolation of the poet in modern society, making the writer — the apostle extolled by Victor Hugo — a fanatical egoist, a sort of *bonze* of art, shutting himself up in a temple into which penetrates only a softened and poetised rumour of the doings, cries, complaints, and acclamations of the multitude.

In the epilogue to the poems he completes his idea. Not only must the poet live, think, and feel apart from his contemporaries, but he must keep his conscience and his thoughts from certain promiscuities. He must in the beginning distrust his inspiration. Wise and proved advice. Good poets thoroughly instructed in their art reach a point at which they can with difficulty write fluent verse. Boileau, that excellent authority, counselled that a poem be returned a hundred times to the loom, comparing it doubtless to a piece of silk woven by a laborious and patient worker. Verlaine bids the poet beware of facility ; warns him against the dangers of the commonplace, not in his subject, for beautiful, great, immortal subjects are commonplace, but in its expression ; and against that terrible invader the stereotyped, the dog-grass of the literary field which it is so difficult to eradicate, springing up again and again as it does with a deplorable fertility. He recommends knowledge achieved by lamplight, and vaunts those two principal virtues of an artist—perseverance and determination.

These precepts, although set forth vehemently, are at bottom a mere reproduction of the counsels of the learned Boileau, who recommended the young poets of his day to work at leisure, ignoring the urgency of prince or publisher, and not to be incited to a foolish rapidity. At the same time Verlaine anathematised in the name of the young school later to be known as the " Parnassienne," the Lakists, not only the English, such as Wordsworth, Coleridge, or Collins, but the vapid imitators of Lamartine, who expressed themselves in ecstatic elegies, or foolishly sighed out drivelling, low, and puerile romances.

The *Poèmes Saturniens* had no success with the public. The press was silent, with the exception of the *Nain Jaune*, in which Barbey d'Aurevilly, who talked largely about the young school, and yet mingled contempt and mockery with his admiration, wrote :

" A Puritan Baudelaire, an unfortunate and droll combination, without the brilliant talent of M. Baudelaire, and with reflections here and

there of M. Hugo and Alfred de Musset, such is
M. Paul Verlaine."

There is little truth in this criticism, but Barbey
was solely desirous of appearing vehement and
picturesque. Verlaine's principal quality in the
Poèmes Saturniens was that of lucidity. He expressed abstract ideas clearly, and subtle sensations
logically, no mean merit. Afterwards he adopted
an absolutely reverse method, and sought for
imperceptible shades and blurred contours. Later
on he formulated his new views in regard to poetry
in the verses setting forth simultaneously rule and
example after the manner of classical treatises on
metre and prosody which begin :

" De la musique avant toute chose, . . . "

His poetic method in the *Fêtes galantes* was
different from that of the *Poèmes Saturniens*. Far
from "dire les torts de la rime" the poet declared
that he hated " la rime assonante" like the pretty
wife and the prudent friend. The wife and the
friend were only introduced by way of a joke, but
the rhyme itself was a serious matter; its richness
was not to be trifled with. Verlaine poured contempt upon feeble rhymes ; he adhered to the
strict rules laid down by Théodore de Banville
in his treatise on versification. The words elevated
to the dignity of rhymes were weighed letter by
letter, the supporting consonant being absolutely
essential for right of admission to the place of
honour in the verse. One of Verlaine's grievances
against Alfred de Musset was that he did not
rhyme well; he even quoted lines by the poet of
the *Nuits* which did not rhyme at all.

The saturnine poet classed among the Parnassians, known as the "impassible ones" before the *Parnassus* was invented, affected the utmost personal insensibility. "Nature, nothing in thee can touch me," he said superbly with Goethe. This was pure affectation and simple "literature," for he was greatly impressed by the monotonous grandeur of northern scenery, and the sad severity of the surroundings of Bouillon charmed him. He was a devoted friend, adored his mother, and was never known to blush at the vulgarity of sentiments wholly in accordance with Nature. He never sought to dissimulate emotion save when he rhymed, and then was not infrequently unsuccessful.

In this youthful collection, the *Poèmes Saturniens*, there is no hint of personal feeling, no self-revelation, no word of confession on the part of the man who was afterwards to use, even to abuse, the autobiographical method to describe himself to the public in prose, verse, speech, and even in drawings. A young poet exhibiting himself thus as an impersonal being is a very rare phenomenon. Baudelaire in his *Bénédiction*, and some other poems in *Les Fleurs du Mal*, alludes to his mother, his mistresses, his travels, and his tastes. Verlaine did not follow the master in these poems of his which were more directly the result of admiration for *La Légende des Siècles*, and surprise at the *Poèmes Barbares*. There is not a single piece in the whole volume which has any relation to a definite event in the life of the poet, a sensation experienced, a joy or sorrow felt; like Goethe in his *Divan* (he read the great German a great deal at this period in Jaques Porchat's translation) he

only dealt with abstract, objective, and compound
emotions. The poems to women were addressed
to no real living creature whom he knew. The
griefs of which he speaks and sings are merely
suppositions. Doubtless he had forewarnings of
the future, but when in 1865 he wrote : " Happiness
has walked side by side with me," the lines charged
with despair applied to no actual fact in his life ;
as yet he had experienced no real troubles. He
was young, in good health, not in love, content
with the pleasures within his reach, possessing
sufficient money to give him a sense of satisfaction,
drinking when he left the leisured precincts of his
office one glass or another of joy-inspiring liquid ;
in fact he was living without thought of the future
peacefully and regularly under his mother's roof.
His melancholy plaint was quite fanciful and
abstract, and at the same time he was busy writing
a burlesque, destined for the lively and far from
saturnine stage of the Gaîté-Rochechouart. He
was so possessed by the idea of entirely disregarding himself in his verse, rhyming only on subjects
which had no connection with anything that was
his, that when his father died (the publication of
the *Poèmes Saturniens* was a year after this event)
he consulted me on the advisibility of allowing the
the poem entitled *Sub Urbe* to appear in the volume.
It begins :

> " Les petits ifs du cimetière
> Frémissent au vent hivernal."

This melancholy description of an imaginary
cemetery, which bore no resemblance whatever to
his family burial-place, ended up with an appeal

to life, to the sun at springtime, and to the song of birds soothing the quiet slumbers of the beloved dead. He feared lest it might be construed as an allusion to his own grief, a lamentation, a kind of personal elegy. I advised him to let the piece stand just as it was written two years before the sad event. The public would certainly only see in the poem what the poet had intended to convey— a general impression received in a cemetery in winter. With regard to that other poem "Je ne sais rien de gai comme un enterrement," I certainly sympathised with the feeling of decorum which made him omit it. I preserved it, however, in its original form, and have already narrated how it came to be published twenty-three years later.

This first volume begun on the benches at school, continued during an idly followed course of law, and completed in the first tranquil months of life in a Government office; thus covering the happiest, most peaceful, and untroubled period of his existence, is charged with a pessimism, baseless, imaginary, wholly fictitious. He was the most lighted-hearted youth, untouched by the ordinary troubles and mortifications of middle-class life, when he wrote the little poem entitled *Chanson d'Automne.* At that time (1864-1865) he had experienced none of the icy blasts of adversity, and the sorrows he claimed to feel were merely artistic conceptions, figments of the imagination. I will conclude these comments on the impersonal nature of Verlaine's poetry, and the objectivity which characterised his poetic method at this period by referring to a poem at first entitled *Frontispice,* which under the title of *Vers Dorés* I quoted in the *Echo de Paris,*

16th May 1889; and which sets forth in definite
and abbreviated form the theories of impassibility
already formulated in the famous verses of the
Poèmes Saturniens, commencing:

"Est elle en marbre on non, la Vénus de Milo?"

Such was the poetic method which characterised the Verlaine of the *Poèmes Saturniens*, deaf
to all the calls, complaints, and exaltations of the
world within him, projecting his sensations outside, materialising his dreams, exteriorising his
impressions and treating poetry as plastic material.
He was to change in its entirety this manner of
seeing, feeling, and expressing his ideas, sensations,
reveries, and visions.

The same impersonality, and an even more
refined and artistic objectivity, dominates that
precious and surprising volume the *Fêtes galantes*.
No borrowed inspiration is to be found here; it is
a synthesis of the Art of the eighteenth century,
a presentment of the manners, conversations, and
diversions of that dainty and superficial period.

What sentiment or idea inspired Verlaine to
write this series of poems, perfect in their unity,
the composition and arrangement of which clearly
indicates a work of art, conceived, taken in hand
and completed in accordance with a definite scheme
quite apart from any personal impression? I should
find it difficult to give an exact idea of the genesis
of the *Fêtes galantes*. Verlaine undoubtedly showed
me, as he wrote them, the various poems which make
up the collection, but he composed at the same time
some pieces of verse of a very different character:
Le Grognard, which was dedicated to me and after-

I

wards published under the title *Un Soldat Laboureur* (in *Jadis et Naguère*), *Les Vaincus*, etc. In my opinion, these exquisite Watteau poems were intended to be collected together, perhaps to make up a set, but were composed without any idea of a complete conception.

I suppose two contemporary events directed the poet's mind towards the marquis and marquises, the little black boys, the pierrots and the columbines, and all the gay throng in the sylvan glades of Lancret and Fragonard; where the sound of the fountains is heard in the moonlight among the marble statues. For one thing Edmond and Jules de Goncourt had just published several very beautiful studies of the eighteenth century and the charming artists of this fascinating period, the Saint-Aubins and Moreaus; and they had narrated the life and adventures of the great actresses, the Guimard, and the Saint-Huberti, and written the only true and not defamatory history of the Dubarry queen of *Fêtes galantes*, whose end was so tragic and disproportionate. It is possible that from these works Verlaine acquired a taste for poetical dalliance in the world evoked by the Goncourts. Then again, the Galerie Lacaze in the Louvre had just been opened to the public, and we never wearied of going to admire the Gilles, the embarkation for Cythera, Fragonard's swings, Nattier's interiors, the Lancrets, and the Chardins; all the art at once intimate and idyllic, realistic and poetical in which Greuze, Watteau, and Boucher are past masters. Perhaps, too, we owe the *Fêtes galantes* to the very strong impression produced by *La Fête chez Thérèse* in the *Contemplations*, a poem for which Verlaine felt an admiration so great that it is the only one by a well-known author which I ever heard him repeat by heart. He had not a good memory, and very few quotations are to be found in his prose works.

The volume was not very successful; the press hardly spoke of it. The first edition, which is very attractive and much prized by bibliophiles, was in-18, on Japan paper, with fifty-four pages. The title-page runs : " Paul Verlaine—*Fêtes galantes*." The publisher's trade mark, and at the foot : " Paris, Alphonse Lemerre, éditeur. Passage Choiseul 47. 1869." On the back of the half title : " Du même auteur : *Poèmes Saturniens*." In preparation : *Les Vaincus.* On the last page : " Achevé d'imprimer le vingt février mil huit cent soixaute-neuf, par L. Toinon et Cie, à Saint-Germain, from Alphonse Lemerre, libraire à Paris."

I was away from Verlaine when the volume appeared, probably early in March 1869 : I had just been sentenced to a month's imprisonment at Sainte-Pélagie for an offence in connection with the press. My incarceration had been hurried on. The cells at Sainte-Pélagie were never left vacant, one occupant immediately succeeding another, and the departure of Edouard Lockroy to a hospital for the completion of his term left free for me the cell known as " Petite Sibérie." I had only time to scribble a few rapid words to my friend on a card, to be left with his mother, who was then living at 26 Rue Lècluse, in the Batignolles.

Verlaine, to whose readiness to take offence I have several times alluded, was hurt by my unavoidably hasty warning, as the following letter shows :

"*11th March* 1869.

"MY DEAR FRIEND,—From the comprehensive
card you were so good as to send informing me
of your imprisonment, but without expressing the
faintest desire to receive a visit from me, or giving
any suggestions as to how one could be made, you
will doubtless be no more astonished at than you have
been preoccupied with the matter of my absence;
it will be religiously continued until the receipt of
a letter (which might have been less delayed)—
Sainte-Pélagie being far, and my time taken up.

                                      "P. VERLAINE.

"RUE LÉCLUSE 26, BATIGNOLLES."

His annoyance was not lasting.   I hastened to
send a friendly letter, dated from the gaol, inviting
him to come on the following Sunday and share
the prison fare, which was backed up by abundance
of victuals from the outside world, and washed
down by no ill liquid.   I explained that I had been
obliged, before asking him to visit me, to ascertain
the necessary formalities, and apparently visitors
might be received at any time, after their names
had been put down on a list which was submitted
to the authorities and signed by the chief of the
police.   This formality required two or three days.

He did not come on the Sunday, excusing
himself in the following letter, which is very
different in tone from the angry effusion quoted
above:

"MY DEAR FRIEND,—If I have not availed
myself to-day, Sunday, of your kind invitation,
you must put it down to the publication of the
enclosed book, which necessitates the doing of a
hundred and one things, and would have prevented

my going to Pélago, even if it had not happened
that my *concierge* only handed me your letter at
ten o'clock this morning. But count on me for next
Sunday at the earliest possible hour; you know
what time I have in the week! I send you the
Fêtes galantes, not for nothing! An article, bursting
with praise—or death! A fig for Woinez! I shall
send it perhaps to Barbum. (Charles Woinez,
literary critic of the *Nain Jaune.*—Barbum, Barbey
d'Aurevilly).

"Till Sunday then, and a hearty handshake,
"P. VERLAINE.

"*P.S.*—While awaiting decapitation at the hand
of Rigault, shake his old fist for me. (Raoul
Rigault, afterwards attorney to the Commune, was
with me in Sainte-Pélagie.)

"*2nd P.S.*—If you may write to me, try and
do so; you ought to have time."

He was very anxious for an article on his
Fêtes galantes, and mentioned the matter again in
the following note, but I could not fall in with his
suggestions either for the article or the appointment
at the meeting at Belleville, which was probably
organised on the occasion of Gambetta's candidature.
On the date indicated I was still in prison.

"*8th April* 1869.

"MY DEAR FRIEND,—Are you going to-morrow
evening to the meeting at Belleville? I shall be
there at eight o'clock, 8 Rue de Paris. There will
be grand doings after the probable dissolution.
By the way, you are naught 'qu'un pitre et qu'un
Berthoud' (from Banville) for not having yet spoken
of the *Fêtes galantes*. I count on receiving a

number of the journal on the day you put it in.
The thing is worth the trouble, and the delay will
be condoned only on these terms.

" To-morrow at eight o'clock.   In any case I am
always at the ' Ville ' from half-past ten till four.—
Ever yours,   P. VERLAINE."

One cannot always do what one likes on the
press any more than in life, particularly in the
matter of placing an article of a eulogistic nature
on a volume of verse.   Verlaine was not deceived
with regard to the curiosity of the public, nor the
eagerness of newspaper editors ; he simply ignored
them.

At the end of July, for some reason or other,
the promised article had not appeared.   Verlaine,
who had gone to his relatives in the north, where
he was joined by Charles de Sivry—it was at the
time when there was first talk of the marriage which
took place a year afterwards—recalled his *Fêtes
galantes* to me in forcible terms :

" FAMPOUX, 31*st July* 1869.

" That wretched Sivry, who is stopping here,
tells me he forgot to deliver a letter I placed in
his charge for you.   In it I told you I was leaving
here, and that I was not very well ; I am now
better, thank goodness !   Apparently, foul creature,
you are no longer to be found at Battur's (Baptiste,
waiter at the Brasserie des Martyrs).   What crime
are you then meditating in secret ?   Naught to
do with my fame, shameless scribbler, for I have
no news of an article from your pen in regard to
the famous and exquisite *Fêtes galantes*.   Be a
great poet now, and have the condescension to
press the hands of the villains in Room 7, and give

them the customary *bock*, so that they may compound for you a passable concoction of advertisement in their miserable papers, which always fall short just when one thinks they may be turned to some advantage.

"And Mérat's *Parnasse?* Woinez is obscene. (Charles Woinez borrowed through the medium of Verlaine and myself the volume of the *Parnasse Contemporain*, belonging to the poet Mérat, for an article on the Parnassians which never appeared.) I hear that Nina's grand *soirée* was very *chic*. Olympe Audouard was there, but *Brididum* (*La Vieillesse de Brididi*, a vaudeville by Henri Rochefort) was not played for lack of the principal actor (I, if you please). Have you been to Meurice's lately? What news is there in Paris? Here I am in absolute exile and know nothing of anything. Have you sent something to Lemerre for the *Parnasse?* (for the second volume). It seems that Mendès' Swedenborgian poem has appeared in *La Liberté*. I am in a lazy mood, and for two days have not touched that ridiculous thing called verse. I believe I have a counterpart on the banks of the Seine in you. I hope, vile wretch, you will answer my letter soon (Fampoux, Pas-de-Calais, chez M. Julien Dehée), and tell me all you are doing; of course, whatever it is, is infamous. Awaiting your reply, I press your fins, and am, your very cordial enemy,   P. VERLAINE.

"*P.S.*—My respects and compliments to your people."

I do not know if this famous article on the *Fêtes galantes* now appeared in the *Nain Jaune*. I have not the numbers by me, and have kept but few of my articles belonging to that period. One is very careless about such things in early youth.

I made it up to Verlaine afterwards. As I had charge of the *Chronique Parisienne* and the dramatic criticism in the *Nain Jaune* when Barbey d'Aurevilly was away at Valognes writing his truculent *Chevalier Destouches*, it was difficult for me to review books. That was the domain of another colleague who took fright at the least indication of encroachment, but I had some influence on the journal, and therefore several poems of Verlaine's were inserted in it, one of which, *Le Monstre*, partook of the nature of a political allegory. He thanked me as follows:

"MY DEAR EDMOND, — Besides the volume promised I send you some verses which seem to me not unworthy of the honour of print. If you wish to stand godfather to them with G. G. (Grégory Genesco, the manager of the journal), and through that influence which Paulus found to such advantage, procure an asylum for them in the *Nain Jaune*, reply (if you please) to Rue Neuve 49, and you will merit the gratitude of their father.

"P. VERLAINE.

"*P.S.*—Viotti wishes success to the fruits of your pen, and to let you know through me that the Sieur Sivry, counterpointist, has not yet deserted Normandy.

"In case of success, correct the proof *very carefully*, and return me the manuscript.   P. V."

A second and more forcible letter reproached me with not having corrected the proofs of his poem with sufficient care:

"TUESDAY.

"FEATHERBRAIN,—You have not attended to my instructions at all. I wrote 'rhythme' distinctly, and it has been printed wrong. Don't you see clearly? The 'A xxx' and the date have been omitted, why? You know I never send the printer anything I do not wish printed, and therefore feel aggrieved when some printer or another takes it upon himself to mutilate my MS.

"After fault - finding, compliments, you have given proof, dear Edmond, of real good-will and charming persistence. I beg you to accept herewith my most sincere and affectionate thanks.

"P. VERLAINE.

"Kind regards to your family.

"I enclose a sonnet, *J'use J'abuse.* . . .

"When M. Woinez has finished with Mérat's *Parnasse* please let him have it back at once.

"On Saturday, Rue Chaptal or at Battur's.

"P. VERLAINE."

At Battur's, as I have said, meant at the Brasserie des Martyrs, where the waiter who served us was called Baptiste, corrupted to Battur. Rue Chaptal, in other words Nina's, was an amusing lively, odd house, where we passed many pleasant evenings. It, too, had some share in bringing together the literary and political youth of 1869, and therefore a description of it is indispensable to a study of Verlaine and his strange and powerful genius.

CHAPTER VI

AT NINA'S—THE *CONTEMPORARY PARNASSUS*

(1868-1869)

Madame Nina de Callias was, in 1868, a young woman of twenty-two or twenty-three, small, plump, vivacious, clever, excitable, a little hysterical, and very attractive, who left behind her a deserved reputation for eccentricity, daring, and free-handed hospitality. In the last days of the Empire she loved to get together in her modest and simply furnished apartment in the handsome house, No. 17 Rue Chaptal, young people interested in literature, art, and politics, who were attracted thither by its gaiety and free and easy ways, and induced to remain by the amiability of their hostess. Once there we found ourselves among friends; it was like a club minus rules and baccarat. One could drop in at Nina's, no matter how late it was, certain to find amusing society, to hear the latest verse, exchange news and talk ill of the Government, or successful literary men, according as one was political or literary, for the two sets fraternised without actually mingling. I belonged to both in virtue of my double qualifications of Parnassian and Republican journalist, recently imprisoned.

Ah, what a strange, fairy-like little creature was

Nina, so excitable, so laughing, so fascinating; we all retain the happiest recollection of her. Verlaine wrote: "Some of us were often to be found at the charming Nina's, of whom, and her artistic nature prematurely devoured by its own fire, I have spoken here and there inadequately."

She was a very good musician, playing the piano like a professional, and occasionally composing, but never inflicting her nocturnes and concert caprices on us. She adored poetry, and possessed the merit of refraining from writing it. Eager to learn everything, feverish to do everything, indefatigable and complex, she was in advance of the women of her day. The first time I saw her she wore a breast-pad and short petticoat, and was taking a lesson in fencing from an assistant of good Maître Cordelois. She had a passion for everything, politics, literature, philosophy, mathematics, and spiritualism. Magic had a special attraction for her. As the fencing master went out the professor of necromancy came in to give his lesson in all seriousness, and in the meanwhile there were scales and exercises on the Erard grand piano. She had met Henri Rochefort at Geneva, and had conceived for the celebrated pamphleteer a friendship which, had circumstances been favourable, might have degenerated into a more positive sentiment. She wrote in remembrance of him on notepaper with a lantern as heading.

Cordial and familiar with every one, she had no recognised lover, at least in the first years of her Bohemian career. Charles Cros, the poet of the *Coffret de Santal*, the inaugurator of monologues

(Le Hareng Saur), and the inventor, before Edison, of the phonograph, was very attentive to her. He performed the functions of obliging secretary and steward, and passed as being specially favoured. With his woolly hair and negro type of face, the whimsical and ingenious Charles seemed ill equipped for the rôle of lover. I believe the part he played was merely that of general utility man. Bazire, a singular young man with an intermittent stutter, a colleague of Rochefort's on the *Marseillaise* and afterwards on the *Intransigeant*, and a violent Republican who was proceeded against for having abused the Emperor Napoleon III. one day when he was walking on the terrace of the Tuilleries near the revolving bridge, was also credited with being on the footing of a lover. This supposition might have been true later on, after the war, when Nina went to live in the Rue des Moines, Batignolles, under the name of Nina de Villars; but I had lost sight of her then.

She was the daughter of a Lyons barrister, M. Gaillard, and had been in possession of a considerable fortune, of which there only remained an assured income of 20,000 francs, and this she spent to the last sou; happily the capital could not be touched. She lived with her mother, who was, I believe, the largest contributor to the household expenses. Madame Gaillard looked a strange figure as she moved amongst us, clad always in mourning, sombre, imperturbable, and apparently unconscious of our wildest uproars. She neither approved nor condemned our most outrageous pranks, absolutely ignoring them. Her constant companion was a horrible little monkey, which perched on her shoulder, made grimaces, and sometimes turned his back on us. Nina had only been married a very short time to a well-known and brilliant journalist, Hector de Callias. He, too, was a character and as eccentric as the little wife whom he could neither appreciate, make happy, nor retain. He was a confirmed absinthe drinker, and presented to the good citizens who beheld him sitting at table in the "Rat Mort" or the "Nouvelle Athènes," a perfect copy of the popular caricature of a literary Bohemian. Hector de Callias lacked neither wit nor talent. He had distinguished himself in the large circle of well-known journalists. At the *Figaro* he had won the interest of Villemessant, who in his will bequeathed him a small income sufficient for food, or rather drink.

When his wife died, Hector de Callias, although separated from her for long years, thought proper to attend the funeral, which took place at Montrouge. In dignified fashion, dressed in black with the conventional white tie, he headed the mourners, and did the honours of the sad ceremony to the few present.

Poor Nina had finally succumbed to the effects of the over-excitement, late nights, and freaks, which were the normal conditions of her existence. The guests of the bizarre evenings in the Rue des Moines were other than those of the Rue Chaptal. The former *habitués* had now become academicians, famous, married, or had died, and with the exception of Léon Dierx, Sivry, and a few others, no old friends came to the new " Maison de la Vieille " described by Catulle Mendès. The decadent, the mystic, the superb elbowed poet-smokers from the Brasseries,

and vague anarchists come to talk of secret
bombs and new explosives amid the popping of
champagne corks at three francs a bottle, which
liquid flowed as in the past, in a continual stream.
The unfortunate Nina lost her reason in the tumult
which had been her joy. She had quaffed the cup
of uproar, as her husband poisonous alcohol, once
too often, and died a lunatic.

The presence of this husband long lost to
sight, although a shock, made no one angry; no
formalists nor prudes had haunted Nina's, and,
moreover, it was possible that during some lucid
interval in her last moments the poor demented
one had expressed a desire to see once more the
man whose name she had borne. Moreover, the
behaviour of Callias was perfect throughout the
ceremony. Those ignorant of the history of this
singular couple might have deemed him an afflicted
widower rendering the last tokens of respect to
a much-regretted wife.

But once the childish coffin was lowered into
the grave, Callias, regardless of appearances, did
not stay for the final handshakes of the departing
guests, but disappeared across the tombs. The
world is not always censorious, and seeing that
he had been separated from the dead woman, some
thought this seemly conduct, and Charles Cros
took his place. But this charitable view was an
erroneous one. Callias went because he could
no longer endure his thirst. The occasion was a
trying one, and for the five hours occupied by the
procession, the ceremony in church and in the
cemetery, he had not moistened his throat.
Having resolved to respect the conventions, he

had resisted the temptation to leave the *cortège*
on the way for an absinthe in one of the innumerable cafés lining the route from the Batignolles
to the Porte d'Orléans. But there was a limit
to his power of resistance, and when the dead
body had been confided to the earth, he hastened
from the scene in order to fly to the nearest counter
and quench the thirst that rivalled a shipwrecked
sailor's.

Three days afterwards he was encountered at
two o'clock in the morning in the Quartier Pigalle,
carefully picking his way and haranguing the gas-
lamps, still in the black suit and with a tie which
had once been white. He had not been home
since the funeral ceremony, and had only reached
his own quarter after prolonged stoppages in the
Quartier Latin, the Halles, and the Faubourg
Montmartre, at all the drinking - shops on the
way; thus making up on the return journey for
his abstinence on the outward.

It was seldom that Hector de Callias was
intoxicated in his evening clothes. He was a
professional drunkard with definite customs and
methods. When he received his pension at the
Figaro, he arranged the manner in which he would
return after his visits to the cafés of the Quartier
Pigalle. He took care of his elegantly cut and
spotless garments : velvet breeches, braided shooting coat and soft felt hat—the uniform of his kind.

After this lengthy funeral outing, Callias now
and again deserted the Quartier Pigalle. He had
taken a fancy to the wine-shops of the Quartier
Latin as he returned from the cemetery, and in
his Bacchic wanderings he came across Verlaine.

They fraternised, glass in hand, and unconsciously drifted into talk about their wives; one dead, the other divorced. They vied with each other in regrets, laments, and abuse, cursing even while they mourned the lost ones.

From time to time, urged by friendly doctors uneasy at his condition, Callias went for a sort of cure into the country, to breathe fresh air and drink fresh milk. It was all very well for a few days, and then he suddenly quitted the farm for an inn, and ordered an absinthe. Having thus taken breath, he regarded himself as cured, and took the train back to Paris, where he at once resumed his usual habits. It was during one of these cures that he succumbed at Fontainebleau to a congestion. Probably it was the milk which killed him; he was not accustomed to it.

However, to return to the *salon* in the Rue Chaptal, where Verlaine was a frequent visitor; it was composite and eclectic, easy and yet difficult of access. It was necessary to belong to the set, to be a budding academician or youthful legislator; it mattered little whether your aspirations were literary, artistic, or political, but one of the three was essential. Other folk were not admitted, and if one managed to creep in, he never came again; the raillery, rough, sometimes intolerable, of which he was the butt, proved too much for him.

Some one among the young poets, artists, painters, journalists, and politicians of Montmartre would say at the Café de Madrid or the Café de Fleurus : "Let us go to Nina's," and off they would troop at once in a body. Thus were organised pleasure parties at night after a society function, a gathering at the Sous-Prefecture, or a day in the country, when the regular establishments had closed their doors, and sent away their customers. There was no closing hour at Nina's; the door was always open and the table spread. There were three sofas often occupied after the departure of the bulk of the guests, by those who lived at a distance, and feared to return home in the small hours. At whatever time one retired one was not the last. I never could make out when Nina, at length left alone, went to bed for a well-earned repose.

Growing notabilities and coming celebrities found themselves cheek by jowl at Nina's. To be seen were François Coppée, with his First Consul face, reciting in melancholy fashion his *Intimités*; Léon Dierx of the poetic isles, tossing back his beautiful black hair as he declaimed his *Filaos*. Charles Cros describing in mocking tones the oscillations of a red herring, suspended from a wall bare, bare, bare at the end of a thread long, long, long; a tale invented to amuse the children, little, little, little; Anatole France, Mendès, Mérat, Valade, and all the *habitués* of the *Salon Ricard*, while Charles de Sivry improvised at the piano, Dumont played Hungarian airs on the zither, Francès, the splendid comedian of the Palais-Royal, with the shrewd face of a country curé, recounted, swelling his voice and rolling his eyes as fiercely as he could, how Sarragossa was taken, Henri Cros, modeller in wax, quietly reproduced in a corner the little head of the mistress of the house, and Villiers de l'Isle-Adam grimaced and reeled off the most unexpected apothegms of Dr Tribulat Bonhomet, heroic Prudhomme and huge Homais.

K

Among the politicians were Abel Peyrouton, one of the originators of the public meetings at the Pré-aux-Clercs and the Redoute, a nervous barrister of abrupt speech and authoritative gesture, who had delivered a vigorous harangue over Baudin's grave, which had recently been discovered among the tombs in the cemetery Montmartre. This chance occurrence, the subscription in the *Réveil*, and the notorious case brought against Charles Delescluze, laid the foundation of the oratorical and literary fortune of Léon Gambetta. Among the Republican *habitués* were the big good-hearted Emile Richard, editor of Delescluze's *Réveil*, and afterwards President of the Municipal Council ; Gustave Flourens, a revolutionary apostle, destined to a tragic death at Chatou by a policeman's sword ; Raoul Rigault, the famous attorney and Prefect of Police under the Commune, who at supper would willingly take upon himself to carve the blushing ham, manipulating the large knife as lovingly as if he were brandishing the legal sword over the necks of the *réacs*. He would propose a toast to Chaumette or Anacharsis Klootz, in between a pantoum of Mallarmé's and a *Fête galante* of Verlaine's, recited by the authors, or the waltz of the *Sylphes*, played by Ferdinand Révillon, pianist and popular agitator, afterwards manager of the Customs under the Commune.

The amusements were of the most varied kind. Charades were improvised, Jeanne Samary, the future Martine of the Théâtre-Français, opened the treasure-box of her laughing mouth, reciting fragments of her *répertoire* ; her incessant laugh rippling forth as if set in motion by a spring. Catulle Mendès shaking his fair hair slowly and gravely sang " Les vaches au flanc roux qui portent les aurores." Coppée parodied Théodore de Banville. Imitations were given of popular comedians, Gil Pérès, Lassouche, Brasseur. Military anecdotes were narrated, long before they formed part of the *répertoire* of Polin, who reproduced them, and lastly, laments were chanted, and burlesque Christmas carols intoned, reviewing the events of the year in vaudeville couplets. Nina's *salon* was to a certain extent in the mockery, fantasy, nonsense, and modernity of its poems, songs and little plays, all invented in the highest of spirits, the predecessor and forerunner of the *Chat Noir*.

There was even to be heard a species of that literary slang, which was in time to obtain a great vogue and make the reputation of Aristide Bruant and his wine-shop. Verlaine first gave this coarse and popular note, afterwards to be greatly abused, in a bizarre and altogether exceptional poem, of which I have the original embellished by a pen drawing representing the personage, with whom it is concerned in clerkly costume : check trousers, open waistcoat, swelling shirt, tie in a sailor's knot, high cap, and with hands thrust deep into pockets. This caricature, both words and sketch, was doubtless inspired by a nocturnal expedition made by Verlaine and myself, clad in blouses and peaked caps obtained from the emporium, patronised by the gentlemen of La Villette, of the hatter Desfoux, Rue du Pont-Neuf.

We had taken it into our heads to explore the haunts of Le Combat and Ménilmontant. At the Bal Gelin, then held at Ménilmontant, Verlaine with his flat nose, his piercing eyes, and his strange aspect, inspired the *habitués* of both sexes with terrified admiration; they took him for a *mec* who would not hesitate to draw his knife. We quaffed mugs of *vin bleu* in company with two or three of the fair dancers at this ball, where such a thing as a high kick was never known, and the gaiety had a mournful constrained aspect, chastened into seeming quiet by the severe, all-pervading eyes of the municipal guards, chosen from among the strongest and most energetic members of the corps. Thanks to my knowledge of the slang, we were able to sustain our parts, and not incur the suspicion, fraught with peril directly we were outside, of being police in disguise. Verlaine talked little; he observed, smoked and drank persistently. The adventure went off without any incident except an unexpected colloquy as we made our way out, with a thin, pale, sharp youngster, fifteen at most, who offered oranges, apples, cakes, and sweets for sale, in a flat basket suspended from his neck.

"Allume," said he to the poet in a hoarse whisper, "à gauche de la gonde, y a d'l'arnacle. . . ." Adding still more indistinctly " Je suis rien fauché, vieux, r'file - moi un patard." Verlaine stood bewildered, rather uneasy. Happily I understood. "Look," the urchin had said in his allegorical way to the author of the *Fêtes galantes*, whom he seemed to take for a distinguished kindred spirit; "to the left of the door are secret police." And as a reward for this information, which was perhaps trumped up in order to throw us off our guard, the rogue having divined our disguise, he added, "I have no money, give me two sous."

I *r'filai* our informant the ten centimes he asked for, and hurried Verlaine away through a dimly lighted corridor, and out of the door of egress. Having lighted our pipes we gave ourselves the pleasure of a stroll along the outer boulevard, past the numberless girls posted under the trees. Some thought they recognised us, and made signs to which we responded with a friendly patronising gesture. On approaching the Café du Delta we pulled off our blouses in the shelter of a newspaper kiosk, and with our peaked caps presented the appearance no longer of "terrors" out on the spree, but of peaceable citizens come for a neighbourly glass. Moreover, Verlaine was known at this café, and his presence attracted no more attention than his headgear.

This escapade, which recalled the adventures of the hero of the *Mystères de Paris*, with this difference, that no Fleur-de-Marie presented herself to our view, indeed we had not gone to the Bal Gelin for the purpose of discovering, as good Prince Rodolphe did, the pure among the prostitutes, inspired Verlaine with the masterpiece of slang aforesaid, entitled *L'Ami de la Nature*. Recited at Nina's, its originality and picturesqueness made it a great success. The style was then completely new, the literature Montmartroise not having been invented. The piece is included in the supplementary volume of the complete works; it does not add to Verlaine's lyrical fame, but affords an illustration of that curious element in his character and talent — saturnine gaiety.

At Madame de Ricard's, after the recitations and charades, towards one o'clock in the morning,

when the number of guests had begun to thin, we
frequently used to retire into a little *salon*, and
seating ourselves round a small, circular table,
covered with a cloth, make up a party sufficiently
attractive to detain us from sleep until dawn. We
played for low stakes some game of chance,
lansquenet, now altogether forgotten, or more
rarely baccarat. L.-X. de Ricard did not play, and
Verlaine seldom sat down, but Coppée and Dierx
were born gamblers.

At Nina's we never played, but our vigils were
even more prolonged, for we supped and we drank—
which pleased Verlaine better than cards. Want
of sleep greatly contributed to the development
among many of us of nervousness, irritability, and a
kind of permanent feverishness, not very pleasant
for other people in our everyday life.

Verlaine was very excitable, and more than
once I had proof of the unfortunate state of
tension of his nerves. The trial in Belgium, in
consequence of the unfortunate shot fired at
Rimbaud, full details of which will be given later,
was kept from me at the time as from every one
else. Had I been informed at once I could have
borne witness to the fact that Verlaine, in certain
moments of excitement, when under the influence
of drink, was liable to commit violent, rash, blind
acts. He was not defended as he should have been
before the Brabant magistrates ; his occasional irre-
sponsibility being a proved fact.

One Saturday, leaving Nina's at dawn on a
pleasant day in spring, we took it into our heads
to go out into the country and breathe the fresh
air. We lounged along the outer boulevards towards

the Bois-de-Boulogne, and talking, smoking, dreaming, arrived at the Pré-Catelan, where we stayed
to drink milk and discuss new-laid eggs. There
were a good many customers in the place, it being
the final halt for the nightbirds that issued from
the all-night restaurants, the bars of the Halles,
and the cellars of Hill and Frontin. Verlaine had
an altercation with a party seated near, but I
interposed and led him away. It must be confessed
that after the milk and eggs he had asked for coffee
and gin, and drunk largely of it. We were walking
down one of the alleys leading to the lake and the
avenue, then known as l'Impératrice, when Verlaine
conceived the idea of returning to the Pré-Catelan.

He wanted another drink, and the gin beginning
to take effect, he experienced a desire to go in
search of the people with whom he had quarrelled,
probably with the intention of renewing the dispute.
His eye looked vicious, his speech grew short and
abrupt, and he brandished his cane angrily. I
tried to calm him, and when he turned to retrace
his steps took him by the arm to urge him forward, whereupon he turned on me with a stream
of abuse, and drawing the stiletto from his sword-
stick endeavoured to close with me. I retreated,
and did my best to parry the increasingly furious
thrusts with which he pressed upon me excited by
the struggle. I begged him to be reasonable, calling out that it was a dangerous game, and one or
other of us might get hurt. He would not listen
to me. The contest was unequal, for I had only a
light cane with which to defend myself. I tried by
aiming at his wrists to make him drop his weapon,
but it was a short one, and the manœuvre was

difficult, as Verlaine wielded it with wonderful
energy.

At last I took to my heels without any
shame in so doing, and rushed among the under-
growth whither I surmised Verlaine, confused with
intoxication, would not be able to get at me, nor
to remain for long in an upright position.   I had
not calculated amiss ; as he came violently after
me, slashing at the bushes with his sword and
calling down vengeance upon my head, the skirts
of his macfarlane caught on a bough, and stumbling
heavily forward he dropped his weapon.   I sprang
upon it, and replacing it in its sheath gave Verlaine
as I released him my inoffensive stick in exchange.
After which I lectured and reasoned with him, but
he continued to growl and threaten, and possibly
in spite of me would have carried out his obstinate
drunken idea of returning to Pré-Catelan, had not
the noise of heavy footsteps and snapping twigs
made us turn our heads ; an old keeper of the
Bois was hastening towards us, evidently intent on
capture.   He must have been greatly taken aback
when he saw the assailant and assailed make off
in company among the trees, helping and encourag-
ing each other in their mutual flight, for I seized
Verlaine, now half-sobered and quite docile, and
dragged him as best I could in the direction of
Paris ; we could hear behind us the old keeper
puffing and blowing, and his cries of stop ! stop !
spurred us on to greater efforts, which we did not
relax until red, perspiring, breathless, we reached
the station and jumped into a train that had just
come in.   Once seated, Verlaine began to snore,
and I could not arouse him in time to alight at the

Batignolles, and we were carried on to Saint Lazare. Having recuperated ourselves with white wine and crescent rolls at a shop in the Rue Amsterdam, in company with postmen and scavengers, we returned to our homes in a more or less exhausted condition. It was half-past six.

This irregular and unconventional mode of life seemed like a revival of that followed by poets and artists in the days of the battles of *Hernani*, or the fantastic and reckless Bohemia of Petrus, Lassailly, and other romancers. Many of us, however, had certain serious, or at least less frivolous duties to perform during the day ; Coppée, Verlaine, Mérat, Valade, and Dierx had offices which claimed them for stated hours. They protested in the evening by various prowls, conversations, and gatherings prolonged far into the night, against the regularity and monotony of their diurnal existence. They were true neo-romantics, and moreover enthusiastic for Art, believing they had a mission for its revival, and hearing mysterious voices like Joan of Arc, which urged them to run counter to vulgarity, platitude, middle-class comedy, realistic novels, and the commerce and production of paying copy. They were ready to fight and to overcome in order to deliver Art and to place it crowned on its reconquered throne, not at Rheims but in Paris.

It was necessary to those adventurous vanquishers of form and artists who claimed to be labourers in the cause of Art, to have a place of meeting, a flag, and a name. All the political, literary, artistic, philosophical, scientific, university, commercial, and sporting circles were known by some distinctive appellation. The *Pléiade* and

Romantiques were examples to follow, but what
name should they adopt, for sometimes the ensign
is a sorry one, and a derogatory sobriquet is con-
ferred? We had already been branded by the
press and mockers on the boulevards by various
nicknames : the *Foôrmistes*, because I had published
in *L'Art* an article entitled " L'Idee et la Forme,"
in which I maintained, while reviewing Destutt de
Tracy and Maine de Biran, that as there can be
no thought without words, so there can be no
artistic idea without form : the form does not clothe
the idea, it creates it, just as in the physical world
the body creates the heart. But this name did
not catch on ; the *Impassibles* was next tried and
was more popular ; it originated in an article by
L.-X. de Ricard. The *Fantaisistes* and the *Stylistes*
were also suggested, but were considered in-
sufficiently sarcastic, in fact eulogistic. At last a
word dawned which was destined to survive, to be
included in the catalogue of literary history and
to designate a whole generation, even now active,
militant, triumphant : some one said, let the *Parnasse* be, and the *Parnasse* was !

We have already seen how, thanks to Ernest
Boutier, we had joined forces with the enterprising
bookseller of the Passage Choiseul, with the result
that Alphonse Lemerre became agent for the journal
L'Art and afterwards issued successively Ricard's
Ciel, Rue et Foyer, Verlaine's *Poèmes Saturniens*,
and Coppée's *Reliquaire*.

As the journal *L'Art* did not pay expenses nor
please the public, its *clientéle* being practically a
free one, Ricard discontinued its publication, and
a few sous still remaining to him to be spent on

printing, he published, on the advice of Catulle Mendès, and with the assent of the good counsellor Lemerre, the *Parnasse Contemporain*, a collection of new verse. Whence this rococo title! The name of the inventor has never precisely been known, several claimants having come forward. I believe, although I cannot vouch for it, that the title was suggested by a philologist who frequented Lemerre's, M. Ch. Marty-Lavaux, to whom the bookseller afterwards entrusted the publication of the poets of the *Pléiade*. Ronsard, the prince of poets, rehabilitated by Joseph Delorme and Banville, was held in great esteem by the *habitués* of the bookshops in the Passage Choiseul. However it was, the name caught on, was banded about, generally recognised, and finally the *néo - romantiques* were definitely grouped together under the title of the Parnassians. Parody was not wanting, and a dissident group of fantastic *littérateurs*, among whom were Alphonse Daudet, Paul Arène, and Jean du Boïs, published under the title of *Parnassiculet*, a satiric compilation in which the efforts of the Parnassians were imitated and ridiculed. There were hints of protestation and strife in the air, but duels at the point of the sword; Mendès against Arène, and fisticuffs—Verlaine against Daudet, were unknown.

The *Parnasse Contemporain, recueil de vers nouveaux*, first edition, on slightly tinted Whatman paper, with white cover, *format* small in - 8vo., sixteen pages, appeared in March 1866. It was an eclectic publication. If the youthful poets, several of them still unpublished, who first of all met and grouped themselves together in the Revue Fantaisiste, Passage des Princes, then at Mme. de

Ricard's, afterwards in the *salon* of Nina de Callias, in Lemerre's bookshop where the journal *L'Art* was published, at Leconte de Lisle's, Boulevard des Invalides, at Paul Meurice's, Avenue Frochot, and at Banville's, formed an important nucleus, a large and honourable place indeed was reserved for their chiefs. These masters not only illustrious but famous, and also some little understood more obscure ones were received with attention. The Parnassians did not hold with the doctrine of chronic and systematic disrespect; doubtless they heartily despised the practical school, and excommunicated from the temple of Art the Scribes and the Ponsards, but they were hospitable to poets whose works and ideas had little in common with the *Parnasse* and the Parnassians.

The *Parnasse* was announced as follows: The *Parnasse Contemporain*, a collection of new verse containing unpublished poems by the principal poets of the day, is issued in parts of sixteen pages, which will appear on Saturday. The publication commencing on the 3rd of March will be finished on the 14th July. Terms of subscription: 8 francs for Paris; 9 francs for the country. Each part may be obtained separately at all booksellers. Note.— A few copies for collectors will be printed on Dutch paper. Price: 16 francs. Paris, Librairie d'Alphonse Lemerre, publisher of the *Pléiade Française*, 47 Passage Choiseul, and at all booksellers, 1866. With the device: a man thrusting his spade into the earth (the rising sun was not added until later), the inscription: *Fac et Spera*, and the monogram A. L. I need not tell collectors that copies are now almost unobtainable.

Part I. began with some poems by Théophile Gautier : *Le Bédouin et la Mer*, *Le Banc de Pierre*, *Le Lion de l'Atlas*, *A. L. Sextius*, and *La Marguerite*. These were followed by a long, unique piece of verse by Théodore de Banville, *L'Exil des Dieux*, and the part concluded with sonnets by José-Maria de Heredia.

Part II. was entirely devoted to Leconte de Lisle. Part III. consisted of sonnets by Louis Ménard, poems by F. Coppée, and verses by Auguste Vacquerie. Part V., most interesting of all, contained the new *Fleurs du Mal* by Charles Baudelaire.

Then followed in succession the publication of verse by MM. Léon Dierx, Sully - Prudhomme, André Lemoyne, Louis-Xavier de Ricard, Antony Deschamps, Paul Verlaine, Arsène Houssaye, Léon Valade, Stéphane Mallarmé, Henri Cazalis, Philoxène, Boyer, Emmanuel des Essarts, Emile Deschamps, Albert Mérat, Henry Winter, Armand Renaud, Eugène Léfebure, Edmond Lepelletier, Auguste de Châtillon, Jules Forni, Charles Coran, Eugène Villemin, Robert Luzarche, Alexandre Piédagnel, Auguste Villiers de l'Isle - Adam, F. Fertiault, Francis Tesson, and Alexis Martin.

I have not omitted any one from this long list. It forms a remarkable medley of poets, some already famous, well on in years, survivors of the romantic period, such as Théophile Gautier, the two Deschamps and Auguste Vacquerie, others younger, but also possessed of fame, almost of glory, such as Théodore de Banville, Charles Baudelaire, Arsène Houssaye, Auguste de Châtillon and Philoxène Boyer, and lastly, the new generation of real Parnassians, of whom only three or four, such as Catulle Mendès, Ricard, Verlaine, and Coppée, had as yet published volumes of verse.

The *Parnasse* made some noise in the literary world, owing chiefly to the trumpeting of the terrible Barbey d'Aurevilly. That impetuous critic published in the *Nain Jaune* of November 1866 a series of portraits, or rather caricatures, evidently malicious in intent, but very clever and amusing, under the title: *Les Trente-sept médaillonnets du Parnasse Contemporain* (the thirty-seven medallionists of the *Contemporary Parnassus*), in which we were presented to the public in more or less ridiculous fashion. Barbey struck at us with his most crushing adjectives, and with his club-pen ground us in pieces.

I will give two or three of the *médaillonnets*, as they are essential to a complete picture of the *Parnasse* of 1866.

To begin with the greatest and also the first, the *Médaillonnet* of Théophile Gautier. The poet of *Emaux et Camées* opened the series of authors invited to take part in the *Parnasse Contemporain*, and headed the procession of poets, young and old, unpublished and celebrated, whose authoritative and dogmatic creed was displayed before the eyes of a rather indifferent public in the shop in the Passage Choiseul, a branch of the Helicon, *annexe* of other holy places, and cradle of the sons of Apollo.

Jules Barbey d'Aurevilly, the violent critic, the seldom amiable, but never insipid nor common-place eulogist, the piler-up of truculent epithets, the exhauster of colossal blame, the paradoxical and terse appraiser, whose very numerous articles on philosophers, religious writers, poets, historians, and blue-stockings, bristled with prejudices, heresies, unconventionalities, and brutalities, but also contained original points of view, surprising deductions, just appreciations and judgments, which time might mellow, only to make the more lasting, and which can be read with a few mental reservations, with the articles of *Père Duchesne* and Hébert. He had already published in the *Nain Jaune* an article on the *Parnasse Contemporain* and the Parnassians as a whole.

This article created some sensation among the poets, and Louis-Xavier de Ricard thought it right to enter a protest. The *Nain Jaune* at first refused to insert his letter as wanting in interest, and constituting an advertisement of the series, but Barbey d'Aurevilly prevailed on the manager, Gregory Genesco, to allow it to be included, and it appeared accompanied by the contemptuous comments of Barbey.

"This letter," he said, "is not a reply to our first article on the *Parnasse Contemporain*, in which we expressed our opinion supported by reasons, whether good or bad, those competent can judge. No! it is simply a little *raconto istorico* that might have been used as a preface, but which it has been insisted should be inserted as a reply. It is the history of the kitchen of the *Parnasse Contemporain*, wherein it appears M. de Ricard holds the handle of the pan; and, more especially, of the provisions that are not prepared there. How can the details of this kitchen interest the public and us? . . . We have found the thing served up to us detestable. Is that a reason why those who concocted it should be more annoyed than those who swallowed it?

" But poets are always the same — *Genus irritabile vatum.* Eternal comedians !

" ' I maintain that my verses are very good.'

" ' You have your reasons for finding them so,' etc. But we had counted upon this. Prose-writers judged as harshly as the poets of the *Parnasse Contemporain* would not have turned a hair, but the vanity of poets is only equalled by the vanity of vain women."

After some reflections on a piece of verse by Amédée Pommier, which the *Parnasse* had not inserted, and which Barbey d'Aurevilly considered good and worthy to figure in the volume, the journal gave the letter of the founder of the *Parnasse.* It bore the date of 30th October 1866. M. L.-X. de Ricard expressed himself thus :

" Before entering upon the subject of this letter it is fitting that I should advise you of my motive in writing. As the founder, with M. Mendès, of the *Parnasse Contemporain*, I think I have the right to correct certain inexact statements in the article which M. Barbey d'Aurevilly has published on the series. I bring no complaint against the brutalities of the critic.

" These are the facts : he has reproached us with having forgotten the contemporaries without whom, to a certain extent, we should not have existed, viz., Victor Hugo, Lamartine, Musset, de Vigny, Auguste Barbier, Sainte - Beuve, and Amédée Pommier.

" Now I answer that, with regard to Victor Hugo, the publisher, Lemerre, possesses a letter from the great poet in which he says that in consequence of his contract with his publisher, it is difficult for him to publish verses in the *Parnasse*

Contemporain ; however, he will endeavour to furnish some next year.

"It is true we have asked nothing from M. de Lamartine, who, according to M. Barbey d'Aurevilly, has the proud honour of no longer being popular with us. It is also true that we have asked nothing from Alfred de Vigny nor Alfred de Musset, for the reason that they are no longer alive, and the *Parnasse Contemporain* is not a selection from the works of the poets of the century, but merely, as the sub-title indicates, a collection of new verse.

"To continue, M. Antony Deschamps has been good enough to give M. de Heredia and us an introduction to M. Auguste Barbier, who informed us quite recently that he had nothing in his portfolio.

"Finally, M. Sainte-Beuve replied to a request by a very kind letter, in which he said he had searched among his papers in vain for unpublished verse.

"These are the facts I oppose to the statements of M. Barbey d'Aurevilly."

M. de Ricard afterwards gave the reasons which had caused him to refuse the verses sent in by M. Amédée Pommier.

The objection, or rather the criticism of Barbey d'Aurevilly, had apparently some grounds, and it might be asked why certain poets were admitted to the *Parnasse* and others with the same claims excluded. It seemed almost as if the choice were limited by the exclusiveness of a school, a sort of *coterie*. If, indeed, only the work of young poets, such as L.-Xavier de Ricard, or beginners who had read their first attempts in the *salons* of Mme. de Ricard or Nina de Callias, or at Catulle Mendès, Rue de Douai, where green tea

L

was drunk, handed round by a vicious young urchin, known as Covielle, to the strains of Wagner, or the recitation of Hindoo poems, had been accepted in the *Parnasse*, surprise might have been felt at finding beside the names of Mendès, Coppée, Verlaine, Léon Dierx, and Mérat, authors as yet almost unpublished, the famous, even illustrious names of Baudelaire, Emile, and Antony Deschamps, Arsène Houssaye, Auguste de Châtillon, and Auguste Vacquerie, and, above all, the magisterial presence of Théophile Gautier, then in the zenith of his fame. His collaboration in the juvenile, rather rash and possibly unsuccessful enterprise of the Parnassians threw into greater relief the absence of Victor Hugo.

Ricard's letter, therefore, meant more than an angry poet's irritable repartee to an intolerant critic. It explained the absence of Victor Hugo and the non-participation of certain poets, such as Auguste Barbier and Sainte-Beuve. Moreover, these masters figured, as their letters gave warning, in two interesting pieces in the second volume of the *Parnasse Contemporain* in 1869. One great contemporary poet alone does not appear to have been solicited, Lamartine, and this was an injustice and an error. Ricard's letter preserves a discreet silence on this point.

Barbey d'Aurevilly replied to Ricard's letter by the publication of his *Médaillonnets*. Here is that of Théophile Gautier:

"Let us begin by turning it face to the wall or covering it up like the portrait of that Doge of Venice who was beheaded for treason, for, as I have already said, M. Théophile Gautier ought not to be here; he is out of place, out of proportion, among these *Médaillonnets*. If he took proper pride in his talent, his record, and his age, he would not be seen at the head of this volume of the *Parnasse*, but easy - going, indolent king that he is, seeking, perhaps, for popularity with these young men who call him Master, he has passively allowed himself to be set on the summit of this *Parnasse Contemporain* which they wished to adorn with his name.

"These poetic bastards, having need of a father, have sought for one in M. Théophile Gautier, although, as a matter of fact, it is not he, but M. Théodore de Banville, or, best of all, M. Leconte de Lisle, who, much stronger than M. Banville, and whom I regard as in other respects vigorous, should lead this troop of imitators."

After the *Médaillonnet* of Théophile Gautier followed that of Théodore de Banville :

"The poetry of M. Théodore de Banville is, in fact, nothing more than a vague decoction, in an empty Bohemian glass, of the poetry of M. Victor Hugo and of André Chénier ; not M. Victor Hugo the great 'genuine,' but Hugo at work, alas! on mythology and Renaissance archaism, for he has such sad days. Imitation is so much in the air of this age without ideas or heart, that it shoots up like an ill weed even in the very face of genius. As a Greek weeping over a dead Venus, whom he calls 'Aphroditè' with an accent grave over the e for the whole of his invention, M. de Banville, who has derived from André Chénier his method of finishing a clause in the following line of his verse, abusing it to contortion and distortion, is more insupportable to me than a superb hollow model. His flute has more than seven holes, or, rather, it has only one, in which the instrument itself disappears. He has been described truthfully, if unkindly, in the words : ' He is only a pitcher which believes itself a jug.' "

Next comes the portrait, rather highly coloured, of the poet who then exercised true supremacy among the Parnassians.

" M. Leconte de Lisle is not content to hang on to and everlastingly balance himself, like Sarah la Baigneuse, between two imitations. He has thirty-six for trapezes. He is energetic and likes variety. He too imitates M. Hugo—M. Hugo, the fate, the *ananké*, of all of them !—but *bast !* he imitates many others as well. Who would believe it ? He goes to the length of imitating Ossian ; he puts a false beard on his chin. He is Scandinavian, Barbarian, Greek, Persian—more especially Persian. He would astonish Montesquieu ! In short, he is anything rather than a Frenchman and poet of the nineteenth century, a man who simply occupies his own place in the scale of humanity. M. Leconte de Lisle has chosen to excel in systematic imitation.

"It is a pity. He might, perhaps, have had originality. Let us tell him the truth in the symbolical language he adores. M. Leconte de Lisle is the veritable Hanouman of this *Parnasse Contemporain*. Hanouman, as he knows, is the monkey god of Indian mythology, the son of Pavana, the God of Winds (and hollow poets !), who is represented with a long tail, followed by a troop of monkeys, and holding a lyre or a fan. . . . A fan ! Not always on account of the warmth of his verses."

This picturesque and amusing opinion, full of

rosserie (hard hits), as we say nowadays, was also full of injustice.   Leconte de Lisle was, as a matter of fact, the soul of the *Parnasse Contemporain*, and, far more than Victor Hugo, a divinity whom they worshipped and venerated at a distance, the pontiff in presence surrounded in permanent fashion by the Levites of the new cult of form and beauty.

Barbey d'Aurevilly reproached Leconte de Lisle with not being a poet of the nineteenth century, a contemporary.   There was some truth in the observation.   Poets, according to the idea of Leconte de Lisle and all those who took part in the poetic revival of 1866, known as the *Mouvement Parnassien*, ought to live or pretend to live outside their own time.   Their doctrine was not so much that of impassibility as indifference, isolation ; the poet, floating above all that is actual, which he regards as vulgar and troublesome, ought to make no practical mark on his century.   What he says, thinks, and desires must be apart from the contingencies which agitate, subdue, or excite the society amid which he lives ; he must appear to have fallen from the moon, or to have escaped from a place reserved for genius.

There was at this period, and we, together with the Decadents, Symbolists, and Naturalists, saw the development commence at close quarters, a double movement of separation : the poets took one road, the public another, with contempt on both sides. They mutually turned their backs, affecting not only remoteness but ignorance of the other's existence.   Thus the public became more and more estranged from the poetical movement, and the poets appeared to have no place, interest, nor

utility in modern society. At most, they were
admitted in dramatic form or at literary matinées,
allowed to furnish interludes which were listened
to abstractedly, and always less appreciated than
prose monologues and songs. The *chatnoiresque*,
imitative, ironical, poet band were only able to find a
public in a few newspapers and wine-shops qualified
as artistic. Fashion always held aloof from these
acrobats of rhyme, fascinating as some of them
were.

Leconte de Lisle, who witnessed the rupture and
had even contributed to its birth and growth, secretly
chafed at the isolation set up and the indifference
displayed. Although surrounded with discreet
homage, respectfully saluted by the literary *élite*
and almost immediately invested with the supreme
honours reserved for recognised, licensed, official,
decorated, and academic literary men, he inwardly
yearned after the popularity for which he had
never sought, certainly, but which he had desired
to receive. He wanted to experience the satisfaction of repulsing the homage that the public
had never thought of offering him, and of shutting
himself in his Ivory Tower, or rather his pagoda,
away from an idolatrous crowd who did not dream
of prostrating themselves on its steps.

Leconte de Lisle retained a secret rancour from
early attempts on behalf of the people. Arriving
from the Isles, full of political enthusiasm and consumed by a fever of democracy, already chilled in
the first battles of 1848, afterwards carefully suppressed, the young creole of the Réunion threw
himself into the Republican struggle, he the future
Olympian King of the Impassibles, the calm, cold

spectator, dignified and superb as a Buddha on his throne, in his artist's arm-chair. He brought to it the fire of his Southern nature ; he was a club orator, an agitator of new creeds, a partisan of the people, an admirer of the masses. He prepared, in conjunction with other young democratic creoles, such as Melvil Bloncourt, plans of reform ; he joined revolutionary societies ; he aspired to the glory of representing some of the simple, unlettered, and ignorant to whom the books he had in mind and his future songs could never be anything but indecipherable texts, incomprehensible sounds, in an unknown tongue.

All his life, like Renan, he retained in his heart the bitterness of having been disdained by universal suffrage, which he in his turn despised. It had remained in his soul like a persistent aroma of this political efflorescence. From this resulted the ironic curl of his lip, the moroseness of his manner, the mordant sallies which escaped him, the cruel fixity of his regard under his monocle, which accentuated the aristocratic carriage of his lordly head.

In spite of the calculated frigidity which he erected like a barrier around him, we loved and respected him in our youth in the early morning of the *Parnasse*. He shone upon us with his growing glory, which to us was already at its zenith, in the obscure bookshop of Lemerre. With what indignation we might be heard crying to the passers-by : " But read *Hypathie, L'Agonie d'un Saint, La Mort de Tiphaine, Midi roi des étés, Le Manchy, Le Corbeau*, read and admire, you pack of imbeciles." No one listened to us ; Leconte de

Lisle remained utterly unknown. Night brooded
over his books, silence around his name. Unjust
as was Barbey d'Aurevilly's diatribe, it had its
advantage. The *Médaillonnet* already quoted at
least served to make the name of the poet sound
in the ears of the great public, those who read
newspapers and not volumes of verse. Some time
afterwards the *Figaro* published one of the finest of
his unprinted poems, *Le Cœur de Hialmar*. Thus
were the foundations of his celebrity laid down,
and dawning glory penetrated the shadows of
indifference.

Leconte de Lisle had a considerable influence
upon the poetical generation of 1866. Sully-
Prudhomme, Coppée, Verlaine, José-Maria de
Heredia, Léon Dierx, and Armand Silvestre all
proceeded from him. His gatherings on the
Boulevard des Invalides were largely attended.
He was listened to as a professor of the Beautiful.
His faultless style, his magisterial objectivity, his
intense colouring, his magnificent imagination, and
his marvellous reconstruction of the heroes of the
nebulous ages renovated poetry. He replaced the
Christolatry of Lamartine and the chivalrous, feudal
verse of Victor Hugo, with evocations of far-off
lands, interpretations of mysterious religions, para-
phrases of barbarian cosmogonies. Melancholy
snow-covered landscapes of the north visions of the
Scandinavian fiords and Celtic forests alternated
with his pictures of tropical vegetation lying beneath
the noonday sun. He conjured up vast prairies,
solitary islands, the rocks of the Skalds and Runic
circles. Thus he set up permanent monuments of
poetry, solid blocks of robust art, which will remain

immutable as long as the French language endures ; an intellectual cataclysm alone could overturn his mighty edifices.

He had no need, the great artist, to seek new words, special methods, extravagant rhymes, bizarre ellipses in order to describe the world within him, to create the plastic forms he knew so admirably how to cast in indestructible poetic moulds ; intelligible words sufficed for him. His dictionary was every man's, and his grammar contained nothing unusual ; he respected his own tongue, and preserved the dignity of metre. Never for a moment did this chief of the Parnassians uphold nor encourage the Symbolists and Decadents. Strength, and simplicity were his attributes. Like the bird of the Andes, of which he has so magnificently sung, he floated above the pettiness of the world, and when death struck him with its immutable rigidity, he remained poised in immortality, asleep in the clear cold atmosphere of glory, with outspread wings. Barbey d'Aurevilly was unfair and cruel to this poet. The outrageous severity he evinced in the *Médaillonnet* of Leconte de Lisle detracts from the vigour and authority of his other portrait caricatures. I have already quoted a part of Verlaine's *Médaillonnet* ; it concludes with the words :

"He has said somewhere, speaking of I know not whom, a fact without importance :—

" ' . . . It has
The inflection of dear voices which are dead.'

When we listen to M. Paul Verlaine, we could wish that his voice had a similar inflection."

This remark may be witty, but it is inadequate from the point of view of criticism.

I will conclude these reminiscences of the *Médaillonnets*, now forgotten, valueless, and interesting merely in retrospect, by quoting, if I may, my own. I have given sufficient proof of my admiration for Barbey d'Aurevilly, both in these papers and elsewhere, to make it clear that he did not even spare those who, like Verlaine and myself, had a perhaps exaggerated deference for him. Although I had the honour of being his friend, and was his colleague on the *Nain Jaune*, and had on several occasions performed his duties as dramatic critic to that paper, leaving to him, of course, his emoluments while he reported himself at Valognes-en-Cotentin, where he wrote the fine novel, *Chevalier Destouches*, it will be seen that he was no more indulgent to me than to my friends and our masters.

This is my *Médaillonnet* :

"Exaggerated echo of André Chénier, echo of M. Hugo Renaissance, an echo of an echo, since the latter echoes M. Théodore de Banville, M. Edmond Lepelletier, has given two pieces to the *Parnasse Contemporain*. The second, *Le Léthé*, unhappily does not make us forget the first, which is called *L'Attelage*, a Grecian mythological poem. The author has essayed to sound the old hunting-horn of Grecian mythology which hangs at the doors of all second-hand dealers, a poetical relic of carnival time. He sings *Cléobis et Biton*, a subject worthy of the resurrecting hand of the painter of Lycus, or of Homer, but which is here nothing more than an old engraving that would prevent a room in an hotel from being let."

All the Parnassians were dealt with in similar

fashion by Barbey d'Aurevilly, and his amusing, violent criticisms helped to draw attention to them, to make known the name they had adopted, and to prepare the ear of the public to listen to their future works. Barbey d'Aurevilly afterwards explained in a final article in the *Nain Jaune* the intention of the *Médaillonnets.*

"What I wished to prove beyond question," he said, "is the exclusively imitative character of a volume with extravagant pretensions, and I think I have done this in my examination, poem by poem, and word by word, of the work of the thirty-seven poets of this pleasant *Parnasse.* Owing to the impossibility of quoting all the verses in a book, which would have to be entirely reproduced in order to convince the reader of the inanity of its contents, and the immense weariness to which it gives rise, I have pointed out the source of each poem in this unhappy collection, distinguished by no hint of originality, and coupled with each of these servile Parnassians the name of the man whom he has imitated."

He concludes by the following violent apostrophe :

"The noble objection has been raised, while I have been writing the *Médaillonnets* of these Parnassians, who are all alike, that I was wrong 'at a time when literature is justly accused of being at a low ebb, to attack unreservedly the poets who have given expression to the most elevated literature obtainable.' This would certainly be true if the poetry of the *Parnasse Contemporain* were defective only in form, but it is radically bad right down to its very inspiration, and therefore it is necessary to be implacable! The poetry of the Parnassians has neither thought nor feeling. It is a mere vile exercise of rhyme, cadence, and incomplete lines. It sings neither of God, Fatherland, nor self-sacrificing love, nor any of the virtues which find an abiding place in our poor hearts. Only the more guilty, degraded and worthy of the whip and lash of the critic in that it believes simply in matter and material attachments. Classed among sinners are those who commit sacrilege by prostituting to unworthy or puerile uses the consecrated vessels of their altar."

It is severe, unjust, and inexact, but it is capitally put all the same. In 1869 the second volume of the *Parnasse Contemporain* was issued under the special direction of Alphonse Lemerre, now become an important publisher. Leconte de Lisle assisted in the arrangement of the lyrical encyclopedia. Some of the poets who, for various reasons, and notably Sainte-Beuve and Auguste Barbier, as has already been said, were not included among the authors in the first volume, were invited to take part in the second. Among these new names were those of Mmes. Nina de Callias, Louisa Siéfert, Blanchecotte, Louise Collet, and Augusta Penquer; and MM. Henri Rey, Victor de Laprade, Anatole France, Léon Cladel, Alfred des Essarts, Joséphin Soulary, Armand Silvestre, Laurent Pichat, Antonin Valabrègue, Gabriel Marc, André Theuriet, Jean Aicard, Georges Lafenestre, Alexandre Cosnard, Gustave Pradelle, Robinot-Bertrand, Louis Salles, Charles Cros, Eugène Manuel, Claudius Popelin, and Edouard Grenier.

In spite of the reinforcement of rather minor poets, such as Cosnard, Louis Salles, Robinot-

Bertrand, Mmes. Blanchecotte, Penquer, Siéfert, and the poor excitable Nina de Callias, whose contribution Charles Cros had certainly put into verse, or at least revised, the second publication of the *Parnasse* produced no sensation. It was a venture repeated, and possessing no special attractions. It did not receive the honour of further *Médaillonnets*, nor of any criticism whatsoever in the Press; moreover, the Parnassians began to separate. The great success of Coppée's *Passant*, unexpected but certainly merited, although a triumphal *début* for the new poetical contingent, gave rise to many jealousies, which resulted in personal ruptures, and many secessions from the school.

Verlaine and I were always Coppée's friends, and delighted at his very great success, but many of our comrades did not feel the same sentiment. Dissimulating their petty envy under protestations in the cause of Art, they asserted that the *Passant* was poetry for the middle classes, and that Coppée was not sufficiently Hindoo. The *salons* in which the Parnassians were wont to meet were no longer frequented by the same guests, some still continued to go to Leconte de Lisle's and Lemerre's, but that excellent publisher's bookshop, became alternately a place for gossip and an academic *salon*, and many of us only went to the Passage Choiseul in connection with publishing business, or by chance. The war of 1870 finally dispersed the Parnassians.

Yet a secret *camaraderie* continued to exist between them, and later on, when pursuing the various paths of literature, art, and politics, they still felt linked together by the powerful chain of

early friendship and mutual literary struggles. They
had been brothers-in-arms, and when they met in
after years, they recalled with pleasure the days
when fame had not yet come to them, and they
had believed that their future lay within the cycle
of the *Parnasse*, and the bookshop of Lemerre,
that dispenser of printed glory.

Louis - Xavier de Ricard, who has published
in *Le Temps* some very interesting articles on the
Parnasse Contemporain, which he was better able
to do than any one else, said, in conclusion, and
this will be the final judgment on the *Parnasse* :—

" I do not believe that the Parnassians were
the supreme poets Verlaine imagined, nor that all
the poetry before, and even more especially since,
ought to be decried; persuaded as I am that
we did good, salutary, serious, useful, and necessary
work, I also believe that the Parnassian movement
is now superseded by the younger generation.

" The *Parnasse* was not a school nor a club, and
least of all the set against which many were greatly,
unadvisedly, and sometimes insincerely irritated.
The *Parnasse* had no creed nor æsthetic dogma,
neither had it any official theory, by which I mean a
collective belief regarding the method of composing
poetry. Although accused of being mere rhymers,
they did not even profess the same opinion as to
the superiority of the full rhyme.

" The Parnassians had no common theory, even
a superficial one, of philosophy, politics, or sociology.
Some of us, on the contrary—I make the statement
without prejudice — professed an actual contempt
for all these questions. Look at the survivors ; they
are scattered among all the professions. Having
thus no doctrine, even on the subject of æsthetics
or poetry in the classical sense of the word, what

was the *Parnasse*? What common bond united us? An idea, no more! But an idea so great that it did not impede nor hinder the personal evolution of any one of us.

" If you are sceptical, compare, as Verlaine said, the works of the Parnassians, one with the other, and observe that they neither resemble those of their glorious masters nor one another's. . . ."

In 1876 the third volume of the *Parnasse Contemporain* was issued. Paul Verlaine did not figure in it. By that time he was known as the author of the *Romances sans Paroles* and *Sagesse*, but an evil reputation surrounded him, and very few of his old friends dared to utter his name. He was forgotten and misunderstood as well as calumniated, dead while yet he lived.

CHAPTER VII

MARRIAGE—*LA BONNE CHANSON*

(1869-1871)

THERE was only one actual event in Verlaine's life. He passed his existence outside the great, and even the smaller happenings of his time. A Republican, he took no part in any of the conspiracies, agitations, or movements so frequent during the last years of the Empire; he had nothing to do with the affair of the Café de la Renaissance. He, who certainly did not hold cafés in abhorrence, never frequented the Brasserie Serpente, the Brasserie Glaser, nor the Café de Madrid—places where the youthful opponents of Imperial rule were wont to meet and men were liable to become involved in violent squabbles, in cases like those of the Treize, to arbitrary arrest, fines, police surveillance, and even to imprisonment at Mazas, followed by a trial for conspiracy and high treason before the High Court sitting at Blois. He circled round, without being drawn into the various political whirlpools. A patriot, he made war from afar, almost as a spectator, and he acted sentry, as it were, in an arm-chair. Although he was living in Paris during the terrible siege he took no part in what went on in public places, and was a dumb inactive figure in the drama of the Commune, remaining peaceably seated on his leather stool at the Hotel-de-Ville. Except for the *Invectives* he did not raise his voice in any of the bitter literary polemics of his time, and never acted in a duel. Like all the rest of us he experienced cruel losses in his family—his father first, his cousin Elisa, and, heaviest blow of all, his excellent mother, but these were only the ordinary trials of everyday life.

That he came to want was not the result of any unexpected catastrophe, but of careless expenditure ; and that, coupled with losses of capital and of the emoluments proceeding from regular work, rendered poverty in the end inevitable. Day by day, almost imperceptibly, he descended the ladder of distress. His disastrous agricultural enterprises at Juniville and Coulommes deprived him of a large portion of his private income, and a swindle on the part of the Abbé Salard did away with the remainder, but this was not the reason of his ultimate ruin.

One fact dominated and poisoned his destiny ; this was his marriage. It is impossible to reconstruct the life of a man, to take a horoscope after death, and it is futile to try and imagine a Verlaine always a bachelor, a Government clerk receiving his salary regularly, living in unpretentious comfort with his mother up to the end of her life, and leading a comparatively regular existence, interrupted only by visits to the cafés and an occasional *amour*, writing leisurely in the quietude of his office and the solitude of his bedroom, and under the inspiration of absinthe, poems more or less studied and polished, and accepted by some review with artistic pretensions—a Verlaine grown wise, staid, correct,

with clothes from La Belle Jardinière, a punctual
tax - payer, laureate of the Académie Française,
having led the life of a sinecurist, monotonous but
happy and pleasant, like some of the comrades of
his youth who finished their careers in an easy
official arm-chair, such as Albert Mérat, or, better
still, at the Institute, like José-Maria de Heredia.

Perhaps if his fate had been thus encompassed
and regulated, if the river of his life had flowed
along steadily and tranquilly between the smooth
banks of an official career, if he had never abandoned
his domestic habits, Verlaine might have continued
to produce good verse in the objective and descriptive style of Leconte de Lisle, but he would not
have been the poet, strange and impressionist,
every fibre of whose being thrilled to the touch of
that inner life which sent through his nerves a
quiver of unexpressed art, to be interpreted by him
into something quite new, something undreamed of
before.   Perhaps those things which went to make
up his personality, his originality, that assured him
a place apart in the wondrous assemblage of poets,
and even the glory which illumines his grave, arose
one and all from this same marriage.   Verlaine
unwed might have been an esteemed and estimable
poet and nothing more.   No matter who his wife
was, marriage for him could not have been happy
nor possible, although he complained in that famous
poem in the *Romances sans Paroles* :

"You have not always been patient. . . ."

The evil destiny of the poet, therefore, was not
due to her who was his choice, but rather to the
conjugal state itself, for which he was ill-suited, with

his excitable temperament, his passionate exuberance, and the deplorable facility with which he allowed himself to drift into evil ways.

The ordinary reasons which impel men to seek marriage were entirely absent from Verlaine's sudden decision. Doubtless he had love for the young girl, the sight of whom moved him so profoundly; he has himself narrated how he was transfixed by the traditional arrow, but his determining sentiment was a feeling of humility and personal inferiority. His abrupt extravagant resolution, resembling one made under the influence of intoxication, to demand (and of her half-brother, a young man not in a position of family authority) the hand of a young girl seen for some few minutes only, was like a protestation against the injustice of chance in the matter of his physiognomy, a defiance of the fatality of his physical appearance.

Verlaine, it must be remembered, was afflicted with exceeding hideousness. In later life his plain, odd, irregular face, bald head, and flat nose were quite passable, illumined as they were by the brilliance of intellect and surrounded by the aureole of talent. One had grown accustomed by that time to his face, like a faun's when he laughed, his sinister aspect when grave. His flattened features, prominent teeth, and appearance generally which recalled that of a classical death's - head, produced an impression of unique ugliness, which, under certain circumstances, might interest and even please. But in his youth he was grotesquely ugly; he resembled, not as has been stated the Mongolian type, but the monkey, and his baboon-like originality could inspire in any woman he met only feelings of repulsion, repugnance, perhaps fright and disgust. If I emphasise these physical peculiarities, it is because criticism and also philosophy and history attach too little importance to the sexual life. Historians, psychologists, and moralists are provokingly contemptuous of the large part played by the instinct of generation in the human drama.

The poor fellow was well aware of the repulsive effect he produced; he used to joke about his *gueusard de physique*, and scribble on the covers of exercise books, in the margins of volumes, silhouettes, sketches, and drawings which confirmed the notion that he was lacking in physical advantages. He caricatured himself mercilessly.

Moreover, he was timid and awkward in the presence of women. He had none of those ingenuous flirtations and charming intrigues common to the twentieth year, and which often contain all the poetry of those who do not compose verse. The letter from Lécluse in September 1862 shows that he did attach interest to these first innocent encounters with the fair sex. He remembered the quadrille in which he had taken part with the headmaster's daughter, Mdlle. Hiolle. But this quadrille led to nothing. No attempt was made to retain him after the dance by a smile or promise to see him again, and he slipped away, sad, disillusioned, trying to forget the little person who showed no desire to continue his acquaintance. He felt himself separated from women by an abyss; a recluse to whom love held out no possibilities. I do not believe, I who never lost sight of him for a single day during the eight years which preceded his

marriage, that Paul had the smallest love affair, or
attempted to court any woman whatsoever, grisette,
cocotte, or artist; had he done so he would certainly
have confided in me, or I should have discovered his
secret. Opportunities were not lacking. Young
women who had had adventures, and girls not
wholly honest used to come to Mme. de Ricard's,
and at the gayer house of Mme. de Callias he met
many amiable young persons, easy of access. He
had, moreover, like every other man, the opportunities afforded by walks, evening parties, theatres,
concerts, and journeys, of finding himself in the
society of desirable and pleasing creatures, with
whom he might have entered into relations ending
in the ordinary way. But it was not so.

In his youth he never had a mistress to whom
he clung either through love or pure sensuality—*i.e.*,
a woman, married or unmarried, recognised as his,
if not exclusively, at least by preference, tenderness,
or possibly interest. He did not even frequent
women easy of access regularly, intermittently, or
in the character of a temporary lover. His amorous
adventures were of more than ordinary simplicity;
he only addressed himself to those unfortunates
who sell love like a commodity—going for his fill
of caresses as he would for absinthe to the nearest
place of sale. He himself has narrated elsewhere
with his ingenuous cynicism how he lost his innocence in a shuttered house in the Rue d'Orléans-
Saint-Honoré.

He had therefore never loved, and his early
poems doubtless owed to his ignorance of passion,
desire, striving, and suffering, an ideality and an
imperturbability such as few poets before him could

boast, and of which marriage was soon to deprive
him.   It is in fact very unusual for a poet to
attain the age of twenty-five without having loved,
and sung his hopes, dreams, sensations, jealousies,
triumphs, disappointments, and suspicions.   Verlaine
knew nothing of the ecstasies, desires, joys, and
sorrows of first love, too often disastrous and
enduring in effect.   In the ardent springtime he
had not experienced the wild delight which succeeds
discouragement, or that terrible moment when the
beloved has escaped, and the whole world seems
tumbling about one's ears.   He was ignorant of
the alternations of happiness and sorrow which
make up love.   The sensual spasm is an absolute
illusion, for without the brain being struck with
certain identities, any woman would satisfy any man.

I never saw the youthful Verlaine give his arm
to one of the opposite sex.   He never joined any
of those delightful excursions into the country with a
party of four, six, or eight, which leave such happy
recollections in the mind.   I would often row on
a Sunday to Joinville-le-Pont, but he would never
accompany me, not that he objected to the boating,
the country, nor the light refections in arbours, but
that he felt alone, uncompanioned, and dared not
hazard a chance encounter in the course of the
outing.   He never took part in our frolicsome
rambles along by the hedges, chanting the choruses
of popular songs, and gathering violets or black-
berries, according to the season.   He was never
one at our gay repasts in the tea gardens of
Montmartre, the Butte, Montrouge, or Châtillon.
Once, indeed, I managed to inveigle him into the
company of a set of young people who held their

meetings at the balls of Montmartre, the Elysée, and the Château-Rouge ; but this set called *La Collective*, a co-operative society for refreshment and amusement, did not attract him ; he was content to watch us laughing, dancing, and flirting. In solitude he steadily emptied glass after glass while we engaged in romping quadrilles and rapid waltzes with the frivolous *habitués* of the place, or sat beside them flushed and breathless after our exertions. He appeared to my friends, journalists and Government clerks, a rather lugubrious boon companion, and one of them, Louis Advenant, the future explorer, added, when saying good-bye to him : "There is not much go about you ! When Death comes for me I shall appreciate your society !"

He used to go away alone, generally under the influence of drink, to the low haunts in which, as he has himself confessed without shame, he made his first essays in passion, where poor girls, spiders of pleasure, watched behind a lamp for passers-by whom they could lure into their toils. Verlaine never wanted any one to accompany him on these escapades. He very seldom mentioned them even to me ; they were always the same, and not of a character in which he could possibly take pride. In his twentieth year love therefore only existed for him, great idealist though he was, in the most material of forms.

But one day chance brought him into the presence of a very young girl, little more than a child, Mdlle. Mathilde Mauté de Fleurville, at the house in the Rue Nicolet, Montmartre, afterwards to become the scene of his domestic tragedy.

He had gone to see the composer, Charles

de Sivry, who lived there with his stepfather,
M. Mauté de Fleurville, an ex-notary and perfect
type of citizen, with mutton-chop whiskers and gold
spectacles, when some one knocked at the door of
the room in which Sivry and his visitor were talking. Oh! that tap-tap, gay and penetrating! It was
to resound for ever in the heart of the poet. A
young girl appeared in a frilled dress of grey and
green, a charming brunette. Verlaine has described
her most delightfully in the verses which begin:

"En robe grise et verte, avec des ruches."

The first interview was simple and decisive.
Curiosity had doubtless impelled the young girl
towards her brother's room. She put her dainty
little head round the half-opened door and made
a feint of withdrawing it with confused protestations and charming grimaces.

"Stay," said Charles, "Monsieur is a poet. . . .
It is Verlaine. . . . Don't you know him? . . ."

In fact he had often been spoken off in the Mautés'
house. I have already mentioned the schemes for
operettas which were then engrossing Verlaine.
Charles de Sivry, future conductor of the orchestra
of the Chat-Noir, was desirous of obtaining verse
of the kind suitable to set to music. He dreamed
of *Petit Faust* and *Belle Hélène*. Besides, Sivry
frequented Nina's *soirées*, and naturally he had
talked of the coming celebrities he met at that
lively house, and even brought home with him
Verlaine's works, the *Poèmes Saturniens* and the
Fêtes galantes. The young girl may have dipped
into these volumes indiscreetly; they had had no
special interest for her.

At her brother's invitation, therefore, Mdlle.

Mauté remained and joined in the conversation. She told Verlaine she liked his verses, although they were a little strong for her, and the poet was touched both in his pride as author and in another feeling as well.

It seemed to him — was it an illusion? very possibly not—that the young girl regarded him with different eyes from those of the majority of the women he had met; he saw nothing of the irony, disdain, cruelty, insolence, fear, or distress which had filled the orbs bent on him hitherto. The young girl did not seem to have any fear of him. Had she not remarked his ugliness? Perhaps, after all, he did not appear so repulsive to her as he did to himself. Did this compassionate child regard him with more indulgent eyes than others of her sex, than his friends, than himself? Was this mere chance? . . .

He dared not follow up so flattering a supposition, but a warm glow pervaded his heart, and he looked curiously at this young girl, a few minutes before unknown, ignored, unsuspected, treated with indifference, as a child. He examined her with the deepest attention, while she on her part seemed to be stealthily regarding him, not without some interest. He was not insignificant and merited attention, he thought with vanity. This happy hypothesis accelerated the workings of his excited brain, and, without a word of warning, into his heart there crept a new and sudden love destined to revolutionise his life. It was as if a rare and beautiful flower had suddenly blossomed within him. Until now he had only dreamed of real affection, and unexpectedly it had come upon him, filling him with an intoxicating sweetness.

On her side the young girl on the verge of
womanhood, which opened a new world before her,
probably felt a sudden impulse, a momentary but
intense excitement, a desire to respond to the
ardent feeling she felt she had evoked in the poet.
Whatever it was this at least is certain, that for
that one and, alas, fleeting hour, there reigned
between these two beings the harmony of perfect
union. I dare assert that both were instantaneously
pleased; the proof of it, as far as the young girl
is concerned, is that Mdlle. Mathilde Mauté, very
young, and living in comfortable circumstances, was
in a position to look forward to marrying at leisure,
with the approval of her family, a Government
employé, an official, a merchant, or perhaps a man
of letters. She could afford to wait and choose;
yet she somewhat precipitately accepted a marriage
that she might have put off for an indefinite
period, and finally refused after reflection and
comparison. There seemed nothing in the union
to attract her; of money there was merely a competency, and our friend could hardly be regarded
as a seductive cavalier. No thought of ambition,
no desire for independence entered into her calculations. She was in no sort of haste to quit her
father's house, where she was made much of, spoilt,
flattered, adored, and wanted for nothing. She
had no romantic tendencies, but already gave signs
of the practical commonsense and shrewd self-
possession afterwards to distinguish her. There
was no question of her losing her head, and she
never permitted her lover to grow bold, with
precocious wisdom and unflagging self-control
restraining his masculine impatience.

Living in surroundings where literature was a frequent topic of conversation, and artists extolled, hearing her mother, a very good pianist, eulogise notabilities, and her brother, Charles de Sivry, speak familiarly of the coming men with whom he consorted, there may have been something particularly attractive in the literary promise which Verlaine held out; and perhaps, too, she was dominated by the force of the passion which emanated from him. Doubtless, it was love at first sight on both sides, and the union immediately projected was a true love match.

Verlaine has himself narrated how completely his life was altered by this meeting. It was a veritable moral cyclone. When he went to the Café du Delta for his usual absinthe, he quite forgot to drink it! Love overcame his desire for the green liquid : a miracle not to be repeated.

The poet now left Paris; he set out precipitately, either to give another direction to his thoughts, or to reason with the love by which he felt himself invaded. He went to the north, his refuge and consolation, and from thence he wrote me this hurried little note, for he had gone away without a word of warning to any one :

"FAMPOUX, chez M. Julien Déhée (Pas de Calais) près Arras.

"Very suffering suddenly, equally sudden departure. Letter from my mother to my Chief. Details later, or prompt return in accordance with expected reply. Don't forget the *Forgerons.* Write to me. Keep well. Your devoted

"P. VERLAINE.

"4*th June* 1869."

In the tranquillity of the country he reasoned
with himself, put his thoughts in order, tested his
moral pulse, found himself very much in love,
decided that he had reason to be, and abruptly,
perhaps under the influence of some inspiring
draught, wrote a long letter to Charles de Sivry.
This missive did not conform to the etiquette
usually observed in such circumstances. Verlaine
boldly, even roughly demanded from his friend
the hand of his sister. He forgot that Charles
de Sivry, unmistakable as was his musical talent,
was only a young man, and without authority in
the family; moreover, as merely the half-brother
of Mdlle. Mathilde, he was hardly in a position
to bestow or withhold the little hand demanded.

But Verlaine cared little in this moment of psychic
exaltation for the question of family precedence.
He entirely forgot M. Mauté, the father; he did
not even think of the mother, with whom he was
on quite friendly terms. He wrote in an access
of fever. He threw the letter into the box as if
he were relieving himself of some compromising
document, and still under the influence of strong
excitement, returned to the Déhées with hasty
step, abstracted air, and shining eyes. Without
a word to any one, he threw himself on his bed
and slept profoundly until he was called to dinner.
The Déhées thought he had been drinking, and
his sleep aroused no comment among these good
people, who were tolerant of over indulgence in
beer or gin.

A letter from Charles de Sivry soon arrived,
the reply so impatiently expected. His future
brother-in-law told him that, taken aback by the

very unexpected request, he had communicated its contents first of all to his sister. This was another grave breach of the conventions, but no notice was taken of it. Sivry had then placed the matter before his mother, who referred it to her husband, M. Mauté. The letter ended up with the good words that he might hope. M. Mauté hardly counted. His wife and daughter approved in principle, that was the important thing. There was room for belief that a happy termination might be expected. But Paul had to realise that he could not expect an immediate reply, still it was more than probable he had not to fear a refusal. Sivry urged him to remain some days longer in the country, and promised to join him very soon and take him back to Paris. Then they would be able to see their way, and matters could be arranged.

In order to explain the promptitude with which the Mauté family agreed to the project of marriage, we must remember that they had two daughters and their fortune was inconsiderable. Moreover, Verlaine, physique apart, was not a match to be despised. He was not a mere starveling poet. Employed in the Préfecture de la Seine, he had a substantial and secure position, greatly appreciated in the middle-class world. He was a *Bachelier*, and consequently might hope, through examinations, to obtain an even better appointment. Moreover, an only son, he would have 10,000 good livres a year from his mother, to say nothing of other relations whose heir he might eventually be. Finally, he had written to Sivry that he loved Mathilde and would take her for herself. The

famous *sans dot!* (without dowry) is still the best
"open sesame" in middle-class marriages.

Verlaine was transported with joy; he read
the comforting words over and over again. His
imagination advanced events; he saw himself
accepted, hopeful, received, loved, affianced, and
permitted to woo; and then he thought of himself
as husband, happy husband! He learned by heart
Sivry's much-prized letter, and in his emotion
forgot to drink. For two days he was not to be
seen in his usual haunts. A significant symptom.

Every hour was now enchanted. A fairy tale.
Every night he dreamed of the Jacob's ladder of
lovers which led up to Paradise. During these
weeks of suspense the poet was subject to a
hallucination. He created an ideal. Certainly
he longed for, loved, and adored her who became
his wife, and whom he afterwards regretted and
yearned after. Yet there was in his passion a
large element of the artistic imagination. He
loved objectively, and Mathilde was but the
representation of a conception of his mind.
Hitherto he had known nothing of passion accompanied by respect; and this love of his founded
on admiration for purity and sweetness, opened a
new world to him. No one had ever loved nor
seemed to prefer him. He had had experience
of bought caresses and knew their insincerity.
His consciousness of physical imperfection, and
the difficulties he would have to overcome if,
experiencing passion, he desired to inspire it,
intensified the entirely new feeling of joy and
pride which had taken possession of him when
he found himself singled out, appreciated, perhaps

even desired by a young girl brought up among
conditions of complete innocence and honesty ;
and, moreover, as he thought to himself with proud
satisfaction, he would certainly be the first who
taught the young Mathilde how to love.   She
was so young, as he frequently remarked, a great
qualification and yet a grave defect.   It was not
long before he realised this.

Directly the idea had entered his impressionable brain that it was possible for him to be
loved by a pure innocent being, with feelings
as yet unsuspected in which he would be her
initiator, than, like Pygmalion with his animated
statute, he was dominated.   The possibility intoxicated him, turned his brain, suggested to him
hypotheses, visions, situations, and combinations,
such as the condition of drunkenness induces.
These imaginations of his soon appeared to him
in the light of realities.   By force of concentrated
thought, such transformations are affected.
Verlaine in the sylvan solitudes of the Pas-de-
Calais, smoking pipes, emptying glasses, wandering over the melancholy plains green with the
leaves of the beetroot, and along the silent stretches
of white road, put into practice that marvellous
theory, established by the *savants* of Nancy, auto-
suggestion.

The result was that he fell really in love, and
found it quite possible to believe that, loving and
desiring, he too was loved and desired.   At length,
Charles de Sivry followed him to Fampoux and
brought him the favourable response already hinted
at, and by the lover taken for granted.   He confirmed his first letter ; his mother and sister were

disposed to accede to M. Paul Verlaine's demand, but time for reflection was necessary, and Madame Verlaine's opinion must be ascertained, for Paul had forgotten to acquaint his mother with his matrimonial projects. Afterwards the Mauté family were going to stay with friends in Normandy for two months, and on their return the matter should be definitely decided.

This week, passed in the society of Charles de Sivry who, for distraction, took the organ on Sunday, and played his own improvisations, *airs de ballet*, and operetta choruses in the church at Fampoux, only increased Paul's desire for the acceptance of his proposal, since it had not been refused and no serious objection had been raised. He returned to Paris with Sivry, and informed his mother. Madame Verlaine, a little surprised at her dissipated son's unexpected determination to make an end to youthful follies and settle down, evinced no dissatisfaction. The Mauté family, with whom she was slightly acquainted through my mother and Madame Bertaux, appeared to her suitable. At the same time she raised her eyebrows when Paul told her that a dowry was not to be expected. But what was more important to her mind than any other consideration, was the regular existence that her son would henceforward lead. A married man cannot continue to frequent wine-shops. She had found Paul one morning lying on his bed fully dressed, with his high hat covered with mud still on his head. He would certainly acquire, thanks to the conjugal state, better habits.

Already she observed a notable change in her

son. He had come from the station without
stopping at the cafés of the Gare du Nord, and
when embracing him on his arrival she had not
detected any odour of liquor. This happy state
of affairs continued ; in the days that followed his
return Verlaine did not drink to excess. He feared
lest he should be invited to commence his wooing
without having had time to dissipate the fumes of
alcohol. He was sufficiently aware of his weakness
to distrust circumstances and temptations. It might
happen that at the first interview, for the other
hardly counted, he would have to present himself in
a disconcerting state of excitement, with haggard
eye, wild gesture, and broken speech, which would
be disastrous and completely destroy the scaffold-
ing of happiness erected by his imagination ; he
therefore kept a watch over himself. He also
became a more punctilious clerk, and was complimented by his chief. His absence was remarked
at the Café du Gaz. He returned home early, and
did not resent his mother's proposal to accompany
her when she visited friends at the Batignolles,
where *bézique* was played at a farthing a thousand,
accompanied by tea and dry cakes.

He had, however, managed, with Charles de
Sivry's aid, to exchange letters with the young girl
in Normandy, pages as innocent in matter as in
style, for he not only kept a guard over his thirst
but over his pen. Mdlle. Mauté announced her
approaching return to Paris, and recommended him
to be wise and patient, and think of the future.
The little lady reasoned with magnificent gravity
that the match was suitable in every respect both
as regards age, tastes, education, position, and even

N

money, and spoke with certainty of their speedily approaching happiness. She made economical and prudent suggestions, and indicated the kind of apartment to be chosen : a light and airy one, even though high up, would be best. They were young, and had legs with which to climb the stairs. She occupied herself with the consideration of how the conjugal nest was to be furnished, and even suggested that his bed should be a plain wooden one, while hers should have pink and blue silk hangings.

Verlaine therefore had to do his courting by letter, a circumstance greatly to his advantage. His epistolary efforts were always interesting, humorous, and amusing, moreover he often wrote in verse, keeping pace with his feelings, desires, and impatience in the delicate and charming stanzas, afterwards collected together in the volume *La Bonne Chanson*, a title that later on had a sound of irony. This poetic labour finished the conquest of his heart. Composition, choice of words, study of rhymes were all as fuel to the flame he had himself kindled and daily stirred into greater intensity with his ardent verses.

At length the Mauté family returned from Normandy, and the long-looked-forward-to interview took place in the Rue Nicolet one evening after dinner. He has himself described quite simply what occurred on this occasion; one on which there must always be a certain amount of stiffness and formality on both sides. Like every other man in similar circumstances he had taken exceptional trouble with his toilet, and over and over again his mother had tied the knot of his *cravate Lavallière*.

When he was ushered into the *salon* of the Rue Nicolet the mother of the young girl came forward and encouraged him with a handshake and a smile. She then presented him to her husband, M. Mauté, an ex-notary with the ruddy face and shrewd air of a countryman grown rich, kind-hearted in reality, but with a keen eye to his own interests, and the unintellectuality and suspicion of a business man.

At last the young Mathilde entered; she no longer wore the costume immortalised in *La Bonne Chanson*: "La robe grise et verte avec des ruches;" but Verlaine was too much overcome at the time ever to be able to recall in what manner his *fiancée* was dressed on this momentous day. Here was the apparition which had haunted his dreams, here in the flesh, living and smiling before him! She appeared to him even more delightful and charming than on the first occasion. The reality surpassed his imagination. They seated themselves round the table and began to talk, saying little things that sounded insignificant, but were full of promise for the two beings whose destiny was soon to be irrevocably knit together. The consent of the parents was obtained; the claimant was accepted, and every evening henceforward Verlaine appeared at the house in the Rue Nicolet, at the earliest possible moment. I had scarcely any letters from him during this year. He almost entirely neglected his café companions, and his best friends only saw him for a few minutes at intervals. He was seldom at Lemerre's, and his visits to Leconte de Lisle and Banville practically ceased. I was not often in his company, and

rarely went to see him at the Hôtel-de-Ville as
I was very much occupied by journalism, and the
violent political struggles then in progress.   His
letters to me were only on the subject of the
Forgerons, now in abeyance, and to which marriage
and later events were to put a stop for ever.

While his courting proceeded Verlaine continued
to compose *La Bonne Chanson*.   This period of
waiting extending over nearly a year had but
intensified the desires of the young wooer.   All
the necessary details had been arranged except
the date of the ceremony.   The end of the spring
or the beginning of the summer of 1870 was
suggested.   But the proverb of the cup and the
lip is often verified : illness abruptly intervened, and
one day when he presented himself in the Rue
Nicolet with his usual smile, Verlaine found his
fiancée in bed with chicken-pox.   Although he
was of a rather timid and fearful temperament, on
this occasion passion had the upper hand and made
him bold, even rash ; he insisted on seeing the
sick girl, and was allowed to enter her room ; but
having heard incoherent words fall from the feverish
young lips moving in delirium he retired discouraged, overwhelmed, the blackest phantoms
haunting his homeward path to the Batignolles.

The marriage which had been announced was
indefinitely postponed.   He analysed in very clear
fashion the feelings of irritation, misgiving, and
sorrow which assailed him in this hour :

"With the very real unhappiness, which like
all very real unhappiness, moral or physical, was
quite pure, was mingled, how can I confess it
without blushing, a certain vile carnal disappoint-

ment. Here was my marriage postponed to the
Grecian Calends. This meant prolonged abstinence
—an abstinence to which I was ashamed to give
a name. I was in the position of one—excuse a
vulgar simile to express a vulgar sentiment—to
whom more butter than bread had been promised,
and neither was forthcoming."

But at last the illness abated, convalescence set
in, and the marriage was fixed for the first fortnight
in July. Now came a new misfortune ; the mother
was taken ill in her turn ; the epidemic seemed to
be running through the house. However, Madame
Mauté quickly recovered. It was decided the
marriage should take place in the month of August,
and Verlaine went to Normandy for a few days.
He had been invited thither by the Marquise de
Manoury, a very excellent woman, not beautiful,
provincial in manner, open-hearted, and destined to
a series of singular adventures which came before
the Courts, for she was successively despoiled by
several unscrupulous gallants, to whom she had
imprudently yielded herself. Very hospitable,
generous, and with a certain fortune, she sought
out poets, artists, and Bohemians, and welcomed
them to her Norman manor, which became a
regular *annexe* of Nina's.

Verlaine's impatience had redoubled as his
wedding day drew near, until he became so irritable
that it was feared he might fall ill in his turn, and
Mathilde had therefore commanded him to go
away for a week, and he had obeyed with docility.
During his absence he wrote numerous letters and
composed many poems, the greater number of
which were unfortunately lost, and do not figure

in *La Bonne Chanson.* On his return to Paris
the final arrangements for the marriage were completed, the legal announcements had been made,
and there was just time for the tailor, dressmaker,
jeweller, and the furnishing of the young couple.

But a tragic incident troubled the young lover.
Three days before the wedding one of our friends,
a young writer and *habitué* of the *Salon Ricard,*
Lambert de Poissy, having lost an adored mistress,
blew out his brains at Passy. He had informed
Verlaine of his fatal decision, and charged him with
various commissions. As the latter was returning
after the burial of this poor comrade, depressed and
dispirited, he sat down at a table in the Café
Madrid to read the newspapers and quench his
thirst. The town was at the time in a feverish
and tragic state of agitation. The war had just
begun in terrible earnest; the first cannon balls
had been fired, and already the sinister phantom
of defeat upreared itself on our invaded frontier.
Moreover, a baseless joy filled Paris with ferment.
A false telegram had announced a great victory
and proclaimed the defeat of the army of Prince
Frédéric-Charles. MacMahon was reputed to be
master of the situation with cannons and standards
captured from the enemy. All the boulevards were
gay with flags; cries of joy went up from every
throat; in the cafés animated and excited conversations spread from one table to another. Men and
women embraced, talked familiarly to any one they
met, and recounted with amplifications the details of
the victory. "Prince Frédéric-Charles had been
surrounded by the Chasseurs d'Afrique and compelled to surrender." "Not at all," said another

narrator who appeared better informed, "it was Captain So-and-so of such-and-such a regiment." In another group the arrival in Paris of the flags taken from the enemy was announced, and it was suggested that they should be exhibited on the boulevards before they were suspended in the tomb at the Invalides. . . .

Suddenly at the Bourse arrived a blunt contradiction. They had been defeated, and MacMahon was in full retreat. It was a complete rout, lugubrious presage of defeats to come.

Verlaine, who had spent the day before in arranging with the police magistrate and Government officials at Passy for the burial of poor Lambert de Poissy, had not had time to read the newspapers, and fell into the midst of the uproar without an idea of what was going forward. At the Café de Madrid he met some friends who speedily acquainted him with the matter, and he was very soon at one with the general enthusiasm —particularly so after swallowing two stiff drinks in rapid succession. A regiment passed along the boulevard ; the friends in question, Delescluze, Charles Quentin, Peyrouton, Jules Ferry, Henri Maret, Lissagaray, myself, and many others since disappeared or dead, nearly all of whom were journalists on the side of the opposition raised the cry of "Vive la République!" Verlaine, standing among them and conspicuous by reason of his very tall hat, mourning garments, and the umbrella he brandished in his hand, joined his voice to theirs to the indignation of a bystander who angrily called out, "You ought to cry 'Vive la France!' There is no Republic here," at the same time pointing

out the poet to the police, who came forward as
if to arrest him. The *habitués* of the Café de
Madrid were luckily in full force, and ready for
collisions with the police, which were then of almost
daily occurrence. These were the days of the
" Blouses Blanches." One evening two policemen
had besieged the café, and we had barricaded it
with chairs and tables. Resistance was customary ;
the police were once more repulsed, and Verlaine
was dragged away and told to slip off as rapidly
as possible by the Passage Jouffroy. He did not
need to be told twice. On the way home, however, he stopped for further refreshment, for he was
very hot and his excitement had made him thirsty.
The evening papers were just out, and buying one
his eyes fell on the following announcement :

" The Empress Regent has promulgated . . .
the following law : All unmarried men belonging to
the division of 1844-1845 who have not joined the
army, are now summoned to serve under the flag."

Verlaine belonged to the division of 1844. He
was exempt by his number, by having furnished a
substitute, and, moreover, by being the son of a
widow ; but the decree had been passed—he would
have to serve. His patriotic sentiments vanished
for the moment. He no longer thought of crying
" Vive la République ! " nor " Vive " anything at
all, and bringing down his fist violently upon the
table he cried, " My marriage is off ! . . ." and
thereupon ordered another absinthe, which he drank
savagely.

Now the marriage was fixed for the following
day. He poured out his fears to his *fiancée's*

family, but they soothed and reassured him. The rapidity with which the ceremony was to take place would probably enable him to evade the new law. Verlaine asserted that he would conform to it very willingly once the marriage was consummated. He was not afraid to serve his country, but that his long-expected happiness would be postponed again perhaps indefinitely, for war is not play, and those who embark on it may never return.

Verlaine had kept me informed of his impatience, his fears, and his long and passionate expectation ; but I had gone off with my regiment directly war was declared, a little uncertain as to the conclusion of the marriage. Grave events such as those which were preparing have terrible effects upon private interests. I was, therefore, not present at the ceremony, though in spirit I was with the young couple, for hearing that it was after all to take place, I sent from the 13th corps of the army of the Rhine to M. Paul Verlaine, lyrical poet, and Madame Paul Verlaine, Rue Lécluse, a poem, a sort of epithalamium, which, if it reached them in time, would recall me to the remembrance of the pair, and signify my part in the simple ceremony. The hour was a tragic one, the wedding one under sinister auspices. Verlaine's witnesses were Léon Valade and Paul Foucher. The ceremony took place at the Mairie at Montmartre, and at the Church of Notre Dame de Clignancourt. Among those present was a woman destined to rather extraordinary celebrity, Louise Michel, then a schoolmistress at Montmartre, a connection of M. Mauté's.

Paul Verlaine's honeymoon was sullen and

blood-red, and his nuptial hymn lost amid the roar of cannon. To set up housekeeping in the midst of the general disorder could only end in confusion. I have already referred to the circumstances attendant on Verlaine's service as official and national guard during the siege and under the Commune, and also the first misunderstandings between the young couple which were created and developed by the strife and convulsions around them. Yet this gloomy period was in the literary history of the nineteenth century that of *La Bonne Chanson*.

La Bonne Chanson was composed during the winter of 1869 and the spring of 1870. The majority of the poems contained in it, and doubtless others afterwards lost, were addressed by Verlaine to his *fiancée* during her two or three visits to Normandy. It consists of twenty-six short poems, and was published during the war—"A flower in a bombshell," as Victor Hugo said. The original edition was printed on tinted Whatman paper; *format* in-32, and on the cover: "Paul Verlaine —*La Bonne Chanson*." Publisher's trade mark— "Paris, Alphonse Lemerre, éditeur, Passage Choiseul 47, 1870." The volume contains only thirty-eight pages, and on the last sheet are the words: "Achevé d'imprimer le douze juin mil huit cent soixante-dix, par L. Toinon et Cie., pour A. Lemerre, éditeur à Paris." We only possess a selection of the tender and loving poems which Verlaine wrote during his period of eager suspense.

"Many of these almost spontaneous productions," he wrote in the *Confessions*, Part II., "were suppressed when the final MS. was sent to Alphonse Lemerre, and, as a matter of fact, I now regret them. . . . The pieces sacrificed were certainly equal in value to the others, and I have asked myself why this ostracism . . . Puritan perhaps."

Verlaine seems to indicate that the poems were sacrificed on account of their warmth, yet they were destined for a young girl in his relations with whom he observed the most scrupulous delicacy. One piece was retained which was certainly couched in more passionate terms, a sort of initiation, but this he declared he only sent her in a modified form.

"Alas," added the poet, surprised in retrospect at his scruples, "ought I not to have sung other songs (e.g., *Chansons pour Elle*, *Odes en son Honneur*) from which every trace of hyprocrisy, or to speak more plainly, restraint was carefully banished, and in connection with which there would be no need of repentance, for, on the contrary, they would have lulled my almost entirely material desires, only to awaken more ardent and eager."

Verlaine gave proof more than once of his special predilection for this volume. In the first place, it testified to days of happiness; these poems of true love recalled past ecstasies and joys long since fled, putting back the hands of time's clock until it struck once more the hours of happiness. Moreover, in *La Bonne Chanson*, Mathilde, his wife, loved, desired, and madly regretted, appeared as the enamoured imagination of the poet always pictured her, adorned with every virtue, every charm, loving, sweet, gentle, and happy in the happiness she bestowed. Considering it from the purely literary point of view, we cannot share Verlaine's fond preference. In our eyes the chief interest of this marriage bouquet, whose flowers have been jealously hidden away to dry in memory's herbal, is that it reveals a new poetic method on the part of him who fashioned it.

La Bonne Chanson is a transition from objective, descriptive, plastic verse to personal expression, the soul's confession. It is the substitution of one method of art for another. To sentiments rece:ved, suggested, and developed rather than felt, to imaginary passions, invented sorrows, sensations obtained from reading, conversation, hypothesis, and human companionship, has succeeded intimate, subjective, personal poetry, the result of feeling, living, and suffering.

It was no longer the Victor Hugo of *La Légende des Siècles*, but the poet of the *Feuilles d'Automne*, and the *Contemplations*, whose influence was henceforward in the ascendant. The transformation thus begun, continued in the *Romances sans Paroles*, and completed in *Sagesse*, owed something also to certain personal poems by Madame Desbordes - Valmore, and Sainte-Beuve. With what admiration has Paul quoted to me fragments of that exquisitely delicate poem : *Toujours je la connus pensive et sérieuse.* . . .

Love, longing, and the delight of revealing himself in the language of poetry which he knew far better than that of everyday life, all combined to impel him to this change in his art. It was like a first conversion, and later on we shall see this new method of the poet's which now was almost instinctive, spontaneously generated from the events of his life, and inspired by the incidents of his amorous adventure, develop and take definite shape.

In the hour when the poet sang *La Bonne Chanson*, that unforgettable hour which most of us have experienced, and the delights of which only an artist can transcribe, he cast away the cloak of abstraction, and poured forth his love like the wild bird of the woods, forgetful of all but the one for whom his melodies arose like a fountain at night among the marbles.

How magnificent in its abandonment to genuine feeling is that enthusiastic appeal to the Beatrice henceforward his guide, his rescuer from the hungry maw of that Hell into which he had been rapidly disappearing; it begins:

"Puisque l'aube grandit, puisque voici l'aurore,
   Puisqu 'après m'avoir fui longtemps, l'espoir veut bien."

This is an echo of De Musset, the poet Verlaine violently decried, the dead god he desired to throw down from his altar of clay; it is one of those Titanesque sobs of despair and disgust with which Verlaine was afterwards to be shaken by his intense desire to follow in peace and happiness the smooth and tranquil path along which the "heart's companion found at last" beckoned him. Here are open raptures testifying to the deep and elevating tumult of his being in this springtime of storm and tempest in the disastrous year of 1870, afterwards to be known as the Terrible Year, which for him always remained amidst the thunder of artillery and the crash of empires the happy year, the blessed year, the good year of *La Bonne Chanson*.

He was sincere when he made the vow, even

as a young priest might have done on the eve of
ordination :

> "Oui, je veux marcher droit et calme dans la vie,
> Vers le but où le sort dirigera mes pas,
> Sans violence, sans remords et sans envie : . . ."

He had hope and faith ; marriage for him was
a true sacrament, an initiation of the soul. He
had never loved, never been loved before. It was
the most wonderful moment in his life. Afterwards, in the midst of cries, blasphemies, psalms,
elegies, invectives, hiccups, and benedictions, there
often sounded in the ears of the poet, cursing
and cursed, the consoling words of his divine
ritournelle :

> "De sa chanson, bonne ou mauvaise,
> Mais témoignant sincèrement
> Sans fausse note et sans fadaise,
> Du doux mal qu'on souffre en aimant."

We shall see how quickly the sky changed and
night fell upon this heart as it lay basking in the
sun of love, and blossoming with hope. In 1870
Verlaine found everything beautiful and good, for
joy was in his heart and love in his eyes. He
admired travelling by train across the sombre plains
of the north, even the telegraph posts, the wires,
had a strange charm seen through the carriage
windows. The odour of coal and water, the noise
of chains, the grinding of axles, had no power to
trouble him rapt as he was in the contemplation
of the white vision which made his heart rejoice.
The sound of the voice of the well-beloved seemed
to mingle with the rattling of the prosaic train,

making it melodious. In Paris he found the
suburban route he had to take bright and splendid,
with its noisy wine-shops, muddy footpaths, and
rattling omnibuses, its workmen pipe in mouth,
its damp walls, its slippery pavement, all the
abominable surroundings of the outer boulevards
from Montmartre to Clignancourt, because he was
going to keep an appointment, and paradise lay
at the end of his journey. He believed in this
paradise, and all of us in one way or another have
had the same illusion. Verlaine's *Bonne Chanson*,
with its beautiful artistic title, is an autobiography
only in its details. It is rather a stanza taken
from the eternal poem of youthful love, and therefore it will live.

CHAPTER VIII

THE RUPTURE—ARTHUR RIMBAUD

(1871-1873)

LA BONNE CHANSON was only sung for a season;
epithalamiums are the poems of a day. We have
already alluded to the first domestic grumblings,
forerunners of violent storms, and the final cyclone
which was to sweep away the conjugal happiness
and family life of the poet. I am far from putting
the entire blame on the wife—whom he adored and
cursed in a breath—and recognise that my friend
was greatly in the wrong; but as he said reproach-
fully in that wistful stanza of the *Romances sans
Paroles*, she had not sufficient patience nor gentleness. Verlaine was easily led, and could without
difficulty have been persuaded to accept tranquillity,
regular work, and a peaceful and orderly existence.
It is difficult for a woman to whom her husband only
displays indifference, and frequently gives cause for
jealousy, and sometimes, worse still, replaces by a
permanent and acknowledged rival, to entice him
back to her side and re-establish peace in the home;
but Verlaine adored his wife, she could have led
him where and how she would—he was wholly
hers.

The conjugal knot was soon strengthened by

GEORGES VERLAINE
Son of the Poet.

the anticipated birth of a child. All his life Verlaine spoke with emotion of his son Georges, whom he was never to hold in his arms. He wrote to Stéphane Mallarmé, when a professor at the Lycée Condorcet, for information about young Georges, whom he supposed had become a pupil there; and later still, he begged me to make enquiries at Orléans, where the young man was working as a clockmaker. His son and his wife were two chains from which he never entirely broke free, for he loved them, these legal shackles. Broken or cut it would have been easy to join them together again, for he desired it.

The great difficulty was to struggle against drink, to conquer the terrible disease which was the prime cause of the scenes, reproaches, and violent quarrels between the two. I have already alluded to Verlaine's fatal alcoholic progress: in early youth during visits to his indulgent relations, the Dehées of Fampoux, the Dujardins of Lécluse, and the Grandjeans of Paliseul, he had acquired a taste for beer, gin and *bistouille*; as a Government clerk with a little money in his pocket, the desire for heady liquids had grown upon him, and the siege of Paris, with its dearth of victuals, and abundance of liquids, its enforced inactivity and compulsory *camaraderie*, still further developed his fatal dipsomania. When sober, Verlaine was the sweetest, most amiable of companions, and I imagine of husbands; but intoxicated with absinthe, curaçao, gin, or American grogs, he became, even with his best friends, disagreeable, aggressive, quarrelsome, in short, insupportable; and if he were like this in the cafés one can imagine his return to the conjugal hearth, often at a very late hour, after final solitary drinks when he had quitted us.

A second cause of misunderstandings arose from life in common with his wife's parents in the little house in the Rue Nicolet. A third cause, resulting from the first one, was the cessation of his duties as clerk, the perpetual holiday, the increased facilities for stationing himself in cafés, and the livelier temptation to pile up saucers in front of him, nothing producing thirst like drink.

During the siege and the Commune, Verlaine and his wife lived in an apartment with a balcony at No. 2 Rue du Cardinal-Lemoine, at the corner of the Quai de la Tournelle ; but believing it necessary in consequence of what happened during the Commune to relinquish his employment, and as it were, hide himself, he took her back to the little house belonging to her parents M. and Mme. Mauté de Fleurville, No. 15 Rue Nicolet, at the foot of the hills of Montmartre, close to the Rue Ramey.

We have already pointed out that Verlaine's political and judicial apprehensions were exaggerated and without foundation. He had taken no part in the insurrection ; he was guilty merely of having remained at the Hôtel-de-Ville instead of rejoining M. Thiers at Versailles. He was the object of no enquiry, no investigation. It might have been supposed that at this period of merciless repression and general suspicion Verlaine's absence from his office, when order was re-established, would be regarded as an admission of guilt ; nothing of the kind, and Verlaine did not take flight. He did not abandon his usual haunts ; he went with the same frequency to see his mother in the Rue Lécluse, where he might easily have been surprised if his retreat in the Rue Nicolet was unknown to the police. But no notice was taken of him ; so inoffensive a subordinate was not considered worth pursuing.

He had taken alarm too easily ; perhaps, at bottom, he wanted to take advantage of circumstances. A little tired of servitude, however light, of the office, aspiring after independence, which, truly, is favourable to poetic inspiration, doubtless he did not regret the political pretext which permitted him to return no more to the Hôtel-de-Ville.

The desire to conceal himself by changing his quarters, and also the necessity of reducing expenses by cutting off the rent of an apartment of 1,500 francs, in order to compensate for the loss of his official salary, led him to the Rue Nicolet. Life in common with his wife's parents had this inconvenience that Verlaine's Bacchic entrances, unperceived or unnoted in a separate abode, now had witnesses, naturally intolerant. The quarrels with the wife which ensued furnished the father and mother, supporting and pitying their daughter, with grievances, which, accumulating, required but the classic last drop of water, to make the cup of conjugal happiness spill over.

The climax occurred about the month of October 1871, when an element of discord was introduced into the household : Arthur Rimbaud, fatal guest, evil genius, knocked at the door of the house in the Rue Nicolet, and, unmindful of evil, it was opened to him. There are moments in life when a destiny is completely altered, an existence, perhaps more than

one, completely disorganised and spoiled by the
chance arrival of some person, who unknown the
day before at once assumes an excessive importance,
exercises a most baleful influence without any pre-
sentiment having forewarned the victim.   Such
ills one is powerless to avert.

Arthur Rimbaud played too important a part in
Verlaine's life for us to pass him over without giving
some details of his career.   He was an Ardennais,
and consequently a compatriot of Verlaine's.   He
was born at Charleville, where his mother lived
with her father Nicolas Knief, on the 20th October
1854.   His family had originally come from the
south, and his father, like Verlaine's, had been
a captain, but in the infantry.   Young Rimbaud
attended the local grammar school, and was quite
a satisfactory pupil, particularly in Latin ; he won
several prizes, notably that for Latin verse.   His
was a precocious, inventive intelligence, which his
masters termed fertile.   For this he obtained praise
which stimulated his already active vanity.   He
soon took to literature, and composed while still
at school several bizarre poems which were afterwards published and admired : *Les Premières Com-
munions, Le Bal des Pendus*, etc.   While still very
young he manifested revolutionary and atheistic
sentiments, for his were the talents of a satiric poet,
and the disordered aspirations of an anarchist.

During the German war, on the day after
Sedan, impelled by the vagrant spirit which was
later to drive him to Harrar and Ethiopia, he sold
the books he had received as prizes, and thus
furnished with money, set his face towards Paris,
but with a naïve and clumsy cunning, desirous of

economising his slender resources, and supposing that he would be able to slip out of the train unperceived on arrival, he only took a ticket for the first station after Charleville, accomplishing the rest of the journey without one.

At the Gare de l'Est he was stopped as a traveller without a ticket, and was found to be without references or papers; having indeed all the appearance of a boy escaped from a reformatory. Accordingly he was taken to the Depôt, but, sullen and contemptuous, he refused to answer any questions as to his origin, means, or the motives which had impelled him to take the train and escape from some place or authority he did not wish to reveal. His secrecy and stealthy glances right and left caused the police to regard him with suspicion; he was retained and sent to Mazas with open instructions. After a few days of detention, however, he made up his mind to give the name of one of his old professors, M. Georges Isambard of Douai. This gentleman, informed by the authorities, sent the money demanded for the railway ticket, and Rimbaud set at liberty was taken back to the station and despatched to Douai, for it was impossible for him to return to Charleville, the communications having been cut off by the Prussians.

This was Rimbaud's first contact with Paris. Once again he escaped from his parents, and went to Charleroi with the idea of joining the staff of a newspaper in that town; but he was not accepted. It must be said that his appearance, that of a vicious and sickly boy, was hardly prepossessing, and the editor of the journal could not believe that such a troublesome vagabond was likely to

prove of any service. Rimbaud therefore returned
home, where he remained quietly until the end of
October 1870. During this period he composed
several poems, among others *Les Effarés* and *Le
Cabaret Vert.* He had some correspondence with
a friend, M. Delahaye, who knew Verlaine. Soon
the desire to go to Paris reawakened in him, but
he knew that the Germans surrounded the capital
with an iron ring, and the fear of not being able
to break through it, kept him for some time longer
in his native town. He inveighed against the war
and against the Parisians for the resistance which
upset his plans. He avidly demanded news,
keeping himself informed every day at the Hôtel-
de-Ville, or in the cafés, of the progress of the
invasion. He declaimed against the length of the
siege, and considered the defence absurd and useless. He said that in the besieged city all thought
was for food, and no notice was taken of poetry.
"Paris is nothing but a stomach!" he asserted.

The gifted urchin gave proof of an extraordinary
force of resistance and proud self-confidence.
Before leaving Charleville he addressed to M.
Isambard, who had rescued him on the occasion
of his first escapade, a sort of profession of faith
which he called the *Littératuricide d'un rhétoricien
emancipé.*

He declared himself absolutely disgusted by
all existing poetry, past or present. Racine, *peuh!*
Victor Hugo, *pouah!* Homer, . . . oh! *lala!* . . .
The Parnassian school diverted him for a moment,
but *pfuitt!* he could not speak of it afterwards
without rancour. Verlaine alone, whom he had
never seen, but whose *Poèmes Saturniens* he had

read, found favour in his eyes. Apart from this poet he admired no one under the sun, and believed only in himself.

Rimbaud took leave of his family to go to Paris in February 1871, and arrived at André Gill's. Why? Perhaps because on the way his eyes had happened to fall on some caricature of the celebrated artist's. He walked into Gill's with amazing effrontery. Cool audacity and disdain for conventions of any kind was one of his most salient characteristics. The artist was absent from his studio, and with his usual trustfulness had left the key in the door. When he returned he stopped on the threshold rather surprised to find an unknown guest stretched upon the divan and snoring vigorously; but it was only a boy, and no thought of evil intent entered his head. He shook the sleeper and asked : "What are you doing here? Who are you?" Arthur Rimbaud gave his name, said he lived at Charleville, and that he was a poet who had come to take Paris by storm, adding as he rubbed his eyes that he regretted having been awakened so soon as he was having delightful dreams. "I, too," responded Gill with his usual jovial good nature "have fine dreams; but I have them at home!" The sleeper excused himself : he was a poor youth, a solitary rhymer, a lost child. Gill had a kind heart and felt sorry for him, but could hold out no hopes of anything being done for a poet in Paris. He gave him ten francs, all the money he happened to have, and urged him to return home.

Pocketing the ten francs, but disregarding the advice, Rimbaud began to wander about the town with anger against everything and every one in his heart, yet guided by the ardent desire to publish, to speak to men, to aim a resounding blow at public opinion, to make himself known, to move the great indifferent, deaf, hostile town. At last, tired physically and morally, his stomach empty, recognising that the reality was too much for him, and resigning himself to Fate, he decided to return to Charleville on foot, by easy stages, traversing the localities where the Germans were encamped.

With the low cunning, bordering on dishonesty, of which he gave many proofs during his life, and which, doubtless, served him in his business dealings with the Ethiopians, he passed himself off as a *franc - tireur* in the villages through which he passed, thus often securing sympathy, food, and lodgings—sometimes money. When the country people turned a deaf ear, for the *franc-tireurs* were not popular everywhere, and some feared to provoke reprisals by sheltering those whom the enemy had placed outside the laws of war, Rimbaud audaciously applied to the mayor, and exacted lodging and food.

After this return to Charleville he only remained two months with his parents, and then for the third time, in May 1871, he took the road to Paris on foot once more, through the German lines scattered over the country. On the outskirts of Villers-Cotterets he nearly fell into the hands of a patrol of Uhlans, but saved himself by diving into a thicket.

He found Paris in a hubbub of insurrection; presenting himself at the gates, he declared that he had come from the country, that he was heart and soul with the Communists, and wished to join them. The *franc-tireur* became for the time being a federate. He was received with enthusiasm; but as the insurrection was nearing its end he was neither equipped nor armed. He lodged in the Babylone barracks; but escaped in time some days before the arrival of the troops from Versailles.

Traversing anew the German lines, he returned to Charleville, composing strange verses as he went along; among others an ode entitled *L'Orgie Parisienne*, a recollection of his experiences in the ranks of the insurgents. This time he remained four months at Charleville, writing verse and prose poems, and exciting the indignation of the towns-folk by his reckless appearance and behaviour. He made the acquaintance at this time of a certain Breton, a friend of Verlaine's. This fellow was a "rat de cave," *i.e.*, a clerk in the Customs. Verlaine designated him as a very good fellow, a great beer-drinker, at times a poet, musician, draughtsman, and entomologist. This Breton, who was an obscure fantasist, making, essentially whimsical verses, was unequalled, it was said, in the way in which he drew up the most detailed and accurate statements of frauds on the part of sugar manufacturers.

It was at Charleville, in 1871, that Rimbaud composed the poem which caused him to be recognised as a poet on his next arrival in Paris. It was a fine thing, despite its strangeness: *Le Bateau Ivre*.

Haunted continually by the desire to return to Paris, he wrote to Verlaine, the only poet living, whom, as we have said, he admired, and sent him the poem.

Verlaine, surprised and perhaps flattered by this

exceptional admiration on the part of a beardless
novice who professed universal disdain even for
the most brilliant and indisputable geniuses, and
struck by the originality of the specimen verses
submitted to him, sent a letter of encouragement,
enclosing a post-office order to the youth; at the
same time warning some of his friends of the
approaching arrival of a young prodigy "who will
put all our noses out of joint."

The phenomenon was awaited with rather
sceptical curiosity.   Verlaine had offered him
hospitality.   "Come beloved great soul," he
wrote, "we await you and want you."

It was not in his own house, but in his father-in-
law's, that Verlaine thus granted board and lodging
to this vagabond of letters.   M. Mauté was absent at
the time, but his wife and young Madame Verlaine
having been prejudiced beforehand in favour of the
mysterious guest, received him kindly.   It was not
long, however, before they regarded him very
differently, with angry eyes and twitching hands.
The first impression was certainly disconcerting.
Verlaine himself, ready as he was to be enthusiastic
over the author of the *Assis* and *Le Bateau Ivre*,
could not restrain a movement of surprise when he
caught sight of the pale, beardless, meagre boy in
place of the grown man he had expected to meet.
The second impression was not much better, except
in the case of Verlaine, who soon recovered from
the first shock.   They seated themselves at table,
and Rimbaud ate voraciously without uttering a
single word, except to reply with an air of fatigue
to the questions which the ladies put to him regarding his journey and life at Charleville.   He did not

condescend to furnish any details regarding the composition of his poems to a guest, Charles Cros, who questioned him amiably on the subject. The last mouthful swallowed, Rimbaud pleaded fatigue, lighted a pipe, and with a "good-night," retired to bed.

He showed himself equally uncouth, taciturn, and unsociable on the following days; so much so, in fact, that Verlaine was asked to send away his young *protégé.* M. Mauté was about to return, and he would not be able to support the presence in his house of the ill-bred, disagreeable youth. It was agreed that Rimbaud should go and lodge with some friends of Verlaine's and await events. Banville, among others, took him in for a time, and then Madame Banville bought a bed for him which was placed in Charles Cros's laboratory. In this way he slept successively in the quarters of a number of hospitable and generous artists and poets, who had barely room for themselves. They clubbed together to enable him to live. He received three francs a day to allow him to devote himself to art independent of money. He was always in the cafés in company with Verlaine, and his labours chiefly consisted in digesting food and absorbing drink, for he ate like an ogre and drank like a templar.

Proud of his prodigy Verlaine displayed him everywhere, extolling, eulogising, and exciting his nervous vanity. Victor Hugo, to whom he was introduced as a direct successor, greeted him with his grave beneficent irony as a "child Shakespeare." The master did not mean what he said, but he loved to lavish hyperboles of eulogy and prognostication on the beginner whom he wished to number among his disciples.

Verlaine, becoming more and more wrapped up in his companion, obtained his inclusion in Fantin-Latour's *Coin de Table*, a picture exhibited in the *Salon* of 1892, which displayed the physiognomies of poets and writers in the dawn of fame, viz. : MM. Jean Aicard, Léon Valade, Emile Blémont, Pierre Elzéar, Bonnier-Ortolan, Ernest d'Hervilly, Camille Pelletan, Verlaine, and Rimbaud. This picture is now in the possession of M. Emile Blémont.

The youthful prodigy, however, was scarcely a success in Paris. In the first place he drank and gave up making verses. His contemptuous silence and arrogant airs wearied the kindest - hearted. Two of his biographers, MM. Jean Bourguignon and Charles Houin, who published in the *Revue d'Ardenne et d'Argonne*, January-February 1897, a very interesting and detailed article on Rimbaud, could not conceal what a failure the great man of Charleville was in Paris :

"In the midst of the literary and artistic world Rimbaud led the strange abnormal existence of a drunken visionary. He systematically intoxicated himself with alcohol, haschish, and tobacco ; he experienced the sensations of insomnia and sleep-walking ; he lived in a waking dream, possessed by fancies and inward visions. This period was not fertile in verse. . . . Except for some enthusiasts the majority of those who were frequently in his company neither understood nor comprehended him, and were completely in the dark as to his person-ality. His ways, his attitudes, his conversation astonished, disquieted, stupefied and frightened a number of people who saw in the poet an 'insufferable coxcomb '—and something worse. . . . In this literary and artistic world where are to be found in greater prominence than anywhere else vanity, raillery, the tone of authority, and the care of individuality, Rimbaud did not bend his spirit of perfect independence, nor modify his tenacious, self-willed yet timid character, in which a strain of cold calculation mingled with a natural and delicate sensibility. For the majority he was an enigmatic visitant who aroused contempt and jealous suspicion, and left behind him a recollection of ambiguous and contradictory stories. This seems to be the explanation of what might be called Arthur Rimbaud's moral defeat in Parisian life."

Rimbaud's unsatisfied vanity, consciousness that he had not caught the Parisian fancy, and conviction that the impression he had made was of the slightest and easily effaced, made him leave the capital abruptly, in revolt against its domination. An adventure in a wine-shop doubtless contributed to hasten his departure.

It was our custom at that time to assist at a sort of co-operative repast given by the Parnassians, and the frequenters of the *Salons* Ricard and Nina and Lemerre's bookshop. We met once a month to dine and talk literature. Several outsiders, less advanced than ourselves, but already more or less famous, came from time to time. Poems were recited and readings given; Richepin's *Chanson des Gueux* and *L'Etoile* were thus heard for the first time. We called ourselves *Les Vilains Bonshommes*, which title arose out of an article by Victor Cochinat in which he thus contemptuously designated us, and defiantly we retained it. The dinner was held at various restaurants on the left bank, often at a wine-shop at the corner of the Rue de Seine. The *ménus* were illustrated. One of them which I have preserved represents the back view of a nude figure, a Venus Callipyge holding a tablet on which is inscribed "Sonnets." At the foot of the drawing is written : "Invitation to the dinner of the *Vilains Bonshommes*." The drawing was always by a clever artist : Regamey, Forain, and Bracquemond designed several of these dinner cards.

At one of these dinners, to which naturally Verlaine had taken Rimbaud, an altercation arose during the reading of poems which terminated the repast. Rimbaud having gone so far as to talk aloud, and laugh scornfully during the declamation of a poem, which doubtless did not correspond with his code of æsthetics, the excellent Etienne Carjat who happened to be present and showed great admiration for the poet reading his verses, Jean Aicard, imposed silence on the young disturber, and as Rimbaud answered insolently that he should talk if he pleased, Carjat said to him : "Brat, if you are not silent I shall pull your ears !" Thereupon the youth, furious, ran to a corner of the dining-room and swiftly armed himself with the sword-stick which Verlaine always carried at this period, and which more than once nearly occasioned disaster. Rimbaud then rushed towards Carjat, and we had all the trouble in the world to disarm him, Carjat even being slightly wounded in the hand. Rimbaud was handed over to a young painter, a splendid fair young artist, Michel de l'Hay, nick-named "Pénutet," who led him away to sleep off his drunkenness in the tranquillity of the painter's studio. The insult produced a bad effect. The gentle Valade, Albert Mérat, and other peaceable poets, decided that Rimbaud should not again be invited to the *Vilains Bonshommes*. If Verlaine liked to come he would be always welcomed at the friendly gathering, but he must not bring with him the intolerable boy, who supported so ill both wine and poems which were not his.

Verlaine showed great vexation at Rimbaud's exclusion; he attributed it to a supposition which had not then entered any one's head. This was certainly the beginning of his voluntary separation from the friends of his youth, and the rupture which was never to be healed. Rimbaud was not, it is true, a very agreeable companion. To please Verlaine I once invited him to my house in the Rue Lécluse at Batignolles, and it required all my energy to keep him in order. In the first place, he did not open his mouth at the beginning of the meal except to ask for bread or wine, in the tone he would have used at an hotel; and then, at the end, under the influence of a heady Burgundy to which Verlaine helped him liberally, he became aggressive. He launched out into provoking paradoxes, and aphorisms intended to arouse contradiction. His chief pleasantry was to call me "saluter of the dead," because he had seen me raise my hat when meeting a funeral. As I had lost my mother only two months before, I ordered him to be silent on that subject, and looked at him in a way which he took in bad part, rising to his feet and advancing threateningly towards me. He seized a dessert knife in foolish nervous fashion, probably with the intention of using it as a weapon.

I put my hand on his shoulder and forced him to sit down, telling him that I went out to make war, and not having been afraid of the Prussians it was hardly likely a ragamuffin like him would intimidate me. I added half jokingly that if he were not satisfied and persisted in quarrelling, I would help him downstairs with a few kicks at the back. Verlaine interposed, begging me not to get angry, and excusing his friend; and Rimbaud, doubtless profiting by the lesson, was silent until the end of the repast, contenting himself with drinking deeply, and surrounding himself with smoke, while Verlaine recited some poems.

I only saw Rimbaud once or twice after this, but I know he did not bear me any good-will. He affected ironically when speaking of me the use of such terms as "saluter of the dead," "ancient troubadour," and "voider of copy." This was quite inoffensive, and I bore him no ill-will, even writing afterwards, when there was talk of raising a monument to him at Charleville, some articles rendering homage to his talent, which was genuine and great. At the same time I acknowledged his tenacity and energy as an explorer, and expressed pity for the sufferings of the last years of his life, and his wholly distressing death in the hospital at Marseilles.

To resume the history of Arthur Rimbaud, he left Paris, as I said, far from enthusiastic, and the disdain perhaps mingled with discouragement that he felt for the inhospitable literary world sowed in his mind the idea of changing both climate and life. He already began to think of renouncing art, poetry, and dreams for travel, commerce, and action.

He continued to correspond with Paul Verlaine, who, as we shall see later on, rejoined him, and travelled in his company. Quarrels followed, then the accident of the pistol shot, and at last the definite and final separation of the two friends. They never met again after the tragic day in July 1873.

Rimbaud, having returned to his mother to be waited on and spoilt, wrote in the tranquillity of Les Roches, near Charleville, his bizarre and vigorous work *Une Saison en Enfer*. This little book was printed in Brussels; but hardly had the volume come from the press than he threw it into the fire. Only three copies were saved. Exaggeration of the outward vision, false colouring of impressions, the blending of the real and the unreal and undue obtrusion of personality, which were Arthur Rimbaud's chief characteristics, were more marked in *Une Saison en Enfer* than in any other of his poems, satires, caricatures, and parodies. At the moment of writing I have in my possession Paul Verlaine's copy lent by his son Georges. It is printed in clear, fine characters: *format* small in-18, fifty-three pages, and on the grey cover is: " A. Rimbaud " (in black at the top) " *Une Saison en Enfer* " (two lines in red in the centre of the page). A little below in rather large black lettering between two waved lines is: " Prix un Franc." In three lines in black at the foot: " Bruxelles, alliance typographique (M. de Poot et Cie) 37, Rue aux Choux, 37 "; and beneath the date of publication: " 1873." The cover has a frame of thin black lines. The volume opens with a sort of preface, having no title, which begins with these words:

"Formerly, if I remember aright, my life was a banquet at which all wines flowed, and all hearts were opened.

"One evening, I seated Beauty upon my knees, and I found her bitter, and I reviled her.

"I have risen up against Justice.

"I have fled. Oh, sorcerers, oh, misery, oh, hatred! It is to you that my treasure has been confided.

"I have succeeded in banishing from my mind all human hope. To strangle all joy I have sprung upon it like a ferocious beast.

"I have called upon the executioners to beat me to death with the butt ends of their guns. I have called upon the plagues to stifle me with sand and blood. Misfortune has been my god. I have stretched myself in the mud. I am dried up in the atmosphere of crime. And I have played hide-and-seek with madness.

"And the spring - time has brought me the ghastly laugh of the idiot. . . ."

All this certainly lacks coherence, order, and sequence; it is the triumph of the anacoluthon. From it may be seen that Arthur Rimbaud was a precursor.

This singular introduction concluded with an invocation to Satan, quite in the style of Baudelaire and Prudhomme. Rimbaud, who did not lack a certain summary of erudition, probably took his Satanic doctrine from certain theological books, dealing with a sect called the Luciferians who existed in Germany in the thirteenth century. They adored the fallen angel, vanquished by Heaven, who symbolised humanity struck down, tortured and cursed by the implacable Divinity. The romantic preface is followed by short rambling digressions in nervous, highly-coloured prose, interlarded with poetical fragments. The titles are often of the diabolical order : *Mauvais Sang*, *Nuit de l'Enfer*, *Délires*, *Vierge Folle*, *L'Epoux Infernal*, *L'Alchimie du Verbe*, *L'Impossible*, *L'Eclair*, *Matin*, *Adieu*.

In *Mauvais Sang* the author begins :

" I have received from my Gaelic ancestors my pale blue eyes, narrow brain, and awkwardness in warfare ; my clothes are as barbarous as theirs. But I do not grease my hair. . . .

" From them I have received my idolatry and love of sacrilege . . .

" Oh! every vice, wrath, licentiousness — splendid licentiousness—and especially deceit and idleness. . . .

" I have a horror of every kind of work. . . ."

The young man boasted overmuch. He was not so vicious as he wished to appear. He did not hold work in such horror, seeing that he chose the hard calling of camel-driver and purveyor of negroes in Harrar, Arabia, and Ethiopia. Later on he cries out in a sort of profession of demoniac belief :

" Priests, professors, masters, you err in delivering me over to Justice. I have never been a Christian. I belong to a race who sing while they suffer ; I know no laws ; I have no moral sense ; I am a brute : you deceive yourselves. Yes, my eyes are closed to your light. I am a beast, a negro. But I can be deaf. You are not true negroes, you ferocious, miserly Moors. Merchant, you are a negro ; magistrate, you are a negro ; genius, you are a negro ; . . ."

Evidently the ebony he was afterwards to become acquainted with haunted the feverish brain of the interesting youth. He took care of his skin, in spite of this *Magnificat* in honour of the king of shadows: "Am I an old maid that I should fear to love death?"

Rimbaud was neurotic and hysterical in his youth, but not to any great extent, being sufficiently robust to undergo a speedy reaction and become a rough, unsentimental cultivator of reality. When we sing of sorrow, we no longer feel it; when we argue about our madness, it is past, and reason and health have returned.

"To me the story of my follies!" cried Rimbaud, and he narrated how he loved idiotic pictures, decorations, mountebanks' tricks, flags, posters, out-of-date literature, Church Latin, ill-spelt, erotic books, old-fashioned novels, fairy tales, children's books, old operas, silly choruses, simple rhymes; he tells how he invented colours for the vowels: *a* black, *e* white, *i* red, *o* blue, *u* green. "I wrote down the silences of night," he said again. "I noted the inexpressible. I fixed vertigoes. Many old, worn-out, practical things went to my alchemy of words. I explain magical sophisms by the hallucination of words."

In this last formula a whole future school of poetry was foretold, founded, greeted.

The destruction of the book *Une Saison en Enfer* was the annihilation of Arthur Rimbaud's existence as a poet. After having definitely broken off all relations, not only with Paul Verlaine—he refused to meet and even to receive the poet, who, after his liberation from the Belgian prison, went to rejoin him at Stuttgart, where he had gone to learn German—but with his old friends at Charleville, and the literary world generally, Rimbaud began a new life of travel and adventure. The vagabond in him survived the poet, voluntarily killed. Serving his apprenticeship as trader and explorer at a distance, Rimbaud set himself to learn German, English, Italian, Dutch, Russian, modern Greek, and Arabic. He travelled over nearly the whole of Europe, and in order to maintain himself, followed the most diverse, and often the hardest and most anti-literary callings: he was successively, like an emigrant in a new world, working-man, labourer, professor, interpreter, clerk, and sailor. He ended by establishing himself in Cyprus, where he opened a branch on behalf of a Marseilles house, MM. Bardey & Co., for whom he travelled through Arabia and Abyssinia, and opened another branch at Harrar. He entered into relations with the Abyssinian authorities, with Makonnen, and even with Menclik, and M. Félix Faure, then Minister of the Navy and the Colonies. He had to negotiate diplomatically for the landing at Obock of the plant necessary for the manufacture of cartridges for the King of Abyssinia.

Having realised a certain fortune by his labours, he made up his mind to return to France; it is the desire of every traveller's heart to go back to his native land. He met with an unfortunate accident while riding, and, on arrival at Marseilles he was obliged to go into hospital and have his leg amputated. Afterwards he returned to

Charleville, suffering, irritable, and helpless. He
soon made up his mind to set out again for
Abyssinia, but was obliged to stop at Marseilles,
where he died in the hospital of the Conception
on the 10th November 1891, aged thirty-seven.

His death passed unnoticed. His name, however, was no longer unknown. Verlaine had
dedicated a eulogistic article to him, and some
quotations from his strangest verses had attracted
attention. The sonnet of the vowels was celebrated; but no one knew what had become of the
errant poet. His poems were published first of
all by M. Rodolphe Darzens — which publication
was the occasion of an action for piracy and a
seizure — then M. Paterne Berrichon took them
up. The latter, who had married the poet's sister,
Mdlle. Isabelle Rimbaud, also published a complete biography of Rimbaud, with his letters from
Abyssinia. He it was who described the existence,
so long unknown, of the poet adventurer, enriched
by trading, and made known the curious ups and
downs of his commercial life at Harrar, and his
tragic end in the Marseilles hospital.

Arthur Rimbaud played a decisive and fatal
part in the private life of Paul Verlaine. He was
the alleged cause of Mme. Verlaine's departure,
and of the action for separation; he encouraged
his friend's unfortunate drunkenness until it became
dipsomania, for robust and able to resist the effects
of alcoholic intoxication as he was, he could support
doses of spirits which deranged Verlaine's more
delicate organism. He dragged him away on
journeys and aimless wanderings. He was the
occasion of his long detention in Belgium. He

has caused him to be suspected of unnatural passions which, brought forward in the action for separation, influenced the magistrates to pass a sentence afterwards interpreted as a divorce. In the minds of many persons, whether informed or ignorant of the facts hereafter to be recorded as they actually happened, these suppositions, due to Rimbaud's continued companionship, still persist and tarnish Verlaine's memory.

These are the misdeeds, unpunishable by ordinary laws, of this vicious and gifted scamp, who ended up his varied career as an energetic, active, hard-working, and enterprising man. He had a most malign influence over poor, weak Paul Verlaine. He dominated, bewitched, and spoilt his life. He was certainly the author of all the wretchedness, moral and physical, which engulfed Verlaine. Did he render him any service from the intellectual point of view? Did his influence affect the poet of the *Romances sans Paroles*? Was Verlaine's new art of poetry the result of intimacy with the author of *Le Bateau Ivre*? I do not think so. His imprisonment, extraordinary religious conversion, and prolonged reflections in the tranquillity and silence of his cell, gave opportunity for the crystallisation of a poetic theory which for a long time had been floating in his head, modified his style, and endued his verse with the original and impressionistic character which differentiated *Sagesse* from the *Poèmes Saturniens*.

Rimbaud's literary influence is doubtful; but that which he had upon Verlaine's actions and sentiments is, unfortunately, only too apparent.

CHAPTER IX

(1872-1873)

THE misunderstanding between the young couple had grown, and after frequent violent scenes the poet who was, moreover, fearful of being denounced as having participated in the insurrection, lent an ear to the more and more imperious suggestions of his adventurous comrade, Arthur Rimbaud, and meditated, arranged, and realised departure.

In the beginning there was no question of a definite rupture sanctioned by law. A temporary separation only was mentioned; apart, the couple would recover their equanimity, and the occasion of their quarrels would no longer exist. They would forget the exchange of unkind words, reproaches, invectives, and bitter recriminations. Time would restore peace to the home, the wife's parents said aloud, while under their breath they hoped that the son-in-law, once he had gone, would never return. It already entered into their calculations that their daughter would live happily with them. They certainly did not foresee the solution of divorce permitting a second union, a new existence, for there were no signs of the great change in legislation, and the voice of

232

Naquet had not yet been heard; but separation
seemed to them preferable to miserable married
life for their child. They were already preparing
material for a case, and the departure of their son-
in-law was too favourable to their secret desires
for them to show any eagerness to retain him.

More toleration could and should have been
used in dealing with Verlaine with his nervous
temperament, fevered by alcoholic excess. He
was docile and manageable, and would have
allowed himself to be retained and led. He only
asked to be forgiven, comforted, consoled, and
cared for; though there would have been need,
doubtless, of great indulgence and multiplied
forgiveness.

Two persons acted upon him—his mother and
his wife. His mother, too indulgent towards her
son's errors, annoyed with her daughter-in-law's
parents, whom she reproached with having been
too zealous in the interests of the bride at the
time of the marriage settlements, did not interpose
at all energetically, and consented to the departure
of her son. She even furnished him with money—
an unfortunate encouragement. Without means
Verlaine could not have embarked upon the
wandering life, from which he derived no kind of
profit, and which was bound to lead him into evil
paths. As to the young wife, wearied by her
husband's roughness, which succeeded in the
moods produced by alcohol, fits of passionate
tenderness, she sighed for deliverance from the
conjugal yoke. She made no attempt to keep
him near her, to save him from himself. Grown
indifferent to his plans, his literary talent, his

dawning fame, she only regarded his failings. In her youthful and frivolous heart all love for him had died, and desire for liberty dominated every other sentiment. This was the initial misfortune, and the young wife, now married again, and the happy mother of a family, was largely responsible for the irregularities in the subsequent career of the poet, if she will permit me to tell her so, her whom I have known almost from a child, long before her meeting with Verlaine, and who, I hoped from afar, under the flag that August day in 1870, would make a permanently happy man of the poor, delicate, sensitive, sickly genius she had bewitched. For he loved her deeply; he loved her always and only, and this love, the proof of which is to be found in all his works, and the numerous letters I possess, survived scandal, legal proceedings, cries of hatred, calumnious imputations, defamatory statements, and more than all, a second union, contracted and maintained in happiness under the despairing and envious eyes of the unfortunate poet.

Far be it from me to impute all the injury to the wife, abused, wounded, often solitary, and at times of crisis ill-advised. Daily quarrels, constant irritation, outrageous words, even threats, wretched scenes of every kind multiplied by drunkenness, rendered life in common insupportable, and made both parties regard separation as preferable, even desirable. But Verlaine was good at heart and affectionate, and he should have been treated as one suffering from illness. Cure was possible, but it was indispensable that the young wife whom he adored should act as nurse, sister of mercy, even

surgeon to the ulcerated heart of her husband, and
as gaoler to his rebellious person. She could not or
would not undertake this sublime task of healing.

Verlaine has himself sorrowfully stated the lack
of sympathy he encountered in the touching complaint in the *Romances sans Paroles* :—

> " Vous n' avez pas eu toute patience,
> Cela se comprend, par malheur, de reste ;
> Vous êtes si jeune ! et l' insouciance,
> C' est le lot amer de l'âge céleste ! "

A separation therefore took place, later to be
made legal. Verlaine decided to travel northwards
through Belgium to England in company with
Arthur Rimbaud. His departure, which resembled
a flight, had a singular prologue ; the two companions had a sort of rehearsal of their projected
expedition one morning in July 1872. Taking
train for Arras they arrived there early, and while
awaiting the hour when Verlaine's acquaintances
in the town would be ready to receive them,
they installed themselves in the station buffet where
they drank until the garrulous stage of intoxication
set in, when they embarked upon the most extraordinary conversation. Rimbaud, who affected a
precocious insolence and haughty silence, made up
his mind to frighten the travellers in the buffet,
and Verlaine, with his usual good-nature, fell in
with the idea. They talked of assassinations,
robberies, old women strangled, prisons, locks,
and escapes ; they gave details seemingly precise
of penitentiaries, and all in a voice loud
enough to enable their uneasy and soon terrified
neighbours to suppose that sitting beside them,
drinking in the peaceful buffet, were two escaped

prisoners perhaps fresh from the committal of a crime. They played their parts so well, thoroughly frightening their honest neighbours, that suddenly two policemen, informed either by a traveller or the waiter, entered and invited the friends to accompany them. They went out amidst winks, chuckles, and alarmed faces, and a rumour quickly spread through the town that two celebrated assassins had been arrested, together with circumstantial details of the age, sex, and position of their victims, and the size of the wounds they had inflicted.

Conducted to the Hôtel - de - Ville, the two suspects were interrogated. Rimbaud, confronted by the representative of justice, resumed his childish aspect and fell to whimpering. Verlaine, questioned in his turn, confirmed his friend's denials, and as the officer of the law began to excuse himself, recognising the policemen's error, Verlaine having on him letters from the Hôtel-de-Ville, diplomas, receipts for rent, and other papers establishing his identity, and the possession of certain funds, the poet, who had not yet recovered from the effects of his libations, raised his voice and menaced the official. Assuming a terrible aspect he declared that he was not going to condone this matter of arbitrary arrest (rolling his r's in the fashion of the villain in a melodrama), that he would write about it in the press, and agitate his Republican friends, and they would resent such treatment of two comrades, peaceful, honourable citizens, untouched by the slightest judicial suspicion. He added that having been born at Metz, he had the choice between France and Germany, and in face of the violent usage to which the French police had subjected him, he should put himself under the protection of the German police who, at least, only arrested scoundrels! This tirade appeared to make a certain impression on the officer, who summoned the policemen and said to them, "Conduct these people to the station, and see that they take the first train to Paris."

This was, perhaps, more arbitrary than the arrest, for when once the prisoners had established their identity, thus proving themselves entirely innocent, there was no reason why, being French, they should not remain in Arras, or go where they liked. However, Verlaine and Rimbaud were taken back to the station. On the way they stopped for refreshment, of which the policemen partook, and then departed for Paris. Arrived at the Gare du Nord they alighted, lunched, and set out immediately afterwards for Belgium. From there they went on to England without hindrance.

From London Verlaine wrote me numerous letters, interesting especially on account of their picturesque, vivid, humorous, and original description of English life. He also gave me some indication of his personal sentiments, labours, and plans, and frequently alluded to the proceedings for separation already set on foot by his wife, at the instance of her parents. I have no detail of Verlaine's and Rimbaud's arrival in London, but here is an undated letter, received in October 1872 :

"My dear Friend,—You are certainly aware of all that has been happening. It appears that my wife, after having written me various illogical and insane letters, has returned to her excessively practical and loquacious self. Does she not demand an income of 1,200 francs, and does she not desire to lay a prohibition upon me? And all this because I do not wish to live under her father's roof. I do not wish to remain in the Rue Nicolet, because my whole life since I was so foolish as to go to my wife's parents, all my letters, my actions, and my words have been under espionage. It appears a clamour has been raised over my departure with Rimbaud. What is there compromising in a man travelling with a friend? They forget that my wife stayed by herself at Périgueux for two months without giving me her address.

" But what is the good of worrying you with all this which you know and understand as well as I do myself? The fact is, I am horribly in love with my wife . . . too much so! You saw me, and your sister also, in that fatal February, but though suffering then even to the point of death, I have endured greater anguish since from the pin-pricks inflicted upon me in that accursed house in the Rue Nicolet.

" It is true I ardently desire that my wife should return to me. That is the sole hope which sustains me, but God knows if it comes to pass and she recognises the sincerity of my incessant protestations, I will never return to the house from whence all manner of vexations, indelicacies, searchings in drawers, and other mean provocations drove me out full of hatred and defiance, I who am all affection and simplicity, alas!

" But enough lamentation! You will please, me greatly by writing to me . . . for if you have an ill tongue, I believe you are a good friend, and you know that I am yours most sincerely. Write to me, therefore, quickly. . . .

" *P.S.*—It goes without saying that I have

nothing against Madame Mauté, who has always been good, and Sivry, who has only one fault, that of being something of a coward. . . ."

I had been present at the commencement of the conjugal misunderstanding, having lived, during the winter of 1871-1872 in the same house as Verlaine's mother, 26 Rue Lécluse. There I had very often seen him, fresh from the Rue Nicolet, nervous, overcome, taking refuge with his mother, chewing his irritations, and ruminating over his despairs. He recounted to me his troubles, grievances, and subjects for complaint, in the course of long evenings, interspersed with the smoking of pipes and the absorption of bottles of bitter beer, obtained from the grocer opposite, and accompanied by heady literature. He did not conceal his own errors; spontaneously confessing his frequent accesses of *soulographie* as he called it, which led to domestic reproaches and scenes with his wife, but he insisted chiefly on the misdeeds of his father-in-law and the plaguing of which he was the object. Very quickly disaffection had entered into his wife's heart. She incessantly talked of a separation; she evinced an intense desire to live, without her husband, with her parents, and to break all ties with Verlaine. There was an irresistible impulsion in these preparations for the rupture. A separation which at first appeared problematical, almost chimerical, impeded by a thousand obstacles, conventions, feelings, legal intervention, division of property, regulation of interests, change of manner of life, etc., soon came to be faced as quite possible and near at hand.

This vital act was eventually regarded as a simple and easy operation.

Verlaine had tears in his eyes while he revealed these sad domestic events. As he continually repeated in his letters, he loved his wife, and suffered cruelly from the situation. Evidently he was to a large extent its originator; but his sorrow was none the less acute on that account. He was weak, he found it impossible to resist temptation; drink had seized hold of him, and when intoxicated he was master neither of his words nor his actions. Moreover, Rimbaud was a large element of discord, and, like an acid, his presence ate away the last bonds which united the pair.

Mme. Mathilde Verlaine taking advantage of her husband's relations with Rimbaud, and assuming the truth of the gossip that had arisen regarding the intimacy of the two friends, refused to allow him to enter her room. Thus the rupture assumed definite shape, and each party secured a solicitor. It was to escape all these worries, to try change of air, that Verlaine resolved to leave the country, at least for the present. For some time previously he had isolated himself, having broken with many of his comrades, and ceased to frequent Lemerre's, who relates "that at this period—1872—the poet became nervous, melancholy, capricious."

It is not true, all his letters and criticisms contradict it, that he was offended at the successes of his friends. Verlaine was never jealous of any one; envy was a sentiment altogether unknown to him. He rather rejoiced, as in a personal gain, at the fame achieved by the Parnassians, and willingly joined in the applause. Whenever one of our com-

rades published a book or had a play performed he
never failed to manifest his interest or satisfaction,
even at the most troubled moments of his life abroad.
Lemerre went on to say in the letter reproduced by
M. Ch. Donos :

" He had been one of the first to predict to
me Coppée's great success, but alcohol rendered
him subject to terrible fits of anger, and all meetings with him had to be given up ; he felt himself
watched and humoured, and came no more."

To Verlaine's letter recently quoted I replied,
advising him to resist the demand for legal separation instituted by his wife. I urged him not to
condemn himself by acceding to it, and thus lending
colour to his wife's statements and grievances in
spite of his denial of them. I indicated briefly
with a reserve easy to understand the motives
which dictated my counsels. I was certainly of
opinion that life in common was hardly possible
for the pair, and that from this point of view the
sentence of separation would be a good thing for
both of them. At the same time, in the interests
of my friend, not only present but future, I advised
him to resist, to dispute the facts brought forward,
to insist upon an investigation, and in short to do
all that would constitute a serious defence in an
action for separation or divorce, particularly in
regard to certain statements made by his wife. I
feared that if he acceded to her demand, and no
enquiry was made, credence would afterwards be
given to the caluminous imputations brought against
him, and more especially that which concerned his
relations with Rimbaud.

Verlaine answered by the earliest post :

" MY DEAREST EDMOND,—. . . Most certainly I
am going to defend myself and attack myself too.
I have whole packets of letters, a regular stock of
'avowals' which I shall use since the example has
been set. For I feel that to my very sincere
affection, of which you were a witness that winter,
has succeeded complete contempt, something like
the feeling of a heel of a boot for a frog. I thank
you for taking my part, and congratulate you upon
doing so, it is a proof of your old friendship first,
and of your good judgment next. Oh! what an
unloading of spite, of clumsy intrigue and mis-
management! Some other day I will tell you about
my interview at Brussels with my wife. I have
never gone in for psychology, but since the occasion
is offered me, the memoir I am preparing for my
solicitor will be the basis for a novel I have in
contemplation. My connection with Rimbaud is
very curious from every point of view; I shall
analyse it in this next book; he laughs most who
laughs longest. . . . And now . . . to the Tower
of London!"

Here is one of his first impressions in England.
They are simple, sometimes naïve, often amusing,
never pedantic. His notes of commonplace things
and rapid surveys make up a description of the
outside of English life, still true, although more
than thirty years have passed since these hasty and
superficial traveller's sketches were written. They
are original, fresh, and sincere, as any one who
visits London will recognise, and although they do
not merit separate publication, yet included here
among Verlaine's letters as he wrote them, they
complete the biography of the poet as traveller.

"London, England, Poste Restante.

"I will not lament like Ovid, but at once embark upon the chapter: *London Sketches*. Flat as a blackboard London! Little dark houses or great 'Gothic' and 'Venetian' fronts; four or five cafés for drinking! Battur would laugh at them. All the rest are dining-rooms, where no drink is to be had, or coffee-houses, from which spirits are rigorously excluded. 'We do not keep spirits,' replied a maid to whom I put the insidious question: 'One absinthe if you please, Mademoiselle.' A host of boys in red shine your boots from morning till night for a penny. To obtain by the aid of their syrupy mixture the gloss, the secret of which Labertaudière believed he had monopolised, they positively lick your shoe and set to work with a will, soft brush in one hand, hard brush in the other, and the boot shines, *sacrebleu*. . . .

"Here may be seen the triumph of rags, impossible to dream of such tatters; but thanks to the abominable multiplications of the little red shoeblacks, there is not a single beggar whose shoes, heels and toes included, do not shine like the fire of Cyrus itself. I will tell you about the better cafés presently; never has anything been seen so poor, so ill-provided; dirty, clumsy waiters, tarnished gilding and paintings which would make Jean de Redon and Ducornet-sans-bras themselves blush.

"And the theatres! The odour of humanity! Actors of the time of the late virtuous Moêssard, cries like those of animals, actresses thin enough to make one weep. . . . In the middle of the ballet in *Le Roi Carotte* a quadrille of Clodoches is introduced, danced by women. In the music-halls, the Alhambra, Grecian, etc., a jig is danced between two 'God save's.' Well, well, how they revile the Jesuits, and how extraordinarily those foremost in doing so resemble Leconte de Lisle. To continue,

the Thames is superb.   Picture to yourself an
immense expanse of mud.   . . .   Bridges, truly
Babylonian, with hundreds of cast-iron piles, thick
and tall as the late Colonne (Vendôme), and painted
blood-red.

"When I arrived the weather was superb ; *i.e.*,
imagine a sunset seen through a grey veil.   But
thanks to the extraordinary circulation of carriages,
cabs, omnibuses, tramways, trains incessantly passing over the massive bridges, incredibly rough
passers-by, brawlers (ducks must be of English
origin), the aspect of the streets is, if not Parisian—
oh, blasphemy!—at least very distracting.

"More details in another letter, and drawings.

"*N.B.*—What I have said with regard to rags
only applies to the best parts of the town, Regent
Street, Piccadilly, Leicester Square, Trafalgar
Square, Mansion House.   Wait till I have seen
the really poor districts!   As a whole, however,
it is very unexpected, and a hundred times more
amusing than Italy, and Paris, and the banks of
the Rhine. . . . I enclose a new poem.   Is it
promising?

"Of French here I have only seen Régamey—
very jolly.   Perhaps I shall take on Vermersch's old
room, he has just married, the idiot!   I hope to
see all the *bons bougres* soon."

Other letters of the same period continue his
impressions of England.

"I have seen the wax-works . . . and the more
than regal enthronement of the Lord Mayor ; excitement everywhere, trumpets, bands, flags, shouting,
and hurrahing.

"I take advantage of this letter to curse, as I
must, the abominable 'ox tail soup!'   Fi, the horror!
There is also 'coffee plain, per cup,' a ghastly
mixture of dried chicory and milk!   Most horrible!

And the gin! Extract of sewage. The fish is horrible; sole, mackerel, whiting, etc., . . . all soft, sticky, and flabby. They give you fried sole with a piece of lemon, as large as a duck's heart; meat, vegetables, fruit, all good, but too dear. Warm beer. The English drinking establishments, properly speaking, merit the description, 'outside it is fine, but inside it is poor' (refrain from an operetta).

"The front is in wood the colour of mahogany, but with great copper ornaments. To the height of a man the windows are filled with coloured glass, flowers, birds, etc., like Duval's. You enter by a terribly thick door kept half open by a formidable strap, which (the door) catches you in the back after having knocked off your hat. The interior is quite small, a zinc slab covers the mahogany counter, beside which either standing or perched on very high, very narrow stools drink, smoke, and talk through their noses well - dressed gentlemen, disagreeable, poor porters and drivers as swollen and hairy as ours. Behind the counter are waiters with their shirt sleeves turned up, or young women, generally pretty, with untidy hair, elegantly dressed in bad taste, who are playfully prodded by a finger, a stick, or an umbrella to the accompaniment of coarse laughter and apparently coarse words which do not seem to shock them. . . .

"Yesterday evening in Leicester Square a band of German musicians began their noise in front of the cafés, when suddenly an Englishman, horribly drunk, seized hold of the music stand of one of the poor devils, and amidst general indifference struck him repeated blows on the head until the unfortunate fell down. Arrest followed. . . . To-day is Sunday: *aoh!* Very dull! Everything shut. No business. Letter - boxes also closed. No shoeblacks. Eating places open at meal times are submitted to frequent visits, with the intention of finding out if one is drinking too much. . . . I met Oswald who has turned sculptor. I am going to see him to-morrow. We are learning a little English, and know enough to find this town absurd . . . 'and the English ridiculous' (quotation from an operetta). If you have time and opportunity to copy again for me the six sonnets of *Les Amies*, I should bless you."

Les Amies of which Verlaine speaks, is a small collection of verse, very unrestrained, of which I possess the original manuscript, or at least a careful copy in Verlaine's own hand. *Les Amies*, which are now included among his complete works, vol. ii., edition Léon Vanier, 1899, were sent by Verlaine to Poulet-Malassis, and appeared in a little booklet, now unobtainable, under the name of *Pablo de Herlagnez*. A very few copies of this book were printed, the majority of them being seized by the police; they had a warrant, it was said, authorising the seizure. These sonnets, of the Lesbian order, are now inoffensive in consequence of later publications in France, both in prose and verse, by numerous writers on the same dangerous subject; but at that time, even for Poulet-Malassis, it was an audacious undertaking.

Continuation of *London Sketches*, London 1872.

"While awaiting a letter from you relative to my miserable affairs here are some more London details.

"I have seen Lissagaray; he now lives at 30 Newman Street, Oxford Street—he is to reply to you soon; also Matusziewicz (officer in the army, compromised in the Commune). Most useful information with regard to paying papers for which to write.

"The fog is beginning to show the end of its dirty nose ; every one is coughing except me. It is true that I, you know me, wrap myself up in flannel, with a comforter and cotton in the ears, all precautions as ridiculous in Paris as they are honourable here.

"Grogs and punch inaugurate their syrupy empire . . . also pale-ale and stout; I am as well as my poor head, baffled by all these villainous manœuvres, permits me to be.

"And then, it rains, and rains. Enough to melt a certain hard heart that you know, alas less well than I !

"All the theatres overflow. I am going this evening to Hervé's *Œil Crevé*, adapted for the English stage (Opera Comique, Strand), and I am writing to you in the Café de la Sablonnière et de Provence, Leicester Square, a nice little place which I recommend to all travellers. At least no Bordelais nor Italians : no one except the eaters at the *table d'hôte*. In the dining-room are two ale-drinkers—myself and another.

"Chapter on women : Incredible chignons, velvet bracelets with steel buckles, shawls red as blood, as Vallès very justly remarked. All pretty, with a bad expression and the voices of angels. One cannot believe all the charm there is in the little phrase, Old C——,' seek its equivalent in French, addressed every evening to old gentlemen better dressed than balanced by exquisite misses in long satin skirts, variegated with mud, spotted with drink, and with holes caused by cigarettes. These conversations are generally held in Regent Street, Soho, Leicester Square, and other Franco-Belgian districts. It appears that in the city it is worse! I shall go and see.

" Negroes, as if it rained them, in the music-halls, streets, everywhere.

" Photographs in the windows : Stanley, Livingstone, Eugénie. Oh, the Eugénies! more than thirty-two positions. It is overdone, my word! Daudet appears, but not Abeilard. So much the better! Still Busnach and Clairville were very cruel to marry the latter. I have met Vermersch at last, very amiable, and his wife very charming.

" I have seen *L'Œil Crevé*—very amusing. The *Langouste Atmosphérique* is replaced by a drinking song which the bailiff sings. . . . The part of Alexandrivore is played by a woman. The Duc d'En-face is very gay. I have seen *Macbeth*, the orchestra begins with the overture from *La Dame Blanche*, and in the *entr'actes* plays Olivier Métra's quadrilles. Fine scenery! it is at the Princess Theatre. Oh! my friend! the matches, they burst like an explosion, but never catch alight, do you understand, never! A fortune might be made by importing French matches in spite of their price, and what a service to render to poor smokers : I am thinking of it.

" I count on entering, in a few days, a great house here where the pay is good. Meanwhile I am doing some American work, fairly well remunerated. I vegetate less than the *bons bougres* of the Rue Nicolet expected, although I am always very sad at the behaviour of my wife, for whom, as you know, my mother has done everything, and I have submitted to everything. Write to me quickly, always 34-35 Howland Street, W.

" Vermersch is going to give a lecture on Théophile Gautier. That will make a fine sensation in the wretched press, I shall be there and will tell you about it."

Here is another letter :

"In greatest haste I send you a few lines with regard to the Vermersch lecture. It was given on the first floor of a public-house, 6-7 Compton Street, Soho. Vermersch very elegant. . . . His lecture was quite literary, very detailed, very anecdotal, and very much applauded by the very numerous English and French, . . . Communists for the most part. The lecture was the first of a series, of which the second will be on Blanqui next Thursday.'

"LONDON, 23*rd September* 1872.

"Thank you for your good letter, substantial but badly written. . . . Thank you also for your compliments relative to my poor verses, which have been carefully denounced, but whither in some *Gazette de Paris* or *Courrier de France* I do not know. If you get wind of it, it would be very kind if you would procure the number and send me the review. And while I am on the subject, when you see Blémont will you kindly shake his fist, and beg him from me to send me the numbers of the *Renaissance.* . . . Make this request to Blémont in a very friendly way, for he has been very kind to me, and is the only one of my friends, with the exception of yourself, who 'deigns' to write to the 'wretched creature' it appears I am.

"I see Lissagaray but seldom, still I could drop him a word regarding your questions—and this I will do to-morrow. To-morrow, alas, is Sunday. Happily there is a monster meeting in Hyde Park on the subject of the police. 'On behalf of the dis-charged and imprisoned constables. Orator, Mr George Odger—Republican.' I shall go and will tell you about it. The notice carried by the sandwichmen is 'Caution—do not heed the rumour circulated to the contrary, and the false reports of the newspapers.' In short it is an attempt on the part of the Radical party there to seduce the police.

" There is a unique curiosity I believe here : it is the Tower's Subway—*i.e.*, a tube submerged about a hundred and fifty feet in the Thames. One descends a hundred steps. It is literally a cast-iron tube with gas jets at about a man's height, with flooring half a yard wide. It is warm, it smells, and it trembles like a suspension bridge under the immense weight of the water. In short, one is very content with having seen it. But when one thinks that it is constructed with all the English rashness and all the indifference to danger of these strange people, one has, on issuing from it, a delicious shiver of relaxation. I must soon go and see the tunnel on the subject of which the English themselves say it is necessary to come down a peg.

" The tube of which I spoke is two steps from London Bridge, the last bridge possible over the Thames.

" Here everything is small, except the City, post-offices, banks, etc., except Southwark, an enormous street full of manufactories and immense warehouses, except the docks, less fine however than those of Antwerp, Belgravia Square, and some gigantic Terminus Hotels. Everything is small : the houses of two stories without visible roofs, at the bottom the doors, *collidors*, door handles, the compartments of the public-houses, comparable truly to the insides of pomegranates, the very small yellow bricks in the walls, which bricks become, at the end of a very short time, obscurely reddened, then altogether blackened ; everything is small, thin, emaciated, especially the poor, with their pallid complexions, drawn features, long skeleton hands, thin beards, miserable light hair, curling naturally after the manner of growth of feeble things, like potatoes in a cellar, hot-house flowers, etc. Words cannot describe the dreadful misery of these uninteresting but very fine, very distinguished wretches.

" Here for a penny one can buy oranges, and incalculably exquisite pears, pomegranates also, apples, etc.

" Give me as many details as possible regarding the ' dear child ' and her august family. Do you see the Sivrys still? Madame Rimbaud is occupying herself very vehemently with the affair. She believes that I should submit to being separated from her son. What do you say? I believe it would prove their one weapon against me. ' They are caned, therefore they are guilty,' whilst we are ready, Rimbaud and I, if necessary, to prove our innocence to all the *clique*—' and that will be the justice.' "

The parents of Verlaine's wife, however, arguing from Rimbaud's stay in London in company with Verlaine, lodged an application for separation, one of the motives for the demand being the intimacy with Rimbaud, which grievance was detailed. Verlaine wanted to reply, to publish letters in the press, to convoke friends, and to hold a tribunal of honour. He went so far, as the letter above shows, as to offer to prove his innocence. This offer, which might have been accepted by the opposing party, must be remembered. If it had no weight with the judges, it would have in public opinion. The silence of the accusers absolved the accused.

I replied, urging him to calmness and silence, except in regard to the legal replies demanded by the procedure. I particularly recommended him not to give too much publicity to the motive in question brought forward in the summons. People always know enough, and the malignity of the public would seize on it only too easily. He

wanted in his rage to go to Paris in order to
seek out his wife's solicitor and break his neck.   I
dissuaded him from such violence, equally ridiculous
and impossible, and told him that in the legal duel
that was to follow, the barristers would fight for their
clients with stamped paper, and urged him to confide
to his solicitor the duty of punishing his *confrère*.
He answered by the following letter, in which he
protested once again against the odious accusation :

" Thank you for your good advice.   I will follow
it although I should have liked to confound at once
the abominable calumnies they bring against me,
for what blackmailing purpose I do not know.   To
this end I have prepared a memoir which will be
useful later.   Therein I clearly state with, I believe,
a communicative emotion, all that the unhappy one
has made me suffer, and everything that led to my
final morosity.   As to the filthy accusation, I have
pulverised it, I think, entirely, and cast back all
the disgusting opprobrium on the authors.   I have
detailed the unheard of perfidies of the latter time,
and show that all this affair against nature that
they have the infamy to reproach me with, is
simple intimidation (blackmailing) for the purpose
of obtaining a larger pension. . . . I expose in
a psychical analysis, very sober but very clear,
without phrase or paradox, the highly honourable
and sympathetic elements of my very real, very
deep, and very persevering friendship for Rimbaud.
. . . You have known all about it from the first
day, and will write me your advice since you are
so kind as to offer me your good offices which
I accept with all my heart.
    " I am going to set about recovering my belong-
ings, which they insist on keeping from me, in spite
of a courteous demand that I sent them in the form

of a very affectionate letter to my wife. It goes without saying that if some of our friends are hesitating, and more especially if they know the grounds for the summons, I authorise you to repeat everything I have said, at need to show them my letters. . . . I have received a kind letter from Blémont and from Victor Hugo, to whom I wrote before receiving the summons. Is it necessary to write them now on the matter? . . .

" My life is entirely intellectual. I have never worked more than I am doing now, freed from the thousand and one annoyances which poisoned my life in that family. Here I am given over entirely to poetry, intellectuality, and conversations purely literary and serious. A very small circle of artists and literary men. And they want to drag me from my quasi hermitage and make me bring forward memoirs and letters before the magistrates. I am working well in spite of it all. I have entered into relations with an editor, and I hope before three weeks have passed I shall be able to send to a few friends, you, of course, among them, a little booklet with (perhaps) a frontispiece, entitled *Romances sans Paroles*. . . . If you see Coppée tell him that all the piano organs grind out his *Sérénade* from the *Passant* (*Mandolinata* by Paladilhe), concurrent with that horrible grand air from *Martha*. Which will survive of these two . . .? That is the question: Diamond cut diamond. There are a great many Turks here; one of them, a tobacconist, is called Economidès, and Italians. . . . The French, *euh !* . . . *euh !* . . . are generally keepers of wine-stalls, newsagents, and ill-bred, except your servant, and some other *bons bougres*.

" If you see my mother, tranquillise her.

" Kind regards to Oliveira, Charly, Notre Nanteuil (Monnantheuil, publicist and violinist), and the Messieurs of *la Renaissance*."

"LONDON, *same address.*

" Leicester Square is an uncultivated place, surrounded by dirty trees, in the middle of which is a zinc horse painted red, which was deprived of its rider, George IV. I believe, on the day of a turbulent meeting. They want to replace the man on his beast ; but the place belongs to a man of spirit who will not permit this reinstatement, . . . and the lease lasts another forty-five years. Forty-five years of joy for the foreigner! The French cafés there are frequented by commercial travellers.

" Is it true that the Communists are all dispersed among the faubourgs, with the exception of Oudet, Landeck, and Vésinier, where they are quite quiet, and issue a very good journal, *La Fédération*, which is said to be maintained by Badingue? I am thoroughly determined to have as little as possible to do with these gentlemen, except Andrieu, a very noble and clever man, and Régamey, very agreeable and very Parisian. I have seen no one I know who is fixed here.

" The tobacco is filthy, and cigars unobtainable here! . . . The city is a truly interesting place. An extraordinary activity in the streets, narrow and black, but flanked with fine houses, offices, banks, warehouses, etc. I went the other day by boat as far as Woolwich—the docks are wonderful —Carthage, Tyre, all rolled into one, eh? Regent Street, the fine quarter, *heu! heu!* like the Chaussée d'Antin in the time of Louis Philippe : provincial finery, pedestrians like dressed-up savages, few carriages, no equipages !

" To sum up, except for its vastness and its very imposing commercial activity, almost terrifying for any one except a Parisian, London is an immense Carpentras—I, who come from the so much decried Brussels, declare it a very charming town (400,000 inhabitants), more beautiful and richer in many places than Paris, overflowing with splendid cafés, restaurants, theatres, and other places, whilst the famous London is nothing more in the eyes of the sage than a clumsy Carpentras; do I calumniate Carpentras? . . . Thank you for useful information. I have written to my wife with regard to the settlement of my affairs. If recalcitrant, I will take further action. Very painful all these wretched details, and worse still this desertion of me by my wife for such a stepfather. I say desertion, since I have never ceased to recall her to my side, and she no longer even writes to me after having insanely abused me and insulted my mother, to whom she *will not even send my son*! Tell that to all my 'astonished' friends."

Another letter.

"Having fled like Lot from the Gomorrah of the Rue Nicolet, without taking anything away, behold me destitute, without books, pictures, or anything else that belongs to me, all being detained by the amiable family you know of, and no prospect of receiving them. Be so kind as to advise me a friendly, or at worst, legal method of obtaining them. There is also the child they want to cheat me out of, and meanwhile are hiding from my mother, who can do no more. As to that, it is an atrocious offence, and will be punished by justice, human or divine. Of the latter, if necessary, I will be the active instrument . . . .

"*London Sketches*: I am working hard. Some serious French papers are being established here; I am intriguing and believe I shall be taken on them. I know the principals; therefore, although far from happy . . . behold me full of courage with my sleeves turned up. . . .

" London is less melancholy than its reputation ; it is true that one must be a searcher like me in order to discover its distractions ; I have found many. But clean cafés, *nix, nix*. One must resign oneself to dirty drinking - shops called ' French coffee-houses,' or to the commercial travellers' boxes of Leicester Square. No matter, this incredible town is very well, black as a crow and noisy as a duck. . . . Everlastingly glutted in spite of ridiculous tracts about drunkenness ; immense, although at bottom nothing but a confused collection of clamouring, rival, ugly, and flat little towns ; without any monuments except its interminable docks (which are sufficient for me and my more and more modern style of poetry). It is well enough, in spite of its numerous absurdities which I have given up enumerating.

" Enclosed are two little poems to follow after the one already sent you. I propose to print them over here next month with others of a similar character, under the title *Romances sans Paroles*. I count on you for advertisement."

Verlaine had quitted precipitately, and, as it were, secretly, the conjugal, or rather his father-in-law's dwelling-place. He had, therefore, left in the Rue Nicolet not only household furniture but a certain number of altogether personal objects which he was desirous of recovering. One becomes attached to things : souvenirs, familiar objects, books, all the intimate garniture of a home. Such things, frequently useless, assume a position of importance in the case of separation. It is the lack of them which often makes travel distressing and saddening ; one feels lost, and tries to lessen the days spent in hotels where everything is strange. In his gloomy and sombre furnished apartments in London Verlaine recalled his domestic gods and evinced a strong desire to recover them. His mother sent me a list of the personal property claimed by her son from the Mauté family, and I sent it on, asking them to accede to the legitimate demand of the absentee. I believe that most of them were sent to Verlaine's mother, who, by reason of her son's unsettled life, took care of them, and almost all of them after her death were taken in default of payment by Verlaine's creditors.

The action for separation proceeded and constantly occupied the mind of the voluntary exile. The following letter explains his feelings at this melancholy, but not yet entirely disastrous, period of his life.

"LONDON, 14*th November* 1872.

" Rimbaud has recently written to his mother informing her of all that has been said and done against us, and I am at present in regular correspondence with her. I have given her the addresses of you and your mother, the Mautés, M. Istace, and the two solicitors ; and you have my authority to act in the matter. How are matters progressing? Have the two solicitors corresponded? It seems to me the logical thing to do . . . but the law is not logical, as every one who has to do with it knows. . . . Do you see my wife, the Sivrys, Carjat, Pelletan? Have any proofs!! confessions!! letters!!! plans, after-thoughts come up? What do the people say who visit my mother? . . . Has she told you of the very idiotic letter beginning ' My dear Mamma,' and signed ' Anna,' dated from Liège for Brussels, which arrived at my hotel three days after my mother's return to Paris, and a day

R

after the appearance at the *poste restante* of a woman . . . who demanded my address . . .? And also that some days before a gentleman made the same enquiry, but although in both cases the address was given no one presented themselves at the house.　The letter in question was absolutely incomprehensible . . . the writing was evidently disguised . . . but the faults in orthography leave me in no doubt, whatsoever, regarding the source of this impudent mystification. . . . Madame Rimbaud, on her part, tells me she has received several anonymous letters against her son.　There is a connecting link between all these circumstances which should and could be broken.　That is why I inform you on the subject, so that you may aid me with your friendly intuition to break the spider's web.

"Enclosed are three copies of *Vers à Bibi*, which appeared yesterday in *L'Avenir*.　They are old, you know them (*Les Vaincus*), but they have come out at last.　Two are for Valade and Blémont. If you see the former upbraid him for his silence, also young Gavroche (Forain), Cros, and Cabaner.

"Felicitations on your translation of Swinburne."

In a letter of a month later Verlaine seemed to have endeavoured to throw off his mind all the worry of the legal proceedings.　He even reproached me with speaking of it exclusively in my letters.　He returned to the *London Sketches*.

"LONDON, 26*th December* 1872.

"I have, contrary to my custom, delayed writing to you.　You must blame yourself.　Why do you only write about that wretched case?　I admit your absorption in it is all on my behalf, but mine does not prevent me when I write from mingling with the pure wine of business, the water . . . of innocent gossip. . . . In this letter there shall be no allusion to the stupid affair."

London Sketches : — " The Grenadiers, splendid men in red, curled and oiled, every Sunday give their arms to a girl, for the sum of sixpence.   But it is a different matter with the Horseguards, with their breast-plates, top - boots, and helmets with white plumes, a shilling ! *dame !*   This was told me by an Englishman.

" The negroes in the music-halls are wonderful ; also the weather, which is, at least this winter, of angelic mildness.   There was a regular May sun to-day.

" It was Christmas yesterday.   Like Sunday, only worse, and to-day is almost as bad.   However, the goose is exquisite.   I get it every day at these islanders at this time of year with apple sauce.

" I am very melancholy, however, and all alone. Rimbaud (whom I alone really know) has gone, leaving a frightful blank.   The rest are all the same, *canaille* ; and this will be shown, but *chut !* *zut !*

" I almost know English, but it is absurd !

" *Beef-steack* does not exist. . . .

" ' Stop,' is only used on boats ; to cabbies one says ' Much obliged ! '

" By the way, it appears that my wife gossips at their house every Wednesday.   In the meantime my mother has been in great danger—erysipelas— and my son is still the little captive of the Mautés ! "

The following letter is more tranquil in tone. Verlaine wrote like a man who has reasoned himself into resignation.   It will be seen that he looked

forward to a new establishment, a recommencement
of life in double harness, a plan which was not to
be realised until just before his death :

"First of all my felicitations on the birth of a
little daughter. May she have a happier fate than
my little stolen one! Amen!

"My life is going to be changed. Rimbaud
returns this week to Charleville, and my mother
comes here. Her presence will not only give me
immense pleasure, but be very useful from the point
of view of respectability. It is probable that we
shall take a little house in a cheap district; there
are many such. Living is a hundred times dearer
than in Paris, but the climate a hundred times
healthier and house-room infinitely easier to find.
Then my life will become happy again, and having
put those wretched people entirely out of my mind,
I shall regain tranquillity, and, who knows, perhaps,
another home. *Dame!* they have authorised me
to any revenge.

"I do not see why, after having suffered,
entreated, and forgiven so much, been attacked in
monstrous fashion, and my venerated mother
insulted and wounded in her most sensitive feelings
by every kind of ingratitude, I should renounce
the joys of honest love, although M. the Mayor of
Montmartre may not sanction it. Only three months
ago I should not have talked thus, but since then
so many injuries have disillusioned me, so many
masks have been thrown off, and so much perfidy
has been cynically revealed, that in truth I fear
everything will be completely ended and nothing
remain for me (except for some miracle which I shall
not invoke, disgusted as I am with my own credulity)
save to accept my position in courageous honest
fashion, baffled, but in time to scorn my present
sorrow.

"Here I am, you will say, a regular resident in England to be pouring out on this country, so many grievances (partly legitimate). What knowledge have I acquired? Well, *mon Dieu*, I mentioned to you, I believe, in one of my letters, my search for what is best in the English character. I believe I have found it; it is something very sweet, almost childlike, very youthful, very innocent, with an amusing and charming roughness and gaiety. In order to find all this one must sink an artesian well right through prejudice and custom; evidently these people do not appreciate us; they are less *kind* than we are in the sense that they are less courteous, and they have a provoking individuality of soul, heart, and mind; but this individuality is really excellent, and there is in this egoism of theirs very great ingenuousness. Their absurdity has nothing odious in it. Family life, which is stupid in France because it is feeble, is organised in such a way here that the most Bohemian can take part in it. These observations are the result of all I have been told, and even heard sung in the music-halls—an admirable mine of information on real life in all countries, are they not?—and also of all I have learned from the people I know here. It goes without saying that I scrawl you this edifying paragraph with reservations and without prejudice to more extended studies which might modify my views. Nothing new here except the presence among other French pictures (by Manet, Monet, Harpignies, Renoir, etc.), of Fantin's *Coin de Table*. We went to see ourselves. It has been bought for £400 by a rich Manchester man. Fantin for ever! There were ten flower pictures sold proportionately well.

"I am going to take to the printer the *Romances sans Paroles*, four parts — *Paysages Belges—Nuit falote* (eighteenth century popular song) — *Birds in the Night*, with this for inscription :

> " ' En robe grise et verte avec des ruches,
> Un jour de juin que j'étais soucieux,
> Elle apparut souriante à mes yeux,
> Qui l'admiraient sans redouter d'embûches,'

about 400 lines in all ; it will appear in January 1873."

Rimbaud had left his friend. The adventurous youth, already practical and very selfish, considered that there was nothing more to be done in England. He had turned to advantage his stay in London at Verlaine's expense. He had frequented the British Museum as much as the taverns, had been initiated in British customs, had learned English, acquired experience, and had, as it were, served an apprenticeship to his future career as explorer, merchant, and business man. This stay in London was very useful to him, and transformed him into a practical man, apt in commercial matters.

Verlaine, separated from one from whom he was considered inseparable, was seized with *ennui* in his London isolation. He ceased sending me humorous sketches. He suffered from a double nostalgia. Rimbaud's departure left him entirely alone with his thoughts, and the remembrance of his wife and anxiety regarding the case then proceeding rendered solitude and exile intolerable. He fell ill and thought he was going to die. He telegraphed to his mother, his wife, and Rimbaud, begging them to come to him. He informed me, but only after several days, of his illness and state of mind, as follows :

" If I have not written to you it is solely because I did not know your new address, otherwise you would have received eight days ago, at the same time as two or three others whom I consider my *serious* friends, a sort of farewell letter, in which I bade them good-bye. At the same time I telegraphed to my wife to come quickly, for I felt myself at the point of death. My mother alone came, and from her I received your address. Two days afterwards Rimbaud, who left here more than a month ago, arrived, and his good care, combined with that of my mother and my cousin, has succeeded in saving me this time, not from certain death, but from a crisis which would probably have been mortal in solitude. Do write to me. I have great need of friendly affection. Tell me all that is going on . . . My weakness is extreme."

Uneasy at the physical and moral state of my friend, I hastened to write to him. He reassured me as follows :

" Many thanks for your cordial letter. I still continue to improve, although my health may be always very precarious, so much so that I fear— shall I say I fear or I hope?—I shall not live very long. My life has been broken by a thousand treacherous and gross injuries, and without being a regular sensitive plant, it has killed me by degrees. However, now that I have drunk the cup to the dregs, and done my utmost to cure my wretched wife of her madness, I have attained, if not the serenity, at least the resignation of a just man. Since they drive me into a corner, I will go on with the affair and get together a report (will you take it in hand as soon as you can?), and meanwhile I will work tenaciously ! . . .

" Although I want to learn English, and Paris repels me immensely, I would follow your advice

and return there, were it not for the certainty
that I should run the greatest risks. Besides the
obliging 'attentions' of the people of the Rue
Nicolet, I have *proofs* that the military authorities
intend to pursue all those whom civil justice has
spared. These proofs have been given me by an
ex-clerk from the Municipal Offices who escaped
only by flight hither from a summons *against all
those who remained*. . . . The death of the great
man (Thiers) cries for vengeance, and the Gaveaus
(Commandant Gaveau) remaining believe they
will render honour to his ashes by pursuing those
Communists not yet imprisoned. It is very serious,
and I give you this information in return for your
advice, which is certainly good ; I shall follow it
directly prudence permits me."

Verlaine's mother, who had come over to her
son in London, was now about to return. She
begged him to come back to France, reassuring
him, on the strength of information received from
me and other friends — as to the danger of a
political prosecution, and giving him to understand that a reconciliation with the Mauté family
was possible. Verlaine hesitated. His mother's
departure leaving him anew in the noisy isolation
of London, for Rimbaud had returned to Charleville, lured him to re-enter France. He wrote
to me on the subject, at the beginning of 1873,
informing me of his apprehensions as to the reception he would meet with in Paris :

"I profit by my mother's return to Paris to
send you these words. Will you when you reply
advise me on certain points ? I intend to return
to Paris shortly, in order to wind up matters. I

count on your assistance in this task, for you know my prodigious inexperience. Only I would wish to be informed who is for or against me among our friends, so as to avoid any unpleasantness, and to know to whom I can hold out my hand. Write me, therefore, fully on the subject. Tell me, also, if there is any way of accelerating matters; they threaten to become ridiculous, all the more so because my defence is so simple. Denial pure and simple of everything, and defiance of their being able to furnish proofs or witnesses, and finally, the supreme thing: it is impossible for me to live with the Mautés, and my wife prefers to break her marriage rather than give in to me on this point."

He left Paris soon afterwards, doubtless because of the state of his health and the need of change of air, but he also secretly hoped that his wife would consent to an interview in Belgium, and that in the new surroundings among which she would find herself with him, far from the influence of her family and the memories of the Rue Nicolet, disunion would cease, the case be abandoned and life in common be resumed. It was an illusion certainly, but it decided Verlaine to leave England at the beginning of the spring of 1873 for Jéhonville, in Belgian Luxembourg, to stay with his aunt, Mme. Evrard.

CHAPTER X

IN THE NORTH—ATTEMPTS AT RECONCILIATION—
PLANS FOR WORK

(*April-June* 1873)

AT Jéhonville, where his mother promised to rejoin him after her return from Arras, whither she was called by family affairs, Verlaine resumed the free, tranquil, country life he loved, and of which he had for long been deprived.

He described in his *Croquis de Belgique*, published by the *Revue Encyclopédique* in May 1881, this northern district, the scenery of which charmed him, celebrating its green of every tint with the blue sky for background, and vaunting the trout of the Semoy, which he qualified as "divine" and "clerical" because eaten in the society of the *curé* of the place. Rambles in this picturesque country, the health-giving breath of the forests, the encircling quietude, the wholesome food, and the simple friendly companionship of relations and friends who had known his father well, recalled to him the happy holidays spent at Paliseul with his kind Aunt Grandjean, and re-established his moral and physical health. Some fine days he spent there — the last; deceptive gleams of sunshine before the storm. He wrote as follows :

266

"JÉHONVILLE, 15*th* *May* 1873.

"I do not know if you are aware of my absence from London, but it is only temporary, for it is only too certain that Paris and France will be dangerous for me for a long time to come. An attempt to cross from Newhaven to Dieppe abundantly proved to me this sad fact, and I only owe it to providential chance . . . to a conversation in English overheard on the boat, an hour before departure, between some men . . . with black moustaches, that I am not now bemoaning on damp straw in *la belle France*, the dungeons of our Republic.

"Therefore, Paris being unhealthy for me, I see only London in which to make hay while the sun shines, and even here I am studying English with all my might; indeed, it is a powerful diversion from all conjugal and other worries.

"My friend, I am going to speak seriously. You have in your rare letters evinced too much real interest for me to ask new and solid proof of it. The commission with which I wish to charge you is, moreover, exceedingly simple; viz., to answer as quickly and fully as possible the following questions :—

"(1) You must know, from denunciations and indiscretions, my wife's position. Young Barrère, (our present Ambassador in Rome) . . . said to me lately on your behalf 'that she was not far from a reconciliation'; but I thought this was merely a delicate and discreet remark of yours to prevent and close all conversation on the subject. On the other hand I was told (permit me to keep silence with regard to my informants), that it was not only time, but *high time* I returned, no explanation being added. Therefore I risked the journey to Paris, so unfortunately prevented.

"A letter from my wife, received at Namur, where, by the way, I again believed myself about to die from some sort of brain attack (say nothing about it, especially to my mother!), intimated to me not to worry her with any more letters. I must tell you that I have never ceased to represent to her, in the most reasonable and touching terms, all the odium, ridicule, and futility of a law-suit which it seems to me I must win.

"It is beyond a doubt that such a change of front on the part of this child of nineteen—for before the incident at Brussels, of which I have spoken to you, there were, in her letters at least, after my departure be it understood, nothing but affectionate protestations and endless appeals, to which I never opposed anything on my side but appeals also, already fearing what has come to pass, and protestations no less affectionate—it is beyond a doubt, I say, that this change of front, which has entailed the abrupt abandonment of my mother, already ill with worry over the matter, is simply a family affair or some infatuation which supposes excessive foolishness. God preserve me from casting suspicion, but, unhappily, I know the house, the 'new' ideas, the 'artistic' environment, the atmosphere of 'vanquished prejudice' in which the strange witch moves. Others in my place might watch with a certain joy for the moment of the inevitable crisis, and make ready to meet it. But I am not of such; for with all my silly head and my eccentric ways, I am sober at bottom, and was intended indeed for tranquil happiness and peaceful affection. The matter is too serious—is it not?—for me to have to recommend you to use every discretion.

"(2) I long to know the general opinion.

"(3) You must know that I attach a great deal of importance to the publication of the volume,

Romances sans Paroles, before the case comes on, for afterwards it might seem that I wish to profit by the advertisement.

"Can I get Lachaud, or Dentu, no matter which—I have too many enemies, why, Heaven knows! to think of Lemerre—to print quickly, in modest fashion . . . 468 purely literary lines? Above all, will you have time (I do not doubt your willingness) to take the matter in hand, and send me the proofs? Who else is there? Blémont? but I believe he too is greatly occupied."

This letter indicates that Verlaine had a certain idea in his head. He asks for particular information after the manner of matrimonial detectives. I hastened to assure him that I had learned nothing suspicious regarding his wife. I should have been very careful to keep from him any evil gossip or food for scandal, if such had existed. He would have been informed of it soon enough, and there was no need to excite or overwhelm him; but, as a matter of fact, there was nothing to conceal. Mme. Mathilde Verlaine was living with her family. If she had nothing to fear from private investigation, on the other hand she appeared in no way animated by a desire for reconciliation, nor for the return of her husband. She seemed satisfied with the existing state of affairs, and happy in an expected deliverance.

In his next letter he seemed pacified, and almost confident of a favourable outcome. It will be remarked that, as a consequence of his mind being set at rest as to his wife, he conceived an abundance of literary projects which he confided to me, at the same time evincing a desire for haste with regard to the publication of the *Romances sans Paroles*. He was undecided how to behave to his wife. He always secretly hoped for a reconciliation. His mother had almost guaranteed it. The departure of Rimbaud contributed to the uncertainty. Mme. Verlaine and her advice, however, in no way disarmed him. I begged Verlaine to engage a business man to watch over his interests, take note of the progress of the affair, and act as a go-between at interviews with lawyers, barristers, etc., as it was impossible for me to take the matter in hand. I was on the point of leaving Paris for Sens, to edit a newspaper which had formerly been run in Paris, but having been suppressed by General Ladmirault in consequence of the siege, we had revived it, with Valentin Simond as manager, at Sens, that place being near Paris and yet outside the zone under martial law. My enforced stay at Sens and the installation there of printing offices for the daily publication of *Le Suffrage Universel* had a direct effect upon the history of Verlaine's works, for there it was that I was able to print and publish the *Romances sans Paroles*.

Verlaine wrote to me from Jéhonville:

"*6th May* 1873.

"I received a letter from M. B. . . . offering his services. Recommended by you he is accepted; you can tell him so. But before entering into relations with him I want to know from you—what I asked you in a letter still unanswered some time ago—what is being said . . . about my wife? I am at this moment preparing a memoir which, extremely detailed as it is, will be inefficient if I remain in ignorance of what concerns my wife, and distressing to me supposing there is any hope whatever for me. I beg you to write to me quickly if only two lines, telling me what you know and what you think. It will be of more than a service! That is why I beg for no delay. As soon as it is received I will write to M. B. . . . As to the report, I believe he has all the materials in hand."

The hope of a reconciliation was always present with Verlaine in the tranquillity of the country, and while he cast his line into the cold and rapid current of the Semoy which sheltered trout in its deep holes, he considered the situation and thought incessantly about his wife. It is evident he longed for pardon, forgetfulness, reunion. Also the idea that she might have given him a successor haunted and tormented him. Like all who are jealous, he pretended he wanted the real truth, were it ever so unpleasant; but a revelation of infidelity on the part of her whom he always considered his wife, his legal property, would have reduced him to despair.

"Jéhonville, 16th May 1873.

"I received yesterday your letter of the 12th, delayed by these indolent Belgians! I am happy in your assurance of the lack of gossip, evident symptom that all is well.

"What I want now is very simple; listen:

"After more than six months of actual separation, without there having been on my part the slightest desire for it, but the contrary, after a judgment which takes away from me all power over my wife and son for an indefinite period; and, lastly, after all the rumours which have been circulated in conversation and on stamped paper, I believe that

an amicable separation, besides not preventing my
adversaries from again resorting to legal proceedings, under such circumstances nothing more nor
less than blackmail, would be a half measure equal
on my part to a tacit acknowledgment. In a word,
it is impossible. What I require is, I won't call it
a reconciliation, for I have never been 'angry'—
my wife's immediate return to me. I have written
to her quite recently to this effect, warning her that
this is the last time. I await her reply, and it is
clear that if she does not give me satisfaction in
a very short time, I shall be forced to take further
steps, for it would be too ridiculous for me to wear
out my life in a suspense equally prolonged and cruel.

" I have said everything, done everything, I have
left London and the promise of a competence, to
come here for Her. I have entreated, reasoned,
and appealed to her good sense, heart, and even
maternal love. I have been answered that I was
afraid of the Law and therefore I said affectionate
things ; that she was not afraid of the Law, because
she knew herself to be quite secure. Now, you
know the purport of their second demand—the rejected exaction of a friendly pension of 1,200 francs,
just as you know that the motive of the first demand
is my refusal of an authorisation to live for an
indefinite period in a problematic south. If, therefore, you see Mme. Bertaux (Mme. Léon Bertaux,
the sculptor)—even go to see her if you can—tell
her if she sees my wife, and gets a favourable
opportunity, to put plainly before her all the madness, immodesty, carelessness of the future of her
son, unhappiness for herself, for me, and for the
child, which the pursuance of a line of action so
revolting as this abominable and grotesque law-suit
would imply and evince. Mme. Bertaux might
add that if they render me desperate to such an
extent, I am determined to defend myself to the

utmost of my power; that I on my part believe
myself secure, but that nevertheless I fear a law-suit,
because I know the happiness of both of us would
have to give place to every kind of remorse for her
and regret for me.   There it is!

" At the same time, if you see any better course,
please advise me.

" My health is altogether disordered.   Ah! if
I had a happy heart my head would be well enough.

" My brain is swarming with new ideas in poetry,
truly fine plans.   I have done a prose drama . . .
Madame Aubin,—a sublime deceived husband, not
like *Jacques*, but an extremely sarcastic modern,
who could give points to all the swindlers of
Dumafisse.   I am finishing an *opéra - bouffe*,
eighteenth century, begun two or three years ago
with Sivry.   That, with the music yet to be composed, will be for the Alcazar of Brussels, where
were produced *Les Cent Vierges* and *La Fille de
Madame Angot*.   Then I contemplate a prose
romance . . . to be very crisply written—a series
of sonnets in which *Les Amies* (if you can re-copy
them, send them to me) will be included, and of
which I send you the prologue in the rough, but
sufficiently explanatory of the work I believe ;—and
the preface to *Les Vaincus* . . . in which I explain
some of my ideas I think good ; I will send it to you
one day, and you will see it is good.   All this means,
I think, some work.

" I should like as soon as my head is all right,
to compose a book of poems . . . didactic poems,
if you like, from which ' Man ' will be completely
banished.   Landscapes, things, the mischief of
things (if you have the book with this title by
Arthur de Gravillon send it to me), the goodness
of things, etc.

" Here are some titles : *La Vie du Grenier*,
Sous l'Eau, *L'Ile*.

" Each poem will contain 300 or 400 lines.   The
lines will be in accordance with a system I have
worked out; very musical, without Poe's puerilities,
yet as ingenuous as that rogue's.   I will talk to you
about him another day.   I have read all his work in
English.   It will be as picturesque as possible—
La Vie du Grenier of Rembrandt; *Sous l Eau*, a
genuine Undine song; *L'Ile*, a great flower picture,
etc.   Do not laugh before you know my system.   It
is perhaps a foolish idea after all.   You will receive
on Tuesday or Wednesday the manuscript (of the
Romances sans Paroles).   Before you acknowledge
it talk to Lechevalier a little about price, etc., etc.
I could write to him.   What do you say?   I should
like the *format* to be the same as that of *La Bonne
Chanson* (Ah! zut!)   If it could appear soon, what
luck!   Finally, I confide this child to you, make
it 'happy'!"

The *Romances sans Paroles*, which Verlaine had
not been able to get published in London as he
had announced in one of his letters, did not find
a publisher in Paris.   Lechevalier, to whom I
applied in accordance with Verlaine's wishes,
refused.   Other publishers I approached also
answered in the negative.   I kept the manuscript,
awaiting an opportunity.   The times were not
propitious; we were in the midst of a parliamentary
upheaval.   M. Thiers had been deposed, and, at
Versailles, royalty had nearly issued, for an instant,
from its tomb.
The conjugal affairs of the poet were scarcely
better.   His projects of reconciliation had vanished.
Stamped paper was flying about, and judgment of
the civil courts pronouncing a separation, for
divorce as yet did not exist, was expected.   Arthur

Rimbaud, recalled by Verlaine, had rejoined him at Bouillon, his return being celebrated by a serious bout of drunkenness. Verlaine and his companion wandered for some time in the Ardennes, and then set out for England, which they both desired to revisit.

The following letters announce this return to London :

"JÉHONVILLE, 19th May 1873.

"You will receive at the same time as this letter the famous manuscript (of the Romances sans Paroles). As soon as you can, put it in hand. Hardly show it to the comrades, and acquaint me with the intentions of this Chevalier or Claye. . . . Mine are solvency, scrupulous honesty, and the desire for publicity. I ask of him moderation in price—credit, if possible, though, if necessary, I will pay cash. . . . It has been thoroughly revised. You will send me the proofs after examination, and I will return them to you on the following day. I should like it to be done quickly ;—four hundred odd lines, it is a matter of fifteen days. I particularly wish the book to be dedicated to Rimbaud, first as a protestation, next because I wrote the verses when he was with me, urging me to their composition ; and, above all, as a token of gratitude for the devotion and affection he has always shown me, particularly when I was at the point of death. The law-suit must not make an ingrate of me. You understand? However, write me if you see any objections other than a respect for others which would be quite misplaced. I intend to return to London in a week and will send you my address."

"JÉHONVILLE, May 1873.

"I set out to-morrow for Bouillon, where I have an appointment with some comrades from

Mézières and Charleville, from there to Liège, a fine town unknown to me, from Liège to Antwerp, and from Antwerp to London, eighteen hours by sea, without counting the Scheldt and the Thames. But it is cheap, and I am not ill on the sea. I calculate within five days to be in the 'Fog's City.' As to the land of soup, *pomme sauté*, serpents (police officers), and fathers-in-law, I mean Paris, I shall return there perhaps in the autumn, once I know English thoroughly. But I wish to be sure that I shall not be encircled by the said serpents.

"All that any one can have a grudge against me for after remaining in my office at the Hôtel-de-Ville, is that in London I belonged to a club for 'Social Studies,' founded by Lissagaray, and composed of Communists, a perfectly inoffensive club in which the whole of my participation has been the requisite 'three shillings by month.' It is true that I was proposed by Andrieu, whom I knew long before my political days, in the quality of colleague at the Hôtel-de-Ville, and friend of Valade and Mérat. Then, it is true, I have seen Vermersch. But I remember the time when Coppée was not a great man, in the days of the Café de Suède. All this constitutes a case against me, according to you? Write. Then there are the Mautés and their lack of scruples. See. Write.

"Having acquired the conviction that my wife and her family do not wish to come to any understanding, I am going to act very soon and very drastically. You shall be advised in time. . . ."

"LONDON, *29th May*.

"I arrived here the day before yesterday from Antwerp. A crossing of fifteen hours of extraordinary beauty. I just throw this into the box to give you my new address. . . .

"8 GREAT COLLEGE STREET, CAMDEN TOWN, N.W."

I received the manuscript of the *Romances sans Paroles*, all of it in Verlaine's own handwriting, on sheets of notepaper, without any of the drawings, scratchings out, or additions, which usually characterised his missives. He had copied it carefully, remembering the time when, ex-pupil of a disciple of Brard and Saint-Omer, he announced to me triumphantly that he had just passed "his writing examination" at the Hôtel-de-Ville.

Having read, with an interest easy to understand, the precious manuscript, I sent my felicitations to the impatient poet, postponing observations and reservations, particularly as regards certain innovations in the matter of rhymes, etc., which might appear daring.

He instantly replied :

"I am enchanted that my little book pleases you in spite of its heresies of versification. I am preparing you many others equally disconcerting, if the terrible state of my health allows me to live to fill in the work of which I wrote to you the other day. To speak truth, I am not ill-satisfied with it, although it is very far from what I wished to make it. I do not want any effort to appear, but hope to arrive as soon as I have completely mastered my system at Glatigny's facility, naturally without his banality and by quite different methods. I am tired of whining poetical Jeremiads. I am meditating my reform very seriously and modestly. . . . Meanwhile I am reading Alfred de Vigny over again. Ah! my friend, what a man! Poet and thinker, he heaps together sublimity.

". . . Some words in Vermersch's lecture. Subject : Alfred de Vigny. All that the newspapers say regarding his want of success is quite false. On the contrary, he is a very great success. Literally, the whole French colony was crowded into the room at Old Crampton Street. An error of the *Rappel*: Vermersch's wife is not English but Dutch, she is not a governess but a dressmaker. I may add that she is charming, very simple, and that it is a case of true love, *rara avis*.

" But to return to *Gustave* (as he called the *Romances sans Paroles*), if you think well : *cut, but hear.*

" None the less, the gossips will be sure to find something to clamour at; but devil take me if in the course of composition I considered whether there was anything *imphame* (infamous) or *infemme* if you prefer. The short pieces, the *Piano*, etc. . . . *Oh! triste! triste! était mon âme* . . . , and *J'ai peur d'un baiser* . . . , *Beams*, and others, bear witness to necessity (seeing my perfect love for the *sesque*), so that the *Notre amour n'est-il là niché* cannot be reasonably reproached under pretence of *Terre Jaune* as impossible for the tongue of honest men. Further, what is there audacious in dedicating a volume which is partly impressions of travel, to the one who was with me at the time these impressions were received? But I repeat, if you prefer, censor friend, cut (here Verlaine, in accordance with his custom of illustrating his letters with his pen, drew a pair of scissors, emblem of *Anastasia*). And since we are on the subject of names for dedication, as Petrus Borel said (another whom it is necessary to re-read), will you accept in *Les Vaincus* the part called *Sous l'Empire*, the largest in the volume, and containing *Le Monstre, Le Grognard, Soupe du Soir, Crépuscule du Matin, Les Loups*, all things you know, and in no way compromising? The things on the Commune will be dedicated to some proscribed friend."

A rapid letter at the beginning of June 1873 :

" I only write you a word, being overwhelmed with work, to scold you for your silence. What has become of *Gustave*? I do not see why politics should interfere with this frail youth, vowed in advance to a special and therefore rare sale.

" I give French lessons, which brings me in something between 100 and 150 francs a month. . . . It kills me with *ennui*. Great point.

" What of the report?

" Try to push through at least one of my three volumes (even by paying extra), and forward it to me here, for my literature lessons *by a poet*. It is the best testimonial for the hair-brained, who pay you half a sovereign for each lesson on versification and the 'artifices of poetry.' Therefore, my commission is all the more serious and urgent. It is understood that I will reimburse you. If you cannot take it in hand yourself, and you see Blémont, charge him with it."

This letter is the last I received before the catastrophe at Brussels. There was no foreshadowing in Verlaine's tone or temper of the disasters which were to accumulate so unfortunately.

CHAPTER XI

(1873)

As narrated in the preceding chapter, Verlaine and Rimbaud were together in London in June 1873, the former giving French lessons, upon the returns from which he lived, largely helped by subsidies from his mother. A quarrel arose between the two companions, and was followed by others, occasioned by the despotic character of Rimbaud and Verlaine's nervous and capricious temperament. Helped on by drink, these disputes quickly assumed a bitter tone. It must be added that in accordance with the proverb which explains why horses fight so readily when there is no hay in the manger, on days of misfortune the two comrades found themselves the one more tormented, and the other more imperious.

Suddenly Verlaine, like a prisoner who breaks his chain and escapes, left London and embarked for Antwerp without informing Rimbaud, or, it appeared, leaving him any money. This flight was an unfortunate proceeding. Verlaine ought to have acted with greater deliberation, and brought greater calm and energy into his decision if he wished to renounce the onerous and troubling company of

Rimbaud. He had only to signify to him that
he had had enough of this life in common, giving
occasion for calumny and furnishing arguments for
the law-suit his wife was projecting. Rimbaud
would have returned to his mother at Charleville,
as he had done before, when he had sufficiently
mastered the English language, and Verlaine would
have gone where he intended, viz., Brussels.

Why did Verlaine take the sudden and
apparently foolish step of separating himself from
Rimbaud, probably for ever, and leaving London,
where he could give lessons, in order to return
to Belgium, where he had no assured occupation
and could only spend money? He had earned
nothing regular for nearly two years, and therefore
lived on his income, and that being insufficient,
he drew upon his capital, already broken into for
the money sent him by his mother.

When we deal with Verlaine's reported poverty
later on, it will be necessary to remember that
although his small fortune sufficed for his wants
when he was earning a regular salary, he could
not live solely upon it, and travel continually.
During the years 1871, 1872, and 1873, up to the
month of July, Verlaine in Belgium, the Ardennes
and England, incurred double expenses, Rimbaud
being without money, and although they may both
have lived in a modest way, yet they never denied
themselves at taverns, bars, and wine-shops, which
they assiduously frequented. During these two
and a half years Verlaine certainly spent 30,000
francs of his capital. He reflected in a moment
of sobriety and wisdom that he could not continue to live in this way, that he must moderate

his expenses and seek another mode of existence. Reconciliation with his wife appeared to him the only advantageous issue from the difficulty in which he found himself. This door of deliverance must be opened. He thought to facilitate return to conjugal life by breaking away thus abruptly. He had not sufficient courage to arrange the affair. In abandoning Rimbaud in London by a sudden flight, he intended to give his wife a pledge that he desired to terminate the friendship, and at the same time render practically impossible any later reunion with the companion, until now regarded as inseparable.

Perhaps also Verlaine made the resolution, the vigour of which contrasted with his customary feebleness, in an access of alcoholic excitement. Naturally he did not inform me, and we are reduced to conjectures regarding his precipitate departure and abandonment of Rimbaud and of England, which was shortly afterwards to result in the quarrel at Brussels, the shot, the trial, and the condemnation.

Verlaine's psychological state at this period was distressing, almost morbid. I have already said that he detested and adored his wife. Alternately he cried for her, longed for her, cursed and overwhelmed her with reproaches and insults from afar. He wrote to her in one of his moments of conjugal nostalgia, begging her to rejoin him at Brussels, promising to give her no further occasion for reproach, and adding that he would kill himself if she did not respond to his appeal. Probably to decide her he announced that he was no longer remaining with Rimbaud, but would go alone to Belgium. In this state of feverish exaltation he set out. His mother perhaps in her touching hope of having her son with her once more in Paris, out of the reach of the irregularities and expenses of life abroad, fostered his conjugal illusions, and caused him to foresee a reconciliation which existed only in the desires of the good lady, and thus influenced his flight from London and separation from Rimbaud.

Evidently therefore he informed her of his departure, and asked for a meeting with his wife. Arrived at Brussels Verlaine found his mother at the appointed place, but suffered a cruel disappointment, for she had to tell him that his wife refused to respond to his appeal; he could not, for the moment, count on a reconciliation. Always optimistic and consoling, Mme. Verlaine entreated her son not to despair; time would perhaps effect a change. It was necessary to be patient, and above all not to recommence his wandering existence with Rimbaud.

The banality of these consolations and the vagueness of these hopes excited Verlaine. He received his mother's counsels with an ill grace, and went off to a neighbouring wine-shop, and there drank steadily to drown his troubles. Under the double influence of disappointment and drunkenness, animosity against his wife regained the upper hand, his affection for Rimbaud revived, with remorse for having left him in London without a sou, and he despatched a telegram to his evil genius, asking his pardon, and begging him to rejoin him in Brussels in order to resume their previous mode of existence. Rimbaud hastened to respond to the invitation, but with no intention of taking up again his life with Verlaine. The intimacy, while it no longer amused, appeared to him insecure, in the light of Verlaine's recent desertion. He came to Brussels solely to obtain the subsidies necessary for a stay in Paris he projected. Verlaine, irritated by the idea, refused the money, which Rimbaud had already vainly endeavoured to extort from Mme. Verlaine. A violent quarrel ensued, ending in the tragic scene, in the course of which the poet was arrested and dragged before the Belgian Courts. Verlaine described this scene half humorously in his book, *Mes Prisons*, but his narrative is incomplete. Here it is full of extenuation of the conduct of Rimbaud, who had caused him to be arrested. Verlaine was always quick to repent.

"In July 1873, in Brussels, during a dispute in the street following upon two revolver shots, the first of which having slightly wounded one of the parties, friends, pardon had been immediately demanded and granted, the culprit, still excited by absinthe, said something so energetically, feeling meanwhile in the right-hand pocket of his coat where the weapon charged with four remaining balls, unlocked, unfortunately was, in such a significant fashion that the other, afraid, ran off as fast as he could across the wide road (de Hall, if I am not in error), followed by his furious friend, to the amazement of the *pons pelches* in their mid-day apathy under a blazing sun.

"A police officer who was sauntering by hastened to seize both delinquent and witness. After a very summary interrogation, in the course of which the aggressor denounced himself rather than that the other accused him, both escorted by the representative of armed force presented themselves at the Hôtel-de-Ville, the policeman holding me by the arm, for it is time to say that I was the author of the outrage, and its attempted repetition, the object of which was none other than that Arthur Rimbaud, the strange and great poet, should die thus unhappily on the 23rd November last." (1873).

These two long sentences of *Mes Prisons* do not properly convey the scene. I have the exact narrative from Verlaine's mother, the only witness of the accident—in reality this act of violence, regretted as soon as committed, was a mere accident, a tragic mischance, an impulsive and unconscious action, performed in the mental confusion of semi-intoxication. Belgian justice sought in it for the elements of a crime, desiring to find a criminal where there was nothing but an imprudent irresponsible being momentarily maddened by alcohol.

Verlaine's mother made a third in the small room at the Liègeois Hôtel, Brussels, where the two men quarrelled on the occasion of Rimbaud's announcement of his departure. The latter asserted that he had only returned with the firm intention of setting off again immediately. Money, and he turned on his heels. Both were under the influence of drink. Verlaine, feebler or more excited by alcohol, grew irritated. In vain his mother begged the two friends to sit down to table and postpone their explanation until the following day, when they would be calmer. Rimbaud would not hear of it. He declared in his ungracious way that he was going to set out at once, and with the authoritative gesture habitual to him, added that he must have money. He kept on repeating, in a sing-song

way, like a music-hall refrain, his imperative demand
for "de l'ar-gent! . . . de l'ar-gent! . . ."

Verlaine had bought a revolver, perhaps with a
vague intention of suicide, tormented as he was by
the recollection of his wife, and his heart tortured
by the separation which her refusal to meet him
at Brussels had rendered definite. For some time
miserable hallucinations had surrounded him, and
at night he was haunted by black demons set loose
by the fumes of alcohol. In an impulse towards
violence he dragged the weapon from his pocket
and pointed it in the direction of Rimbaud. The
movement was sufficiently slow to permit the latter
to put out his hand instinctively as if to seize the
revolver. The first ball grazed Rimbaud's right
wrist, the second, fired after his attempt to avert
the shot, went into the floor, the point of the revolver
being lowered. For a moment the three personages
in this scene stood motionless, and then Mme.
Verlaine dragged her son into his own room. He
wept, expressing the most lively regrets, and returning to Rimbaud, who did not utter a word, he cried:
"Take the revolver and kill me!" Mme. Verlaine
endeavoured to calm the two young men. She
bound up Rimbaud's wrist, and at his urgency,
for he would not relinquish his fixed idea, she
gave him 20 francs to return to his mother at
Charleville. It was believed by all parties that
the matter was terminated, and Rimbaud's insignificant scratch, already half healed, seemed unlikely
to have any result medical or legal.

Rimbaud, insisting on taking the next train back
to Charleville, Verlaine accompanied him to the
station, and on the way thither became a prey to

another access of violent excitement. Rimbaud believed that at a certain moment he was fumbling in his pocket for his revolver for another shot. This, at least, is the explanation he gave afterwards. Whether it was the effect of fear or some sort of diabolical machination, quite in accordance with his character, to rid himself once and for all of Verlaine's importunity, Rimbaud ran towards a policeman, calling out "An assassin!" Verlaine followed him like a madman, running, gesticulating, shouting, perhaps threatening. Rimbaud pointed him out to the officer and he was arrested. An explanation at the police-station followed, Verlaine was searched, and the pistol deemed sufficient proof of attempted assassination. The arrest was confirmed, the weapon confiscated, Rimbaud's complaint lodged, and the unhappy poet imprisoned in l'Amigo, while Rimbaud callously took the train home, dreaming of new wanderings and distant adventures.

Verlaine was transferred to the prison of the Petits Carmes at Brussels, under the plea of attempted murder. The matter became serious. He narrated afterwards with much good humour his interview with the superintendent, a stout little man with a face disappearing among grey moustaches and whiskers, and piercing eyes under his spectacles.

This functionary held a letter in his hand as he began to examine the prisoner. He said politely: "Will you kindly sit down, M. Verlaine!" which were the first courteous words that had been addressed to the poet since his arrest. Fresh from his sojourn at l'Amigo and the rough handling of the police, the poet did not know to what motive to attribute this unexpected kindness on the part

of his keeper. The explanation was soon given :
" I have just read, monsieur, as is my duty," said
the superintendent solemnly, "a letter addressed
to you, and I am astonished, having such corres-
pondents, to see you here ; but read for yourself! "
He held out the letter to the prisoner. It was a
reply to a hasty and desperate appeal he had
sent to Victor Hugo, to intervene on his behalf.
Tormented by the memory of all France held dear
for him, evoking in his distress his broken happiness,
Verlaine had made this last attempt, begging
Victor Hugo to bring his great authority to bear
upon the hard-hearted wife, and to endeavour to
lead her to an unhappy prisoner who implored
grace, pity, and pardon.

The great man replied in the following laconic
rather sibylline note :

" My poor Poet,—I will see your charming wife,
and speak to her for you, in the name of your little
boy. Courage, and return to the truth,
" Victor Hugo."

What did this exhortation to return to the
truth signify ? To what did it allude ? Verlaine
was imprisoned for assault. He needed to be
made known to the Belgian authorities, not as
the vagabond, drunkard, suspected Communist, and
man of ill - repute he was designated in the
famous police notes, but rather the nervous, impressionable artist incapable of a bad action,
but susceptible of being led into an excusable
momentary violence, and, moreover, by his talents,
his social position, his family and education, not to
be confounded with the rogues and scoundrels of

Brabant. What place was there in all this for the advice to return to any truth whatsoever? Further, Verlaine had begged Victor Hugo to attempt to bring about peace and reconciliation with the wife from whom he had voluntarily separated. What connection had this friendly and generous mission with a sort of exhortation to the prisoner to remove himself from error? It would seem as if the illustrious poet had been consulted on a question of philosophical or religious orthodoxy. The apocalyptic letter had, however, the good result of inspiring the superintendent with a certain consideration for the prisoner, who at first, on the evidence of the police notes, he had taken for some ordinary evil-doer.

Verlaine's mother, on her side, had written to the magistrates. The superintendent informed his prisoner:

"Your mother has solicited Monsieur le Procureur du Roi on your behalf to authorise your admission to the *Pistole.* And he added, with a certain kindness, which comforted the poor prisoner: "In consideration of this letter I take it upon myself to give you the authorisation while awaiting my instructions which I think will confirm it."

By virtue of the system known as *La Pistole,* Verlaine, a paying prisoner, was lodged alone in a cell with permission to have his food from outside, and also to walk by himself in the yard, thus being spared the society of the other prisoners. An enquiry was set on foot in Paris, and the information obtained from *concierges,* neighbours, and tradespeople in the quarter where Verlaine's wife

T

lived with her parents, always very hostile to their son-in-law, proved most injurious. Drunkenness, and domestic quarrels reported by vague witnesses, and garnished by the exaggerations of servant-maids, were added to the ill name of Communist which the poet had earned by pursuing his employment at the Hôtel-de-Ville after the 18th March. Verlaine's father - in - law, very badly disposed towards him, repeated in his deposition at the Commissioner's several of the clauses in the application for a separation set on foot by his daughter. Among them the imputation concerning Rimbaud. These unfavourable reports served Belgian justice as a pretext for keeping back the affair, and transforming a simple police case into a criminal action.

In accordance with our code in force in Belgium, as it was only a case of minor violence involving no incapacity for work, the misdemeanour proved, together with the carriage of prohibited arms, was liable only to punishment as an ordinary offence—a fine and five days' imprisonment at most. This statement of the facts which caused Verlaine's case to be brought before the High Court of Justice in Brussels is corroborated by all the papers relating to it. I will quote the two following extracts from "The instruction attendant on the accusation of Paul Verlaine: Case No. 148 of 1873, placed on the registers of the Court of Appeal sitting at Brussels," documents absolutely unpublished, which it has been difficult for me to procure, and the authenticity of which is established by the signed register itself as follows: "No. 318. Copy of the 19th August 1897, signed illegibly."

Deposition of the witness, Arthur Rimbaud, dated 12th July 1873.

"About two years ago I made the acquaintance of Verlaine in Paris. Last year, in consequence of disagreements with his wife and family, he proposed that I should go with him abroad. We were to gain our livelihood by some means or another, for I have no personal fortune, and Verlaine has only the produce of his work and some money given him by his mother. We came together to Brussels in the month of July last year and stayed about two months; seeing there was nothing to be done in this town we went to London. We lived there together until quite recently, occupying the same lodging, and having everything in common. In consequence of a discussion we had at the beginning of last week, a discussion arising from my reproaches with regard to his indolence and his manner of acting towards some acquaintances of ours, Verlaine left me almost unawares, without even informing me of his destination. I supposed, however, that he would go to Brussels or pass through it, for he had taken the Antwerp boat. I afterwards received a letter from him headed 'at sea,' which I will place before you, in which he announced that he had recalled his wife, and that if she did not respond to his appeal within three days he would kill himself. He also told me to write to him, *Poste Restante*, Brussels.

"I afterwards wrote him two letters, in which I asked him to return to London, or to consent to my rejoining him at Brussels. He then sent me a telegram to come here, to Brussels. I desired that we should be reunited, because we had no motive for separating; I therefore left London. I arrived at Brussels on Tuesday morning and rejoined Verlaine; his mother was with him. He had no settled plan. He did not wish to remain in Brussels, because he feared there was nothing to be done in this city. I, on my part, did not wish to consent to return to London as he proposed, because our departure must have produced too disagreeable an effect on the minds of our friends, and I resolved to return to Paris. Sometimes Verlaine manifested an intention of accompanying me, in order, he said, to get justice done on his wife and her parents. Sometimes he refused to accompany me, because Paris recalled such sad memories. He was in a state of very great exaltation; nevertheless he persisted in his desire that I should remain with him. Sometimes he was in despair; sometimes he fell into a rage. There was no sequence in his ideas. On Wednesday evening he drank to excess and became intoxicated. On Thursday morning he went out at six o'clock, and did not return till noon, when he was again in a state of drunkenness. He showed me a pistol he had bought, and when I asked what it was for, he replied jokingly: 'It is for you, for me, for every one!' He was greatly excited.

"While we were together in our room he descended several times for drink. He persisted in endeavouring to prevent the execution of my project of returning to Paris. I remained resolute; I even asked his mother for money to make the journey. Then, at a given moment, he locked the door of the room leading on to the landing, and sat down on a chair in front of it. I stood upright with my back against the wall, facing him. He said to me then: 'This is for you, as you are going away,' or something to the same effect. He pointed his pistol at me and fired, hitting me on the left wrist. The first shot was almost instantaneously followed by a second, but this time the weapon was no longer directed towards me, but lowered to the floor.

"Verlaine immediately expressed the most acute despair at what he had done. He precipitated himself into the adjoining room, occupied by his mother, and threw himself on the bed. He was like a madman. He put the pistol into my hands and entreated me to discharge it at his head. His attitude was that of profound regret at what he had done. About five o'clock in the evening his mother and he brought me here to have my wound dressed. On returning to the hotel, Verlaine and his mother proposed that I should remain with them to be taken care of, or return to the hospital until the cure was complete. The wound not appearing to me to be serious, I manifested my intention of returning to France the same evening, to my mother at Charleville. This news plunged Verlaine anew into despair. His mother gave me twenty francs for the journey, and they went out with me to accompany me to the Gare du Midi.

"Verlaine was like a madman. He did everything he could to detain me, at the same time keeping his hand constantly in the pocket of his coat where his pistol was. When we reached the Place Rouppe he went in front of us for a few paces, and then stopped and faced me. His attitude made me fear he would commit some new excess. I turned round and ran off, and it was then that I asked a policeman to arrest him. The ball which I received in the hand has not yet been extracted. The doctor here tells me it cannot be done for two or three days.

"Q. On what did you live in London?

"R. Principally on the money that Mme. Verlaine sent to her son. We also gave French lessons together; but these lessons did not bring us in much—about a dozen francs a week towards the end.

"Q. Do you know the cause of the disagreements between Verlaine and his wife?

"R. Verlaine did not wish his wife to continue to live with her father.

"Q. Did she not also bring forward as a grievance, your intimacy with Verlaine?

"R. Yes, she even accused us of relations, but I do not wish to give myself the trouble to contradict such calumnies.

"Read, confirmed, and signed.

"*Signed*: A. RIMBAUD; TH. SERSTEVENS; C. LIGOUR."

The Court of Justice, in spite of the slight nature of the offence, condemned the accused to two years' imprisonment and a fine of 200 francs. In his summing up, the magistrate described Verlaine as a Frenchman, a Communist, and a poet. These three qualities had something to do with the severity of the sentence.

On the advice of his counsel the condemned moved an appeal; but the magistrate, finding the sentence too light, moved on his side an appeal *à minima*.

A new hearing took place, and the witness, Arthur Rimbaud, made a second deposition as follows:

"I persist in the declarations I made to you before, *i.e.*, that before firing at me with the revolver, Verlaine used all sorts of entreaties to induce me to remain with him. It is true that at a certain moment he manifested the intention of returning to Paris in order to endeavour to obtain a reconciliation with his wife, and that he wished to prevent me from accompanying him there. But he changed his mind every moment.

He never persisted in any plan; also I can find
no serious cause for the attack he made upon me;
but his reason had completely gone.   He was in
a state of intoxication; he had been drinking in
the morning, as he was wont to do when left to
himself.

"Yesterday the revolver shot, by which I was
wounded, was extracted.   the doctor tells me that
in three or four days the wound will be healed.
I intend to return to France to my mother, who
lives at Charleville.

"Read, confirmed, and signed.

"*Signed*: A. RIMBAUD; TH. SERSTEVENS;
C. LIGOUR."

The Court rigorously maintained the first
sentence, and at least the magistrate's movement
of appeal *à minima* had no effect.   It is not for
us, at a distance of thirty-three years, to discuss the
thing judged.   Verlaine worked out his sentence.
His supposed victim, who had only a slight wound
on the wrist, is since dead.   The condemned has
acquired the amnesty of fame.   One remark only
may be made, viz., that the wording of the
accusation expressly contains proof that Verlaine
was condemned for having at Brussels on the
18th July 1873 "voluntarily inflicted injuries and
made wounds entailing personal incapacity for
work on Arthur Rimbaud"—nothing more.   It is
quite evident that with the hostility the accused
encountered in the authorities, and the small
indulgence shown him by the Belgian magistrates,
if there had come up in the examination the least
proof in connection with the legend regarding his
relations with Rimbaud, the Belgian courts would
not have failed to bring up this overwhelming

charge, and apply to the infamy of the accused all the rigour of the circumspect, adding their quota to the severity of the condemnation. It can be seen by these authentic papers, by all the facts of the case, that there is no truth whatsoever in the calumny which has been circulated in the literary world, reproduced in numerous articles devoted to the poet Verlaine, and is still the basis of much unkind criticism in conversations in which the name and personality of the author of the *Romances sans Paroles* occurs.

The trial at Brussels clearly established that Paul Verlaine was condemned with exceptional severity it is true, but solely for violence, shots, and wounds consequent upon a quarrel in which morality had nothing to reprehend. The quality of foreigner, the eccentric ways, intemperance, and irregularity of life of the poor Bohemian poet, and the unfavourable reports received from France in response to enquiries pursued in the manner described above, explains the merciless sentence and its subsequent confirmation.

Although mention was made in the course of the action for separation of this imputation, supported principally by literary gossip, the tittle-tattle of servants and tradespeople of the Quartier Clignancourt, and although it was even alluded to in the police reports, the silence of the Belgian magistrates is sufficient to prove that it was entirely without foundation. Of this accusation, therefore, the poet's memory must be relieved.

The allegation, without proofs, of a woman desirous of obtaining a sentence of separation, and gossip at bottom more idle than malevolent,

for in the world of poets, artists, and journalists
scandal is propagated without more importance
being attached to it than to professional backbiting
and current humbug, ought not to be regarded
as correct and proved fact.   It is only right in
obedience to the wishes of the dead man, who
expressly desired me to do so, to destroy this
scandalous legend once and for all; and I execute
his constant and supreme desire by bringing a
searchlight to bear upon all the obscurities of
the glorious and unfortunate life of the author of
Sagesse.

CHAPTER XII

IN PRISON—*MES PRISONS—ROMANCES SANS PAROLES*

(1873-1875)

VERLAINE was condemned to two years' imprisonment by the Brussels magistrate on the 8th August 1873, and this severe sentence was, as we have seen, confirmed on the 27th August 1873 by a decree of the Court of Brabant. The steps made to procure a reduction of the sentence led to nothing. I went to Mons and Brussels in 1874 to try and interest the Belgian notabilities in the fate of the unhappy poet—but in vain. In company with Lissagaray, who had been proscribed, and sought refuge in Brussels, I paid various fruitless visits. Everywhere we were met by a courteous but firm refusal; and it was impossible for us, unfavourably as we were regarded at the time by the French Government, to ask for the intervention of the Ambassador.

I returned to Paris without having received a glimmer of encouragement, or even permission to visit Verlaine in his prison. I had, therefore, kept from him my journey to Belgium and its ill success, for fear of depressing and driving him to despair. His mother, who made long stays in Brussels in order to see her son, also vainly solicited several personages of the Belgian Court. No one cared to speak or write in favour of the poet, condemned and calumniated, and, moreover, suspected of being a Communist. Victor Hugo himself, in spite of his broad-mindedness and habitual tolerance, did nothing. Verlaine had to finish out his time, for, although he was freed in January 1875, *i.e.*, after eighteen months' imprisonment, it was not by favour but in accordance with the law; he merely benefited by the reduction accorded to all those who were sentenced to solitary confinement.

He has himself described his harsh captivity without emphasis or acrimony, but rather with shrewd good - humour and ironical resignation. Although it differed both as regards origin and gravity from his other enforced sojourns in a police cell, in the course of a vagabond existence, he has confounded his imprisonment in the Petits-Carmes, Brussels, and at Mons, with the narration of his incarcerations as an insubordinate student or disorderly drinker.

All these interruptions of his life as a free man served him as a pretext for autobiographical details and humorous observations. He collected, under the title *Mes Prisons*, several articles which appeared in literary journals a long time after the events. These articles must be included among the biographical and anecdotal writings of Paul Verlaine: *Confessions*, *Memoires d'un Veuf*, *Mes Hôpitaux*, and *Les Poètes Maudits*. The volume *Mes Prisons* only contains eighty-one pages. It was published by Léon Vanier, *format* small in-18, and bears the date 1893.

Mes Prisons begins with an account of the first captivity of Paul Verlaine : confinement in a room at the Institution Landry for an error in a Latin lesson, accompanied by insubordination. He did not retain an unpleasant recollection of this first cell, having indeed a special toleration for gaols.

"A very suitable cell, light, without rats, mice, bolts, anything on which to sit down, and the least facility for writing, and from which I came out at the end of two short hours, probably as learned as before, but certainly very hungry." (*Mes Prisons*, p. 5.)

His second prison, although more serious in point of time and place, was equally lacking in terror. During the siege, when he was acting both as National Guard and Government employee, Verlaine neglected the rampart for the office, preferring, when the first fire of patriotic enthusiasm had died down, and he had thoroughly savoured the joy of wearing a helmet and managing a sword, the office stool to the camp bed. It must be said in vindication of the culprit that he was newly married and much in love with his wife, to whom at the end of his official day he was free to return ; the reverse being the case when he was on guard. He was punished by his superiors with two days at the police station. There he found a numerous and amusing company.

" The acquaintance of my companions, workingmen confined there for breaches of discipline similar to my own, was quickly made, thanks to my particularly sociable temperament." (*Mes Prisons*, p. 9.)

With drinks smuggled in from outside, the
smoking of pipes, political discussions, and a
certain partridge pie, sent by his wife and enjoyed
in secret — "in these conditions, acceptable as a
whole"—the forty-eight hours passed rapidly, and
the chastised National Guard returned home in high
good humour, to be met there, in response to his
thanks for the succulent partridge pie, with the
remark : "Indeed, I have always understood that
the rat was a great delicacy."

The third prison was at Arras in 1872, simply
a matter of being detained at the police station
in company with Rimbaud—an incident already
narrated. The fourth, the serious, the real, was
that of Brussels and Mons, for the Rimbaud affair.
The fifth incarceration is rather more obscure, and
Verlaine has not been very explicit on the subject.
It was at Vouziers—

"a town charming in the extreme," said Verlaine,
"where I was imprisoned on the charge of threatening my mother, a crime, according to the penal
code, punishable by death. . . . *O maman!* . . . *O
maman!* . . . *O maman*, indeed, forgive me this
one speech : 'If you do not come back home I will
kill myself!' . . ." (*Mes Prisons*, p. 69.)

The curious and interesting volume *Mes Prisons*
is no tearful narrative emulating that of Silvio
Pellico; Verlaine was not of a whining temperament. As we shall see in *Mes Hôpitaux*, at his
worst times he only complained gently and humorously. He never cursed destiny, nor shook his
fist at hostile gods, nor apostrophised society and
these members of it with whom he had come into
unpleasant contact. He never showed himself a

grumbler, agitator, nor anarchist. With one or two exceptions, of which *Les Invectives* bears the trace, although the outbursts of indignation therein contained are mere fits of irritation, he never attacked nor defamed any of those who worked him ill, either directly or indirectly. In the fragmentary memoirs in which he speaks of his places of captivity, and those who guarded him, he displays no hatred nor sense of injury. In recounting his tribulations he never grows angry nor protests. With a very rare sincerity he recognises that the greater number of his misfortunes were due to himself, his errors, his faults, and his weakness.

He even takes a pleasure in self-accusation; with proud humility he confesses all his sins. He pushed this absence of rancour and lack of animosity against men, institutions, and things so far, that he did not even criticise the penitentiary system, despite his experience of its excessive, useless, and inhuman rigours. Nay, he goes so far as to regret the cell he looked upon as a refining crucible, wherein the impurities and dross of the soul are drawn off, and he admires and celebrates, as an artist, the lugubrious building, describing it as "a mansion which gleams quite red and sleeps quite white," in which he was shut up for sixteen months. He not only refrained from displaying any of the hostility usually felt towards anything that is associated with suffering and oppression, but he even experienced a sort of nostalgia for his prison long after he had left it, and exhibited a strange gratitude towards his gaol and his gaolers. Prison chaplains ought to read from Verlaine to their prisoners on Sundays, by way of a lay sermon.

In prose and in verse Verlaine preserved an excellent recollection of this prison at Mons, and in *Mes Prisons* he expresses himself thus flatteringly in regard to it (it was all he knew of the town, for he did not visit Mons until very much later, when he was travelling to Holland in 1892):

"The prison of the capital of Hainaut is as pretty a thing as possible. The outside of pale red brick, almost rose-coloured, this monument, this veritable monument, is white with limestone and black with tar inside, and with sober architecture of steel and iron. I have expressed the kind of admiration raised in me by the sight, the very first sight of this, henceforward my *château*, in the verses that may be found amusing in the book *Sagesse*, the greater number of poems in which are dated from thence:—'J'ai longtemps habité le meilleur des châteaux. . . .'" (*Mes Prisons*, p. 45.)

In a poem from *Amour*, and not from *Sagesse*, as Verlaine wrongly states, headed "Written in 1875"—and which is dedicated to me—composed at Stickney in England, where he was a professor, Verlaine celebrates first the architecture, then the interior, and lastly the furniture of the penitentiary. He found the decoration admirable, and the furniture perfect. He had a table, a chair, and a narrow bed, sufficient light, and enough space, and he records, moved by these recollections, his regrets for the two years passed in *la tour*. There he found real and lasting peace; the silence and the solitude suited his sad heart. Like one wounded, he had need of shelter and tranquillity. He reproduced Pascal's famous saying: "Our calamities all arise from this, that we do not know how to live in one room." To this sentence of the great thinker's he added a superb line, worthy of the author of the *Provinciales*: "Unhappiness is certainly a treasure we dig up. . . ."

He clearly and admirably described his happiness at that time: the possession of good things that no one envies, the sentiment that has no trace of jealousy, the disdain of vain glory, for the desire of men's good opinion underlies all earthly things, and even, according to Pascal, forces those who write against fame to have the fame of being good writers, and he expressed the serenity of this recluse existence, divided between the two benefits, prayer and study, with for recreation a little manual labour. Thus did the saints live, said he.

And so his conversion came about. He considered with disgust and repentance the sinner he had been. He showed satisfaction in being included "among the hidden, reserved hearts that God makes His own in the silence," and he felt himself growing good and wise. He had the dignity of security, a serious rendering of the humorous reflection of Alfred de Musset's, when he was conducted to Les Haricots for neglecting the summons of the National Guard: "They do not arrest any one here!"

In this laudatory poem is to be found, with a rare power of colouring, the silent impression of the place:

" Deux fois le jour, ou trois, un serviteur sévère,
　Apportant mes repas et repartant muet.
　Nul bruit. Rien dans le tour jamais ne remuait,
　Qu'une horloge au cœur clair, qui battait à coups larges. . . ."

It concludes by a blessing on the prison, "that castle of enchantment, wherein his soul was born," and from which he issued forth ready for life, armed with gentleness and faith.

Long afterwards, when travelling through Belgium and Holland on a lecture tour, he passed by his old enforced retreat, and looked without much emotion at "the austere asylum in which he had suffered greatly nine years before." He describes thus in prose the castle "qui luit tout rouge et dort tout blanc" :

"I want to speak of the prison which I had never properly beheld from the outside. It is situated at the extremity of the town, and is in the form of a wheel enclosed in four walls constituting a rectangle, the whole terminated by the polygonal dome of the chapel. The entrance door, framed in grey stone, has an artistic appearance, and plays the Gothic fairly well. Distance and the rust of years showed them to me then, as the verse of which I have just quoted a fragment evokes them for me now, blood red : these bricks which had seemed to me of yore, viewed close at hand and soon after the building had been erected, almost pale rose." (*Mes Prisons*, p. 77.)

With great resignation and an unexpected firmness of mind, for he had nothing of the stoic in him, Verlaine supported the excessive penalty so roughly imposed upon him. He armed himself with patience, stored up his energy, and courageously set to work to count out the days without overmuch bitterness. But he had hours of torture in his isolation : the memory of his wife was always with him, tormenting him, haunting his dreams at night

U

and his thoughts by day. He was as if bewitched by the love philtre of ancient legend, a sort of auto-suggestion, he saw incessantly in thought the one who greatly desired to withdraw herself entirely from him. There was doubtless in this curious sentiment, love increasing with resistance, longing intensified by absence, the usual phenomena of passion ; but in the case of Verlaine, there was also a desire for a regular orderly life, conjugal union, forgetfulness, and pardon. The conversion on which he felicitated himself, the absolution he had solicited and obtained, seemed to him incomplete without the return of the wife who could not be induced to pardon him. The thought of his son, whom he was never to embrace, added to his desire to resume married life and blot out the past. The following letters, written from the prison of Mons, clearly establish Verlaine's new state of mind. In almost all of them by the side of the absent one there is question of the *Romances sans Paroles*—his mental consolation.

The following is the history of this delicate and subtle collection of verse, perhaps Verlaine's most intense work, in which are to be found blended together his two styles: the objective with its representation of forms, imaginary conceptions, and exterior recollections (*Paysages Belges, Ariettes Oubliées, Aquarelles*), and the subjective, with its expression of personal sensations and description of real sorrows (*Birds in the Night*).

As has been seen in the preceding chapters the poems, of which the volume *Romances sans Paroles* is composed, were all written between 1872 and 1873, during Verlaine's stays in Belgium, the

Ardennes, and London. He had not succeeded in finding a publisher for it; neither had I. Volumes of verse do not attract publishers. Those necessary intermediaries between the author and the public become fractious at the sight of MSS. with unequal lines. Even when offering to meet the expense of production the unfortunate author has a difficulty in finding any one to print his rhymes; and in this case the difficulty was enhanced by the sort of ostracism Verlaine was enduring. He had sent me his manuscript before his return to England in 1873. I could not get any bookseller to put his name on the cover. Then came the accident at Brussels, and I decided to publish the poems myself, for better, for worse, knowing how much it would please him.

I had left Paris owing to circumstances to which I have already alluded. M. Thiers had been overthrown, and the Maréchal de MacMahon had taken his place. Paris was in a state of siege. The Republican journal for which I wrote the *Peuple Souverain*, an organ in small *format* at five centimes, the precursor of the *Petit Parisien* and the *Lanterne*, for at that time there was only the *Petit Journal*, similar in *format* and price, among the political organs, had been abruptly suppressed by the order of General Ladmirault, the military governor of Paris, under the pretext of an article which would nowadays be considered perfectly inoffensive, on the liberty of the press, entitled *Un Edit de Louis XV.*, by Edouard Lockroy.

The disappearance of this journal meant loss of work and daily bread for five hundred persons, and, moreover, deprived the democracy of a redoubtable champion. The manager, my friend, Valentin Simond, who has since founded other newspapers, among them the *Echo de Paris*, resolved to continue the publication of the paper by transferring it to a territory outside the range of martial law. Sens, two and a half hours from Paris, was chosen as the most convenient place, and I went thither to act as editor. We installed our printing and publishing office in this unrepublican city, and utilising the plant of a local printer, Maurice Lhermitte, who published the *Courrier de l'Yonne*, we managed to issue the journal which was afterwards to succumb to law-suits and fines.

I found in our printing - office some type sufficiently elegant for a volume of Verlaine's poems. I bought some Whatman paper, and after having superintended the composition and correction I sent the poet a specimen, showing the *format*, style of type, etc. It pleased him as he told me in a letter quoted later on. Not very many copies were printed, five hundred I believe, and they were not sold in the ordinary way. I sent copies to Verlaine's mother, the names given me by Verlaine and the press ; but not one of the papers even quoted the name of the book. I have preserved some copies, now very rare, and regarded as bibliographical curiosities ; I afterwards distributed copies among some friends of Verlaine's, writers, who like M. Henry Baüer, were ignorant of the poet, and despised the man, and who, being impressed by the little volume, were transformed into sincere admirers and ardent defenders of the poet's.

A correspondence of necessity constrained, by reason of the prison formalities, was exchanged

between the prisoner and myself in regard to the
details of publication with, in his case, the everlasting, mournful refrain of regrets, raptures, male-
dictions, and despair with which the attitude of
his wife inspired him. These letters, some of which
were put in the post clandestinely, and even without
stamps, "one is poor in prison," wrote the prisoner,
are on dirty torn notepaper, with the word *Bath*—
which must have made Verlaine smile more than
once—in filigree lettering at the top—paper of the
canteens. Several came to me almost illegible,
being written to economise paper and postage, in
a microscopic hand blotted by the thick blue prison
ink. This is one of the first letters I received
from the Carmes about six weeks after the
condemnation :

"BRUSSELS, *Sunday, 28th September* 1873.

"As soon as this letter reaches you, please
answer it. You will understand why I make a point
of this. For the last three weeks I have had no
more visits, my mother having gone, and I have
only received one letter from her in that time. I
wrote to her last Sunday, and am still awaiting her
reply. In the state of sorrow and anxiety in which
I know she is and all alone, and with her uneasy
temperament, the least delay in a letter makes me
uneasy in my turn. I invent a thousand evils, thus
augmenting the discomfort of my deplorable situation. Certainly, any moment a letter may reach
me, but that does not prevent you from hearkening
to my prayer; it is such a great pleasure a letter
to a poor prisoner. Make it as long as possible,
and as legible as possible, not on my account, for
I am used to your scrawls, but for the prison
authorities, so that there may be no delay. Tell

me about Paris, our comrades, and if you have any
news from the Rue Nicolet. Do the Paris newspapers by chance speak of this unfortunate affair?
Is Victor Hugo in Paris? Kindly send me his
address (the great poet did make a vain attempt
to obtain a remittance of the sentence).

" My mother has told you the great importance
I attach to the prompt publication of my little book.
I have a thousand literary projects, particularly
dramatic, for I intend when I come out to set to
work seriously to gain money by my pen. I will
write you later at greater length. I do not know
when I shall come out; it may perhaps be any
moment — so write to me very quickly. I have
asked Laura (my sister, Mme. Alphonse Humbert)
to go as often as possible to see my mother, and I
thank her for the interest she takes in the matter.
My depression, particularly during the last fortnight,
has been atrocious, and my health is not good. I
have frightful headaches sometimes, and am more
nervous than ever. Say nothing about this to my
mother, I entreat you, and if you see her before
I write to her again, tell her you have heard from
me, and that my health is good. Kind regards to
Blémont and Valade."

Here is a second letter of the same period :

" Thank you very much for your kind remembrance of me, and I send Laura all my gratitude for
her kind letters to my mother. . . . *Hein!* what
unhappiness it is to have a bad wife, backed up in
her foolishness. She might have been so happy,
if, thinking of her son, and remembering her true
duty, she had rejoined me when I begged her,
especially that last time when I warned her of all
the unhappiness that would happen if she insisted
on preferring her family to me. How can I speak
of that family? You and your sister have both

been witnesses of my grief, my forbearance, and my sacrifices. You have seen me in a terrible state, alone, and thinking only of this wretch, and trembling and crying at the idea that I shall never see her again—and you see what she has done! I retain no bitterness against her. God is my witness that I would forgive her everything and make her happy, if she would only open her eyes to the enormity of her conduct to me and to my mother, who was so good to her, and is so deserving. I ought, it seems to me, if they persist in their infamous action, to resist to the end; but to do so I must be on the spot. . . . Shall I obtain a year's remission? My mother will speak to you about it. I am very anxious that my book should appear this winter. . . . I shall very soon be installed in the prison at Mons, and able to give ample details; perhaps they will permit me to correct my proofs. . . . I am working hard at English, *of course for I am to live at London henceforth.*

"A hearty handshake, and looking forward to seeing you again, if not very soon at least I hope in good health and good luck. Your old unfortunate comrade and friend. P. V.

"From Brussels, *de mare tenebrarum.*"

Another letter from the Carmes, full of interpolations and erasures, while thanking me for taking the *Romances sans Paroles* in hand, he again urges haste in regard to it, and speaks of plays he intends to write in prison, and place before some of the French comedians, when in London. "They will be modern," he writes, "elegant, moral, and everything! literary, too, but not lyrical nor pedantic, etc., etc. In fact eminently practical."

Transferred to Mons, he sent me a letter in quite different handwriting, inclining very much downwards—a certain sign of hopelessness and depression.

"MONS, 22nd *November* 1873.

"This is chiefly an earnest entreaty; write to me from time to time. Would it be possible for you to do so every fifteen or twenty days . . . giving me news of friends, events in Paris. . . . It is four months and a half since I read a newspaper. . . . As to what is happening in literature I know nothing. I have some English books— I have just read *Fabiola* without a dictionary. My occupation up to now is to pick coffee; that takes a little time. I go out for an hour every day during which I may smoke; all the rest of the time is solitary confinement in the strict acceptation of the word. I am on the *pistole* with a good bed and good food. Always feeble in health, and the courage which sustained me at Brussels seems about to abandon me, although I have more need of it now than ever. I must hope that I shall not have much longer to endure; that I shall obtain a remission. They are very kind to me, and I am as well as possible. But my poor head is so empty, so resounding, with all the recent troubles and worries, that I have not been able to acquire that species of somnolence which seems to me to be the *ultimum solatium* of a prisoner.

"Also, need I ask for some remembrance of me on the other side of the wall, that is why I persist in the entreaty I made above with all my might. I therefore count on a prompt reply. . . . I shall be more grateful than you can imagine for this mark of friendship.

"Address: To M. the Superintendent of the prison at Mons (Hainaut) Belgium, and at the head of the letter put: Kindly hand to the condemned prisoner, Paul Verlaine, *pistole*, Cell 252."

I sent him in accordance with his desire a specimen page of his book, and awaited his remarks. Although afterwards he criticised the *format*, which certainly gave something of the appearance of a political or medical pamphlet to the little volume, but was unavoidable on account of the limited range of a newspaper printing office, at first he declared himself satisfied, being occupied at the moment with another matter. He was undergoing a new and violent emotional crisis, and his thoughts were distracted from poetry and publishing, as the following letter shows. A singularity in the date is noticeable; he did not know whether it was the 24th or the 28th—the days passed by unnoted in his cell.

"MONS, *24th* or *28th September* 1873.

"I received your note and the specimen . . . it is very nice. Do not trouble to send me anything else just now. When the book is finished will you forward a certain number of copies to my mother, or if she is still here send her one that she can give me. . . . As I told you last Thursday I am much discouraged, and at times very sad. Can you believe that my wife is still one of my troubles? It is extraordinary that she should be afraid of her father and mother. I pity her with all my heart for what has happened, knowing her to be amid uncongenial surroundings, far from the only being who understands something of her character— I mean myself. But so much has been done and insisted upon, that now she is practically in honour bound to persist in her design. In reality I am sure she is consumed with sorrow, perhaps remorse. She knows she has deceived herself, she knows who and what I am, and of what I am capable for her happiness.

"From the fact that she saw me drunk, and they put it into her head that I cruelly outraged her, I must conclude that her desire for a separation was spontaneous . . . done for effect. . . . For a moment at Brussels last year I saw that her eyes were opened, but it passed ; her mother was there. The unhappy girl certainly knows that here, in this ignominy into which I have been thrust, I am thinking these things. She knows it, she wishes to return and cannot. Therefore her father's house is indeed a hell for her ; it is chiefly this which afflicts me.

"You laugh perhaps at my psychology! You are wrong, all this is true. I am not yet sufficiently blessed to be able to shut my eyes to everything. I intend, when I come out, to re-enter France armed with legal rights. A legal struggle with M. Mauté has nothing in it terrifying for me. . . . As to the dear child, I shall always be just the same to her ; gentle, patient, and with open arms. But enough of this subject, I shall speak of it again."

Evidently he still had some illusions with regard to the reality of his wife's sentiments towards him, and all hope of recovering lost happiness had not vanished at this period.

However, the *Romances sans Paroles* soon claimed his attention again, and shortly afterwards he wrote :

"If there is still time in the poem : *Oh ! la rivière dans la rue !* line 4, please put : 'Derrière un mur haut de cinq pieds' instead of 'entre deux murs.' I remember that there was in reality only one wall, the other side being on a level with the ground.

"In *Birds in the Night*, poem 12 : 'Aussi bien pourquoi me mettrai-je à geindre,' line 2, please put 'Vous ne m'aimiez pas' instead of 'Vous ne m'aimez pas.'

"When you send copies to London, enclose with Barrère's one for Lissagaray, another for Swinburne, and another addressed to Barjau, French newsagent, Frith Street, Soho. You would do well to send the latter a note, and if he writes an article in the *Pall Mall Gazette*, or any other journal, ask him to be good enough to send it to you, . . . if by chance Barrère, to whom I send greeting, as well as to the others mentioned above, is good enough to give me the pleasure of writing to me, his letter will be welcome. Give him my sad address. Recommend him to avoid carefully any Communist allusion or any compromising name, both in the article and in the letter. His address is Camille Barrère, Arts Club, Hanover Square, Oxford Street.

"I am working at the poems of which I spoke to you. I hope when I come out to have completed six acts, one in prose, and a volume of verse, of which you have seen specimens. It will be composed of some fantasies, like the *Almanach* . . . and five or six little poems, one of which you have, *L'Impénitence Finale*. Three of them are finished. Rimbaud has them, and my mother has a copy; they are more or less of the diabolical order. Titles : *La Grace — Don Juan Pipé — Crimen Amoris*,—150, 140, and 100 lines; the volume will be nearly 1,200 lines."

The *Almanach* to which he alludes was then entitled : *Mon Almanach pour* 1874. It was a single poem divided into four parts with titles, the first of which was *Le Printemps*, beginning "La bise se rue à travers. . . ." It is now included in *Sagesse* and has no title, but is numbered 11. After the 13th line it reads : "J'ai des fourmis dans les talons," while on my manuscript were the

words : "Voici l'Avril. Vieux cœur, allons!"
immediately after which came *L'Été*: "L'Espoir
luit comme un brin de paille dans l'étable" . . .
while in the edition of the complete works, vol. i.,
page 278, *Printemps* continues with this variant :

> "Debout, mon âme, vite, allons !
> C'est le printemps sévère encore,
> Mais qui, par instant, s'édulcore ! . . ."

these eight lines being added by Verlaine afterwards.

L'Été, which figures without a title in *Sagesse*
on page 268, vol. i. of the complete works, and
numbered 3, has also some variants. *L'Automne*
is entitled *Vendanges*, and forms part of *Jadis et
Naguère*.

The prisoner seemed to be endeavouring to
throw off his depression, and to concentrate himself
less on his troubles. He asked me for political
news ; it had a personal interest for him, on account
of the steps that were taken, unfortunately in vain,
to obtain a pardon, or reduction of sentence, no
intimation of any kind from the Quai d'Orsay reaching Brussels.

Hoping against hope, however, the prisoner
wrote to me :

"MONS 1874.

"I am forced to adjourn the famous volume on
Les Choses; it would necessitate too much tension
of the mind, and I find I cannot work very hard
here without getting ill . . . some news would give
me much pleasure. . . . Tell me what publisher
you have in view for my next book. It is ridiculous
this proscription from Lemerre's ; it dates from
the Commune, would you believe it ? Leconte de

Lisle . . . has regarded me as an ogre since then, and after this last affair, probably something worse. Lemerre, I know, has no part in the matter, and I send him greeting.   Tell me a little of what is going on in the political world.

"I have no idea when I shall be set free. According to the system here the fact of my solitary confinement entitles me to a reduction of six months, which with the five already passed reduces the time to thirteen months; but I ought to be able to count on other ordinary little reductions: two months, three months, especially with the good record I have.   Then there are royal pardons to be obtained by petition, which may be plenary.   I have also my quality of foreigner.   My mother and M. Istace are actively occupied in regard to the matter, and liberty may be mine any day, or not for a long time.   As you say, I must be patient, and time is always on the wing.

"Make no allusion to this letter, even destroy it; it is not passing through the hands of the authorities.

"I am making some hymns to Mary like those of the early church; I enclose one.   It has nothing odd about it, except the title, which is a monogram from the catacombs."

In this curious and composite letter — for Verlaine had copied in it some melancholy verses, a *Prisoner's Lament*: *Les Déjas sont les Encors* . . . and a mediocre comic song entitled *Faut Hurler avec les Loups* ornamented with a vague representation of my silhouette, and introduced thus: *Théâtre des Folies-Hainaut, chansonnette par M. Pablo de Herlañez*, sung by M. Ed. Lepelletier — was a second *P.S.* written across the commencement of a poem: *Le Bon Alchimiste*.

"*Ma foi*, to be continued in our next. I profit by a little space to ask you to send a copy to Andrieu; his address is M. William Knock, 32 or 34 Richmond Garden, Uxbridge Road, London, and don't forget the others, Vermersch, Barjau, etc.

"One word more. Shall it be sent to my wife? Decide, I might have, alas! I speak in all sincerity, prepared other verses for her than *Birds in the Night*, which is the true history of Brussels. And certainly, with what is still in my heart for her, it should be a *song of songs*, but *habent fata* . . . you decide. As for me, a poor prison brute, I have no judgment now in such things."

In accordance with what I knew to be his wish, I sent a copy of the *Romances sans Paroles* to Mme. Mathilde Verlaine on publication. I received no acknowledgment. The book was printed and produced in February - March 1874. I received the following list of those to whom copies were to be sent, through Verlaine's mother.

"For the press: Jules Claretie, Ernest Lefèvre, Charles Yriarte, Charles Monselet, Paul Mahalin, Ludovic Hans, Armand Silvestre, Paul Courty, Barbey d'Aurevilly, Jules Levallois, Louis Dommartin, and all the other critics Lepelletier may select. With the note: 'From the author.'

"Paul Meurice and Auguste Vacquerie: 'With the author's compliments.'

"In London: M. Camille Barrère, a souvenir of the author; M. Eugène Vermersch, from his friend P. V.; M. Jules Andrieu, in cordial remembrance; M. Dubacq, ditto; M. Guerreau, ditto; M. Swinburne (through MM. Barrère and Andrieu) with the author's compliments; M. Barjau, a souvenir of the author.

"Send all these to M. Barjau, bookseller, Frith Street, Soho, London.

"To MM. Victor Hugo and Théodore de Banville, to my dear master; Leconte de Lisle, with the author's compliments; Alphonse Lemerre, with kind regards; Paul Foucher de Goncourt, with the author's compliments; Emmanuel des Essarts, Carjat, Catulle Mendès, Victor Azam, Antony, Valabrègue, De Heredia, Villiers de l'Isle-Adam, A. France, Léon Dierx, Louis Forain, Valade, Emile Blémont, from his friend; Stéphane Mallarmé, Mérat, Aicard, Elzéar, Bonnier, Fantin, Maître, Charly, Oliveira, very cordially; Coppée, Mlle. Adèle Aneste, Mme. de Callias, F. Régamey, Charles de Sivry, with cordial remembrance."

Also the following note in Verlaine's handwriting:

"Lepelletier will endeavour to collect the reviews and send them to my mother. He will particularly watch *Le National* on Sunday evening, when M. de Banville's dramatic criticisms appear, which at the end frequently deal with books. The publication of this volume will be a great consolation to me. I commend it to Lepelletier's friendship. It will be like a resurrection, I shall be very grateful to him. He can do as he likes about the dedication, though I should prefer it to stand.

"Add to the books in preparation.

"In the press: Londres: *Notes pittoresques*.

"This little work will reach Lepelletier in instalments, and he will try to get it inserted in some paper, under my name or the pseudonym Firmin Dehée."

I did not have to collect the reviews for none appeared; Verlaine was practically dead and buried.

His resurrection was not to come until later. I sent out the copies, but except for two or three of the recipients, kind-hearted and of lesser importance, I received no acknowledgment to transmit to the imprisoned poet.

He wrote to me again on 27th March 1874, pointing out a few printer's errors, but adding that he was

"very satisfied, very satisfied, and very grateful for all the care that has been taken. And now," he went on, "comes the question of the buyer. As to the price per copy, what do you say to two francs? . . . If it could be any higher I should be a hundred miles from raising any opposition. . . . I await with impatience the promised letter of criticism . . . on the said 'work' as you call it so magnificently. Add L.-X. de Ricard, Charles Asselineau, and Gouzien to the free list. . . .

"It would be a good thing to send it to some English and Belgian papers; I can recollect nothing English except the *Pall Mall Gazette*. Send two or three copies for the purpose to Barrère, besides his own, which I am most desirous he should have. (Then followed some suggestions for the Belgian press, and he concluded with the suggestion that it might be well to let them know that he was a prisoner in the country.) It might help me to come out sooner. P. V."

Verlaine worked in his prison, meditating poems, dreaming of plays, studying English. He even wanted to give himself up to regular translations of contemporary English authors, and to found an agency for translation as will be seen later on. Sometimes, for he had a fund of gaiety, occasionally rather vulgar and vaudevillesque, he amused himself by sending me parodies, recalling the good time when he worked on *Le Hanneton* with Coppée. The following was in regard to a rumour which had spread, but was almost immediately contradicted (I had mentioned it to the prisoner) that our Parnassian comrade, Albert Mérat, had hung himself. The poet of the *Chimères*, far from ending his days in the forest of Fontainebleau, is very much alive still. He has been librarian of the Senate House and never ceased to rhyme.

> "Les écrevisses ont mangé mon cœur qui saigne,
> Et me voici logé maintenant à l'enseigne
> De ceux dont Carjat dit: ' *C'était un beau talent,*
> *Mais pas de caractère,*' et je vais, bras ballant,
> Sans limite, et sans but, ainsi qu'un fiacre à l'heure,
> Pâle, *à jeun,* et trouvé trop c... (chose) par Gill qui pleure.
> ' Mourir, dormir ! ' a dit Shakespeare. Si ce n'est
> Que ça, je cours vers la forêt que l'on connait,
> Et puisque c'est fictif, j'y vais pendre à mon aise
> Ton beau poète blond, faune barbizonnaise ! "

"Kind remembrances to your sister. I often hear of you from my mother, who is not well just now. I know that Laura often goes to see her in the solitude in which I think she is wrong to shut herself up, and I am very grateful for the kind attention. My mother will probably come and see me next month, after Easter. She will doubtless remain some weeks in Brussels, where she will see if it is possible to obtain a reduction of my time, which would be most welcome, for it is dreadfully long, and my health, mental and physical, especially during the last few weeks, has not been without various *impedimenta*. In particular, I have blanks of memory and absences of mind which irritate and make me uneasy. I hope to get over all this, but I repeat a reduction of time would not only earn my gratitude, but restore my courage.

"Indeed prison life is not calculated to stimulate one to any intellectual work whatsoever. You speak of verse—for a good long time that has been *given up and over*. All that I can do is to work away at that everlasting English. Truth to say, I know it well enough now to read, without much reference to the dictionary, the Tauchnitz novels which are in the library here. I mean to translate, with a view to its publication by Hachette, a remarkable work by Lady Gullerton, *Ellen Middleton.*

"Meanwhile, I have all ready for the *Renaissance*, since they pay, a delicious story by Dickens, not yet translated. When my mother comes I will send you through her the little manuscript of the pages. If the *Renaissance* does not accept it, will you do me the kindness of placing it in some other paying quarter, and obtaining the money for me? Misfortune has its advantages, and once outside, I am counting on utilising my new acquirement in enterprises of this kind. In London there are a number of good writers full of talent, perfectly unknown in France, who would agree with enthusiasm to translations of their works into our language. The difficulty is not to find them—they swarm— but to find a publisher to undertake to pay for translations, other than those already in circulation. At the worst I would establish a "house" (there are no small traders). Such an enterprise would have no risk. There is money in it, and besides that it would help literature.

"This is only one of my schemes, for I intend, when I come out, to return to Paris (after having obtained in London an assurance of my absolute security), and there I hope to settle down seriously. I have learned to leave nothing to chance, and my first step will be to attach myself to that anchor of well-being, an office. Adventures in literature and translation can come afterwards. I have not given up all hope of returning to the Hôtel-de-Ville. After all, I am neither a deserter nor a Communist, like several we know, who are now peacefully pursuing their occupations. And as to my imprisonment, there is nothing, I dare to flatter myself, dishonouring in that, it is a misfortune, but one that can be repaired, I believe. How I go on talking. I will stop to urge you not to be so slow in replying to me. Besides, you owe me information with regard to my book and the reviews of it. Do not be afraid to give me news. . . . When it reaches me the events are too distant and, as it were, too immemorial to cause me any trouble ; so give yourself a free rein, and keep your promise to write soon."

Here is another letter :

"MONS, 1874.

"I have reflected that it would be best when you write to me to avoid any mention of my new ideas, even to approve them. They are too serious to be dealt with in correspondence, and besides, later on, I hope to have plenty of time to explain them to you. Meanwhile, procure an excellent book which will interest you even from the historical point of view, and will perhaps convince you. Do not be daunted by the too modest title, *Catéchisme de Persévérance*, by Mgr. Gaume. All I can tell you now is that I am feeling in a great, an immense degree, what one experiences when, the first difficulties surmounted, one enters upon a science, an art, a new language, and also that wonderful sense of having escaped a great danger. I entreat you not to say a word to any one of what I write — to any one who does not know me, like those of the Rue Nicolet. Tear up my letter, keeping only the verses (of *Sagesse*). Keep my communications entirely to yourself. If any one asks you after me say that you know I am well, and that I am absolutely converted to the Catholic religion, after mature reflection, being in full possession of my moral liberty and my common sense. . . .

"The poem, *Amoureuse du Diable*, is one of a series of which you already have *L'Impénitence Finale*, and which contains three other little poems, *Crimen Amoris*, *La Grâce*, and *Don Juan Pipé*.

"With my new ideas I do not know if I shall go on with my dramatic projects. I should like to. I have two fine subjects, irreproachable, although very daring, some scenes of which are commenced. These are not the important thing.

"Au revoir! I know now what true courage is. Stoicism is melancholy folly. I have something better; and this something I desire for you, too, my friend. But I can still see a joke. I don't think I am an austere devotee, all gentleness towards others, all submission to The Other, that is my plan."

Solitary confinement had certainly an influence upon Verlaine's ideas, opinions, and mental objectives; but the change had not come about so suddenly as he said, nor so definitely as he believed. The prison led to his conversion and modified his temperament, he declared in *Mes Prisons*, but that book was written a long time afterwards, during a totally different phase. However, at this time two transformations were completed in Verlaine. From an unbeliever, if not militant at least avowed, he became a theoretical believer, a fervent Catholic, —almost a devotee; and, moreover, in his poems he finally abandoned the objective, descriptive, impersonal, impassible method, the force and superiority of which the principal Parnassians extolled, and became a personal, subjective, intimate, impassioned, ironical, and sentimental poet. He sang not of what he saw with his bodily eyes, but with his soul's vision, and from the violin of his heart his poetic bow drew forth harmonies sad and delicate, such as awaken slumbering echoes in other wounded hearts. These two conversions were not the unique result of his incarceration, although naturally such abrupt transplantation would modify any human plant.

We have already noted three stages in our poet's interior development. First, in early youth his classical Voltairian education at the Lycée, then his romantic initiation and the culture of the Parnassians, and thirdly, marriage, patriotic enthusiasm, and a certain exaltation, if not revolutionary, at least democratic, anti-religious. With these periods corresponds a poetical conception, descriptive, objective, pompous, decorative, plastic, virulent, and a trifle declamatory: the *Poèmes Saturniens*, the *Fêtes Galantes*, *La Bonne Chanson*, and *Les Vaincus*. In spite of its personal, almost biographical character, *La Bonne Chanson* was partly objective; while the poet set forth his own desires as a lover, he also expressed the sentiments and ecstasies of a lover in the abstract, the lover in himself, to use the pedantic terminology of the philosophers. There was a general echo, a universal cry in this song which chronicled his love. But already in *La Bonne Chanson* there were indications of transition, evolution. Nature abhors a vacuum, and in the transformation of a soul there are no interruptions nor breaks; each link is indissolubly connected with those preceding and following it.

The *Romances sans Paroles* is linked to *La Bonne Chanson*, and the transition is apparent. He had reached the third stage, with its material changes, its violent perturbations : the siege and its temptations to drink, the Commune and its terrible excesses, the fear of prosecution, the abandonment of regular employment, the days of idleness, the meeting with Arthur Rimbaud, the growing influence of that energetic, interesting, imperious youth, with his incoherent yet expressive verse, which sought for and found colour in the vowels ; then the flight from home, rupture of family ties, and an independent wandering, Bohemian life. His poetry naturally follows the variation in his existence. The *Romances sans Paroles* bears witness to a mental revolution. He is no longer the poet of the *Fêtes galantes* describing the familiar features of the Belgian landscapes. The separation and the law-suit it entailed completed the transformation both of his life and his poetry. His ideas, sentiments, desires, and opinions underwent a radical alteration, and with this change in his mind was a corresponding change in his method of writing. He entered upon a new existence. He dreamed of a new style of verse.

It was not the prison which suggested to him the idea of another system of rhythm, a search for new cadences and metres culminating in an entirely original method of versification. Several times in his letters he spoke to me of an innovation he was contemplating, an idea he wished to put into practice. The complete isolation of his cell doubt-less permitted him to reflect more profoundly on the modifications he proposed to introduce into his method and style, but it was not then that he first conceived the idea. Captivity in its separation, both from people and things, while it constrained him to find resource in himself, he who was so open to outward impressions, also inspired him with new reflections, unwonted thoughts. His sensations were different from those he had experienced in a state of liberty. What wonder, therefore, that he expressed in a new manner the impressions of a new environment, and even as his temperament as a poet was modified, so was his character as a man, but less definitely, for his moral conversion did not last long, at least in an ardent and active state. He divested himself of the old man during these sixteen months of imprisonment, because the penitentiary system necessitated an entire change in his habits and manner of life. As a prisoner he was of necessity sober, which altered him physically and morally, and changed the cast of his mind. His customary excitement was diminished, the habitual irritation of his nerves soothed. By degrees he regained possession of himself, came to his mental senses.

A little shame and a great peace rose from his heart to his lips. He grew gentler, no longer swore, nor, as had been his wont, took the name of God in vain. He blushed at the thought of his past, reproached himself with all the blamable, extravagant, ridiculous, and shocking things he had done. He was no longer irritated against any but himself, and the memory of his errors and misdeeds. In the tranquillity of his cell he proceeded to a strict and rigorous examination of his conscience. He found himself, as it were, placed in front of a mirror, which reflected in turn the various events of his life and the images of those with whom he had come into contact. As he recalled his life, he raised that superb despairing cry, " What have I done with my youth? " Discouragement seized him, and he was a prey to violent moral depression, at the end of his energy, purged of his pride : struggling amidst an ocean of recollections, regrets, irritations, and despair, he sought for a buoy to which to attach himself, a rope to hold on to, a boat as refuge.

While in this state of affliction there awakened in one of the recesses of his troubled brain an emotion, a thought that had for long been slumbering : the religious idea. The conception of help from above took shape in his inner consciousness, and even as mechanically, atavistically the least devout at a critical moment cry out " Mon Dieu," like so many unbelievers at the point of death, he called upon the Lord, and his conversion was effected.

Was it deep and genuine? I do not think so. It was a temporary impulse, an emotion in which reason had no part. I do not mean that Verlaine simulated devotion nor that he was attacked by religious mania. I simply doubt the reality of the return of his childish faith and its capability of persistence. He was not converted by force of reasoning, by conviction, but only by the violence of one of life's storms, by the moral and material tempest in which he felt himself carried away. He invoked God in his anguish ; the trouble past, it remained to be seen if the mood would continue.

Verlaine had made his first communion, like all

the rest of us, in his school days. But his fervour had only been momentary, and his faith like ours, superficial. I affirm that in his youth he did not believe; he had not only grown weary of the practice of religion, but put it away from him for lack of faith. We had read together, among other materialistic works, the book then celebrated and regarded as daring, Doctor Büchner's *Force et Matière*, drawing from it scientific arguments, not for the purpose of cavil and discussion—at our Parnassian gatherings we never spoke of religion, and very rarely of politics—but for the sake of instruction and to fortify our philosophical convictions. From reading and reflection we had become persuaded of the non-existence of the supernatural, the impossibility of a tutelary providence and of another world; we no longer believed in the supremacy of an exterior power, dominating and governing humanity, judging, rewarding, and punishing its every action. Verlaine, therefore, at the age of twenty, was an absolute unbeliever, by force of reason, conviction, and study, and not through gross material indifference, as is the case with those who neither know nor think. His atheism was rational and intelligent.

But the religious instinct, the result of heredity and early education—for at eleven years of age we have all sung hymns and listened to miraculous legends—existed in him; it was slumbering, and trouble awakened it; that childish feeling of appeal to God, the Great Physician, who can cure the ills of the soul, our defence against the evils and dangers that assail and menace us. Besides the chastening of confinement and isolation, and the

examination of his past life, for all these depressing
conditions influenced his feelings and made him
invoke the support of God in his distress, Verlaine
received a brutal blow, not entirely unexpected nor
unforeseen, but resolutely put from him by optimistic
hope and favourable hypothesis, until he had come
to regard it as improbable, if not impossible. This
it was which decided the change and brought about
his conversion.

In his book, *Mes Prisons*, Verlaine minutely
described the interior of his prison, explained its
rules, narrated its exercises, and presented a picture
of himself wearing the melancholy penitentiary
uniform. He sketched the superintendent, whom
he called a charming man, and did not forget a
single detail, mentioning even a little copper crucifix
" with which he was later to become acquainted."
In the first weeks of his incarceration no half-
forgotten prayer rose to the lips of the prisoner
accustomed to complete liberty, even licence and
blasphemy. He read, for books were supplied,
but only secular works. He did not mention the
chaplain, desiring neither his intervention nor his
favour, and the visit not being compulsory avoided it.

But one morning the door of his cell opened
and the good - natured superintendent appeared.
He seemed saddened by some melancholy communication he had to make to his prisoner. " My
poor friend," he said to Verlaine, who started up
on his bed with something of the terror of those
condemned to die, " I bring you bad news. Courage.
Read this." And he handed him a stamped paper,
the legal declaration of a separation between Paul
Verlaine and Mathilde Mauté, his wife.

Thus the dreams of peace, reconciliation, restored happiness, and a regular life which Verlaine's mind had harboured, even in the height of his indignation, faded away. While he had been in prison the hope had revived, and knowing nothing of what was going on, for he received no letters, and his mother did not enlighten his ignorance, he had lived in a fool's paradise ; therefore the blow fell heavily upon him and overwhelmed him. He recovered himself, but the wound was deep and incurable. To quote his own words :

"I fell back in tears upon my poor bed. A grasp of the hand and a pat on the shoulder from the superintendent gave me back a little courage, and it was but an hour or two afterwards I begged that the chaplain would come and speak to me. He came and I asked him for a catechism. He immediately gave me the one on perseverance by Mgr. Gaume."

Thus was Verlaine's conversion effected. It would seem from his manner of relating it that there was something factitious in such suddenness. In his loneliness and misery he set out upon this new road, at first with anxiety, afterwards with hope and even joy, but when his circumstances changed he fell back into his old ways.

Once more free, and back again among his old companions, he lost the fervour of the neophyte, and his faith evaporated, leaving only a superficial and poetical taste for religion. There seemed to have been something of hysteria in the manifestations following his conversion, and judging from his narrative I should say that his mystic adoration

was tinged with literary dilettantism. On the
wall of his cell there hung above the regulation
little copper crucifix, a lithograph representing the
Sacré-Cœur. The continual sight of this image
accelerated his conversion; as a luminous, attractive,
dominating point, it exercised a sort of hypnotic
effect.

"Something, I know not what or whom, suddenly
raised me," said Verlaine, "threw me out of bed,
and without even leaving me time to dress prostrated me sobbing and weeping at the foot of the
crucifix, and of that other image which has evoked
the strangest, and in my eyes the most sublime
devotion of modern times."

Again he asked for the chaplain. "I would
have been martyred for my faith," he confessed,
and he cried out for the worthy ecclesiastic, who was
a little surprised at the vivacity of the catechumen in
the excitement of his new experience: "I know, I
believe, I am undeceived," and claimed on the spot
absolution for his sins after a general confession of
them. The prudent chaplain, however, postponed
the unloading of the overcharged conscience of his
urgent penitent, and it took place later. Verlaine
describing it, said:

"I received humbly and contritely, after my very
veracious and conscientious confession, a benedic-
tion, but not at once the greatly coveted absolution.
While awaiting it, in accordance with the advice
of my spiritual director, I resumed my occupations,
varied reading and the making of pious verse
principally. *Sagesse* dates from about this period."
(*Mes Prisons*, pp. 60-61.)

Verlaine's conversion was, therefore, both moral and poetical. Although he had seldom used religious terminology in his early poems he had deep down in his memory a stock of suitable phrases, a vocabulary all ready for the rendering of devotional feelings, and he experienced not only the new birth of his soul, but also a renewal of all the poetical structures, dirty and dusty with time and wear, which he and other poets had built in accordance with set and almost invariable plans. The *Parnasse* had been Pagan, Oriental, Colonial, and Scandinavian, invoking all the divinities issued from the imagination and the terror of men, Baghavat, Yaveh, Kronos, Isis, Odin : Jesus alone had been ignored. Verlaine estimated that without undertaking to sing the Christian cosmogony, there was in the Catholic sentiment, in the preciosity and delicacy of the adoration of Christ and the Virgin Mary, a very rebirth of poetry to be sought for, found, and interpreted. Thus he translated the unction of the catechism of Mgr. Gaume, and set it to metre inspired by Desbordes-Valmore. In this way most of the verses of *Sagesse* were contemplated, rhymed, and written. A large number of the poems figuring in this delightful and affecting collection came to me in manuscript, always on the common bluish or dirty white paper supplied by the canteen with the office stamp in the centre.

After Verlaine's conversion his letters became more rare, either that he feared raillery from me, or that he felt some embarrassment at writing down sentiments so new to him.

A letter he wrote to me, giving details regarding the state of his soul and analysing his religious aspirations, never reached me. At the last moment he changed his mind and sent me merely the following note at a later date :

"Mons, 8th September 1874.

"My letter of the 22nd August for grave reasons was not despatched. I now send you this postscript, dated 8th September : still four months, fourteen days! If a concession is not granted I shall be greatly surprised . . . If you do me the immense kindness of writing to me, make no allusion to this P.S. nor the verses, and do not tell any one that you have heard from me. This is the last poem of which I spoke."

Here the verses followed, and at the end of the P.S. he announced :

"I have absolutely experienced it all, I assure you. It would be necessary to undergo all I have undergone for the last three years : humiliations, scorn, insults, in order to realise the admirable consolation, reason, and logic there is in this religion, so terrible and yet so sweet. Terrible, yes, but man is so evil, has fallen so low . . . I say nothing of the historical, scientific, and other proofs which are dazzling when one has the immense happiness of being out of this abominable, effete, old, foolish, proud, cursed society of ours.

"Have I told you that I am working hard at English? I have read Shakespeare without a translation, and Latin, the Bible, and lastly Spanish for use later. What a language! what things to read! Therefore good-bye for a very little while, for I must return to France to prepare for the law-suit which arises out of no desire of mine. But as on the whole I am less stupid than father Mauté, as certainly I am more honest, . . . he

only deals in lies, inventions, and slanders, I fear
nothing from a good big publicity, which, nevertheless, I would prefer not to provoke. Besides I am
expecting schemes and snares. . . . It is clear
they will try all sorts of things when I am free,
but at each caress or threat I shall cry: ' Down
with your paws!' One day my wife may come to
repentance . . . . in such case she will find complete forgetfulness, pardon, happiness, what am I
saying? But you will understand. If you could
but know how detached I am from everything outside prayer and meditation."

From this letter it may be seen that religion
was gradually transforming Verlaine; moreover, he
was ill, and had but a vague hope of ever resuming
his married life. His troubles grew upon him. He
anxiously awaited a remission of part of his sentence,
but it never came. Official silence was the only
response to all appeals on the part of his family and
friends. He was like one shipwrecked in the darkness, who for the moment inspirited by a deceptive
gleam of light, when once more plunged in impene-
trable gloom, incapable of further effort, abandons
himself meekly to unconsciousness and oblivion.

Yet the prison was to a certain extent for
him an inspiring, creative force — a very rare
phenomenon. In the case of the majority of
writers, philosophers, and poets who have undergone a long term of imprisonment, the imagination
dries up and the impulse to create becomes sterile.
That the air of the prison is poisonous to flowers
of thought many examples prove, but the author of
Sagesse was an exception. Religion did not occupy
all his thoughts and verse. He had fits of lyrical

eroticism of which his later works bear traces. In his penitentiary solitude, between reading Gaume's *Catechism* and writing a poetic invocation to prayer or a hymn to the Virgin, Verlaine composed love poems of an impassioned and not very edifying character.

It was in prison, recalling the discourses of Arthur Rimbaud and his peculiar ideas with regard to metre, that he thought out lyrical combinations, in which a new music of verse played an important part, not only accompanying the idea, but evoking feeling, recollection, association, just as a perfume to the refined senses of certain beings calls up actual visions, distinct images, beings, and things almost tangible. The admiration he had long felt for Baudelaire had part in the new conception. The title, *Romances sans Paroles*, determined upon long after the varied poems which make up this interesting collection were composed, although apparently suggested by Mendelssohn, was a summing-up, a synthesis, of this new theory of verse. With the misfortunes that darkened his life came, as is the case with every poet, the desire to unburden his woe, to perpetuate it in his work. Art was a powerful anesthetic. He treated himself to a course of personal impassioned verse. He renounced the poetry of his early years. The *Poèmes Saturniens* and the *Fêtes galantes* were like flowers cultivated scientifically in the classic *parterres*, French or exotic, of the *Parnasse*, while the *Romances sans Paroles*, *Sagesse*, and the other poems alluded to in his letters from the prison of Brussels and Mons, were fruits of bitterness, watered by tears, ripened in gloom, the untended wild flowers of solitude, like those plants of phosphorescent gleam and extraordinarily contorted shapes, their interiors filled with ashes, which grow in dense forests wherein no sun nor joyous life ever penetrates.

All appeals for a reduction of his sentence were put aside, probably without examination. The Belgians were merciless. We had pointed out that the offence, in accordance with the law, merited at most a sentence of a few days' imprisonment, and the Belgian Government would have earned respect by rectifying the error of its judges, and modifying the excessive penalty. It must be remembered, however, that no such suggestion came from France. Apart from Blémont and myself, none of Verlaine's old friends bestirred themselves on his behalf; and he had three who were already very influential at this period; I will not name them. Almost all the literary lights, whose friendship was under eclipse, have since shone upon Verlaine's glory, and claimed the honour of projecting their lights upon his tomb.

So, like the worst of criminals, he worked out the whole of his sentence. He did not come out of his official tomb until the 16th January 1875.

It may be asserted that the imprisonment, which modified Verlaine's poetical temperament, also changed his character, placed him, as it were, outside society, and predisposed him to the excesses and eccentricities of every kind which troubled his existence and his talent during the third phase of his glorious and miserable life.

Often in prison are unfortunately contracted physical infirmities which cause suffering, and mortal maladies which cause death.

Y

CHAPTER XIII

VERLAINE A SCHOOLMASTER IN ENGLAND AND IN
FRANCE—LUCIEN LÉTINOIS—VERLAINE A FARMER

(1875-1881)

MADAME VERLAINE awaited her son at the gate
of the prison. What effusions! What joy to hold
her dear Paul once more to her heart! It was
eighteen months since she had seen him except
at a distance, under the eye of an official, and
behind a grating. He was conducted to the
frontier by a police escort, being the object of a
special decree of expulsion. His mother, who
made the journey third-class in the same train
as far as the frontier, amidst light-hearted people,
travelling under the same conditions as the poet,
hastened, when his guard had left him, to take
him for rest and the re-establishment of his moral
and physical health to her relations at Arras,
Fampoux, and from there to the Ardennes. Very
happily he went with her. A new life opened
before him; was his heart new too? He wrote
to me from Fampoux some days after he left
Mons.

"FAMPOUX, 25th January, chez M. Julien Dehée,
near Arras.

"I reply a little late, my dear Edmund, to your
kind letter of 31st December last, but the un-

338

certainty of the date of my departure, the *ennui* of writing *per angusta*, and also the desire to surprise you with a sudden visit one morning— a thing much more amusing than a letter—has delayed me until now.   I and my mother have been here since the 16th, staying with very kind relations.   I cannot say if I shall return to Paris shortly.   They are all so kind here, and it is good to breathe the air of the country even in a north wind, and the great town does not tempt me yet.   At the same time, I trust it will not be long before we meet. . . . We will talk over my plans.   You will probably find me very much changed; my health is rapidly improving.   I hope you and yours are well.   You are right in thinking one of my first visits will be to you, my dear friend. . . ."

I saw Verlaine only in passing, as it were, one February afternoon, when we plucked a chaplet of recollections. He set out again for the north and the Ardennes, to pay a visit to some relations there, but rumours of his troubles had got about and he received scant welcome.   Still under the influence of the impressions received in prison, and his conversation with the chaplain, he reflected with gravity upon his situation.   He was in haste to quit the unfriendly hearth at which he found himself.   What should he do?   There was one refuge always open to receive him, one heart always warm towards him, at the Batignolles, where his mother awaited him.   It would be pleasant to live with her, but her income was very small.   Should he compass her ruin by forcing her to break in upon her capital?   No, indeed! It was, therefore, necessary to plan out a life apart, but where, and how? The idea of farming occurred to him, later to be put into practice. At present, although he was greatly disposed towards country life, he put this suggestion from him; probably he had not the necessary capital at his disposal to buy or rent a farm, and he was, moreover, too much of a novice to embark on such an enterprise alone. If one of his cousins, a Dehée or Dujardin, would have gone into it with him, he would certainly have turned agriculturist, but the lack of enthusiasm which greeted the announcement of his intention both in Artois and the Ardennes, caused him to renounce the idea, only, as will be seen later, for a time.

Should he turn towards literature? But what branch of literature? He knew from me and many others the vicissitudes of journalism, how difficult it was to obtain definite employ. He felt no aptitude for it; he could not and would not turn out paying copy, topical paragraphs, reviews, serials. He felt indisposed for novels or critical studies such as a publisher might accept. The drama he knew to be practically inaccessible. As to poetry, his own particular art, as a matter of fact, an income was necessary for its exercise. The four volumes already published, had they not been issued at his own expense? He could not count upon the manuscript of *Sagesse*, which he had brought with him from prison nearly completed, as an instrument of fortune or even as a momentary resource. And then literature meant Paris; he did not want to live in that great town. He had spoken to me very frankly on the matter at our brief interview. He felt as if he had lost his place—become a stranger there. Several of his letters written in prison bore witness to his annoyance at the calumnies spread about him. He knew that the old comrades whom he met would pretend to know nothing of them, but he could not rely upon support and esteem in our old Parnassian circle. He wanted oblivion, silence, effacement, and that was not the way to get on in the literary world.

Moreover, he felt the necessity of beginning a new life which would enable him to forget the old one. He must prove to every one, and especially his mother, in regard to whom he felt some little shame, which accentuated his desire to earn his own living, that he had become another man. Work, and a regular, punctual, middle - class, perhaps one day even family life, would furnish indisputable proof. He desired that there should be no shadow of doubt as to his firm resolution. To leave Paris was the first step; a stay there was perilous. He must not fall back into his old disorderly ways. He had made, as it were, a vow to get drunk no more. Would he give the lie to the sceptical proverb regarding the duration of such promises. In Paris, where temptation abounded, he could not guarantee an affirmative. He doubted his force of resistance among such surroundings. Idleness and aimlessness abandoned for ever, dissipations and the wine-shop avoided even by flight, and regular honest work, without rest or pleasure, such things would prove to his mother, to old friends, to every one—who knows? perhaps even to Her, towards whom his thoughts always insensibly turned—the sincerity of his repentance and the

firmness of his new vocation. Therefore an existence apart, outside Paris as much as possible, and
work bringing in sufficient for a livelihood, this was
the problem to be solved. Thus he put it to himself, and he found the solution with a decision of
which he very rarely gave an example.

The difficulty was complicated thus : he desired
to obtain employment, and at the same time to
be out of reach of the temptation of the wine-shop
and the street. This condition suddenly inspired
him. He examined his means of work. All that
he had at his disposal for the purpose of gaining his
bread, besides his diploma of *Bachelier-ès-Lettres*,
was a little Latin, furbished up in prison, and an
acquaintance, already rather extended, with the
English language.

He resolved to make use of it ; he felt capable
of giving lessons, and realised that it would have
to be in a school. He did not fear lack of liberty ;
he had grown accustomed to that. He, therefore,
sought for an establishment where he could be
lodged, fed, and kept ; and where he would teach
what he knew—French, Latin, and English. He
had heard of boarding - schools in England, and
thither he turned his eyes.

On the other side of the strait were to be found
forgetfulness, tranquillity, peaceful labour, and an
honourable livelihood. He had acquired some
practical ideas during his experience of English life.
He knew what an important part the advertisement plays in every business matter with our
neighbours, and did not hesitate to address to two
or three newspapers through an agent he knew,
M. E. Rolland, Advertising Office, Great Wind-

mill Street, one sufficiently eloquent offering lessons in French and literature in exchange for board and lodging. It was necessary to perfect himself in the English language—hence the modesty of his demands. He had not to wait long for a response, and the following letter, dated 10th April, informed me of his residence in England, and new position.

"STICKNEY.

"Here I am a professor . . . in an English village. There is no one around me who can speak a word of French. . . . I teach French, Latin . . . and drawing. I am sufficiently accomplished for these three labours. And I teach in English . . . what English! but during the eight days I have been here I have improved.

"Family life : Mr Andrews is a young man who reads French as I read English, but who does not speak it . . . charming, cordial, very well informed. My pupils are very well brought up children, who teach me English while I teach them French, which is exactly what I want. How long shall I remain here? Three or six months, according to my progress in speaking and understanding. Then I shall seriously set about earning my living in this country, where my mother, I hope, will join me.

"I have no distractions and seek none. Much reading, walks with the pupils (not in rank and file, nothing of that sort here) across magnificent meadows full of sheep, etc. It is astonishing how well I have become morally and physically in these eight days.

"I sowed on my journey to London the seeds of relations which will be useful to me one day. Nothing of the refugees, of course. . . . Lissagaray, I am told, is in hiding ; Vermersch is in Switzerland ; Andrieu has got his own place. That is all.

"You will send me some news. Some fresh gossip about my 'mysterious departure' must be circulating in the Rue Fontaine, Montmartre (where his wife's family was). If they could see me in my new incarnation I daresay they would be *astonished*.

"More details shortly; drawings, verses, etc. . . . For the moment a recommendation : do not divulge my address until instructed; reasons very serious. You will thank Dierx for his volumes. I await impatiently a long and substantial letter from you.

"My address is : M. P. Verlaine, at M. W. Andrews, Stickney Grammar School, Boston, Lincolnshire.

"My village is Stickney, two or three miles from Boston; but the address is as above. *Silince*."

Thus he lived peacefully employed in regular work in the homely boarding-school. He wrote to me comparatively little during his time there. More than once he declared himself completely absorbed in his occupations. He allowed his muse to slumber. They were months of contemplation and spiritual and material abstinence. He remained a year and a half with M. Andrews.

Ennui and the desire to see his mother again caused him to leave the Stickney establishment. He wrote to his mother, who came to join him at Arras. In that cold and gloomy garrison town he led a quiet, and, judging from the following letter, very regular life, busy with the revision of the manuscript of *Sagesse*, with an idea of speedy publication ; it was not issued, however, until 1880.

"ARRAS, *2nd August* 1876.

"I write to recall to you your promise, and am counting the days until the arrival in my solitude of the first part of the *Chien du Commissaire* (a novel by E. Lepelletier).

"You will accompany it with a very long letter with *plenty of details* about everything, literature, etc.

"Here, I live more and more like a hermit. I have even renounced the Café Sans-Peur, or only go there on Saturday afternoons to see the pictures in the illustrated papers. The rest of the week the *Figaro* bought at a kiosk—for we have had a kiosk here for some time—suffices for the requirements of my present existence. I versify to death, and occupy myself greatly with English. I send you two fragments of my book *Sagesse*, which will be ready in October, when I return to Paris. Be indulgent to these productions, and, if, for yourself, you have something in your portfolio do not forget to communicate it.

"2, IMPASSE D'ELBRONNE, ARRAS.

"Maman joins with me in compliments to you all."

He returned to England and settled at Boston, near Stickney, intending to live by giving private lessons. But whether from lack of pupils or introductions he did not succeed, and sought for another school to which to attach himself. He was soon entered as a professor of French in an establishment directed by M. Remington at Bournemouth.

Several of the poems in *Sagesse* were written at Bournemouth, in particular those numbered XIII. and XV. in the complete works: *L'Eclaboussement des Haies* which in his first MS. Verlaine had entitled *Paysage en Lincolnshire* and *La Mer est plus Belle*, designated by the title *La Mer de Bournemouth*.

In a letter dated from Bournemouth and containing these two poems he spoke of his project of returning to France soon.

"*7th September* 1877.

"I have received the first part of this *Chien*, read it with great pleasure, and only await the remainder to devour it open-mouthed. I will make some trifling observations with regard to it *viva voce*.

"I intend to return to Paris shortly, as it is the time when appointments are to be obtained in schools. One of my first visits will be to the Rue Coq-Héron (my office), to the printing-house Dubuisson (afterwards Bougival).

"I would ask you to be on the alert for any opening for me. If you see Herbault (our old professor) explain to him the case of his ex-pupil. Do all you can.

"I have in my pocket two splendid English certificates, signed by the local authorities, and confirmed at the French Consulate in London. You see I have turned to advantage your excellent advice of two months ago.

"I have masses of verse. A volume very nearly finished. Try to unearth me a publisher not too exacting. You shall see it soon. I enclose a little specimen. . . ."

After a stay in Paris, where he remained in retirement, avoiding rather than seeking his old companions, he found, through his friend Ernest Delahaye, professor in an ecclesiastical college at Rethel, an appointment which he accepted. He determined rather abruptly on the change, and wrote to me about it in the following letter:

"RETHEL, 14*th November* 1878.

"You will have understood that I did not take leave of you nor write to you during the last six weeks, because it was an absolute impossibility. I was counting on at least another week of leisure in Paris, and prepared to give myself the pleasure of asking you for a *déjeuner* in your castle at Bougival, when a letter from the head of the college came, instructing me to set out by the first train on the following day at latest; so I had to re-organise my plans, and put aside all correspondence likely to be lengthy.

" To-day I have a little time to breathe, and I take the opportunity of sending you and yours my cordial greetings. I am a professor of literature, history, geography, and English here—all agreeable and distracting subjects. The system is excellent. Room to myself. No underhand surveillance; nothing which recalls the university 'boxes,' lycées, municipal colleges, or *pensions*. The majority of the professors—Latin, Greek, and Mathematical— are ecclesiastics, and I am naturally on the best terms with these gentlemen, who are cordial, simple people, of a kindly gaiety, and, without animosity, or humbug. In short, it is a sort of haven for me, where I have peace, calm, and liberty to think and act as I like — inestimable benefit. Salary reasonable.

" Of politics I take no heed. I have abandoned myself entirely to literature, not paying—alas !— (and yet!) except in personal satisfaction. I have given a name to the verse of which I will send you a formidable slice, so that you may taste this 'delicate' feast.

" The town is insignificant. . . .

" If, sometime, as an influential publicist you can procure *La Tentation de Saint Antoine* by Flaubert, a book which, it appears, treats the subject intelligently, send it to me, if you please, as soon as possible.

" Write to me, College Notre - Dame, Rethel

(Ardennes), and do not give my address to any one. My family, M. Istace, and Nouveau are the only people in Paris who know my present *Thébaïde* . . ."

Verlaine was, doubtless, a rather unusual professor, and his lessons were certainly stamped by an originality and depth not to be found in those of either his predecessors or successors. It would be matter for astonishment if something from his teaching did not remain with his various pupils at Stickney, Bournemouth, and, more particularly, Rethel.

It is true he was not very strong in Latin and other University subjects, but he had a solid basis of classical knowledge. He knew the Latin authors well, had ideas about Greek drama, and was familiar with our great writers of the seventeenth century. He lacked, perhaps, education in history, and I suspect he obtained his ideas with regard to it from Barbey d'Aurevilly's volume on historians.

But history and mathematics apart, for he knew nothing of figures nor algebraical signs, Verlaine may be considered as having fulfilled, not only conscientiously, but competently, his professional duties. At Rethel he had the two specialities of French literature, in which his knowledge was indisputable, and the English language. He knew English well, although his pronunciation was defective; however, his pupils had to be content with it. Mallarmé, who was also a professor of English, but in a Paris lycée, joked his colleague about it afterwards.

Keeping a watch over himself, and affecting a sedate demeanour without being hypocritical,

Verlaine rapidly acquired the esteem of the college ecclesiastics. The head and the professor of literature, Eugène Royer, found him rather too reserved; the masters among themselves casting aside their professional stiffness. The professor of rhetoric, named Dogny, tried to get to know his uncommunicative colleague, a debatable, linguistic point being the occasion of his attempt. Verlaine, on whom at bottom his aloofness weighed heavily, asked nothing better than to respond to those who appeared desirous of being friendly, and from that time he lived on a footing of very agreeable intimacy with the other members of the staff, and always retained a most happy recollection of his stay in this pious and learned house where they knew nothing of his past.

He was silent in regard to his antecedents. It was supposed from what he let fall concerning his travels and the literary culture of which, in spite of himself, he gave serious proof, that he had occupied a good position, and, owing to a reverse of fortune, was obliged to resort to teaching. No one suspected that the college, so like a convent, was harbouring one of the greatest poets of the age, who had, moreover, been guilty of sometimes excessive extravagances. His punctuality in class and chapel, the grave manner in which he gave his lessons, his edifying demeanour, and regularity in religious observances, left no room for recognising the Verlaine proceeding from Villon. In spite of the pious sentiments of which he gave daily examples, not one of the simple priests suspected in him the author of magnificent hymns, the only modern religious poet.

In several letters at this period Verlaine sang the praises of his colleagues, and of the charm and peace of this almost conventual retreat. He tasted a novel and secret enjoyment: that of being ignored, which is a joy of subtle flavour, and only accorded to a small number of beings.

In his solitary chamber, cell-like in appearance, Verlaine experienced an intense, quasi - perverse pleasure in correcting and copying out verses by turns mournful, sentimental, passionate, religious, and amorous, hiding them away like some secret sin. With an ironical and proud satisfaction he said to himself: "No eye sees me open my mysterious poems, no ear hears the silent chant of my rhythms, and no one among all the good people in this college imagine that I am Verlaine, Paul Verlaine, the saturnine poet, the precious poet of the *Fêtes galantes*, the poet, sensitive, suffering, fantastic, and mocking of the *Romances sans Paroles*, and soon to be the great Christian poet of *Sagesse.*"

Later the good priests learned, not without naïve emotion, what an extraordinary guest they had harboured; but in spite of the explanation given they did not know all about the personage they had seen modestly sitting in their refectory, joining in their simple conversations, interesting himself in the little matters of their everyday life, kneeling with them in chapel, and like them, correcting the pupils' exercises. The professor of rhetoric likened him to Apollo in the house of Admetus. They were neither scandalised nor annoyed. The religious merits of the poet were skilfully emphasised, and to the head, harassed with the difficulties of the time and the hostility of legislators, were quoted the indignant lines on the exiled priests : " Vous reviendrez bientôt les bras pleins de pardons, vous reviendrez, vieillards exquis. . . ." It was said that a master so highly esteemed in the thinking world would do honour to the house in which he had taught, and silence was maintained as to those unfortunate rumours which accompanied the poet's fame. The pupils participated in this feeling. In 1897 the old boys of the college of Notre Dame organised a banquet in Paris in honour of their illustrious professor. On the *ménu* was a bust of the poet surrounded by Fame, with the town of Rethel and its college detached in a nimbus of glory, and at the conclusion of the banquet a eulogy on Verlaine was delivered by one of the organisers, M. Jean Bourguignon of the *Revue d'Ardenne et d'Argonne.*

Verlaine rather abruptly cast off the frock-coat of the professor, leaving the college and the professorial chair for the farm and the plough, to become an agriculturist. This unexpected determination, like everything else, had its explanation ; in the first place, he had a desire which became much more persistent—it manifested itself very strongly some years later, when at his urgent request I endeavoured to obtain his reinstatement in the Government offices — of re-entering the ranks of society, and obtaining regular employment at a fixed salary, poetry to be regarded as a relaxation and consolation in times of trouble. Secondly, he had always had a love for the soil, for country things and rustic life. He came of a family who lived on the land, and was tempted to return to the surroundings so congenial to them.

What decided him, perhaps, was one of his impulses—strange, powerful, and much misunderstood—towards friendship. I have already alluded to the strength of the attachments he conceived for various comrades : one of his Dujardin cousins, Lucien Viotti, Arthur Rimbaud. Science and history have determined the purely platonic character of such feelings. The most celebrated philosophers of antiquity displayed an affection, passing the bounds of ordinary friendship, for some of their disciples. In the case of Socrates, it had the effect of propagating his teachings, attaching hearts, and dominating minds ; a psychic communion being established between master and disciple. Verlaine, who especially in his latter years, had the innocent whim, in certain hours of expansion, of treating his young friends, Maurice du Plessys, Anatole Baju, Cazals, not in secret, but quite openly in the café, in paternal fashion, did not escape the suspicion of the evil-minded ; but he simply shrugged his shoulders and emptied his glass of absinthe in company with the women of his choice, ill - favoured enough, but complaisant and gay : Esthers, Philomnènes, and Eugénies.

Verlaine's new friendship was for one of his pupils, Lucien Létinois, the son of a farmer, born at Coulommes, in the Ardennes, on 27th February 1860 ; a tall, pale, slim, awkward youth, with a melancholy and simple air ; a rough-hewn rustic, slightly pretentious, and rather sentimental ; the shepherd of a comic opera. His father, a shrewd countryman, had put him to college, desirous of making a gentleman, a clerk, perhaps an official of him. Little is precisely known about this peasant scholar. Verlaine has been sparing of details in regard to him in his autobiographies and confessions in prose; but, on the other hand, he has celebrated, poetised, idealised, and extolled him in verse. Not being able, like the Emperor Hadrian, to erect a mausoleum in stone to this Ardennaise Antinoüs, he constructed the *Amour*, a lyrical monument apparently indestructible. He traced a portrait of the young man, doubtless flattering, but with a graceful touch. A distant echo of the *Odes* of Anacreon and Virgil's *Eclogues* murmurs in the delicate lines, in which he pictured his young friend gliding " marvellously " over the ice. Following upon this imaginary description, he shows us his comrade against the majestic and tranquil background of the fields engaged in wholesome rustic labour. The young man was religious, another motive for Verlaine's attachment to him.

Poor rudderless boat, he hoped unceasingly to find a haven in religion. It was not goodwill that he lacked, but true faith and conviction. He had read overmuch in his youth of Louis Büchner, Moleschott, Feuerbach, and other scientific materialistic philosophers. He hoped that this young and simple believer with whom he disputed, and who opposed to his doubts *sa foi de charbonnier*, would support and lead him along the pathway of faith.

Verlaine afterwards evoked a remembrance of his friend as a soldier, for in the poems devoted to him in *Amour* he pictured him in twenty different characters and as many attitudes, real and fictitious. Lucien Létinois went through his military service, brutally cut short by death, in an artillery regiment in Paris. This recollection haunted Verlaine's saddened spirit, and he poured out his grief in some exquisite lines. He partly explained the affection he felt for this young son of the fields. " J'ai la fureur d'aimer!" he clamoured; a cry right from the heart. Moreover, this sentiment for a youth much younger than himself, who was not in the same position and lacked his artistic education, was largely paternal. Verlaine found again in him the son who was lost, dead to him.

Shortly after the poet had left the house of his wife's parents, the scene of daily quarrels, a son was born to his wife. The law gave the child into the charge of his mother, and she out of her modest resources provided for the needs and education of young Georges. When he attained adolescence she married again, and had other children, and desired to apprentice her son to some trade by which he could gain his living. She therefore sent him to a clockmaker's at Orléans; which Verlaine, hearing of, approved, even making some comments favourable to the trade of clockmaker.

Georges Verlaine did not pursue this calling. He returned to his mother in Belgium. He was engaged in military service, and unfortunately ill in hospital when his father died; the two never met. When young Georges had finished his term, he came at once to me in Paris. I was struck with his strong resemblance, with greater regularity of feature and symmetry of visage, to his father at eighteen years of age. He remained with me some time as secretary, and acted in the same capacity to M. Joseph Uzanne. Afterwards he became clerk in a library, and finally I obtained a position for him on the Metropolitain, where he is still. He is married, and I was his witness. He has a great respect for his father's memory, and having no desire to mix himself up in the conjugal quarrel, while loving his mother and recognising her care and sacrifices for him, he conceived a profound admiration for his father's genius, and instituted himself with laudable pride the guardian of his father's fame and works, personally superintending the publication of the last edition of the complete works.

Although he never had the joy of embracing his son, nor the possibility of occupying himself with him, Verlaine often thought of the little being, his sole offspring, born of a unique and great love, who grew up away from him, and perhaps would never know him, or despise him. The boy's destiny occupied his thoughts. What an interesting page that is in which, imagining his son to be of an age for soldiering, he gives him advice, exhorting him to serve his country, and endeavours to make of him a good soldier, an honest man, and also a good Christian. Verlaine wrote this lay sermon in 1874, in his cell at Mons. In it he asked his son when serving under the flag to care nothing for the opinion of others, but to perform the whole duty of a Christian, regardless of the foolish and the wicked. He gave him a perfect code of conduct. He was, alas, experienced in more than one of these matters : he had known and succumbed to the temptations against which he endeavoured to put the young conscript of 1880 on his guard : women and drink. "A little glass of brandy, a common and inoffensive refreshment, invites to a second, which warms you, and to a third which excites you; the fourth habituates you to it, and after that is the beginning of the end, in what disaster!"

Verlaine went a little farther in his wise counsels, imitating those Anglican preachers, the teetotallers. In the same way he exaggerated when, as if he foresaw latter-day conflicts, he advised his soldier son not to serve against "God and His ministers," speaking in the character of the catechumen of Belgian prisons, rather than in that of the son of an officer obliged to submit to any order whatsoever. It is true he finished his exhortation with the words: "Be French, though!"

On several occasions he evoked the image of his son in his poems and in his prose writings. The volume *Amour* concludes with this noble apostrophe to Georges Verlaine:

> "Voici mon testament:
> Crains Dieu, ne hais personne, et porte bien ton nom,
> Qui fut porté dûment."

The exigency of his affection impelled Verlaine, when Lucien Létinois quitted the college, to follow him. He renounced the calm of collegiate life for that of the country. He gave in his resignation, left Rethel, and installed himself at Coulommes with Lucien Létinois. The young man's parents did not view his arrival with displeasure. They had all the rural avidity, and reckoned on making something out of this town gentleman who wanted to turn rustic. Here, then, was Verlaine a countryman, and before long a farmer. There were two rustic periods in the life of the poet. The first, from 1878 to 1881, was comparatively peaceful. Verlaine, after spending some time with the parents of his friend, reading, smoking, dreaming, and writing a little, resolved to become a regular agriculturist. Létinois's parents encouraged and stimulated him. Verlaine persuaded his mother to join him. She, always desirous of pleasing her son, fearing for him the temptations of the town, and not having much of an opinion of the profession of lyrical poet, strongly approved his project. A farm was therefore bought at Juniville. The acquisition was made in the name of Létinois's father. Verlaine pretended that there would be danger in buying in his own name a property which might be pounced upon by his wife claiming provision and costs in the action for separation. In reality he had no such fear, the costs of the action having already been paid. Besides Verlaine could have bought the property in his mother's name. She herself was dissatisfied with the arrangement, which left her son a prey to the Létinois's.

The new farmer interested himself chiefly in the play of sunlight among the leaves, the clearness of the morning, and the splendour of the sunset. He has described in very beautiful Georgic verse his labours and his pleasures in the Ardennes country. He was very desirous of setting his hands to the plough, but they were more accustomed to the lyre. He lacked experience in directing a farm, and often hindered the young Létinois, whose aptitude was greater in his work. They talked and idled. "Our attempt at farming had a sad end," the poet confessed. As the saying goes, they were eating money, and the earth, rebellious against those she regards as intruders, did not yield the townsman even the equivalent of the money he lavished on her. Létinois's father looked on, saying neither "yes" nor "no," and awaiting the climax.

Verlaine, disgusted, losing his head in the face of threats, intimidated by the reception of certain stamped papers, perhaps at bottom tired of farming, and desirous of recommencing with Lucien Létinois the wanderings of former years in company with Rimbaud, resolved to leave and persuade Lucien to accompany him. One fine morning the farm found itself without inhabitants. Létinois's father, in order to take care of the property which was legally his, although he had not disbursed a penny upon it, installed himself at Juniville. Later he sold the farm to his own profit, naturally.

On leaving Juniville Verlaine went with his young friend to his usual goal in time of trouble— London—in order to forget the disappointments of farming, and the gossip of the village which had sprung up in regard to their friendship; but their visits could not be prolonged on account of lack of funds. It was necessary to return to Paris, where Verlaine's mother was. Moreover, Létinois's father, having sold Verlaine's farm, had just established himself at 14 Rue de Paris, Ivry, and Verlaine and his mother took up their abode in the Rue des Parchamps, Boulogne-sur-Seine.

During this period, between two essays at rustic life (1881-1883), Verlaine made the attempt, unsuccessful, as has been narrated above, "to obtain reinstatement" in the Government offices. At the same time he endeavoured to regain his footing in the literary world of Paris. It was at this time that I introduced him to the *Réveil*, and he published *Sagesse* with Palmé, the publisher; it did not create the least sensation. We will return in the next chapter to this period in Verlaine's literary career, confining ourselves at present to the termination of his career as farmer.

A disaster suddenly overtook him. Lucien Létinois was carried off by typhoid fever in the Hôpital de la Pitié, and Verlaine experienced violent grief. In his book, *Amour*, he poured out his sorrow in beautiful lines, equal, if not superior, to those in the *Contemplations*, in which Victor Hugo lamented the tragic death of his daughter Léopoldine. In this requiem Verlaine employed an incomparable simplicity, sorrowful and homely phrases, which cause the reader's inmost being to vibrate as if to the melancholy and grave sounds of the violoncello. Few poems have a deeper intensity than the short piece in which he evoked some of his meetings with his lost friend. He spoke of the gare d'Auteuil as a paradise, since he was to meet him there, and recalled the first sight of him with a mournful joy. Then together the two friends would wander under the trees, discussing points of theology, metaphysics, doubt opposed to faith.

"O tes forts arguments, ta foi de charbonnier ! . . .
Et puis nous rentrions, plus que lents, par la route. . . ."

Verlaine was present at Letinois's death, and followed him to his grave in the cemetry at Ivry. In a noble lamentation Verlaine, remembering

Job, mourned but dared not accuse the Divinity
who had struck so cruel a blow at his affections:

" Mon fils est mort. J'adore, ô mon Dieu, votre loi . . .
Vous châtiez bien fort. Mon fils est mort, hélas !
Vous me l'aviez donné, voici que votre droite
Me le reprend, à l'heure ou mes pauvres pieds las
Réclamaient ce cher guide en cette route étroite.
Vous me l'aviez donné, vous me le reprenez :
Gloire à vous ! . . ."

In all these sad verses of his Verlaine displayed
the most Christian resignation. He regarded his
loss as a punishment, an expiation. He ought
not to have substituted this son by election for
the legitimate one who would return to him later,
realising that his father had *enduré de sottises
féroces.* He ought to have left the young man
in his home. The adoption was forbidden fruit,
and heaven punished him for reaching out his hand
toward it.

To this mystical exaltation, which led the poet
to regard his loss as moral discipline, Verlaine
added an undoubtedly sincere testimony of the
absolute innocence of the friendship. He always
depicted Lucien Létinois as a pure being, the sight
and presence of whom purified him :

" De lui, simple et blanc comme un lys calme, aux couleurs
D'innocence candide et d'espérance verte,
L'Exemple descendait sur mon âme entr'ouverte,
Et sur mon cœur qu'il pénétrait, plein de pitié,
Par un chemin semé des fleurs de l'amitié ! . . ."

When he speaks of the young friend so brutally
torn from him it was always in such terms as :
"l'ange ignorant de nos routes," "le pur esprit
vêtu d'une innocente chair," and "mon bon ange."

He recalled how he had dreamed of marriage for him, and evoked "la parfaite, la belle et sage fianceé." Such lines in *Amour* and others in *Bonheur*, give a perfectly definite character of purity and virtue to Verlaine's affection for Lucien Létinois, absent from the later noisy friendships of the poet. He thus described his sentiment for Lucien, his "guardian angel," "good counsellor," "plank of safety in the shipwreck of passion."

> " . . . Je t'estime et je t'aime, ô si fidèlement
> Trouvant dans ces devoirs mes plus chères délices,
> Déployant tout le peu que j'ai de paternel,
>
> Plus encor que de fraternel, malgré l'extrême
> Fraternité, tu sais, qu'eut notre amitié même. . . ."
>
> (*Bonheur*, xv.)

And he adds this declaration of friendship which should serve as a shield against all the thrusts of calumny :

> " . . . Soyons tout l'un pour l'autre, en dépit de l'envie
> Soyons tout l'un à l'autre en toute bonne foi.
> Nous avons le bonheur ainsi qu'il est permis.
>
> .   .   .   .
>
> Toi, de qui la pensée est toute dans la mienne,
> Il n'est dans la légende actuelle et l'ancienne
> Rien de plus noble et de plus beau que deux amis."
>
> (*Bonheur*, xv.)

These invocations to friendship are touching, and written in charming verse. Death broke the pleasant bond. It was a rough blow for the poet, and an unfortunate one. Verlaine began to descend with ever-increasing rapidity the slope leading to an abyss which was to swallow up not only the health, the tranquillity, the well - being, and the dignity of the poet, but a large share of his fine talent.

CHAPTER XIV

RETURN TO PARIS AND THE LITERARY WORLD—
*SAGESSE—LES POÈTES MAUDITS—LES MÉMOIRES
D'UN VŒUF*

(1881-1883)

VERLAINE, after his return to Paris, lived successively
at Bologne-sur-Seine, in the Rue de Lyon, and at
No. 17 Rue de la Roquette, and having renounced
agriculture for the time being endeavoured to
resume his place in literature. He had entirely
lost touch both with authors and booksellers, and
it was difficult for me to find a publisher for him ;
Dentu and Veuve Tresse (Victor Stock) who
published my first novels would not hear of poetry.
At last the Catholic publisher, Victor Palmé, took
the manuscript, which the poet had been hawking
round with monotonous unsuccess from publisher to
publisher. Palmé accepted the volume, not because
the poems seemed to him to be fine, but solely
because the work of M. Paul Verlaine had been
recommended to him by pious persons as likely to
furnish edifying reading. This was *Sagesse*. It
was not as one of the finest books in our literature,
or as the only religious poem that the nineteenth
century produced, that *Sagesse* was printed, but as
a collection of new hymns likely to vary the

monotony of the liturgical *répertoire*. The un-witting publisher has since acquired indisputable reflected glory from its publication; but, at the time, he made a poor business of it—to his great chagrin.

This book, which was afterwards to place Verlaine in the front rank of poetry, attracted no attention whatever. The first readers for whom it was designed, the poets, were entirely lacking. Not one voice was raised in the press to signal the appearance of this incomparable and sur-prisingly original collection. I certainly wrote a eulogistic article on the poems, the greater number of which I possessed in manuscript, and of which I had the pleasure of being the first reader, but that year I was writing solely in political journals like the *Mot d'Ordre*, and my article on *Sagesse*, of necessity abridged, did not come under the notice of readers interested in poetry. The ordinary *clientèle* of the paper despised a work which appeared to be "clerical."

Sagesse had, moreover, the misfortune of being quite unappreciated by the Catholic circle, and the publisher, annoyed at having been misled into print-ing a book of a character inconsistent with the works of piety, of which he made a speciality, hastened to remove the whole stock to the cellar, and afterwards, to free himself from an incumbrance, sold the whole edition as waste paper, resolving that never again would he publish verse so full of unction, so perfumed with orthodoxy as he had been assured these were. He was right, this merchant of prayer-books; the pious do not buy volumes of verse, and the clergy have not time to read them, particularly nowadays, when they are so much occupied with politics, dividing their reading between newspapers and breviaries.

Palmé was mistaken, but he was not qualified to launch a book of subtle, exquisite, and intense poetry such as this. He would have been consoled afterwards for his initial want of success if one of his clerks had chanced to think of putting aside a few copies of the unsaleable book. The original edition of *Sagesse*, of which there now exist only a few copies in the possession of friends, is greatly sought after by collectors. Twenty or thirty copies saved from the paper merchant would have reimbursed Palmé for the expenses of a publication he considered unfortunate and ill-advised.

The original addition of *Sagesse* is an oblong volume in *format* something like that of an in-8vo. It contains only 106 pages. The type is rather thick and very clear, in the old style. The cover is a greyish yellow; it has on it: "A. Paul Verlaine—*Sagesse*". The publisher's trade mark, a shield with griffins and a lion rampant, tail erect, and head turned, with the motto: *Sustinens palmas Domini*. At the foot: "Paris Société générale de Librairie Catholique. Paris, Ancienne Maison Victor Palmé, 76 Rue des Saints-Pères. Bruxelles Ancienne Maison Henri Gœmare, 29 Rue des Paroissiens. MDCCCLXXXI." On the half title is: "Du même auteur: En préparation: *Amour. Voyage en France par un Français.*" And at the foot: "Evreux, Imprimerie de Charles Hérissey."

The book is dedicated *A ma mère*.

The original edition has a preface, which has not been included with *Sagesse* in vol. i. of the

complete works published by Léon Vanier in 1899.
Why not? I therefore reproduce it.

"The author of this book has not always
thought as he does now. For a long time he
wandered in contemporary corruption, bearing his
part in its sin and ignorance; but troubles, well-
merited, came as a warning, by which God has
graciously permitted him to profit. He now pro-
strates himself before the long neglected Altar, he
adores the All Perfect, and invokes the Almighty;
an obedient son of the Church, least as regards
merit, but full of good-will. The consciousness of
his weakness and the remembrance of his failures
guided him in the elaboration of this book, which
is his first public act of faith after a long literary
silence; nothing will be found in it, he hopes,
contrary to the charity which the author, henceforward a Christian, owes to sinners in whose detestable ways he followed until recently.

"Two or three poems nevertheless break the
silence that he conscientiously imposed upon himself in this respect, but it will be observed that they
bear on public actions, on events too generally providential in their after effects to be regarded as
anything but a necessary testimony; a confession
of which was called for both by religious duty and
hope for France.

"The author published, when very young, *i.e.*,
ten years ago, some sceptical and sadly frivolous
verses. He dares to believe that in those which
follow no dissonance will shock the delicacy of the
Catholic ear: it would be his dearest fame as it
is his most confident hope.

"PARIS, 30*th July* 1880."

The edifying sentiments expressed in this preface, undoubtedly calculated to impress *les oreilles*

catholiques, were not unfailingly persistent. It is true that the above-mentioned ears remained deaf to the pious accents of the converted poet. Subsequent volumes, notably that entitled *Femmes*, printed and published under the rose, showed signs of a return to the verses, if not sceptical and impious, at least light. At the same time, it must be recognised that Verlaine never went back to irreligion, but always reverenced the beliefs and religious practices of his childhood, which he had resumed, at least poetically, after the storms and cataclysms of his maturer years.

Verlaine, in spite of the ill success of *Sagesse*, perhaps by reason of this mortification, seeing his resources diminishing, and his mother, with reason, being less ready to supply him with funds, courageously resolved "to live by his pen." He had always had this desire as many of his letters prove, but had not made much progress in remunerative literary work. He knew very well that verses do not sell except in very rare cases, having published all his first volumes at his own expense. He had only dreamed of works likely to be accepted by editors and publishers. As a matter of fact, he had no aptitude for practical commercial current literature. For this he should be praised. As Edgar Poe, with whom he had more than one point of resemblance, said, "he wrote too much above the vulgar" to be accepted and remunerated by the daily papers. I succeeded, however, as will be seen later, in obtaining regular paid employment for him on the *Réveil*, in which journal, it is true, I had the upper hand. It was an exceptional case. He never published anything even when he had obtained a legitimate notoriety and was surrounded by the halo of misery and the hospital, except in out-of-the-way papers, juvenile reviews, firebrands of audacious schools, tentative publications for a restricted *clientèle*, of which only an infinitesimal number were printed and distributed more often than sold. He was always a poet, dreamer, and fantasist, and could not bend himself to the exigencies of ordinary publication nor popular taste. He never thought at any time of sharing the profits, although they accrued in the case of several of his works; but not until later. He was unable to write a long novel; he lacked the necessary imagination. The construction of a story with characters, adventures, and action was impossible to him. Equally so was a psychological work, although he was well read in this class of literature and knew *Obermann*, *Adolphe*, *Jacques*, and various novels by George Sand. Sentimental descriptions would have been more within his scope, but he had no heart for them. Poetical composition spoilt him for such work, and popular prose came heavily from the fingers accustomed to strike the lyre. In verse he introduced psychology, inspired by Joseph Delorme and Mme. Desbordes-Valmore; but in prose he could not get away from himself, and an author cannot be always in the confessional.

As for plays, they tempted him. We have seen how, in his earlier years, he amused himself with attempting an operatic farce (*La Famille Beautrouillards*, never finished), and also began in collaboration with me a drama, popular and yet superior to traditional melodramas, the *Forgerons*. We meant to depict in five prose acts, destined for the Porte-Sainte-Martin or the Odéon, jealousy in a working man, a sentiment very strong and violent in its manifestations among stunted souls and bodies inured to rough labour. The play was never finished, and I have only preserved the interrupted fragments of the first acts. Perhaps it had in it the elements of a good piece. I have another project for a play, *L'Alchimiste*, which we also meant to write together, and which was never even begun. The two little pieces which Verlaine has left, *Madame Aubin* and *Les Uns et les Autres*, the latter of which was represented at his benefit at the Vaudeville Theatre, cannot be counted as serious dramatic productions.

There remained to him, outside his poetic vein, which was always abundant, original, coloured, and harmonious, a vein of prose to be exploited. He was what the English call an "essayist." He excelled in little pieces prolonged by digressions, often happy and unexpected, in which he noted things seen, impressions felt. He wielded now and then very gracefully the critic's ferule ; but he was much more ready to praise. He succeeded to perfection in humorous descriptions of places seen, landscapes, interiors, and people met. *Les Mémoires d'un Veuf, Quinze jours en Hollande* contain masterpieces of this kind which will figure later in collections of pieces selected from our prose writers. But his personality always dominated him, and the events of his life interposed between him and the outer world. There are few pages in which he makes no allusion to his sorrows and troubles, his lost wife, and her parents who incited him to perdition.

He resolved, however, to realise by his poetical imaginative, digressive, parenthetical prose the ideal of Théodore de Banville's young man, whose improbable destiny we had often merrily evoked: "The lyrical poet who lived by his profession." I encouraged him in this design, and took him on the *Réveil*, a great literary daily paper of which I was editor-in-chief. The offices of the *Réveil*, together with those of the *Mot d'Ordre*, which was under the same management, were on the ground and first floors of No. 19 Rue Bergère, at the corner of the Cité Rougemont. There was in the same building a German brasserie where Verlaine very regularly waited for me; but I was scarcely ever free till seven o'clock. Several of the writers on our papers noticed and were disquieted by the strange apparition. Who was this unknown "type," bald, but thickly bearded, with rough-cast features, and the appearance of a wandering Jew of the Boul' Mich', wearing a thick macfarlane, with the air of a Montmartrois hidalgo, whose mocking smile zig-zagged below a Socratic nose? Evidently he was no ordinary Bohemian. Henry Baüer, who afterwards very cleverly described his first sight of the vagabond poet, in whom he found something sinister and disquieting, interrogated me with regard to him. My strange visitor greatly perplexed the ears and disconcerted the minds of those who observed him. They were surprised when they caught fragments of our long disconnected conversations on literature, philosophy, history, in which we quoted books of divers characters: the *Ramayana, Gaspard de la Nuit*; *Port-Royal*, by Sainte-Beuve; the *Ensorcelée* by Barbey d'Aurevilly;

2 A

Marlowe's *Faust*; Calderon's *Dévotion à la Croix*;
Les Nuits, of Aulu-Gelle; and Petrus Borel's
Rhapsodies.

To Henry Baüer's question regarding my friend,
I replied simply: "It is Paul Verlaine, a great
poet." "Ah yes! . . . ." Baüer said politely, and
went away, apparently none the wiser. A few
days afterwards I lent him a copy of the *Romances
sans Paroles*. He took the little book away, read
it, and said to me: "You are right, Verlaine is a
very great poet," and from that day he has been
one of Verlaine's fervent admirers.

The *Réveil*, forerunner of the *Echo de Paris*,
was a great literary journal, the true precursor of
many other successful papers which founded themselves upon it. It was originated by Valentin
Simond, and contained only a short political
bulletin. At this period it was a doubtful innovation, for a newspaper was not supposed to be able
to exist without polemics. Reviews, authentic facts,
reports, portraits, green-room indiscretions, short
stories, and first-rate novels (the *Réveil* published
Alphonse Daudet's *Sapho*, Guy de Maupassant's
Sœurs Rondoli, etc., etc.) made the *Réveil* an
original and interesting journal; it proceeded from
Villemessant's old *Figaro*, and Aurélian Scholl's
Evénement; but it dealt more in artistic matters,
and was less preoccupied with polemics and political
personalities. It was an ingenious creation; but its
success did not come up to its founder's expectation.
It was premature, an eclectical organ, republican
without violence. The beginning of anything is
often attended with mortification. The *Réveil* was
a novelty in literary and informative journalism, but

the old political and didactic style still carried the
day. Polemics, parliamentary discussions, doctrinal
and sociological theories were all the rage, and one
could hardly foresee outside the Quartier Latin
and some of the boulevard cafés a *clientèle* for a
paper, almost exclusively literary, in which poets
were dealt with, and columns on the first page
devoted to a theatrical representation, the criticism
of a book, the explanation of a mundane scandal,
or the analysis of a legal drama. But sometime
afterwards the *Gil Blas* appeared, and its great and
rebounding success afforded a permanent contradiction to this assertion current in the newspaper
world. Later the *Echo de Paris*, the *Journal*, and
the *Matin*, influenced some of the papers, until
then entirely political, to suppress the doctrinal
article, the "tartine," and to give more space to
news, criticism and topical scandal. Thus was completed the transformation of the press, and thus
grew in popularity and circulation the literary,
mundane news sheets, leaving far behind them
those of the old style, which dragged on a miserable
existence for a little while, or else remoulded themselves on the pattern of the new sensational press.

The *Réveil* was not able to overcome the initial
obstacles. Neither talent on the part of the writers,
nor ability on that of the administration were lacking, to prevent it from following its course : its too
hasty departure in the face of a surprised unpre-
pared *clientèle* was the sole cause of its defeat, for
which Valentin Simond soon took a brilliant and
novel revenge by launching the *Echo de Paris*,
which was a second *Réveil*, only better furnished
with collaborators and money.

The principal writers on the *Réveil* were : Léon Cladel, Jules Vallès, Paul Alexis, René Maizeroy, Francis Enne, Hector France, Albert Dubrujeaud, Henry Baüer, Gaston Vassy, Emile Bergerat, Jules Caze, Paul Bonnetain, Henri Fèvre, Emile Blémont, and lastly Paul Verlaine, and Edmond Lepelletier.

The editor's secretary was Robert Caze, a novelist of much talent, the author of the *Martyre d'Annil*, who was unfortunately killed in a duel with a decadent poet, still obscure in spite of the sensation created by the affair, which arose from his anger at a criticism of his bizarre lucubrations. He deprived our literature of strong and original works, and, moreover, contributed to the wreckage of two other lives : Robert Caze's young wife did not survive her husband more than a year, and their orphan child, left penniless, to grow up as best he could, became a young criminal : he was brought up before the Court of Assizes several years ago for murder and theft, and sentenced to imprisonment. Wounded literary *amour-propre* sometimes takes a terrible revenge, and duels between men of letters do not always terminate in a breakfast as the foolish pretend.

Taking advantage of Verlaine's happy determination to write prose suitable for a newspaper, I introduced him to the manager of the *Réveil*. Although literature was its leading feature the journal was none the less a popular organ intended for the great public. I, therefore, urged the author of *Sagesse* to bring me something which would come within the scope of a daily paper. Verlaine's first essays in this direction were mostly autobiographical in character, and contained allusions to his troubles with his wife's family.

The following letter is an indication of his state of mind in this respect, and the rather strange idea he had of a newspaper.

" *Wednesday.*

" Here is an essay for *Jean qui pleure*, and *Jean qui rit*. I think it is sufficiently general and dramatic to pass.

" If it does pass, I particularly recommend to you the *vieille m . . .!* (Cambronne's famous term). You can guess to whom it refers (to his father-in-law).

" If it is impossible then put it with full stops *vieille m . . .!* or *vieille moule.* But it would please me if it could appear in full."

I had inaugurated in the *Réveil* an idea which has since been imitated, perhaps perfected, and was most popular : *Paris-Vivant*, made up of short articles printed in italics on the first page ; impressions, Paris pictures, sketches, sensations, and scenes taken from life. They were signed *Jean qui pleure* or *Jean qui rit* in accordance with the tone, melancholy or gay, of the subject. I wrote the two first, and then inserted a certain number by Paul Bonnetain, Robert Caze, and others, among them some by Paul Verlaine, although his articles were hardly suitable, even to our journal itself. Naturally I was unable to insert, in spite of his great desire, the epithet to which he referred.

Here are some letters relating to these articles, the insertion of which gave the author great pleasure. The first was partly in English :

"Enclosed is *L'Ami de la Nature* you asked for (a little song of the Bruant species, but written fifteen years before the *Marché des Dos*). . . . It will appear, and then various prose poems from *La Parodie*.

"I recommend myself always to M. de B.

"I will try to go to-morrow to the Brasserie, but have not much hope of doing so. My wretched cold makes me literally ill. . . .

"Don't you think that it would be possible to me to hope for some money in return of my four *Paris - living*? If such was the case, I would manage in order to write one per week. You could perhaps, if I were not able to-morrow to see you at the 'Brasserie,' answer me and deep post a word on the matter.

"Excuse bad English, and believe me to remain. . . ."

"*23rd December.*

"Here is an essay for *Jean qui rit*. . . .

"What of M. de B.?

"You ought to have received a *Jean qui pleure* yesterday at the Brasserie. . . ."

"*Friday evening.*

"In a hurry. Cannot wait for you.

"Enclosed is a *Jean qui pleure*. To-morrow I will send or bring you a *Jean qui rit*: *Auteuil.*

"What of M. de B.?"

The insistence with which, when sending his *Paris-Vivants*, Verlaine enquired about M. de B. was in connection with his application for re-instatement as employee in the Préfecture de la Seine, an application which I had warmly recommended to Charles Floquet, then Préfet de la Seine, and which was supported by my colleague on the *Mot d'Ordre*, M. Jehan de Bouteiller, then President of the Municipal Council.

The greater number of the *Paris-Vivants* Paul Verlaine wrote are reproduced in *Les Mémoires d'un Veuf*, as the following letter indicates :

"BRASSERIE BERGÈRE, *Saturday evening.*

"6.25. Missed you this evening. According to the waiter you hurried off only five minutes ago. I came very much in connection with the 'Ville' and M. de B ; also a little in connection with the affair V. *versus* M. (Verlaine *v.* Mauté) which is less urgent.

". . . Enclosed is a *Paris-Vivant.* Cut or prune if you think necessary . . . but if you can, supposing it is not inserted, keep the manuscript for me. It is to make part, you know, of a prose volume entitled *Les Mémoires d'un Veuf*, which is dedicated to you. You have been, in a fashion, the depositary of the chapters in this little book which you are good enough to accept."

Les Mémoires d'un Veuf were indeed dedicated to me, but, if I am not mistaken, this dedication, which figured at the commencement of the original edition, is not included in the fourth volume of the complete works. The publisher erred in suppressing it, for it contained an interesting and precise definition of this very personal and characteristic prose work of Verlaine's. It ran as follows :

"DEDICATION TO EDMOND LEPELLETIER.

"My dear Edmond, here are some pages, under an enormous title, which are neither a little novel, nor a collection of small bits of news, but rather fragments of a career lived to some extent under your eyes. There are no double meanings in the little work; nevertheless, as the public cannot read between the lines, and would experience no pleasure, even malicious, in doing so, I have been obliged to develop certain passages, which you and two or three others alone will understand, with generalities for the benefit of the unknown reader.

"Many opinions separate us to-day; we have in common only one idea, except as regards initial good sense and literature, ferociously idolised by me, which is to keep intact the old friendship so strong and so beautiful.

"Accept, therefore, this dedication, as simple as my heart, but sincere and warm as my hand when it presses yours."

Les Mémoires d'un Veuf contained, as has already been said, some short articles published in the *Réveil*, which were generally Parisian or country pictures, such as *Auteuil, Les Chiens, Nuit Noire, Nuit Blanche, Un Bon Coin, Par la Croisée, A la Campagne*, descriptive and ironical; or reveries and fantasies, in the style of Baudelaire's *Petits Poèmes en Prose: Quelques - uns de mes Rêves, Palinodie, Mon Hameau, La Morte, Ma Fille, Les Fleurs Artificielles;* or sensations and hallucinations: *Jeux d'Enfants, Corbillard au Galop* (recollections of an impression we received together in the Brasserie, Rue Fontaine, and which I had embodied in a piece of verse in the *Nain Jaune*, 1869); and lastly, some recollections of troubles or personal rancours, such as in *Bons Bourgeois*, a picture of a domestic quarrel, *Formes*, in which the lawyer, Guyot-Sionnest, and his study are portrayed, and *A la Mémoire de Mon Ami XXX*.

It was to this particular fragment that Verlaine alluded in his dedication when he spoke of passages which I and three or four others alone could understand.

This passage, in which Verlaine conjures up, at a table in a café once frequented by us, a picture, seen through slow tears, of a comrade of our youth, the elegant and slim form of twenty years, and handsome head, "celle de Marceau plus beau," as he says in his posthumous enthusiasm, relates not to Lucien Létinois, but a friend of earlier date, Lucien Viotti. This charming young man joined the 69th Regiment of Infantry at the beginning of the war of 1870, on the same day that I did. Indeed, it was through him that I chose the 69th, of which he knew the captain.

Verlaine, in this short *In Memoriam*, cried in accents of distress, like those of Achilles, when he learned the death of Patroclus, whom he had sent into the combat:

"Alas! oh, unfortunate delicacy, oh, deplorable and unexampled sacrifice, oh, imbecile that I was not to have understood in time! When the horrible war in which our country nearly perished broke out, you engaged in it, you died atrociously, glorious youth, because of me, who am not worth a drop of your blood, and of her, of her! . . ."

The private and sad drama which these lines of Verlaine's seem to reveal had escaped me. It is true I had remarked the melancholy of our friend; but he was of rather a reserved nature, and I attributed his sadness to the gravity of the time and anxiety for his country. It was not until a great deal later we learned that a secret unfortunate love for the girl who was about to become his friend's bride was the chief motive of his enlistment, for he was like me, doubly exempt from active service as the son of a widow, and as having drawn a lucky number in the ballot. Verlaine's moving and mournful phrases explain this poetical and tragic adventure of love and sacrifice of the young Viotti.

Les Mémoirs d'un Veuf contains some pages of criticism : among them a succinct and fairly exact history of the *Parnasse Contemporain,* Verlaine very clearly demonstrating the decisive influence of this group on the literary taste and opinion of our time ; and his definition of the mission of the poet, and the action of poetry could hardly be bettered.

Much less just and certainly reprehensible is Verlaine's attack on Victor Hugo. He had greatly admired, and, like all of us, closely imitated the master in his early poems. Moreover, he had been received by him with kindness, and even flattery. There was something of ingratitude in his irreverent attempt to depreciate the greatest poet of the nineteenth century, and in his affected admiration for *Gastibelza* and the *Chanson des Pirates.* But, as we have already said, Verlaine sometimes loved a coarse laugh, and had impulses towards parody, and his exuberant humour must not be taken seriously. He declared, with rude irony, that it would have been better if Victor Hugo had died in 1845, and allowed him three ballads only on which to rest his fame : *Les Bœufs qui Passent,* which, set to music by Lassimonne, one of the conductors of the orchestra at the Elysée-Montmartre, he had applauded at a café-concert ; *Le Pas d'Armes du roi Jean,* the rhythmic and coloured music of which we had praised when our friend, Emmanuel

Chabrier, the author of *España*, improvised it with his indefatigable fingers one evening at L.-X. de Ricard's ; and *La Chasse du Burgrave*. He allowed some merit to *Les Tronçons du Serpent* and the *Orientales*, which he proclaimed a pearl. In prose he admired *Bug-Jargal* and *Notre-Dame de Paris*, which he asserted was very amusing in places, and finally, he classed among the works worth preserving *Le Rhin*—all the rest he consigned to perdition.

" Oui," he cried in a sort of iconoclastic fury, "tout ce qui part des *Châtiments*, et *Châtiments* compris, m'emplit d'ennui, me semble turgescence, brume, langue désagrégée, d'art non plus pour l'art incommensurable, monstrueuse improvisation, bouts-rimés pas variés, ombre, sombre, ténèbres, funèbres, facilité déplorable, ô ces *Contemplations*, ces *Chansons des Rues et des Bois !* manque insolent platement de la moindre composition, plus nul souci d'étonner que par des moyens pires qu'enfantins."

In this mad demolition, vainly attempted by him and by others who had not his merit, the god remaining imperturbably seated upon his intangible pedestal of poems, novels, plays, history, and criticism, he ended by declaring that *Gastibelza* surpassed all Hugo's other works. Here the joke passed all bounds, and Verlaine, in the excess of his truculent and mocking attack, showed the cloven hoof of the hoaxer. Evidently he was jeering at us not at Hugo ; laughing up his sleeve at the credulous *naïveté* of the young innovators of the Quartier Latin who had already formed a circle around him in the Café François Premier, and whom he treated as Hugo treated us.

These young men have now made their mark.

Many of them have quitted symbolist literature for grocery or Government employ, and have assuredly changed their minds as to the *par-excellence* of *Gastibelza*. This attempted destruction of the figure of a great man was a pose and a kind of sacrilege. Verlaine had abandoned himself to the black mass of poetry. I cannot believe him sincere in these excesses of the intellect. No more importance should be attached to such an outbreak, of which Victor Hugo's fame was the momentary object, than to the burlesque *Testament* set down by Verlaine in his *Mémoires d'un Veuf* :

"MY WILL

" I give nothing to the poor, because I am poor myself.

" I believe in God.   PAUL VERLAINE.

"*Codicil.*—As regards my obsequies, I desire to be conducted to the place of final repose in a Lesage cart ("dust-cart"), and that my remains shall be deposited in the crypt of the Odéon.

"As my fame has never prevented any one from sleeping, the choirs can sing, during the sad ceremony, to an air of Gossec's, the celebrated ode 'La France a perdu son Morphée.'

" Made in Paris, June 1885."

These are merely spiritual debauches, doubtless succeeding to others, spirituous.

The original edition of *Les Mémoires d'un Veuf* is a volume in-18 of 222 pages. The cover of glazed, greyish paper is surrounded by a design in black, and bears the following words : Paul Verlaine—*Les Mémoires d'un Veuf.*—Paris. Léon Vanier, éditeur, 19 Quai Saint-Michel, 1886."

On the half title is the following announcement :

" *Ouvrages du même Auteur* : *Poésie* : *Poèmes Saturniens,* 5 fr. ; *Fêtes galantes,* 3 fr. ; *La Bonne Chanson,* 2 fr. ; *Romances sans Paroles,* 3 fr. ; *Jadis et Naguère,* 3 fr.
" En Préparation : *Amour.—Parallèlement.*
" Prose : *Les Poètes Maudits,* 5 fr. ; *Louise Leclercq,* 3 fr. 50.
" Asnières. Imprimerie Louis Boyer et Cie, 8 Rue du Bois."

Verlaine, timidly, having gradually accustomed himself to contact with people and things in the Brasserie Bergère, where the collaborators of the *Réveil* used to assemble, made some appearances in the Quartier Latin, for which he always had a predilection. He was seen at the Harcourt, the Source, and the Louis XIII. He had no circle of disciples at that time ; Germain Nouveau was his most frequent companion. However, he met some young writers, ardent fault-finders, who published a satirical newspaper, exclusively literary and innovating : *Lutèce,* which betokened the dawn of symbolism, and the entry on the scene of the Decadents.

This new generation which had grown up after the war, altogether apart from the authors and their productions of Lemerre's *Parnasse,* treated Leconte de Lisle, Heredia, and Coppée with a scornful irreverence, considering as classics, out - of - date, old - fashioned, the innovators of 1868! These young men, as is customary, attacked the preceding generation with which they were ill - acquainted, and had had no opportunity of knowing. There was between elders and youngers the gulf of 1870. Consequently, they had espoused neither the quarrels nor the rancours of our comrades. They did not turn their backs on Verlaine, murmuring hypocritically tales of conjugal and legal adventures, travestying the facts, and interpreting in their own fashion the Belgian condemnation. They ignored such gossip, and if they had known of it the accusation would have made them smile; might even have recommended the object of it to their sympathy, almost admiration.

They were equally ignorant of Verlaine. The most erudite had vaguely heard of the *Fêtes galantes*; but it was supposed that the author was dead, or had disappeared, retired, become extinguished.

Acquaintances were made. Léo Trézenik, who was the editor-in-chief of *Lutèce*, accepted some of Verlaine's poems, notably the famous *Art Poétique*, which he had sent to me from the prison of Mons, and it attracted the attention of the new poets, Tristan Corbière, Laforgue, and Vielé - Griffin. Verlaine next gave to *Lutèce* some essays on writers, slighted, ignored, or not in receipt of the full measure of fame to which, according to him, they had ample right. These articles brought Verlaine into contact with the publisher Léon Vanier. They appeared afterwards under the title *Les Poètes Maudits*.

Les Poètes Maudits, biographies in which there is a great deal of autobiography, holds a more important place in Verlaine's life than in his work. It consists for the most part of short studies of curious personalities, poets more afflicted with strangeness than abuse, except the gentle, melancholy, and resigned Marceline Desbordes-Valmore, who rather gave the impression, in this circle of wild lyrists, of a virgin dropped into a house of debauch. Quotations abounded. Praise, sometimes hyperbolical, supplied the place of criticism, and Verlaine's personality peeped through the lightly-sketched silhouettes of Tristan Corbière, Arthur Rimbaud, Villiers de l'Isle-Adam, and Stéphane Mallarmé.

The principal interest of these extra-eulogistic notices for the rare contemporaries attracted by such poetic curiosities, was the production in the full light of day of several pieces of verse by Arthur Rimbaud, hitherto kept in the manuscript obscurity of a portfolio. Rimbaud was hardly more than a name. The recollection of him which remained in the minds of those who had met him in company with Verlaine ten years before was confused and unsympathetic; they recalled extravagances and disdainful poses which the most exceptional talent could not justify. The equivocal mystery of the struggle at Brussels, with the severe sentence following upon it, the true motives of which were not known—in this book the exact facts of the case are set forth for the first time—surrounded this bizarre figure with a repellent atmosphere. He had disappeared, and none cared to know what had become of him. The quotations made by Verlaine were like a revelation. The extraordinary sonnet of the vowels was reproduced, commented upon, mocked at, admired, and by the following day Rimbaud was celebrated in a corner of literary Paris. In this notice no allusion was made to the tragic events which led to the separation of the two friends; and no explanation was given of Rimbaud's conduct when he renounced poetry, burnt the copies of his *Saison en Enfer*, destroyed his manuscripts, and went in search of fortune beyond the seas.

Tristan Corbière was the author little read, and nowadays almost entirely ignored, of the *Amours Jaunes*. His biography is insignificant. Some quotations from his poems, curious rather by the arrangement of the rhythms than by the composition itself, on marine subjects in which the drowned, of a fine colour, whom the poet depicts sinking in their boots, and tossed without nails or planks upon the billows, swelling like an amorous body, gives piquancy to a rather insipid portrait; for Verlaine did not trouble to trace for us recognisable features of his model. He informed us that he was a Breton, and loved the sea, which is little enough, and does not convey a lasting impression of this poet who was not without merit, and of whose work one strange line at least is remembered and often ironically quoted : " His sole regret was that he was not his mistress " — the epitaph of one not understood, not satisfied.

Villiers de l'Isle-Adam was a magnificent prose writer rather than a poet. Verlaine justly rendered homage to his powerful dramatic qualities, quoting a scene from his *Nouveau-Monde*, a drama written for a competition founded by a certain Michaëlis. The piece was bracketed with another in the second place, four laureates being singled out from the multitude of competitors attracted by the prize in kind, and the certainty of being played in Paris. The *Nouveau-Monde* was performed without much success at the Théâtre des Nations. The quotation given by Verlaine proved that Villiers possessed the art of managing crowds upon the stage, a very rare gift, and one which, since Shakepeare, Ibsen alone appears to have had.

For Stéphane Mallarmé who was to succeed

him as prince of poets, Verlaine raised a triumphal
pedestal. Mallarmé, a little-known professor of
English, who gave his classes in an intelligible
manner and wrote in very lucid prose, became
obscure and often affected when he touched verse.
He sought in darkness for phrases where others
seek in light, yet his style is seductive and his
sibylline lines beguile and soothe like a musical
idiom murmured by a foreign woman in your ear,
which you divine, you feel, you listen to, but can
neither translate nor retain. He practised the
new *Art Poétique*, the theory of which was formulated by Verlaine.

Desbordes - Valmore, whom Verlaine quoted
more than he studied, and whose sentimental
mystery he could not explain, had always been
extolled by him in spite of her affectation and air
of singer of romances for Louis-Philippe drawing-
rooms. He loved her especially as a compatriot,
one like himself. She had been born in the north
and suffered from sorrow of heart, which, like
him, she poured out in melody. Verlaine afterwards wrote a notice of himself under the name
Pauvre Lélian, an anagram of Paul Verlaine. The
nickname clung to him and he was sometimes
mentioned by it in kindly articles. After having
summed up various phases of his existence, spoken
of his "exceptional" parents, recalled his school
days, and quoted his verse " Je ne puis plus
noter les chutes de mon cœur," he named under
designations easy to recognise his principal works:
Mauvaise Etoile (the *Poèmes Saturniens*); *Pour
Cythère* (*Fêtes galantes*); *Corbeille de Noces* (*La
Bonne Chanson*); and *Sapientia* (*Sagesse*), that

2 B

murdered muse buried in Palmé's cellar; lastly he spoke of the *Poètes Maudits*, which he called *Les Incompris.* " Since then Pauvre Lélian has produced a little book of criticism—oh! of criticism —of praise rather, in connection with some slighted poets."

The original edition of the *Poètes Maudits* only contained notices of Corbière, Arthur Rimbaud, and Mallarmé (1884). The second edition, in 1888, illustrated with six portraits by Luque, contained, besides the notices already mentioned, those of Marceline Desbordes-Valmore, Villiers de l'Isle-Adam, and Pauvre Lélian. Edition in-18 of 102 pages. Léon Vanier, publisher. Printed by Louis Boyer & Cie., of Asnières.

Verlaine sought to turn his prose works into money. He knew that verses find not only a publisher, but a public, with difficulty; moreover, he had become attracted towards remunerative prose. He had had experience with the *Paris-Vivants* for the *Réveil,* and Léon Vanier had just printed and paid him for his *Poètes Maudits.* He resolved to "place" copy.

He had in his portfolio articles which had either appeared or for some reason or another not been accepted by that journal. He collected and completed them, and sent them to Vanier under the title *Les Mémoires d'un Veuf.* At the same time he finished and sent to the same publisher the manuscripts of *Louise Leclercq* and *Mme. Aubin,* and also a collection of verse: *Jadis et Naguère.*

These various works were issued by Vanier; but Verlaine was no longer in Paris. He abruptly left town, desire for the country having again seized hold of him. Once more he turned agriculturist.

CHAPTER XV

(1883-1885)

VERLAINE, without renouncing his pen, returned
to the country. He did not warn any one of his
new resolution. He accomplished the change in his
life as if by magic. I was expecting him, but he
did not come; I thought he must be ill or have gone
away on a visit. He had spoken to me vaguely
of a return to the country, and I thought, from his
laconic telegram, that he had gone to his relatives
at Fampoux or Paliseul. I supposed he wanted
money, and that his mother and he were selling
some piece of land in order to raise funds. They
had indeed done this, but the money was to serve
an immediate purpose of which I had no inkling.
The following letter undeceived me:

"REIMS, *8th October* 1883.

" This is not to excuse my failing to answer your
summons the other month, for on the one hand
I was too ill, and on the other I had telegraphed
to you explaining it, but rather to tell you that I
have left Paris (not without the intention of returning, naturally), and am living in the country in a

387

house my mother has recently bought, and that when you feel disposed you will be received with open arms at Mme. Veuve Verlaine's, Coulommes, near Attigny (Ardennes).

"Write to me often in the meanwhile. . . . I am publishing just now a series of articles in *Lutèce* on *Les Poètes Maudits* (Corbière, Rimbaud, Mallarmé). I am writing by this post to Louis Dumoulin, as I went away without taking leave of him the day after that on which I was unfortunately unable to go to Bougival : I was very unwell then.

" Do write to me from time to time.

" I am at Reims on business, but am returning to-morrow to my village not to leave it often. Write ! write ! will you not ? "

What motive decided Verlaine to make another attempt at farming, after the ill success of his venture at Juniville, some miles from Coulommes, three years before ?

The explanation is rather confusing. Verlaine always loved the country, as a large number of his poems, articles, and letters show, and rural life he especially delighted in, thus justifying his choice of an agricultural career ; but besides inclination, aptitude, knowledge, and practical experience were necessary, all of which he lacked. It was not work in the fields for which he was utterly unsuited that he really wanted, but vague, aimless wanderings across the wide, open country. He loved to walk on the springy turf, to feel the stubble crunch beneath his feet. On the banks of the Semoy it had pleased him to hold a line in his hand, but he smoked and dreamed, stretched in the shade in some hollow of the bank, while the fish more often than not escaped. What he appreciated more than anything in rustic life was the freedom from restraint, the comfortable old clothes, the open hospitality, the talks in the chimney-corner, and the frequent halts at the inn — that friend posted at the corner of the roads. The comfort, homely but cheerful, of the houses in the village, with their open windows in the morning displaying bulky eiderdowns and thick mattresses to the purifying sun, and the health-giving fresh air, seemed to him desirable and delightful when he escaped from the confinement of town.

But the true son of the soil does not appreciate these benefits of country existence in the least; more or less in subjection like the serfs of old he dreams of the emancipation of the town, of shoes instead of sabots, of the clerk's black coat; in an ambitious vision he even sees himself in the uniform of an official. He knows nothing of the beauty of the earth, the trees, the clouds; he does not comprehend the melancholy of the plains dotted by a flight of crows. With his poet's eyes Verlaine could have no peasant's heart. He mistook his vocation as farmer; he was ever a visitor to the fields, a townsman appreciating his holidays in the country, whose longing for the soil does not endure. He was rather fitted for the monotonous existence of the provincial householder, and might have rhymed sonnets as he watched the planting of his cabbages. He could not adapt himself to the laborious anxious life of the farmer, in perpetual fear of rain, drought, hail, disease among the cattle, underselling in the markets, or rise and fall in the price of crops, to say nothing of fires, damage, and bad debts. Nevertheless, his desire to live

the life of the fields is indisputable. In all sincerity
he wrote :

" My idea has always been to live in the real
country, in a village surrounded by fields, in a farm
of which I should be the proprietor, and at the
same time one of the labourers, one of the humblest,
seeing my feebleness and idleness."

Such a desire justified his first attempt, his
installation with his friend, Lucien, at Juniville ;
but the second essay, and the acquisition of a new
home in the country is less intelligible.

I confess I do not thoroughly understand his
abrupt flight from Paris just when he had recovered
his footing in the literary world, formed a new circle
of comrades in the cafés of the Latin Quartier,
found in the journal *Lutèce* the commencement of
fame, and in the publisher Vanier a prospect of
remuneration. Doubtless, it was in a large part
owing to his mother's influence, combined with a
precarious financial position ; the hope of obtaining profits from agriculture perhaps decided him ;
he saw himself with money in his pocket, hitherto
lacking. His mother, inexorable in Paris, would
not refuse to her son cultivating his fields the
money necessary for the absorption of the alcohol,
the habit of which he had resumed in the Quartier
Latin.

Madame Verlaine was as favourable to this
new project of her son's as she had been to his
first attempt at Juniville. This time, she thought,
he would be alone with nothing to distract him
from his work in the fields. Paul became
perceptibly more reasonable. She, therefore,

rejoiced in this return to the country life she
esteemed above all others, coming, as she did,
of a family of rural proprietors.   She might have
preferred to live in a country town, like several
of her relatives, but she accepted the village.
She asked for nothing in reality but to end her
days in some calm retreat, her son with her,
living comfortably on the small competency she
had been able to preserve.

To have left Paris was a great point gained.
She greatly feared the temptations of the city for
her son, imagining he only drank when within
its walls.   No distrust of the village inn had risen
in her mind during the Juniville days.   Lucien
Létinois, a sober and shrewd rustic, had not
produced on her the terrible impression of Arthur
Rimbaud.   The country meant enforced sobriety,
regularity of life and health for Paul.   Above all
it meant a definite rupture with the past *orgiaque
et melancolique*, of her saturnine son.   Moreover,
she respected the labour of the fields, alone productive and certain in her eyes.   Her family had
found a comfortable living in it, her dowry had
come from the produce of the soil ; literary work
she did not regard as serious, an opinion justified
by Paul.   He had never brought home any gains
since he had left the Government employ ; the
few louis produced by the *Paris-Vivants* had been
carefully suppressed by the author.   Not only
would her son lose nothing by quitting Paris,
but besides gaining his own living he might even
be able to save.

As to Verlaine, he obeyed a feeling of lassitude,
disgust ; he wanted to put a distance between him-

self and the scene of his disappointment. He had greatly wished to resume his place at the Hôtel-de-Ville; setting upon it all his hopes of return to a calm, regular, pleasant existence, with ample leisure for literary work, and money coming in at the end of each month with the regularity of clockwork.

I have already spoken of the failure of our combined efforts, in spite of the influence of the President of the Council, the support of Valentin Simond, and the consent of the Préfet, Charles Floquet. Those in authority refused to reinstate Verlaine in the modest employment for which he had passed the requisite examinations, and of which he was thoroughly capable. It was a profound disappointment to him, and he conceived a horror of Paris and the busy world, and craved for the silent fields, the limitless plains, the peaceful village, where forgetting one is by the world forgot. He wanted to slip away, to disappear. His choice of locality seems singular; it was the one in which he had lived with Lucien Létinois. The country is rather monotonous and melancholy between Rethel and Vouziers, but it suited his mood, and he may have wished to intensify his never flagging memory of his friend.

Verlaine, too, was at this period without money, and besides requiring some for his daily expenses, he wished to print the volume of verse he had just completed, entitled *Jadis et Naguère*. The majority of the pieces in it had been composed in England, Belgium, and his cell at Mons—a few only having been produced in Paris. But volumes of poetry are seldom issued at the expense of the publisher, and although Verlaine afterwards obtained a little money from Vanier for poems become saleable, thanks to the notoriety of the author, at this period his poetical works had no other public than those to whom he gave free copies. *Sagesse* had not found a single buyer. Although Vanier was kindly disposed to the author and promised to reprint it, and willingly published *Les Poètes Maudits*, it was doubtful if he would meet the expense of issuing *Jadis et Naguère*.

How was Verlaine to guarantee the necessary amount to the publisher? It is possible that Madame Verlaine, pleased with her son's retirement into the country, would advance it, but I am inclined to believe that Paul was thinking in this connection not only of his mother, but of Létinois's father; not that the countryman was likely to prove a benevolent lender, but Verlaine was probably attracted to him by the hope of effecting a good stroke of business in buying his house at Coulommes.

It was, in fact, Létinois's house that Madame Verlaine bought. As will be remembered the cunning rustic had, on the death of his son, sold the house at Juniville without passing on a penny of the price to the real owner, and it is probable that Verlaine sought to reimburse himself for this loss by taking over the property at Coulommes, consisting of house, outbuildings, yard, and garden, on behalf of his mother, for the sum of 3,500 francs.

Verlaine and his mother thus commenced the peaceful and laborious life amidst the fields of which they had dreamed; but the realisation of dreams is a difficult matter, and the new essay in farming did not succeed. Debts came, and with them quarrels between mother and son. Verlaine was wholly in the wrong. Contrary to the expectation of his mother he had begun to drink again terribly. Moreover, he had fallen in with a band of roystering young rustics, who kept up their revels far into the night, and separated at an advanced hour, singing and brawling, to the great scandal of the village. Money soon became lacking, and Verlaine imperiously demanded it of his mother. Discussion ensued, he being often inflamed with drink.

At last (in April 1884), for the sake of peace, yielding to the importunities of her son, and doubtless, also, in order to be able to evade the expense and results of various actions, occasioned by disputes with neighbouring farmers and tradesmen, Madame Verlaine made over the property of Coulommes to her son. The deed contained a clause prohibiting seizure, and thus assured a dwelling to Verlaine in spite of his various creditors. Paul continued his evil courses during the whole of 1884.

Mme. Verlaine had a neighbour at Coulommes, named Dane, who was not favourably disposed towards the poet. He advised Mme. Verlaine, since she could not prevent her son from drinking and spending his money on the riff-raff of the village, and similar companions come expressly from Paris at his invitation, to separate herself from him. After a more violent quarrel than usual, accompanying an urgent demand for money, Mme. Verlaine determined to follow M. Dane's advice, and intimated to her son that she would no longer live under the same roof with him; immediately putting her resolution into force, and retiring to the shelter offered her by her zealous friend. Her age, seventy-five years, precluded any evil interpretation of such hospitality, nevertheless, Verlaine accused him on several occasions of having exercised an undue influence over the mind of his mother, enfeebled by age and misfortune, in order to wring from her her small remaining fortune.

In consequence of these events Verlaine went to Paris on the 9th February 1885 and stayed at Austin's Hotel, an English tavern. The whisky and stout doubtless attracted him, for it was not his ordinary resort. As a rule when he visited Paris in connection with publishing business he lodged with Courtois, a wine and tobacco merchant at No. 5 Rue de la Roquette. When he left Coulommes he was probably under the influence of drink, and certainly he was not in his right mind, and had lost all sense of moderation and duty when he quitted the hotel on the following day to return to Coulommes.

Thus on the 11th February came to pass a scene for ever to be regretted, which I would gladly efface from Verlaine's life and not mention in this work, but I judge its inclusion necessary, first because it is an important fact in the life of the poet, as he himself recognised in his book *Mes Prisons*, and, secondly, because if the affair at Vouziers is not clearly narrated, it is likely to be misrepresented and exaggerated, and afford an opening for calumny like the affair at Brussels.

These, then, are the facts in all their distressing exactitude :

On the 11th February 1885 Verlaine went back to Coulommes, hoping his mother would have regretted her determination, and, pardoning him once more, return home. His disappointment was therefore great on finding the house empty, and his irritation grew. Some meetings, on the way home, accompanied by the inevitable drinks, had excited his anger. He was told that Dane preferred a hundred accusations against him, defamed him, and boasted of having cut off his supplies ; Mme. Verlaine having promised not to give him another sous, nor to sign another paper without his, Dane's permission and presence. In this state of excitement, acting under the double spur of alcohol and humiliation, he went to Dane's, where he knew he should find his mother, and a confused conversation broken by complaints, apostrophes, reproaches, insults, and threats took place between mother and son, at which Dane was present. He made no attempt to calm Verlaine, nor to arrange matters, and gain time. He ought to have persuaded the poet to return home and rest, and on the following day, sobered and tranquillised, he could have reiterated his demands for money, and begged his mother to return home with him.

But things turned out more tragically. Verlaine forgot himself so far in his excitement as to raise his hand against his mother—so Dane asserted in court. Mme. Verlaine herself declared that her son had subjected her to no evil treatment, but the judge preferred the testimony of Verlaine's personal enemy — for this domestic quarrel was brought into court. Dane had called in the police, who came from Attigny to Coulommes to investigate the matter, and it had gone too far to be stopped. This would seem to indicate the influence of Dane and Mme. Verlaine's dependence upon him, for I who had known the excellent woman for thirty years, and been a continual witness to not only her love but her indulgence to her son, cannot believe that she was a free agent when she consented to her well-beloved Paul being the object of a legal enquiry for lack of respect to her. Left to herself, she would have suffered and wept in silence over his evil doings, and never have delivered him over to justice. For a violent and intemperate demand for money, even a threat, she was incapable of bringing down upon his head a sentence of imprisonment for from two to five years! Her deposition itself bears evidence that it was suggested, exceeded her wishes, and exaggerated her complaints.

The court sitting at Vouziers, although it referred to the aforesaid penalty, did not go so far as to pronounce it.

The case came on on 24th March 1885.

The accusation reproached Verlaine with having used violence towards the person of Elisa Dehée, particularly in pressing her wrists to the point of making her cry out, and, moreover, with having in the same circumstances menaced the said dame with death if she did not give him money. The accusation added that the accused was holding an open knife in his hand at the time.

Verlaine interrogated, began by protesting his affection and respect for his mother. He exhibited a deep repentance for everything that might have offended her in the scene which had led to the prosecution. He contested the gravity of the facts with which he was reproached, and endeavoured to reduce them to more exact proportions.

He recognised that on the day in question he was excited by drink, and in such a state might have solicited his mother rather too violently for the money of which he had urgent need by reason of a law-suit and other engagements. He declared that he had no recollection of having threatened nor insulted his mother. If such unhappily had been the case, he had uttered the insults and threats under the influence of drink without knowing what he said. He denied having drawn a knife from his pocket. One witness alone asserted this aggravating fact, and that witness was his personal enemy, M. Dane.

He might in his anger have menaced the latter, for it was against him that he was animated by violent sentiments. He reproached him for abusing his influence over his mother, and of having induced her to come to his house, in order to inveigle her confidence and seize hold of her property. He also accused him of having slandered him throughout the whole neighbourhood, and of having boasted that he would make him leave the country and take possession of his house. He confessed that he was wrong in frequently drinking to excess, but stated that he had been driven into drunkenness by the annoyances of every kind he had endured at the hands of his mother's adviser. In spite of all the respect he owed her, and the affection he felt for her, he must advise the court that his mother's faculties were enfeebled, and that she allowed herself to be entirely dominated and directed by this Dane, who had resolved to obtain possession of her little fortune and separate her for ever from her son.

These simple and dignified statements, and his evident repentance, clearly testifying to his respectful affection for his mother, produced a favourable effect in court. Mme. Verlaine's deposition was excellent. She declared that her son "had always acted becomingly towards her" —the expression considered suitable in a court of law—until their arrival at Coulommes. Since his residence in that village Paul's character had changed. He drank and frequented those of dissipated and idle habits. She added: "I have nothing to reproach him with on the score of bad treatment. He may have caused me to spend money, but he has never taken any from me." She said nothing of any knife having been raised against her, and attributed her son's misconduct to his evil companions and alcoholic excess.

I am ignorant of M. Boileau's speech in the defence, but I suppose it was able, for he obtained almost an acquittal; but he could not plead, as it should have been pleaded, the cause of the neurotic poet, exposed to the calumnies and malignity of the villagers. He could neither comprehend nor make the Ardennaise magistrates comprehend Verlaine as he really was. They judged the author of *Sagesse* as an ordinary drunkard, who had fought with his relatives over a question of money one evening after a prolonged visit to the inn. Such quarrels are frequent in villages, and rarely come before the courts, but are arranged, if need be, by a justice of the peace.

What principally led to Paul Verlaine's condemnation by the judges of Vouziers was the hostility
displayed against him by his neighbours. He had
shocked and irritated them by his ways, which it
must be admitted were out of the ordinary. He
did not even drink like others. His drunkenness
was of an exuberant character, noisy and aggressive,
and disconcerted the habitual topers of the district.
Between two glasses he would hold ill - advised
conversations, often incomprehensible to his peasant
associates, and therefore regarded with suspicion.
The country people, no worse than others, could
not sympathise with this poet of eccentric behaviour,
who mixed himself up with farming affairs, of
which he knew nothing. Why had he come to
Coulommes, this wicked Parisian? Why had he
not remained in that town, the inhabitants of
which are too polite to be honest? Vaguely he
assumed in their unfriendly gossip the similitude
of one who sought to steal land, and they banded
together against him, as against a foreign invader.
Thus all the witnesses were on Dane's side,
desiring in their hearts to get rid of the Parisian,
and keep his house after the fashion of their
neighbour Létinois.

It is therefore to be remarked, for an exact
appreciation of Verlaine's offence that it was established by openly hostile witnesses ; exaggerated
rumours, and the inquisitive and uncharitable
observation of unsympathetic people giving rise
to suppositions, which received an appearance of
reality from Verlaine's language and manners.
Besides which the reports concerning him from
Paris and Belgium were not of a nature likely

to bias his judges in his favour. Therefore the sentence of a month's imprisonment may be re-garded as a quasi-acquittal, considering the penalties attaching to the offence preferred against him. There is no excuse for Verlaine's conduct to his mother, still it must be recognised that it was not an affair of great moment, but rather one for settle-ment at home by a sharp maternal reprimand to Verlaine sober.

The poet was released on the 13th May, quitting the gaol at Vouziers, of which he has left a sketch both in *Les Mémoires d'un Veuf* ("Un Héros"), and in *Mes Prisons*, one fine spring morning. No one was awaiting him on this occasion, no friendly face greeted him with smiles as the door of the gaol opened. Mme. Verlaine, her heart lacerated, although she had long ago freely forgiven him, had determined against the journey to Vouziers to meet her son. She remembered not with resentment but with sorrow the scene at Coulommes, and intended to punish the heedless and impulsive rake by her absence. Besides, which partly justified Verlaine's irritation, her adviser, M. Dane, had dissuaded her from going to meet Paul.

Nothing could have touched him to the quick like this marked absence. He understood the punishment the one always indulgent intended to inflict upon him, and he at once determined to appear utterly indifferent. His freedom brought with it liberty to drink of which he would make use on the spot. *Dame!* it is pleasant to drink on a holiday, but company is precious to those just come from captivity. With whom should he crack a glass to independence reconquered? *Parbleu!*

2 C

with the companion who was there on the threshold :
the gaoler who had drawn the bolts and jingled
his keys as he politely conducted to the exit the
ex-prisoner with whom he was on friendly terms.
Verlaine invited him, and they went to empty a
bottle of white wine at the " Bon Coin," the usual
resort of the staff of the prison.

This libation in the open air consoled the poet
for the moment. But the gaoler was obliged to
return to his duties, and Paul remained alone, face
to face with a bottle. He pondered over what he
should do. Ought he to go to Coulommes, demand
pardon of his mother, throw himself at her feet
and embrace her? It would be very melodramatic,
and he would be the laughing-stock of the village.
Then, again, where must he go to find her? To
his enemy's, he who had delivered him to justice?
He could not go there, besides his mother had
written to him that she intended to return to Paris
shortly. Country life, naturally, had lost all its
charm. The evil reputation of her son reflected
injuriously upon the unfortunate mother, who found
herself shunned.

Moreover, the judicial position was becoming
grave. Some law-suits had been lost, their credit
was dead, and Verlaine no longer possessed even
the house which his mother had given him, having
sold it to a local farmer, after the miserable scene
which led to the prosecution, for the sum of
2,200 francs. The house is still in existence at
Coulommes, the property of Mme. Rigot Oudin,
widow of the aforesaid buyer.

Verlaine, therefore, returned to Paris to take
up his life there afresh, relinquishing the charm

of the fields. He determined to set to work and live by his pen — a praiseworthy resolution ; but unhappily he came back from the country ill-equipped for the endeavour. He was nearly ruined, and his mother, impoverished and saddened, who followed him, had not her former ability to assist him. Worse still, gout had begun to seize hold of Verlaine. His muscles atrophied, his joints grew stiff. If his brain remained healthy and vigorous, his aptitude for work, never very considerable, had diminished. Even his talent had undergone a perceptible alteration. A few years more of Bohemian life in the Quartier Latin, and the admirable poetic vein of his youth that had produced *Sagesse*, *Amour*, and *Bonheur* would dwindle and change. The return of the poet to Paris in 1885 marks the beginning of the third and most wretched stage of his life, sojourns in hospitals alternating with stagnation in drinking-shops, and soon the great, powerful, genial Paul Verlaine would be nothing more than the "Poor Lélian" of legendary destitution.

CHAPTER XVI

JADIS ET NAGUÈRE — MES HÔPITAUX — DEATH OF
VERLAINE'S MOTHER — IN HOSPITAL — *AMOUR—*
PARALLÈLEMENT—AIX-LES-BAINS

(1885-1890)

WHILE living in his Ardennaise village, "laughing,
drinking, and singing," Verlaine had now and then
endeavoured to re - animate his somewhat torpid
muse. He arranged for a new volume, and collected
together some fragments, previously composed, with
the idea of their publication with Vanier. Soon
after his settlement at Coulommes his volume *Jadis
et Naguère* appeared. He advised me of the fact
in the following undated note :

"COULOMMES.

'MY DEAR EDMOND,—A volume of mine has
just been published, *Jadis et Naguère*, by Vanier,
19 Quai Saint - Michel. One of the poems is
dedicated to you, *Le Soldat Laboureur* (alias *Le
Grognard*) you will speak of it, won't you? and
send the article to your   P. VERLAINE."

Jadis et Naguère is a collection of verse written
some years before publication. Several of the
pieces classed together under the sub-title, *À la
Manière de Plusieurs*, were sent me from his Belgian
prison, where they had been composed. A certain

404

PAUL VERLAINE AT THE CAFE FRANCOIS, QUARTIER LATIN (1889).
" Nos contemporains chez eux "

number date from an earlier period, for instance, *Le Grognard*, afterwards entitled *Le Soldat Laboureur*, was written in 1869. The actor, Frances, recited this poem, which was at once a satire and a eulogy of the old army, one evening at Nina de Callias's. It was a sort of reply to Coppée's *Bénédiction*, recited by the same artist in the same *salon*.

There are in the book, which is one of Verlaine's most interesting volumes, poems written in accordance with each of his styles, and suitable for inclusion in his previous collections.

Thus *Images d'un Sou* seems like a leaf escaped from the *Fêtes galantes* :

> " . . . Voici Damon qui soupire
> La tendresse à Geneviève
> De Brabant, qui fait ce rêve
> D'exercer un chaste empire,
> Dont elle-même se pâme
> Sur la veuve de Pyrame,
> Tout exprès ressuscitée . . . "

Fantoches is like a pleasing mocking echo, in which the poet projects against the moon the gesticulating shadows of Scaramouche and Pulcinella, while the excellent Doctor Bolonais below slowly gathers simples among the brown grass. This poem is contemporary, by reason of its character, composition, and colouring, with the strange lines in the *Romances sans Paroles* :

> "C'est le chien de Jean de Nivelle
> Qui mord, sous l'œil même du guet,
> Le chat de la Mère Michel ;
> François les Bas-Bleus s'en égaie . . . "

Some of the poems in the book were composed

before Verlaine's first wanderings in Belgium and England ; the highly coloured description of *L'Auberge*, for example, might be included among the *Paysages Belges* of the *Romances*. Other verses date from the poet's earliest youth, like *La Pucelle*, a sonnet, of which I have the original pencilled manuscript, composed in 1862, when Verlaine was at the Lycée Bonaparte.

Some belong to the same period as the *Poèmes Saturniens*, and are in the author's objective and descriptive style.

Among the sonnets in the part of the volume entitled *Jadis*, there are some of great beauty, elevated philosophy, and superb workmanship like *Le Squelette*, which might be placed side by side with Baudelaire's *La Barque de Don Juan* ; and there are other short and purely descriptive poems, rivalling in clearness of touch the most polished productions of Théophile Gautier and Leconte de Lisle.

Descriptive poems (*La Princesse Bérénice*), humorous (*Kaleidoscope, Dizain mil Huit Cent Trente, le Pitre*), realistic (*La Soupe du Soir, Paysage, l'Aube à l'Envers*), legendary, and narrative, go to make up this volume, which sums up the entire range of Verlaine's inspiration and style. The poem *Les Vaincus*, with its epic character, belongs to the same category as the *Ode à Metz* ; it is a tribute to the victims of the civil war, calling for fierce reprisals, and was composed in London in 1872. Probably the pusillanimity of Vermersch, one of the refugees of the Commune, helped to inspire Verlaine to this bitter cry of despair, which recalls Alfred de Vigny's *Mort du Loup* :

"Et nous, que la déroute a fait survivre, hélas !
Les pieds meurtris, les yeux troubles, la tête lourde,
Saignants, veules, fangeux, déshonorés et las,
Nous allons, étouffant mal une plainte sourde."

Later on he conjures up a terrible vision of pitiless justice and unbridled vengeance.

It may be said that in *Jadis et Naguère*, the seven cords of the lyre sound, vibrate, mutter, sigh, murmur, menace, and sing. It is not Verlaine's most perfect volume, and many of the pieces of which it is composed were severely omitted by him from the MSS. of previous volumes ; they did not satisfy the poet, and appeared to him to require further consideration and polishing. He discovered imitations among them, and these he grouped together under the ingenuous sub-title : *A la Manière de Plusieurs*. In short the poems, diverse in tone, character, subject, and inspiration, which make up this volume, give it the appearance of a collection of selected pieces, and it was very well received, and regarded as very interesting when it was presented to the public by the publisher Charpentier.

As if in justification of the composite and antho-logical character of the book, there is included in it a little play, *Les Uns et les Autres*, a poetic and delicate lover's quarrel, like an echo of de Musset and Molière, set in a scene by Banville, a *fête galante* adapted for the stage.

After it had been played it was published separately as an ordinary dramatic booklet in-18, 36 pages, with a pale bluish cover, on which was printed : "Paul Verlaine.—*Les Uns et les Autres*, comédie en un acte et en vers. Représentée pour la première fois au théâtre du Vaudeville, par les soins du Théâtre d'Art, le 21 Mai 1891.—Paris, Léon Vanier, libraire-éditeur, 19, Quai Saint-Michel, 1891.—Evreux, Imprimerie de Charles Hérissey." On the half title : "*Les Uns et les Autres*, comédie dédiée à Théodore de Banville."

Copies were sent to :— MM. Krauss, of the Odéon ; Paul Franck, of the Gymnase ; Engel, of the Opera ; Albert Girault and Henri Huot, of the Théâtre d'Art; Mmes. Moreno, of the Comédie-Française; Lucy Gérard, of the Gymnase ; Suzanne Gay and Denise Ahmers, of the Théâtre d' Art.

Les Uns et les Autres was only played once, not that the piece was a failure, but its performance was an exceptional affair and could not be repeated, at least at the Vaudeville. The theatre was taken for a matinée by the young enthusiasts of the Théâtre d'Art, and the affair was managed by M. Paul Fort.

The performance was organised by subscription, the price of the stalls being 20 francs, at least that is what I paid, and I suppose, as the notices stated, there were no free tickets. It was for the benefit of Paul Verlaine and the unfortunate painter of Tahiti, Gauguin. The curtain raiser was *Le Corbeau*, Edgar Poe's poem translated into prose by Mallarmé, the tragedian Damoye interpreting the melancholy and despairing visionary of the poem. This was followed by *Le Soleil de Minuit* by Catulle Mendès, the scenery and very costly dresses of which absorbed the greater part of the receipts. Indeed, although the artists gave their services, after all the expenses of staging, lighting, printing, posters, etc., to say nothing of cabs, cigars, and drinks for the members of the committee, had been paid, nothing remained for the two who were to benefit by the entertainment.

I found Verlaine during the performance in the little American café leading out of the vestibule. Wearied and disgusted, he was absorbing heady liquors, and pouring out angry sarcastic complaints against the organisation of what he called his *maléfice*. I pacified him as well as I could, and remained with him till the end of the programme, which ought to have brought in a good deal if the too costly dresses of the *Soleil de Minuit* had had the success they merited.

Verlaine was preparing *Les Mémoires d'un Veuf*, *Louise Leclercq*, and some biographies for publication in the *Hommes d'Aujourd'hui*, when an attack of gout confined him to his bed, and he caused himself to be transported to the hospital at Tenon. This was his first experience in a hospital. He was afterwards to become acquainted with several others, and grew to regard them as hotels in which lodging was to be had gratis, and with far more comfort attached to it than was the case in the furnished apartments in the Quartier Latin, which formed his temporary abiding-places.

He was grateful to "his hospitals," speaking of them as a landowner speaks of "his lands," where, quitting the town, he enjoys repose and recuperates his strength. He devoted to them, as to "his prisons," a book full of kindliness, tinged occasionally with a rather bitter pleasantry, but with no peevish complaints against the staff, the doctors, nor the management. He was cared for very tenderly in several of these asylums, and never exhibited any grievance against the *assistance publique* often attacked with reason.

One exception, however, must be mentioned: an attendant named Grandmaison, who treated him with harshness, even brutality, but received the punishment he deserved, for the usually forgiving Verlaine addressed an "invective" to him.

This was the sole occasion on which Verlaine uttered a word of censure in connection with his hospital life. At the end of his little book, *Mes Hôpitaux*, he testified his gratitude to those who had cared for him, and, not being able to cure him, had rendered his malady supportable, and addressed the following greeting to the hospitals in which he had stayed:

"*Mes Hôpitaux* . . . adieu! if not, *au revoir*! . . . I have lived quietly, laboriously within your walls, quitting you one after other not without regret, and if my dignity as a man, hardly less miserable than the most sadly destitute of your frequenters, and my just instinct as a good citizen, not wishing to usurp the places envied by many poor people, often hurried me forth prematurely from your doors, blessed both to those who arrive and to those who go out, be assured, kind hospitals, that in spite of all the inevitable monotony, the necessarily strict rules, and the inconveniences inherent in every human situation, I retain a recollection of you unique among many other remembrances infinitely more painful, that life has had and will have for me doubtless always."

Picturesque descriptions, recollections, reflections on books, and autobiographical details form the substance of the seventy-five pages of this

volume published by Léon Vanier in 1891, with
a very successful and life-like portrait by F.-A.
Cazals, of Verlaine standing, dressed in the
hospital garb — long dressing - gown, shirt un-
buttoned at the neck, and cap.

This volume, which was called for in haste by
Vanier, who was desirous of reimbursing himself
for several advances by publishing Verlaine's prose,
for which a small circle of readers existed, does
not convey the exact sentiments felt by the poet
during his various stays in hospital, but rather
consists of reflections made outside, and journalistic
comment.

The following letters, dated from Brussels,
Tenon, Vincennes, and Saint - Antoine, give a
more exact idea of his actual feelings.

He was ailing, rather than ill, suffering from
an hereditary rheumatism in the joints which
hindered his walking.   Finding himself alone,
penniless, without regular work, and with no
shelter except wretched rooms like those in the
Cour Saint-François, the light, clean wards of the
hospital were attractive and desirable.   Moreover,
with the enforced sobriety, his body, freed from
the bondage of drink, was soothed by a diet, if
not abundant and succulent, at least healthful and
regular.   These periods in hospital were better
for him than the life outside, as he openly
recognised.

His mother died in January 1886, which was
a sad and disastrous event for Paul, who found
himself altogether isolated, and without restraining
influence or support.   He wrote me the following
letter soon after :

"PARIS, 26*th January* 1886.

" I have for a long time past been confined to my bed with rheumatism, which is the reason why I did not convey to you myself, as I might have done, the sad news.

" Will you—I entreat you ardently—as soon as you receive this, come and see me, and talk to me for a long time? I am more unhappy than you can possibly imagine!

" Receive my most sympathetic shake of the hand, and come very quickly to see your affectionate friend.

" I am lodging at a wine - shop — entrance through the shop—Hôtel du Midi, 6 Cour Saint-François, Rue Moreau. It is between the Rue de Charenton and the Avenue Daumesnil, five minutes from the Bastille.

" At a later hour.—Come immediately if you can, and as quickly as possible."

I went to see him on receipt of this note, some time after the death of his mother, for I had been absent from Paris when the sad event occurred, and found him lodging amid absolutely deplorable conditions. The Cour Moreau, which is inhabited by the working classes, chiefly the very poor, is situated at the foot of the railway line to Vincennes. Verlaine lodged on the ground floor, and it was necessary to penetrate through the dirty shop in order to gain the poet's chamber. The place was most unfortunate both for Verlaine's health and his purse. The few sous he received either from Vanier, from friends to whom he communicated his distress, or from the wreck of his mother's fortune, only too easily found their way to the bar. His room was small, sordid, sinister, like the cut-throat place at the bottom of which it squatted.

There was no flooring, not even a paving; the foot fell upon the bare earth, which was a little muddy, dampness, brought in from outside by those coming and going having softened it. The pot boy bringing in his food, rare acquaintances from the Quartier who came for a drink at the counter hard by the bed of the sick man, and also an obliging neighbour who talked in the evening with the poet, and lent him newspapers, performing a few of the duties of a nurse, formed his sole visitors.

A little cupboard served as Verlaine's library; into it were crowded several books—waifs of his many shipwrecks—and some manuscripts. A narrow table and two wicker-bottomed chairs completed the furniture of this wretched room. Evidently Verlaine was in a bad state from every point of view, and when he decided to return to hospital it was a change for the better, an indisputable gain.

Tenon, his first hospital, is situated on the heights of Ménilmontant, and he has described it in picturesque fashion.

He came out very soon, cured, or nearly so, of his first attack of gout. A new attack took him back to the hospital again, and on the 13th December he wrote me the following letter:

" I received only yesterday, 12th December, your letter of 25th November, and hasten to answer the questions you put to me.

" For six weeks I have been in the Hospital Broussais, Salle Follin, bed 6, Rue Didot 96,

14th *arr.* (the public admitted on Thursdays and
Sundays from one till three), for a stiffness in the
left knee, the result of rheumatism last winter.

"I spent the months of July, August, and
September in the Hospital Tenon, on account of
swellings in my legs, also the result of rheumatism.
My lodging is always the same, 5 Rue Moreau,
6 Cour Saint-François, 12th *arr.* But until other
advice write to me or come and see me at Broussais.
So much for my health.

"My affairs with my legal ex-wife have been
arranged, naturally to my loss ; *i.e.*, that after having
paid my debts, those of my mother (debts, mine
and hers for board and lodging for five or six
months), and defrayed the expenses of her interment
at Batignolles, there would have remained to me
scarcely enough to live on for some days, if I
had not inherited from my Aunt Rose, who died in
February, the sum of 2,400 francs, three quarters
of which also went in medicine, board, and lodging.
Such is my financial situation.

"My wife, or ex-wife, in reply to a courteous
demand of mine to see my son has said no. I
learned quite recently that she married again in
November last. I think I have some right to see
my son, and interest myself in him. He is over
fifteen, and is a day-boy at Rollin's, to whom I
have been kindly mentioned, and he very well
remembers my visits to him some years ago.
What do you advise me to do?

"I am glad you like my *Mémoires.* Have
you also received my collection of stories : *Louise
Leclercq*? You should send me the *Echo de Paris*
in which you speak of me.

"It is a fact, I believe, that I ought to be
able to earn some money now that my name
has issued from the shadow of the *Parnasse* and
decadence (what a stupid word). So again I ask

you how, where and all the etceteras to write in paying newspapers. With my leg which prevents me from walking, and my awkwardness — my inexperience in these things—I am in as great a difficulty in this connection as in every other.

"Luck and ill-luck; the important thing is that at bottom health and truth remain. As the people say, I am not sick at heart; that being so and without giving way to overmuch despair, I can perhaps extricate myself from the abyss. Easy to say, is this not your own opinion? I should be very glad to see you, and to have a talk by ourselves. When shall we see one another again? I do not know when I shall leave here, and I fear that your occupations prevent you from coming to see me—at least very often. But we can correspond, and I can count on your kind letters of news and advice, can I not?—Very fraternally,

"P. VERLAINE.

"*P.S.*—I have received news of Ricard, and am going to publish a biography of him in *Les Hommes du Jour*."

Verlaine suddenly disappeared. He took up his quarters again in hospital, and during the summer of 1887 several weeks passed without my hearing anything of him. I wrote to him, care of Vanier, and received the following reply:

"PARIS, *7th August* 1887.

" I received your letter at the Hospital Tenon; it reached me through Vanier, but not the newspaper. I will procure one, or if you have time send one to Vanier. I left the Cour Saint-François in April last. Thank you in advance for what you say about the *Romances sans Paroles* which have had the strange fortune to appear when I was—where you know—and to re-appear, thirteen years after, finding me here. *Habent sua fata*, etc. The Sens edition was completely exhausted, as was also that of the *Fêtes galantes* (have you received a copy of the new edition?), and the *Poèmes Saturniens*, and this *Bonne Chanson* which . . . (*rehabent sua fata relibelli*). For, oh derision! I have some success as a poet, 'fame' even, but I can say with as much appropriateness as Lamartine ruined :

"'The more I have squeezed this fruit, the more empty have I found it.'

"Yes, my dear Edmond, *my circumstances* are more deplorable than ever ; and here is my budget :

"Not a sou! The small amount of money Vanier may still owe me cannot be more than a few crowns. I expect, not before the 15th November next, 900 francs from a notary absolutely inflexible in the matter of any advance whatsoever. I speak from experience. You see, dear friend, the situation is very clear. To die of hunger, or to find something as soon as possible, no matter what, now or afterwards. Such are the horns of the dilemma. Ideas I have not. I could give lessons in English and other things, with diploma and references . . . to support me, but to whom, and where? You know the use of advertising in the newspapers! It is only through friends that I could obtain anything. If you know . . . some one who could offer me anything, tell me.

"I have been offered (Mendès) or rather promised work in the press. Perhaps help from the Ministère de l'Instruction Publique. That is a secret!—but for the moment I have nothing in my pocket, and no idea how anything is to come there. I am very grateful to you for your kind efforts. Please pursue them actively. I shall know how to respond to the success of your friendly endeavours. As much as all these worries permit me I work—outside the verse which it is absolutely impossible for me not to make from time to time, it is truly second nature with me—at prose, which I am making as 'possible,' as possible. But when one has acquired the habit, whether of refinements or simplicity, perhaps more refined still and more difficult, what an effort it is . . . to see it become unprofitable.

"I wrote you from Cochin, where I spent a month in August and May. Did you receive that letter? This time I was very careful to put on the envelope 'personal and urgent.' I am here, Hospital Tenon, ward Seymour, bed 5 bis, Rue de la Chine, Paris—probably until Tuesday next week, 9 inst., the day on which I shall be sent to the Asile de Vincennes, Saint-Maurice (Seine), where I shall remain a fortnight or three weeks. But it is possible, seeing how full all the hospitals are now, either that they will keep me here another week or send me away a week sooner. In any case, you will be instructed immediately to what address to write. . . . I press your hand very sadly, but all the same very courageously. P VERLAINE."

He entered for a time the Asile de Vincennes, from whence he wrote to me, asking me to come and see him.

In September 1887 he came out, visited the familiar cafés, had a relapse, and re - entered Broussais.

I invited him many times to come and stay some weeks with me at Bougival, where he would have had a good opportunity to read, work, and get well, with certain precautions, on my part, to prevent too many visits to the wine-shop, but he always postponed his visit, although he knew that it would do him good. After his third relapse, when I renewed my insistence, he wrote as follows:

" *27th September*, 1887.

"I refer to my last letter only to tell you that I ended by returning to the hospital. My present address therefore is . . . Hospital Broussais. . . . All the rest of my letter is of a true absolute : Misery—Infirmity—Hope.

"I am treated here sceptically. Perhaps they will try and bend my leg after putting me to sleep, in a fortnight's time, so I have fifteen days to the good. I confess I would rather go out. Could you procure some sort of shelter and food for me? I shall have very little money. Could you or any one you know advance me 100 francs to be repaid on the 16th November next for certain? To my frank demands kindly answer frankly. Friends always. I shall have all the necessary courage. Besides, I have great hope in the near future, and I am equal to a great effort. Answer immediately, will you not?"

Verlaine wrote me many letters at this period from the Hospital Broussais; their monotonous character renders it unnecessary to quote them all, but the following are some extracts from them:

" PARIS, *9th October* 1887.

"Many thanks for your kind promises of hospitality. I hope not to weary you for long if I am obliged to avail myself of your kindness. I do not yet know when I shall take my departure. I shall try to delay it as long as possible, especially as I am on the mend, and begin to hope that they will continue to treat me by gradual movements. In

PAUL VERLAINE AT THE HOSPITAL.
From a drawing by F. A. Cazals in the Musée National du Luxembourg, Paris.

this way I shall avoid, not without joy, an operation of doubtful success. However, I will advise you, some days in advance when I am about to leave."

"HOSPITAL BROUSSAIS, 21st October 1887.

"First, many thanks for the mention in the *Echo de Paris*. . . .

"I expect to go out soon; in reality, I believe myself incurable, or at least a cure would take so long that it comes to the same thing. A vague but very distressing *amour-propre* makes me impatient. One has the air of being here through charity although perhaps the Association which despoiled me in the form of the Justice of the Peace of the 12th *arr.* owes me a little hospitality. And then from one moment to another I may be sent away, so benevolent are the managers and doctors. Now if I go out suddenly, before the 15th November, I may very easily find myself with not enough money to take the train to Bougival. I should, therefore, be very much obliged to you if you would send me the necessary sum (0.90 c. !!). I assure you that you will be repaid next November. I shall put the sum aside to await my departure, and not touch it. Some friends bring me tobacco from time to time, and Vanier—but it is hard to make him part! . . . I am going to conclude some future agreements not very satisfying . . . with this publisher, intelligent, but I repeat, close!

"I shall drag out the days here as much as possible, and only decide to go when I see they have had enough of me. But as I expect this will be soon, you see I am right in awaiting with impatience what you will be so kind to lend me for the little journey to be made by a quasi-invalid.

"I will not weary you otherwise very much nor very long. If you knew how easily satisfied I have become, though I never was difficult in this respect. I have so few requirements now! Some friends are trying right and left to place copy for me. Perhaps you, too, could give me advice and indications without, of course, losing sight of the idea of my living, if possible, in a private hospital. But I believe I may hope to earn money by literature, and to make up enough for my daily bread (and a little butter) with other slight labours, lessons, writing, etc.

"When I am with you I will read a great deal and bring myself up to date . . . and make plans to be put into execution if I can get 'my' notary to advance me 1,000 francs on a debt of 1,500 francs to be recovered a little later from an old vicar of Saint-Gervais—a hard morsel a vicar of Saint-Gervais, but a pretty morsel: 1,500 francs! . . ."

"HOSPITAL BROUSSAIS, 26*th October* 1887.

"I am counting upon my 943 francs and some centimes about the 16th November next. This sum, together, perhaps, with some probable 'returns,' will permit me, while endeavouring to recover my debt of 1,500 francs, of which I spoke to you in my 'rather agitated' letter, to buy a few clothes, choose a suitable lodging, and wait while working for the newspapers and seeking lessons or an appointment.

"A volume of mine is about to appear, *Amour*. It is Catholic, but not clerical, although very orthodox.

"In it I have dedicated to you a poem in the same simple and descriptive style as the *Nocturne Parisien* and *Le Grognard*. . . . I think this book, which is more varied than *Sagesse*, will have some success and put me in the way of obtaining more lucrative work. It will be followed by *Parallèlement*, an altogether 'profane' collection, a little 'red' and amusing, I think. These two, absolutely finished, are almost in the press.

"I have two short stories ready and several articles for a second series of *Les Memoires d'un Veuf*, . . . also some other prose writings. You see, I have done work in advance. Some friends are trying to place them but . . .! How odd this literary situation is! But I believe if I were sharper, from the publishing and journalistic point of view, I could extricate myself. I am going to try. *Que Diable*! It would be too much to die of hunger. But first I am going to economise. How difficult even with nothing in one's pocket and with most reasonable wants. However, I have been, and can be again, without very much trouble. But I babble. . . .

"PARIS, 28*th November* 1887.

"I owe you this letter, for you may be surprised at my silence, after my resolution several times expressed, to ask you to give me shelter for a time at your Bougival. This is how it is. The 900 francs, on which I confidently counted in November, will not be remitted to me until April, but surely then. . . . I explained to you, I believe, that it was the remainder of a deposit in guarantee of payment for a property sold by me in 1882, said payment to be completed in six years. I made a mistake with regard to the date . . . but it is sure, sure!

"The impossibility of obtaining from Vanier— *spes unica* — sums sufficient to live on outside while awaiting the most welcome payment, has determined me, following the reiterated advice of friends who have been to see me, to prolong my stay here as long as possible. But I have carefully put your loan aside, thanking you again for it a thousand times.

". . . Have you spoken of me to any one who could help me, and do you see any hope? Do you, at least, see any means of my placing in the press some short stories, fantasies in the style of *Les Memoires d'un Veuf*, criticisms, translations, etc.? Vanier, with whom I have agreements, but so unremunerative, would not be offended ; on the contrary, I believe he would be pleased to see a prose work of mine issued by some other publisher. Do you see any possibility of an agreement between me and one of his *confrères*, with some advance on a book, nearly completed, of short stories and articles, two or three of which are rather stiff, but can be modified if necessary? . . . And lessons? . . .

"I am always much the same, lame, but able to walk a little, almost enough : but at the same time sufficiently afflicted to interest them here. I am very dull although I work very hard. What a life, what surroundings, what burial, remote from any possibility of speaking for myself, and the absent are always wrong! I am none the less grateful to you for your kind digressions and flattering allusions to me. When there are any in your newspapers, try and send them to me. My volume, *Amour*, will soon, I hope, appear. . . . I have another, I ought to have written to you about it, nearly ready, equally daring and *orgiaque*, and not too melancholy ; it makes part of a whole, of which *Sagesse* is the frontispiece, *Jadis et Naguère*, a part, and *Parallèlement* another part, *Bonheur* being the conclusion. A second series of *Les Poètes Maudits* is in the press (Desbordes-Valmore, Villiers de l'Isle-Adam, and Pauvre Lélian [P.V.]) . . . *Dame !* I shall have time to arrange everything when I have *some money for such a purpose*. . . ."

GEORGES VERLAINE AND HIS FRIENDS.

×

"*3rd January* 1888.

"Always in hospital, where, 'as regards the leg,' I get better only imperceptibly. However, my general health is good, and outside a number of kindly articles seem to be preparing for my future publications — my store cupboards are full — a pecuniary reception from publishers, and in the meanwhile, from editors. I count always upon your kindly efforts in my favour. . . . I shall do my best to prolong my residence here, as it is salutary from every point of view, for at least I work in peace in this very calm Broussais.

"My book *Amour* will soon appear. The piece in it dedicated to you appeared in *La Vogue* in 1886. It is entitled *Ecrit en* 1875, and has to do with my *Villégiature* at Mons, in 1873, 1874, and 1875. I would send you a copy, but my manuscript is with Vanier, and you know what a poor memory for verse, whether my own or others, I have. I hope you will like it.

"An employee in the offices of this hospital, M. Désiré Vally, police magistrate, at the Palais (Morbihan), from February 1880, then at Château-neuf (Charante), where, at the end of July 1883, he was dismissed, hoping that the reasons which decided the administration to use so rigorous a measure, would not now prevent his reinstatement, is soliciting a new appointment from the Minister of the Interior as police magistrate or inspector. This gentleman, who has always been very obliging to me, has asked me to do what I can for him, so I recommend you his application, which is not sent yet, but will be when I hear from you, if you see any method of supporting it. Send me your *Morts Heureuses.*"

"PARIS, **21***st February* 1888

"This is to tell you that I am still in the same

state, neither good nor bad, at the Hospital Broussais.
My finances are a little better, and I hope when
I go out to have some money to go on with until
I receive the amount which will give me time
to look about me.   Have you taken up the matter
of good M. Vally?   I recommend it to you again.
Could you insert enclosed advertisement in one of
your papers, the *Mot* or the *Echo*?   He would be
very grateful to you.   You might send me the
number in which it appears and I will hand it to
him.   He is a man worthy of every confidence. . ."

Verlaine came out of hospital and occupied
himself with his affairs, particularly in connection
with his mother's will, wrote some articles for
Vanier, and then, utterly disheartened, crushed by
life and his recent loss, stunned by isolation
tormented by disease, uneasy about the future,
seeing himself almost without friends, having broken
with all the companions of his youth except me,
who, unhappily, was very much occupied and could
not keep him company, nor spend my time in
visiting the wine-shops, he fell back into chronic
drunkenness.   Dragging his diseased leg, supporting himself with a stick, but with body upright, head
held high, and a sarcastic smile, he went on his
wretched way through Paris, sitting at the tables
in the cafés of the Quartier Latin and rhyming
verses, writing by fits and starts short stories,
and talking and drinking endlessly with the young
poets attracted by his growing fame.

One fine day he was no longer to be seen at
the François Premier or the Café Rouge—the
establishments he usually frequented—where he had
his little court and had been photographed for a
series of our literary men as " Verlaine at Home."

His disappearance caused no comment unless some one asked carelessly " Do you know in what hospital Verlaine is ? "

In the *Echo de Paris* I wrote an article pointing out with a certain emotion the ill-health and needy condition of the poet. Some of his café companions suggested that in depicting his misery I had attacked his dignity, which was ridiculous. A little newspaper published in the Cour des Miracles announced that Verlaine had written to blame me, which was an error. The following matter establishes the facts.

"PARIS, 17*th February* 1889.

"DEAR FRIEND,—I hear that an article by you has appeared in the *Echo de Paris*, in which you speak of me in amusing and affectionate terms. I will try and procure the number ; meanwhile I seize this opportunity to thank you for your kind remembrance. What did provoke me, I confess, in the article of the 12th inst., was to read of myself as having been seen crushed with misery in the hospital of legends like Gilbert, H. Moreau and all the rest of the lyrical, consumptive, interesting, brotherhood, one of whom Heaven forefend I should ever be regarded. As you can understand, one is at times rather easily annoyed at such suppositions, and I am quite sure you would never reproach me with being proud, even if I were sometimes a little too much so.

"With my hand and all my heart P. Verlaine, Hospital Broussais.

I have just received your card, not only without anger, but with another handshake."

Verlaine meanwhile had published *Amour*, and *Parallèlement* was in the press.

I have already indicated the circumstances and state of mind in which the poet wrote the majority of the pieces composing these two volumes. It is not necessary to attribute to *Parallèlement*, certain pages of which border on a looseness only to be qualified as imaginative, the authority of an autobiography, or of confession. It must not be forgotten, when reading these pages of vicious, rather boastful fiction, that Verlaine said : " Of course I am not speaking of *Parallèlement* in which I rather pretend to be in communication with the devil " (*Mes Prisons.*) It was in the solitude of his Belgian prisons that Verlaine conceived and executed the majority of these little poems which are characterised by an intense pruriency. The distorted, bizarre and capricious verses recall the cocoanuts patiently carved into faces by the convicts of old times, which they offered with a simple and mischievous air to the nervous citizens visiting the hulks at Toulon and Brest.

Verlaine wanted to go for a time, when he came out of hospital, to Aix-les-Bains, as the following letter shows :

" 15*th July* 1889.

" That . . . . Vanier, has he sent you *Parallèlement* and the new edition of *Sagesse*? As for me I have no longer any connection with him, and am ready to make him dance. . . . I may even beg you one day to insert a letter of mine which will please him but ill. . . . Could you by any chance see if you could obtain for me a railway pass to Aix-les-Bains, I have a bed and excellent recommendations to the hospital there? I have returned here, for my leg torments me dreadfully, and I wish to have done with it, even if it takes me six months or more of serious treatment. . . ."

He was able to go to Aix-les-Bains, where he had rather an amusing adventure in a hotel. The landlord did not want to take him in, being startled by his rather wild air and Bohemian dress. A well-known doctor, however, to whom Verlaine had been recommended, arranged the affair for him.

In letters written from Aix to his young friend Cazals, Verlaine enumerated his literary projects. He was working at *Bonheur*. He had an idea for the second edition of *Parallèlement*:

"A dialogue between youths and virgins in the style of Virgil. The subject will allow me the utmost liberty. Title: *Chant Alterné*, I shall lengthen the lament on L. L. (Lucien Létinois) in *Amour*, but shall undoubtedly leave *Sagesse* as it is. Therefore *Parallèlement* being augmented by 400 or 500 lines, the volumes of my tetralogy, if I may thus speak of my elegy in four parts, will be of equal importance."

This fragment shows that there was a great deal of "composition" in both the audacious passion and despair of his verses. He heightened his lament for Lucien Létinois, like an actress who wrote to Dumas that she was "working up tears" for a moving fifth act. It would therefore be incorrect, as I have already said, to take as the expression of personal sentiments and desires all the passages, often extreme, in this "tetralogy," in which Verlaine combines the duly proportioned parts with art and artifice.

On Verlaine's return to Broussais, the hospital he preferred, he became impatient at not seeing his works published in the newspapers. I did what I could both in the *Echo de Paris* and elsewhere, and was fortunate enough to get some of his prose and poetry accepted; but Verlaine's copy was not always easy to place in a great daily. The following letter shows his rather excusable irritation:

"PARIS, 8*th January* 1890.

"MY DEAR FRIEND,—What does this silence signify? What makes you angry with me? I am compelled to formulate this question and put it to you. Nothing, I believe. And I have written to you so often about such important things.

"You offered once to send a story of mine to the *Echo de Paris*. I sent you one (*Extrêmes Onctions*), but have received no acknowledgment, in spite of three or four letters. But it appears that on the *Echo* I have an enemy, a M. B. . . . G. . . ., ready to do me an ill turn, for in the affair of the Boucicaut legacy, I, after much unpleasantness, only received a hundred francs, while others almost unknown, obtained three and five hundred!

"I had also, it seems, ill-wishers on the committees of the syndicates to which I have sent verse and prose, as I told you. Let us pass over, then, the *Echo de Paris*, in which, I have it on the best authority, there is nothing to be done for me, but have you not the ear of several other journals for which I could work?

"I am not a beggar, but a known literary man, and almost dying of hunger—ill, moreover—who asks himself what is the use of friends if they are so neutralised by others in authority. I dare ask nothing more of you, except to indicate to your pen my situation as an author whom a publisher (Vanier) keeps in poverty by agreements which he himself does not observe, and who can do nothing except, on the one hand, provoke in his (P. V.'s) favour a press campaign against Vanier, or, on the other, print his works himself in spite of every one.

"Can I at least count on you for this? Please advise me, and send me the numbers in which you reveal this real scandal, dreadful and dishonouring to the country in which it has occurred."

I succeeded in obtaining the insertion of some poems for him in the *Echo de Paris*, for which he thanked me, asking at the same time anxiously for payment.

He went out of Broussais in the spring, to enter it again in the autumn.

"PARIS, 3*rd November* 1890.

"I am writing you this from Broussais, now become proverbial, but none the more amusing for that, to tell you about a plan for a fairly long book — impressions more or less pleasant and humorous, without any malice — entitled: *Mes Hôpitaux!* . . . I have twelve closely written pages, and the thing can be extended to double this length; and it will be extremely easy for me to carry it out to the end, so much I possess my subject, or rather, alas! does my subject possess me! Now, could this work be included . . . in one of your journals? . . .

". . . I do not know when I shall leave here. I will spend one or two days with you at Bougival, not, of course, without warning."

He had a fresh attack of rheumatism at the beginning of 1891, and changed his hospital for that of Saint-Antoine.

"14*th January* 1891.

"For the last three days my cursed rheumatism, doubtless aroused by the intense cold, has seized me again, this time in the left wrist, so much so

that I am disabled all one side of my body!
And wretched! I immediately 'established' myself
in the Hospital Saint - Antoine . . . where I am
allowed to hope for a possible and comparatively
rapid cure.

"Xau recently sent me a letter inviting me to
do an article on society women, drawing-rooms,
elegances, fashions, etc. Difficult to do, especially
for a savage like myself, and paralysed by rheumatism. I am going to write and excuse myself,
and find out if he has really anything for me
to do. . . ."

"*15th July* 1891.

". . . A little country air would do me the
greatest good, and enable me to finish some great
works which should at last free me from embarrassment. Besides, I hope soon to have finished with
this five years' misery! . . .

"BED 25, WARD WOILLEZ, HOSPITAL COCHIN."

Verlaine, in the various hospitals in which he
stayed, was, therefore, well treated and cared for;
he enjoyed, even from the patients, ignorant of
the quality and literary importance of their room-
mate, particular consideration. He was up in all
the traditions of the hospital, the object of the
doctors' attention, and the sympathy of the patients.

One of the physicians who showed the most
kindness to and interest in him was the excellent
Dr Tapret. This will surprise no one, as Dr
Tapret is not only one of our most eminent
practitioners, but also a friend of the arts, and
a connoisseur in literature, painting, and music.

He was not able to cure Verlaine, for his
complaint was incurable, but the care of the
learned man, to whom I myself owe gratitude

for the almost miraculous cure of an attack of
gout, so checked and diminished the progress of
the disease, that Verlaine returned no more to
hospital. Sainte-Antoine was his last hospital,
and Dr Tapret his last physician. But for the
irregularities and excesses of his later life, Verlaine
might, doubtless, have been definitely freed from
the rheumatic attacks which tormented his mature
years.

The hospital was a shelter, a refuge where he
could work, a haven where he was safe from the
shipwrecks of debauch; a sanatorium, moral and
physical.

CHAPTER XVII

LAST YEARS — EUGÉNIE KRANTZ — DEATH IN THE
RUE DESCARTES—FUNERAL—A MONUMENT TO
PAUL VERLAINE

(1892-1896)

PAUL VERLAINE's last years were rather regrettable.
I shall give few details of his existence in the
Quartier Latin from 1892. He lived in various lodgings, all equally squalid, and dragged his diseased
leg and his withering talent into all the wine-shops
and bars on the left bank, in company with Eugénie
Krantz, Philomène, or Esther, light-o'-loves, anxious
to empty his glass and his pocket. This period,
however, was neither unproductive nor sterile.
After *Amour* and *Bonheur*, the two last works
of his best period, he published several unequal
volumes. In some of these tortured poems, ellipse,
anacoluthon, and disordered phrase too often correspond with incoherence of idea ; and absurdities,
and plays upon words abound. Besides various
fragments in prose, biographies, travel - notes,
fantasies, he published successively in his last
years *Les Elégies, Dans les Limbes, Les Dédicaces,
Les Epigrammes, Chair, Chansons pour Elle,
Liturgies, Intimes, Odes en Son Honneur.*
    Several of the poems in these different volumes

432

date from an earlier period. They had been neglected or buried by the poet, and afterwards exhumed. In spite of his loose life, his numerous changes of domicile, and his sojourns in prisons and hospitals, Verlaine preserved and published almost everything he wrote. In his letters the insistence with which he asked me for any poem he had sent me a copy of is remarkable. Still a few poems went astray, some of which I have reproduced, and various fragments which were buried in dead publications and youthful verses have been included in the last volume of the complete works, under the title *Œuvres Posthumes*.

As its title indicates, the book *Dédicaces* is only a bouquet of rhymes offered nominally to personal friends for the most part. A dedication addressed to me begins the volume, a sort of frontispiece, with a fac-simile of Verlaine's handwriting.

I will add to the list of Verlaine's last works a booklet of erotic character, entitled *Femmes*, which was privately circulated, and could not figure even in a complete edition.

One volume stands apart, but must not be overlooked, viz. : the collection of poems issued by Charpentier, under the title *Choix de Poésies*. A fine portrait, poetic and melancholy, by Eugène Carrière, adorns this volume, made up of excellent poems, chosen with taste from among the principal works of the poet, the *Poèmes Saturniens*, the *Fêtes galantes*, the *Romances sans Paroles*, *Sagesse*, *Jadis et Naguère*, *Parallèlement*, and *Bonheur*. The collection may not be of much account to those who love poetry and desire to possess the complete Verlaine, but it is sufficient, especially

2 E

for a foreigner, to give a good idea of the work of the great poet. I may add that the *Choix de Poésies* could be put into any hands and figure in any catalogue of the classics.

There now remains for me to speak of only one book, and that is one the publication of which I deplore. It is entitled the *Invectives*, a posthumous work. I do not wish to stir up the controversies revived by the publication of this book. The publisher Vanier is dead. I will only declare anew that if Verlaine had lived, he might wisely, loyally, and advantageously have omitted certain of these *Invectives*, viz. : those which have aroused most hostility to his memory as poet. These *Invectives* it is which have arrested the efforts of the committee for the monument, and alienated a large number of persons otherwise favourably inclined. By means of a few crowns Vanier doubtless acquired these *satirettes* which are unworthy of the poet, lampoons rather than poems. Verlaine scribbed them off to amuse himself, to ease his spleen, just as he drew caricatures on the margin of his letters, without attaching any importance to them. One laughs at such skits among friends, and never thought that these improvisations, often unpolished, and always spiteful—except two or three pieces, such as the famous *Ode to Metz*, inserted by the publisher to lengthen the volume—would ever go beyond the circle of café companions.

Pressed for money on certain days of idleness and great thirst, Verlaine "tapped" his publisher, who, "on principle" he said, would not part with 10 francs except in exchange for a morsel of copy.

Then Verlaine took out of his portfolio an *Invective*, or perhaps improvised one in a neighbouring café, and the publisher handed over the coveted pelf.

But at least half of this poetic dross should have been rejected by the crucible. The *Invectives* might have been quoted in the back part of a brasserie by poets and poetasters, but their appearance in daylight was treason to the memory of the poet, and created an obstacle, surmountable doubtless, but serious to his glorification in public places. For instance, Senator Cazot, treasurer of the Senate, believing himself badly treated in one of the *Invectives*, under the guise of the Magistrate Cazeaux, prevented the placing of a bust of the poet in the Luxembourg Gardens.

Verlaine once had for a moment the idea of presenting himself for election to the Academy, with no intention of irreverence towards that learned company. Rather was it an act of homage on the part of the Bohemian poet, for that Institution is more often than not attacked and ridiculed by the juvenile circles of the Quartier. I did my best to dissuade him, and took the trouble to explain to the public in an article in the *Echo de Paris*, that in my opinion Verlaine had every literary right to a seat under the cupola between his friends, François Coppée and José - Maria de Heredia, but that there were indispensable conditions regarding regularity of life, etc., which the candidate was unable to fulfil, and which would therefore prevent his election.

Verlaine, at first dissatisfied both with advice and article, quickly came round to my point of view, and thanking me, gave up the idea. As a poet of superior merit, as a powerful and original writer Verlaine assuredly merited admission, but his Bohemian life, his errors of conduct and ill repute rendered his candidature impossible. It must not be forgotten that Leconte de Lisle having died, Verlaine had been singled out, by the votes of a large number of poets, as his successor to the title " Prince of Poets." He who was the object of so flattering and well-merited an election might very well also be considered entitled to succeed Leconte de Lisle in his seat in the Academy.

The following letter gives Verlaine's opinion on the matter :

"My dear Edmond,—I thank you with all my heart for your article of three days ago. It delighted and touched me. A thousand and a thousand very sincere and hearty hand-shakes, I assure you.

"Certainly, yes I shall be happy to see you. I am always here and do not leave my room yet. But the afternoon is best ; in the morning there are hindrances, and in the evening I go to roost, like the chickens.

"You will receive a book from M. de Montesquieu, a very devoted and very kind friend of mine, to whom you will give great pleasure as well as to myself by speaking of his book, *Le Parcours du Rêve au Souvenir*, as it merits, in one of your next articles. . . .

"I naturally wrote the desired article on M. de Montesquieu, who, with Maurice Barrès and some others of our friends, often replenished the poet's empty purse."

Several detailed articles in newspapers and

magazines and even a volume (*Verlaine Intime*) have appeared, which give a complete idea of these last years of the poet. His feminine *liaisons* of this period have been recounted with a great many anecdotes by his latest friends. Although to the end I maintained the happiest relations with Verlaine, I saw him less during these last years. Greatly occupied, I could not follow him in his interminable peregrinations among the cafés and wine-shops of the Boul' Mich' and the Rue de Vaugirard. I went, however, from time to time, to "visit" him at the François Premier, Café Rouge, and Mürger, and he came to have a drink with me fairly often in the near neighbourhood of my Editorial Offices; also I helped him to the insertion of some articles. His correspondence with me, therefore, did not amount to much, and consisted principally of postcards or notes sent by hand "to await reply," which contained little beyond the suggestion of an appointment, demand for money, or thanks. He also invited me to his literary Wednesdays, very modest but interesting evenings, which combined originality of discussion with excess of certain appreciations.

A rather curious photograph, serving as prospectus to F.-A. Cazal's work on Paul Verlaine, represents the poet's *salon* with the following assistants: Mmes. Rachilde and Sophie Harlay, MM. Jean Moréas, Villiers de l'Isle - Adam, Laurent Tailhade, Gabriel Vicaire, Henri d'Argis, F. Clerget, F.-A. Cazals, Ary Renan, A. Desvaux, Jules Tellier, Paterne Berrichon. It is entitled: *Une Soirée chez Paul Verlaine in* 1889.

There were others invited to this *salon* of the

Rue Royer-Collard, from the hospitals, and from the tables of the François Premier, Mürger, and Café Rouge, where Verlaine usually held his receptions : Saint-Georges de Bouhélier, Raymond de la Tailhède, Georges de Lys, Jacques des Gachons, Maurice Leblond, Albert Grandin, Emile Blémont, Raymond Maygrier, Ernest Raynaud, Pierre Devoluy, Léon Durocher, Raoul Gineste, Stuart Merrill, Adolphe Retté, Gustave Kahn, Xavier Privas, Adrien Mithouard, Léon Deschamps, Achille Ségard, Signoret, Maurice du Plessys, etc.

He had some fairly happy periods of work and better health. Once he gave a series of lectures in Holland and Belgium, which had a certain success, partly owing to curiosity and partly to the clever way in which matters were arranged for him ; for Verlaine was only a mediocre orator. He recognised this himself when describing his tour. He read, always an unpleasing thing to do, and in a weak, hoarse voice. He was, however, thanks to excellent and enthusiastic friends, very well received, and brought back some money with him. But this was rather disastrous than otherwise, both to his health and powers of production, for affection and revelry on the part of his companions, as was their wont when the poet had money in his pocket, followed upon his profitable tour in the Low Countries.

As I said, anecdotal and indiscreet details of Verlaine's notorious mistresses have already been given to the public ; they were all vulgar, illiterate, belonging to the lowest strata of the Quartier's temptresses ; but Verlaine was not discriminating, and then he had known so little of women ! It was

not until after he was forty that he attached himself
to any one in particular ; moreover, a certain adapta-
bility was necessary to enable these gay companions
to accommodate themselves to the caprices, whims,
irritations, and even violences of the poet when he
was under the evil influence of alcohol.

One of them, named Philomène, seems to have
been rather amiable, gentle, and sisterly to him ;
but fickle and ungrateful, the poet left her for a
big, stout, Ardennaise, who looked as if she had
been hewn with a hatchet out of a hard block of
wood, and with fingers like sausages, which could,
however, be curved on occasion. This rustic, called
Esther, extorted from him all the money of which
she felt him to be possessed ; when his pocket
was empty she disappeared, safe to return when
Verlaine published another volume or had some
articles accepted in the press. She always heard of
these windfalls ; perhaps some of the poet's young
friends informed her. She came like a butterfly on
fine days, no unusual characteristic of Verlaine's loves.

The best known mistress of the poet, she who
accompanied him longest, and closed his eyes,
was Eugénie Krantz. She, too, squeezed the unfortunate man, but she made him work. Covetous
and provident, she knew that the day after she
had kept him at work like an ox at the plough,
the lines, poetic and prose, hastily scrawled by
Paul, could be exchanged at the newspaper or
publisher's office for silver, and sometimes gold,
to find their way immediately afterwards to the
nearest wine - shop. The lecture tour having
resulted in unexpected prosperity, Eugénie Krantz
radiated amiability. Verlaine, loving tranquillity,
hating scenes, and having retained at heart some

of a citizen's prejudices, conceived the odd idea,
during a tipsy reconciliation after a violent quarrel,
of marrying this woman.

He wrote to her from England:

"Do you speak seriously of marriage? If so,
you will procure me the greatest pleasure of my
life! We will go to the mayor's when you will?
It is besides the surest means of assuring you
something certain after my death. My dear one,
these have always been my ideas! I love only
you, and how much! . . ."

The letter finishes thus:

"Your will is mine: I know too well what it
would cost me not to obey you; you are always
right. . . . We shall meet soon, dear woman. I
embrace you and love you with all my heart!"
(*Verlaine Intime*—Charles Donos, page 235.)

This woman tranquilly deceived him. She was
denounced by her rival, Philomène Boudin, and
there was trouble between the two. When he came
out of hospital Paul found sometimes Philomène
and sometimes Eugénie. The former had a defect
in his eyes; she was married, while the other
woman was free. Consequently Eugénie could
more easily post herself at the entrance and seize
hold of the poet when he came out with money in
his pocket. Philomène was always unlucky; but
she never complained. Provided Paul had enough
to pay for a modest dinner accompanied by libations
somewhere in the Quartier, she was quite content
and amiable.

When his last attack of rheumatism came on,
feeling perhaps that his end was near, he would

not return to the hospital, but made up his mind to remain where he was, and, as he had some money, begged Eugénie to engage a nurse. He thus avoided charitable assistance, the thought of which was now distasteful to him. Verlaine, in spite of his vagabond existence and Bohemian ways, had retained a citizen's respect for the proprieties, and the hospital, tolerable, even agreeable, in his eyes as a place of repose, shelter, and cure, seemed to him an unbecoming place for death ; this prejudice he avowed to me on several occasions.

Therefore, although Eugénie Krantz was far from the worthy, faithful, devoted companion she ought to have been, and although personally I have a grudge against her for failing to warn me in time of my friend's severe illness, I feel grateful to her and forgive her much because she allowed Verlaine to die in a room he could regard as his own. He did not desire the melodramatic ending of a Gilbert or Malfilâtre. His last efforts were exerted to prevent his death taking place in a bed supplied by Government. What irony of fate that a great poet, son of an officer in the army, and a well-dowered mother, should owe it to a chance meeting at a counter with a woman whose favours were for sale, that he did not have to render up his soul to God in one of those great caravansaries. Thanks to this creature, task-mistress as much as lover, who had deceived, ill-treated, and despoiled him, and was incapable of comprehending or admiring him, he was not, in the supreme hour a mere number, a bundle of cold flesh to be taken to the dissecting-room, if his friends did not arrive with sufficient rapidity to claim his remains. He expired in a private room, among familiar objects, having under his eyes and at hand the ordinary accessories of his daily life, which made up the desired illusion of a home. To complete this illusion he only lacked the presence of old and dear friends, such as Coppée and myself, and his son Georges. His son, ill when he had completed his military service, was not, indeed, able to be present either at the death of his father or his obsequies. He had been attacked by some kind of congestion, the effect, it appeared, of hypnotic experiences.

Mme. Delporte, Verlaine's re-married wife, afterwards stated the following facts with regard to her son Georges:

"My husband, myself, and my two little children left Algeria at the beginning of July, leaving Georges, who loved the country, and desired to remain there. I gave him a small sum of money, which would suffice for his modest wants for several months. Suddenly, in a few weeks he found himself denuded of everything. He lost his memory; when he was spoken to he appeared to awaken abruptly; he had the automatic gestures, the entirely different voice, and the manners of a somnambulist.

"He was taken to the hospital. Treated by suggestion he was cured. Feeling himself recovered, and the time having come for his military service, he would not take advantage of the law which makes one year of service only compulsory for Algerians. He went to Lille, and was incorporated in a regiment, but, unhappily, he had been allowed to depart too soon, before his cure was complete, and a lethargic slumber again overtook him.

"Well cared for, he recovered, but his case interested the doctors by its singularity, and he was kept under observation.

" He was to have left in the first days of January, but was not allowed to depart until the 13th, too late, therefore, to assist at the obsequies of his father."

Georges Verlaine, an amiable and rather melancholy young man, acquired an unbounded admiration and very vivid posthumous affection for his father. He had for a long time been possessed with the desire to see him. He had written to him, and, but for his illness, would certainly have been present not only at his funeral but also at his death-bed. Fate intervened between father and son. Mme. Delporte, the heroine of *La Bonne Chanson*, protested against the idea that she hindered the meeting of the two.

" During the twenty-three years that I had not seen Verlaine," she wrote, " I had time to forget the bad days, and in the ten years since I married again and became happy I certainly forgave him. It is, therefore, an error for the newspapers to declare that I systematically kept Georges from him."

I will not dispute this statement; the ex-Mme. Verlaine is not a spiteful person. She has always been very good to her son. It may even be presumed that she has not remained indifferent to the fame of the man whose name she bore, and it is possible that during the last month she consented to, and even facilitated, their drawing together. But as we have seen from Verlaine's correspondence and the narration of his history, he asked in vain for his son's address. It was always concealed from him, and the joy of embracing his son was never his.

It was on opening the newspaper one morning that I suddenly became aware, without any preparation, of Paul Verlaine's death. I learned afterwards that he asked for me and François Coppée in his last moments. His illness had been kept from us, and no telegram was received. Some time had passed since I had heard anything of the poet; but in the vortex of work and business matters, not having time to visit him, I reassured myself with the proverb, "No news is good news," that no aggravation had occurred in the ailing condition to which he was only too much accustomed.

On returning home after the funeral I found a piece of paper, wrongly addressed, informing me that if I wished to see my friend, Paul Verlaine, for the last time, I had only to go to the Rue Descartes. This advice, in any case very late, was signed by Eugénie Krantz, the companion of the poet's last days, in whose presence he breathed his last. She did not long survive Verlaine. Alcoholism, facilitated by the sale of certain autographs and rare papers of the poet's, she had put on one side, in particular a fragment of *Louis XVII.*, carried her off rapidly.

I hurried off as soon as I had learned the fatal news, to No. 39 Rue Descartes, where I found my old friend reposing in the immobility of death. Deeply moved, I imprinted a last kiss on his icy forehead. The lodging was poor, but clean and light, looking on the street. At the back a recess served as a dining-room.

With some of the poet's friends I undertook the charge of the obsequies, and arranged with the curé of Saint-Etienne-du-Mont for the religious service. M. Léon Vanier had already made some arrangements ; but they seemed insufficient considering the religious sentiments of the deceased and the numbers who would probably attend. Indeed the register placed in the humble lodge of the *concierge* of the Rue Descartes was filled with the signatures of men in every class of life, from the highest aristocrats of literature to workmen whom Verlaine had known in hospital and the Cour Moreau.

Let me say here that M. Léon Vanier did not pay the expenses of Verlaine's funeral as has often been claimed. They were met by the sum of 500 francs handed over in the name of the Minister of Public Instruction and the Fine Arts, by M. Roujon, who told me so himself on the day of the funeral. Further expenses, particularly the augmentation of the religious service, were met by subscriptions from friends.

The invitations to the funeral, sent out by M. Vanier, ran as follows :

"You are invited to take part in the procession, service, and interment of M. Paul Verlaine, poet, who died on 8th January 1896, fortified by the Sacraments of the Church, at his residence, 39 Rue Descartes, aged 52, which will take place on Friday, the 10th inst., at ten o'clock precisely, in the Church of Saint-Etienne-du-Mont, his parish.

"*De Profundis.*

"Friends will assemble at the house of death.

"On the part of M. Georges Verlaine, his son, M. Ch. de Sivry, his brother-in-law, his publisher, his friends, and admirers.

"The interment will take place in the cemetery of the Batignolles."

The Verlaine family possessed a lot in perpetuity in this suburban cemetery, where only in exceptional cases do funerals now take place, and which is situated on the right of the Avenue de Clichy, outside the fortifications.

The newspapers sent reporters to the Rue Descartes, and artists and photographers made sketches. A very good death-mask was obtained by his friend Cazals.

The day of the funeral was cold and bright. After the religious service, which was celebrated at the High Altar with chants and music, the great organ being played by M. Fauré, the procession set out across Paris for the Batignolles. The corners of the pall were held by MM. Maurice Barrès, François Coppée, Edmond Lepelletier, Catulle Mendès, and Robert de Montesquieu.

Charles de Sivry, in the absence of Georges Verlaine, headed the mourners.

The funeral orations were as follows :

M. Maurice Barrês.

"The youth of literature place upon this tomb the tribute of their admiration. Paul Verlaine had neither official position, wealth, nor influential friends. He did not belong to the Academy. . . . He was an exile who consoled himself very simply with the first comer from 'l'Academie Saint Jacques' or the last arrivals in letters.

"We shall no longer have the good fortune to meet this popular figure, but the essential part of him was his power to feel and the accents that communicated his sorrows and his flights, French to the core, imbued with those tender and thrilling beauties which have no analogy except, in another

art, in *The Embarkation for Cythera*. All this still
lives . . . in all of us here present.

"That is why we do not come to bewail his
genius . . . but to assert it. Much homage has
youth rendered for the last twelve years to the
master, Paul Verlaine, but now we bring a still
more solemn testimony to this place, where we are
joined in spirit by the literary youth of other lands.
The constant fidelity of the younger generation to
the master, whom all the critics ignored or abused,
is an important fact, the significance of which I
wish to emphasise. If it is admitted, as we maintain, that hero-worship makes the strength of a
country, and upholds the tradition of a nation,
literary men and artists must be placed in the
front rank of those who thus uphold their country
and their race. No others in social life proclaim
so unmistakably the perpetuity of individuality.
When a great administrator, official, manufacturer,
or soldier dies, it is the end of his personal
existence. His effort, however useful it may
have been, is dissipated among anonymous work.
He leaves behind him only silence and a little
dust in the cemetery. What light does he furnish
to the Frenchman who wishes to know himself, to
see his way? But Verlaine, linked with François
Villon by the freedom and the charm of his
genius, helps us to comprehend one of the principal
tendencies of the French type. Henceforward,
his ideas will take their place among those which
constitute the national heritage. And thanks to
whom has this augmentation of the French ideal
been realised? To the younger generation.

"It is by our constant propaganda, our generous
love, our active clear-sightedness, that the work of
Paul Verlaine, repulsed by his friends and rivals—
save some to whom public opinion renders homage
—has triumphed over the obstacles which in 1890

might have seemed insurmountable. The unanimous homage rendered to-day to the illustrious dead is the multiplied echo of the opinions of the literary youth of the Quartier Latin.

" Let us, therefore, now cease to be accused of systematic negation. We are the beginning of our elders' immortality, and transport in our barque only the shades of those we recognise as benefactors of our intelligence."

M. FRANÇOIS COPPÉE

" MESSIEURS,—Let us salute respectfully the tomb of a true poet, and bow ourselves before the coffin of a child.

" We had hardly passed the twentieth year when we became acquainted, Paul Verlaine and I, when we exchanged our first confidences, and read our earliest verses. I see once more our two heads bent fraternally over the same page ; and once more I experience in all their youthful ardour, our admirations, our enthusiasms, our dreams. We were two children, going confidently towards the future. But Verlaine never encountered experience, that cold and sure companion who takes us roughly by the hand and leads us along the rugged road. He remained a child always.

" Shall we complain of this? It is a grievous thing to grow wise, to run no more along the free road of the imagination for fear of falling, to gather no more roses of delight for fear of thorns, nor touch the butterfly of desire lest we should crush it in our fingers. Happy the child who, falling roughly and picking himself up with tears, immediately forgets the trouble and the pain, and opens anew his eyes, still wet with tears, but eager and delighted, to nature and to life ! Happy also the poet, who, like our poor friend here, preserves his child's heart, his freshness of sensation, his instinctive need of love, who sins without perversity, sincerely repents, loves frankly, believes in God to whom he humbly prays in hours of darkness, and naïvely voices all he thinks and feels, with charming innocence, and ignorance full of grace!

"Happy that poet! I venture to repeat it even while I recall how Paul Verlaine suffered in his sick body and sad heart, Alas! even as a child he was without defence, and life often, and cruelly, wounded him; but suffering is the ransom of genius, a word which must be pronounced in speaking of Verlaine, for his name will always awaken the remembrance of an absolutely new poetry, which has assumed in French literature the importance of a discovery.

"Yes, Verlaine created a poetry which was his alone, an inspiration at once naïve and subtle, all made up of shades evoking the most delicate vibrations of the nerves, the most fugitive echoes of the heart, yet, very natural, a poetry fresh from its source sometimes even almost popular; a poetry in which the metre, free and broken, preserves a delicious harmony, while the stanzas sway and sing like the song of a child, and the lines, most exquisite, are full of music. And in this inimitable poetry he has told us of all his ardours, faults, remorse, tenderness, and dreams, showing us, meanwhile, his heart troubled yet innocent.

"Such poems are created to live, and I aver that the companions of Paul Verlaine's youth, who have put all their effort into their art, would renounce the sweets and vanities of a happy life, and accept 'Pauvre Lélian's' days without bread and nights without shelter, if they were certain to leave behind them, as he has done, pages that will never die, and to see the immortal laurel bloom upon their tomb.

2 F

"The work of Paul Verlaine will live. As to his lamented dead body, we can only, in thought, associate ourselves with the touching prayers of the Christian Church, but now recited, which demand for the dead only rest, eternal rest.

"Adieu, poor and glorious poet, who, like the leaves, has trembled more often than sung; adieu, unhappy friend, whom I have always loved, and who did not forget me. In your death agony you asked for me, and I arrived too late. . . . But your heart and mine have always believed in a state of peace and light, in which we shall all be pardoned and purified—for who will have the hypocrisy to proclaim himself innocent and pure?—and there, in the fulfilment of our ideal, I will answer you: here I am!"

M. CATULLE MENDÈS.

"PAUL VERLAINE,—On the borders of night, through my voice, the sorrow of the brethren of your youth says to you: 'Adieu,' and their admiration: 'for ever.'

"You passed away in suffering. Your martyrdom is finished. May your God give you what you hoped for! But among us your fame remains, imperishable; for you have built up a monument like unto none other. By shallow, marble steps, through the melancholy whispering of the rose bays, we mount to a great white chapel wherein fair wax tapers shine! And as the kingdom of heaven belongs to the poor in spirit, so the kingdom of fame belongs to the simple in genius.

"We love you and lament you, poor dead. We adore you, pure immortal."

M. STÉPHANE MALLARMÉ.

"The tomb loves silence.

"Acclamation, renown, eloquence cease, and the

sob of poetry abandoned, does not follow to the place of quietness the one who hides himself here, that he may not dim his glory with a presence.

". . . Yes, the *Fêtes Galantes*, *La Bonne Chanson*, *Sagesse*, *Amour*, and *Parallèlement* will be poured out, from generation to generation, when youthful lips open for an hour, in a melodious stream quenching their thirst with an immortal flow of exquisite French . . . Paul Verlaine, his genius soaring into the future, remains a hero. Alone . . . an example the centuries can rarely furnish, our contemporary faced in all its terror the state of the singer and dreamer, for solitude, cold, discomfort, poverty ordinarily make up the fate of him who with ingenuous hardihood walks through life according to his inspiration. . . . With this homage, Verlaine, we salute your remains in all reverence."

M. JEAN MORÉAS.

"MESSIEURS,—If I speak before this tomb, it is as one of Paul Verlaine's oldest friends among those who are called the poets of the new school. But let us leave schools alone. To-morrow we can, we must take up quarrels again. To-day, here, there is only one thing—poetry ; and, Messieurs, from the latest classics to Victor Hugo, from Victor Hugo to Leconte de Lisle, from Leconte de Lisle to the youngest amongst us, even as from Villon to Ronsard, from Ronsard to Malherbe and Jean Racine, this poetry, the poetry of the French, invites us to lament the loss of one of its greatest exponents.

And certainly, Messieurs, the author of *Sagesse*, *Jadis et Naguère*, and *Amour* must be admired as an illustrious poet in the absolute sense of the word, and, moreover, if our muses are to go back to classical tastes, we can, I think, consider Verlaine as one of the most genuine artisans of the happy return.

"Adieu, therefore, Paul Verlaine, and whatever may be the divers chances which await poetry in your country of France, your name will not perish."

M. Gustave Kahn.

"I have not come here with a speech prepared, I desire merely in my name, and those of other poets younger than I, to bid a last adieu to the most profound, most tender, most exquisite of French singers ; the one whom we have loved most of all. Adieu, Paul Verlaine, adieu. . . ."

These, with a few words from myself, are the orations, sincere and eloquent, which were pronounced over the tomb of Paul Verlaine.

Verlaine's friends have formed themselves into a committee for the purpose of raising a monument to him. The anniversary of his death was celebrated with a certain ceremony. An important religious service was held at Sainte - Clothilde, followed by a visit to Verlaine's tomb in the cemetery of the Batignolles. After thanking those present I said a few words, which were more or less as follows. I quote from memory :

"The committee, who are actively endeavouring to obtain the erection of a monument to the memory of Paul Verlaine, believe that the simplicity of this commemoration, which is not intended to be a manifestation, will recall to all the end to be attained.

"The better part of Paul Verlaine is not here, hidden in the fertile earth between the rows of those little yews of which he has sung. It is around his work that the pilgrimage of posterity must be made, and before the bust and group by the sculptor Niederhausern, erected on the soil of the town of Paris in a corner of some public garden that

Verlaine's next anniversary should be celebrated. Except for the family and some particular friends, the tomb in the cemetery of the Batignolles will receive few visitors. The anniversary we celebrate to-day will, we greatly hope, be the last assembly of the friends and admirers of the poet at his place of repose. It is among the living, the passing generations who ought to know his name and admire his work, that we must meet to do honour to the name of Paul Verlaine.

" Next year we shall doubtless have inaugurated the monument, and thanked the subscribers, chief of whom to be mentioned and congratulated is M. Leygues, Minister of Public Instruction and the Fine Arts, whose considerable subscription, 1,000 francs, will permit the committee to clinch their operations, and to set about erecting on a site chosen or generously granted by the Town or the Minister, the statue of the poet. Thus his features will be revived for the multitude, rescued by the permanence of sculpture from the maw of death.

"Thus will be completed the work to which Verlaine's friends and devoted admirers have pledged themselves. The undertaking is not without its difficulties. Various obstacles have arisen : the unfortunate rivalry of the publisher Vanier wishing to act on his side, and to get up a subscription and a monument to serve as an advertisement for his house ; the annoying and illicit publication of certain fragments not intended to be printed, improvised by the poet for his own amusement, and regarded by him simply as satirical or humorous autographs ; and finally, loudly hostile articles, have aroused a momentary fear of the indefinite postponement of the monument.

"The committee has happily not lost confidence nor relaxed its activity. Its president, Stéphane

Mallarmé, whom we have had the misfortune to
lose so suddenly, never doubted its final success.
This committee has to-day at its head the illustrious
sculptor Rodin, whose presidentship is a guarantee
from every point of view, and especially for the
artistic value of the work we are to place before
the town of Paris and submit to the public.

"We hope to find the funds necessary for the
completion of the monument, and rely upon the
sculptor, to whom we have applied, to fulfil his
engagements, and present us in due time with a
work meriting inauguration."

Unhappily, all our efforts have not yet yielded
the required result.

The committee is now composed as follows:

Auguste Rodin, president; members: MM.
Maurice Barrès, F.-A. Cazals, Léon Dierx, Ernest
Delahaye, Edmond Lepelletier, Natanson, and
Alfred Vallette, treasurer.

I asked the General Council of the Department
of the Seine, at the sitting of Friday, 12th July
1901, for a site for a monument to be raised to
Paul Verlaine in the square of the Batignolles.
This place was chosen because Verlaine passed
his youth in the Batignolles. There he composed
his first verse, and his mind was opened to the
world of art, and there, in the cemetery, he rests.
My proposition was submitted to the Commission
of Instruction and the Fine Arts, who regarded it
favourably, and then to the Third Commission, who
dispose of sites in Paris.

Nothing has resulted, except that the Municipal
Council of Paris have given the name of Paul
Verlaine to a place in Paris in the 13th *arrondisse-*

ment: a beginning. After a visit to the cemetery of the Batignolles on the anniversary of the poet's death, the members of the Committee, headed by M. Léon Dierx, vice-president, and other friends of the poet, went on Sunday, 13th January 1907, to the Place Paul Verlaine, and speeches were made by MM. Louis Dumoulin and Edmond Lepelletier.

Victor Hugo did not receive the honours of a monument until fifteen years after his death. Alfred de Musset has only recently had statues erected. We need not, therefore, despair for Paul Verlaine; indeed the passing of the years is favourable to the proper perspective of his glory. But the waiting must not be too prolonged. His friends should still be here, and those who knew and loved him, behold him established for ever in the public gaze. It is for them to fan the flame of good - will, to hasten forward the ceremony of inauguration.

While awaiting that day, which I hope is not far distant, I have raised to the memory and glory of my dear Paul Verlaine this printed tribute. This book, exact, impartial, and sincere, may help to point out and explain the statue of Paul Verlaine, which, for the honour of French literature must be raised in Paris.

INDEX